PHILOSTORGIUS:
CHURCH HISTORY

Society of Biblical Literature

Writings from the Greco-Roman World

John T. Fitzgerald, General Editor

Editorial Board

Number 23

Philostorgius:
Church History

Volume Editors
William Adler (translation) and Everett Ferguson (notes)

PHILOSTORGIUS:
CHURCH HISTORY

Translated with an Introduction and Notes

by

Philip R. Amidon, S.J.

Society of Biblical Literature
Atlanta

PHILOSTORGIUS:
CHURCH HISTORY

Library of Congress Cataloging-in-Publication Data

Philostorgius.
   [Ecclesiastical history]
   Philostorgius : church history / translated with an introduction and notes by Philip R. Amidon.
      p. cm. — (Writings from the Greco-Roman world ; v. 23)
   Includes bibliographical references and index.
   ISBN: 978-1-58983-215-2 (paper binding : alk. paper)
   1. Church history—Primitive and early church, ca. 30–600. I. Amidon, Philip R.
II. Title. III. Series.
   BR65.P473E2313 2007b
   270.2—dc22   2007035239

15 14 13 12 11 10 09 08 07   5 4 3 2 1
Printed in the United States of America on acid-free, recycled paper
conforming to ANSI/NISO Z39.48-1992 (R1997) and ISO 9706:1994
standards for paper permanence.

Contents

vi CONTENTS

Abbreviations

a.	*anno* = year [used to specify the year entry of a chronicle]
A	Appendix (*Anhang*)
AASS	*Acta sanctorum quotquot toto orbe coluntur*
ABD	*Anchor Bible Dictionary.* Edited by David Noel Freedman. 6 vols. New York: Doubleday, 1992.
Aed.	Procopius, *De aedificiis*
a.m.	*anno mundi* = in the year of the world (i.e., from creation)
Ammianus	Ammianus Marcellinus, *Res gestae*
AnBoll	*Analecta Bollandiana*
Anon. Val.	*Anonymus Valesianus*
Ant.	Josephus, *Jewish Antiquities*
ANRW	*Aufstieg und Niedergang der römischen Welt: Geschichte und Kultur Roms im Spiegel der neueren Forschung.* Part 2, *Principat.* Edited by Hildegard Temporini and Wolfgang Haase. Berlin: de Gruyter, 1972–.
AP	*Artemii Passio*
APF	*Archiv für Papyrusforschung*
Apol.	Eunomius, *Apologia*
Apol. Const.	Athanasius, *Apologia ad Constantium*
Apol. de fuga	Athanasius, *Apologia de fuga sua*
Apol. sec.	Athanasius, *Apologia secunda* (= *Apologia contra Arianos*)
Athenaeus	Athenaeus, *Deiphnosophistae*
Aurelius Victor	Sextus Aurelius Victor, *De Caesaribus*
Bab.	John Chrysostom, *De sancto hieromartyre Babyla*
Bab. Jul.	John Chrysostom, *De Babyla contra Julianum et gentiles*
BHG	*Bibliotheca hagiographica Graeca*
BHL	*Bibliotheca hagiographica latina antiquae et mediae aetatis*

Bios	Guidi, Michelangelo. "Un 'bios' di Costantino." *Rendiconti della R. Accademia dei Lincei* 16 (1907): 304–40, 637–62.
Brev.	Rufius Festus, *Breviarium rerum gestarum populi romani*
BSGRT	Bibliotheca scriptorum Graecorum et Romanorum Teubneriana
BSOAS	*Bulletin of the School of Oriental and African Studies*
ByzZ	*Byzantinische Zeitschrift*
BZNW	Beihefte zur Zeitschrift für die neutestamentliche Wissenschaft und die Kunde der älteren Kirche
C. Ar.	Athanasius, *Orationes contra Arianos*
Cassius Dio	Cassius Dio, *Historiae Romanae*
Cedrenus	George Cedrenus, *Historiarum compendium*
Certamen	Simeon Metaphrastes, *Certamen sacrosancti martyris Babylae*
CCSL	Corpus Christianorum: Series latina
Chron.	*Chronicon*
Chron. misc.	*Chronicon miscellaneum ad annum Domini 724 pertinens*
Chron. pasch.	*Chronicon paschale*
Cod. justin.	*Codex justinianus*
Cod. theod.	*Codex theodosianus*
Comp. chron.	*Anonymi compendium chronicum.* Vol. 7 of *Bibliotheca graeca medii aevi = Mesaionike vivliotheke.* Edited by Konstantinos N. Sathas. Venice: Typois tou Chronou, 1894. Repr., Hildesheim: Olms, 1972.
Const. ap.	*Constitutiones apostolicae*
Consul. const.	*Consularia constantinopolitana*
Corp. herm.	*Corpus hermeticum*
CQ	*Classical Quarterly*
CSCO	Corpus scriptorum christianorum orientalium
DEC	*Decrees of the Ecumenical Councils.* Edited by Norman P. Tanner. 2 vols. London: Sheed & Ward, 1990.
Decr.	Athanasius, *De decretis*
DHGE	*Dictionnaire d'histoire et de géographie ecclésiastiques.* Edited by Alfred Baudrillart et al. Paris: Letouzey & Ané, 1912–.
Did.	*Didache*
Diodorus of Sicily	Diodorus of Sicily, *Bibliotheca historica*
Diogenes Laertius	Diogenes Laertius, *Vitae philosophorum*

Dion.	Athanasius, *De sententia Dionysii*
Enarrat. Ps.	Ambrose, *Enarrationes in XII Psalmos davidicos*
EOMIA	*Ecclesiae Occidentalis Monumenta Iuris Antiquissima.* Edited by Cuthbert. H. Turner. 2 vols. Oxford: Clarendon, 1899–1939.
Ep.	*Epistula*
Ep. ad Ath.	Julian, *Epistola ad senatum populumque Atheniensem*
Ep. Aeg. Lib.	Athanasius, *Epistula ad episcopos Aegypti et Libyae*
Ep. encycl.	Athanasius, *Epistula encyclica*
Epit. Caes.	*Epitome de Caesaribus*
EPRO	Etudes préliminaires aux religions orientales dans l'Empire romain
Etym.	Isidore, *Etymologiae*
Eun.	Gregory of Nyssa, *Contra Eunomium*
Eutr.	*In Eutropium*
Eutropius	Eutropius, *Breviarium ab urbe condita*
FGH	*Die Fragmente der griechischen Historiker.* Edited by Felix Jacoby. 3 vols. Leiden: Brill, 1954–64.
FHG	*Fragmenta historicorum graecorum.* Edited by Karl Müller. 5 vols. Paris: Didot, 1841–70.
Frag.	John of Antioch, *Fragment*
Frag. Ep.	Julian the Apostate, *Fragmenta breviora* (*Shorter Fragments of Letters*)
Frag. hist.	*Fragmenta historica*
GCS	Griechischen christlichen Schriftsteller der ersten Jahrhunderte
GRBS	*Greek, Roman, and Byzantine Studies*
H. Ar.	Athanasius, *Historia Arianorum*
HA	Athanasius, *Historia acephala*
Haer. fab.	Theodoret, *Haereticarum fabularum compendium*
Herodotus	Herodotus, *Historiae*
Hist. eccl.	*Historia ecclesiastica*
Hist. Goth.	Isidore, *Historia Gothorum Wandalorum Sueborum*
Hom. Phil.	John Chrysostom, *Homiliae in epistulam ad Philippenses*
HTR	*Harvard Theological Review*
Invent. s. crucis	Alexander Monachus, *De inventione sanctae crucis*
ITQ	*Irish Theological Quarterly*
John of Nikiu	John of Nikiu, *Chronicle*
JQR	*Jewish Quarterly Review*
JRH	*Journal of Religious History*

JRS	*Journal of Roman Studies*
JSJ	*Journal for the Study of Judaism in the Persian, Hellenistic, and Roman Periods*
JTS	*Journal of Theological Studies*
Justinus	Marcus Junian(i)us Justinus, *Historiarum Philippicarum libri XLIV* (a Latin epitome of the *Historiae philippicae et totius mundi origines et terrae situs* by Pompeius Trogus)
LCL	Loeb Classical Library
Leo Grammaticus	Leo Grammaticus, *Chronographia*
Malalas	John Malalas, *Chronographia*
Mort.	Lactantius, *De mortibus persecutorum*
Nat.	Pliny the Elder, *Naturalis historia*
Nat. an	Aelian, *De natura animalium*
Nicephorus	Nicephorus Callistus Xanthopulus, *Historia ecclesiastica*
Olympiodorus	Olympiodorus of Thebes, *Historikoi logoi*
Opitz, *Vit. Const.*	Opitz, Hans-Georg. "Die Vita Constantini des Codex Angelicus 22." *Byzantion* 9 (1934): 535–93.
Or.	*Oratio*
Orosius	Paulus Orosius, *Historiae adversum paganos*
Palaephatus	*De incredibilibus*
Pan.	Epiphanius, *Panarion* (*Adversus haereses*)
Pan. Lat.	*XII Panegyrici Latini*
Pausanias	Pausanias, *Graeciae descriptio*
PEQ	*Palestine Exploration Quarterly*
PG	Patrologia graeca [= Patrologiae cursus completus: Series graeca]. Edited by J.-P. Migne. 162 vols. Paris: Migne, 1857–86.
Photius	Photius, *Ex ecclesiasticis historiis Philostorgii epitome* (see PG 65:455–638)
PL	Patrologia latina. Edited by J.-P. Migne. 217 vols. Paris: Migne, 1844–64.
PLRE	*Prosopography of the Later Roman Empire.* Edited by A. H. M. Jones, J. R. Martindale, and J. Morris. 3 vols. Cambridge: Cambridge University Press, 1970–92.
PO	*Patrologia orientalis.* Edited by René Graffin and François Nau. Paris: Didot, 1904–.
PTS	Patristische Texte und Studien
PW	Pauly, August F. von. *Paulys Realencyclopädie der classischen Altertumswissenschaft.* New edition by Georg

	Wissowa and Wilhelm Kroll. 50 vols. in 84 parts. Stuttgart: Metzler and Druckenmüller, 1894–1980.
QG	Philo, *Quaestiones et solutiones in Genesin*
RAC	*Reallexikon für Antike und Christentum.* Edited by Theodor Klauser et al. Stuttgart: Hiersemann, 1950–.
S	Supplement (translation of material in Bidez, *Philostorgius,* 377–81)
SC	Sources chrétiennes
SOC	*Scriptores Originum Constantinopolitanarum.* Edited by Theodorus Preger. 2 vols. Leipzig: Teubner, 1901–7.
Socrates	Socrates, *Historia ecclesiastica*
Solinus	Gaius Iulius Solinus, *Collectanea rerum memorabilium*
Sozomen	Sozomen, *Historia ecclesiastica*
StPatr	Studia Patristica
StPB	Studia post-biblica
Strabo	Strabo, *Geographica*
Suda	*Suidae Lexicon.* Edited by Ada Adler. 5 vols. Leipzig: Teubner, 1928–38.
Syn.	Athanasius, *De synodis*
Synax.	*Synaxarium ecclesiae constantinopolitanae: Propylaeum ad Acta Sanctorum Novembris.* Edited by Hippolyte Delehaye. Brussels: Carnandet, 1902.
TAPA	*Transactions of the American Philological Association*
Theophanes	Theophanes the Confessor, *Chronographia*
Theophylact	Theophylact, Archbishop of Ochrid in Bulgaria, *Martyrium XV martyrum*
Thes.	Nicetas Choniates, *Thesaurus orthodoxae fidei*
TRE	*Theologische Realenzyklopädie.* Edited by Gerhard Krause and Gerhard Müller. Berlin: de Gruyter, 1977–.
TU	Texte und Untersuchungen zur Geschichte der altchristlichen Literatur
VC	*Vigiliae christianae*
Vir. ill.	*De viris illustribus*
Vit. Const.	Eusebius, *Vita Constantini*
Vit. Pyth.	Porphyry, *Vita Pythagorae*
Vit. soph.	Eunapius, *Vitae sophistarum*
VP	Iamblichus, *De vita Pythagorica*
ZKG	*Zeitschrift für Kirchengeschichte*
Zonaras	Johannes Zonaras, *Epitome historiarum*
Zosimus	Zosimus, *Historia nova*

Introduction

Constantine, the Arian Dispute, and Church Unity

The Council of Nicaea, convened in 325 by the emperor Constantine I to settle the quarrels in the church about the date of Easter and the doctrines of the Alexandrian presbyter Arius, published a creed that occasioned theological controversies that lasted well into the next century and beyond. For several years before the council, Arius had been criticizing his bishop, Alexander (Athanasius's predecessor), for speaking of the Son of God as co-eternal with the Father. The word "son," he argued, implies origin, but what has an origin is not eternal. Besides, to speak of both the Father and the Son as eternal seems contrary to monotheism, if one holds that only God is eternal and that Father and Son are really distinct (as their names imply).

Arius did not hesitate to draw the conclusions he thought latent in his objections: the Son of God, having an origin, does not exist from all eternity with the Father but comes into existence as the Father wills and is therefore a creature. He is the first of all creatures, the Father's instrument in creating the rest of the world, mediating the Father's creative power. Christian monotheism is thus preserved, as is God's impassibility: any suggestion that the Father might be affected by the passion inevitably accompanying the act of begetting the Son, if "begetting" is thought of in the physical sense, is eliminated when the production of the Son is declared an act of creation; and if the Son is a creature and has no part in the Father's impassible nature, then Christ's capacity for suffering seems easily explainable. How that suffering is redemptive Arius perhaps found harder to explain.

Most of the bishops of the council were opposed to Arius's doctrine. However much they might have shared with him the conviction of God's impassibility, they still thought that the worship traditionally offered Christ by the church, and his work of mediation, meant that his unity with the Father must be quite different in kind from any that could be ascribed to even the holiest of creatures. To signify their opposition as effectively as possible, they decided, after long debate, to publish a creed that declared the Son of God to be "consubstantial" (*homoousios*) with the Father. They also published a condemnation of the main articles of Arius's teaching.

The modern reader may find the word "consubstantial" unclear; many who first heard the Creed of Nicaea would have agreed. The letters accompanying the creed had to explain that the word was not meant to suggest that the Son had been begotten in any material or physical sense or by an act of creation; it expressed rather the co-eternal unity of Father and Son in a relationship intrinsic to their very divinity. But the word "substance" (*ousia*), from which it stemmed, was equivocal: it could mean, among other things, an independently existing entity or, by contrast, the essence or nature of such an entity. The latter meaning informed the use made of "consubstantial" by the Valentinian gnostics, by whom it was used to refer to the common nature shared by the deities of their luxuriant pantheon. And if its gnostic odor did little to recommend it to monotheistic Christians, it also appeared, shortly after the council, that there were those, like Marcellus of Ancyra and Photinus of Sirmium, who seemed to interpret it in the contrasting sense; the ineptness of Marcellus's exposition suggested that he thought of God as a primordial unitary deity in which the differentiation of Father and Son emerged only within the dispensation of creation and redemption: the Trinity was neither from eternity nor unto eternity. It was this lack of clarity surrounding "consubstantial" that helped fuel the doctrinal controversies that soon spread over the entire church.

Constantine's convocation of the Council of Nicaea, following the military victories that unified the Roman Empire under his one rule, shows how deeply he felt that God wanted him to do all he could to end the divisions within the Christian community with which he had associated himself. He had already spent much effort (and money) trying to reconcile the Donatist schismatics to the Catholic Church, and he had the bishops at Nicaea draft a plan for reintegrating the separatist Melitian clergy in Egypt.[1] He also encouraged the gnostic sectarians to join the Catholic Church by transferring to it their buildings and withholding from them the economic benefits it enjoyed (Eusebius, *Vit. Const.* 3.64–65).

His efforts did not achieve the results for which he must have hoped. The Donatists remained stubbornly apart, unwilling to be tainted by contact with a clergy suspected of having lapsed during persecution. The plan for the Melitians remained unfulfilled when Athanasius was consecrated in 328 to succeed Alexander. As for the gnostics, many of them seem in fact to have chosen the path of prudence and enrolled as Catholics. But they were by no means converted, for within the church they worked hard to sway its members to their own doctrines, as Epiphanius relates some fifty years after the

---

1. The Melitians did not accept the policy of the bishop of Alexandria of admitting to communion those Christians who had lapsed during persecution.

Council of Nicaea (*Pan.* 26.17.4–9; also 40.1; 58.1.4). The pagans, he complains, assumed that those doctrines were authentically Christian and were so revolted by them that missionary work among them had become impossible (27.3.3–4).

At the Council of Nicaea itself, almost all the bishops subscribed to the Creed. Arius and his closest followers refused and were sent into exile, but their situation did not suit Constantine's policy of comprehension, and in a few years they were back, sheltered by their powerful and astute episcopal champion, Eusebius of Nicomedia.

The ecclesiastical history of the rest of the century, and beyond, is a tangle of faith and order: the church was working out the consequences of the Nicene doctrine, its own organization, and its relations with the imperial government, now that it was free from external persecution and enjoyed legitimacy in civil law. Arius's rehabilitation was strongly opposed by Athanasius of Alexandria and Marcellus of Ancyra, both of whom ardently defended the Council of Nicaea. But Marcellus, as we have seen, might easily be interpreted as understanding "consubstantial" in a sense that denied the primordial distinction of the Persons within the godhead, and Eusebius of Nicomedia lost little time in bringing about his deposition, managing in the process to tarnish the reputation of the very word "consubstantial" among many bishops who had no liking for Arius's doctrine at all.

Athanasius he found harder to remove; he had assisted his predecessor at the Council of Nicaea as a deacon but had been far more circumspect in his use of the central term of its Creed. However, the validity of his episcopal election was contested, and he repaid dissidence with rigor and was accused of irregular ordination and violence toward schismatics and of overreaching his authority; finally, even during the high tide of Constantine's policy of Christian reintegration, he found himself summarily banished by the outraged sovereign upon the charge, brought by Arius's episcopal protectors, that he had threatened to disrupt the grain supply; his biography is in fact a long tale of repeated exiles and restorations in which the part played by the strictly doctrinal issues may be debated until the end of time.

"Consubstantial" in Creed and Doctrine after Constantine

Doctrine was, however, a central player in the history of the time. The use to which some had put the word "consubstantial" provoked various responses. Many bishops thought that the gist of the Creed of Nicaea was better represented by speaking of the Son as *homoiousios* ("similar in substance") with the Father. But the Antiochene layman Aetius, and his illustrious disciple Eunomius, who had become associated around 356, found the term repugnant. In striking contrast to one of Arius's own doctrines and to one of the central features of the gnostic ideology, they insisted that God's very substance or essence is knowable by human reason reflecting on scripture. God, they said, is truly known as ingenerate and known therefore to be essentially unlike anything else; unchangeably One, he must be utterly impassible, and therefore any language that suggests that he can beget as natural fathers do is ruled out of court. God produces the Son by creating him; he also creates the Son's creative power with which the Son in turn brings the world into being. The Son is the "only-begotten God," the God of the creatures he produces, but he is not the image of the God who produced him, since in his substance he is engendered, not ingenerate. He is, however, the image of the Father, since "Father" is the title referring to God in his activity of engendering the Son by creation. That is an activity of God's will, not of his substance, since it is done freely. The Son is the image of the Father, then, because he reflects God's will that brought him into being.

This doctrine did not recommend itself to the conservatives, who labeled Aetius and his followers "Anomoeans" or "Dissimilarians," from the word *anomoios* or "unlike." The ecclesiastical advisers to the emperor Constantine's successor, Constantius II (337–361), were united in their conviction that the Nicene "consubstantial" could not be part of any creed acceptable to the whole church, the unity of which the emperor desired as ardently as had his father. But they were divided over how to word a replacement formula, some favoring the term *homoiousios* (whence they became known as "homoeousians"), while others wanted simply to say that the Son is like the Father, omitting the word "substance" altogether, since it had seemed to occasion such controversy. The emperor ultimately decided for the latter solution, and the Council of Constantinople of 360 promulgated a creed that declared that the Son is like the Father without qualification. All bishops were required to subscribe to it. The supporters of this doctrine became known as "homoeans," after the word *homoios* ("similar").

Athanasius strongly opposed this development, although for long years he had to do so in hiding from the wrath of Constantius, who resented his opposition and suspected him of plotting against his interests. Athanasius became increasingly convinced that the Creed of Nicaea was the true bulwark of orthodoxy and that the homoeans were at best Arian dupes; he is in fact largely responsible for extending the epithet "Arian" to anyone opposed to continued use of the term "consubstantial" in the creed, including many who would quite justifiably have resented the association. He repeatedly accused his adversaries of being unchristian and pagan in the tendency of their doctrine, and when, in 361, Constantius died and was succeeded by the pagan emperor Julian, his claim seemed to receive verification from quite an unexpected quarter. Julian recalled all Christians exiled for religious reasons by his predecessor, hoping thereby to start some disedifying quarrels when the banished bishops returned home to confront their replacements (his hopes were fully justified). Athanasius, who was among those who returned, immediately began making overtures to the "homoeousians," suggesting that their language was compatible with the doctrine promulgated at Nicaea, if the central terms were carefully examined. We may wonder what they thought of his suggestion at first, but the doubtful reputation he had acquired in many quarters of the Eastern church must have been transformed when in 362 Julian singled him out from among all the bishops in the world for renewed exile, making it clear that he was doing so because Athanasius was baptizing members of the nobility. This exile ended at Julian's death the following year, and then even the homoean emperor Valens (364–378) thought it as well to leave the bishop in peace at last.

Valens sanctioned no new creeds, insisting only that the churches in his realm remain in communion with the homoean bishop of his capital. It was during his reign, however, that the alliance of pro-Nicene loyalists and homoeousians proposed by Athanasius began to bear fruit, as Basil of Caesarea and his Cappadocian associates continued to develop the theological language that would allow the doctrine implicit in the Creed of Nicaea to be expressed with greater clarity. Their undertaking was conducted in intense and protracted debate with the "Eunomians" (as the anomoeans came to be called) who feared that the Creed of Nicaea was an opening to the sort of polytheism they saw all too much of in the Gnosticism that had infected the churches in more than one place.

THEODOSIUS I AND THE NICENE DOCTRINE

Their fears were not allayed when the emperor Valens was succeeded by the pro-Nicene Theodosius I (379–395), who summoned a large council to Constantinople in 381; the council promulgated a revision of the Creed of Nicaea that retained the word "consubstantial" to describe the relationship of Father and Son and lengthened into an article the earlier passing reference to the Holy Spirit, now described as equal to the other two. This Catholic faith, Theodosius declared, was henceforth the official religion of the Roman Empire; the Eunomians, like the other nonconformists, were left in a state of increasing isolation: a small sect convinced that it alone guarded the true monotheistic Christian faith inherited from Israel and under constant attack from a polytheistic paganism thinly disguised as Gnosticism or as Nicene Christianity.

Pro-Nicene and Anti-Nicene Historiography

To the Nicene loyalists Theodosius was of course a great hero. When in 402 or 403 Rufinus of Aquileia published his translation and continuation of the church history of Eusebius of Caesarea, the emperor's reign, culminating in the final victory over usurpation and the reestablishment of a single dynasty within the Roman Empire, provided a fitting conclusion to the thoroughly pro-Nicene work. It enjoyed immediate and lasting success. Eusebius's original history, published in 324–325, had acquired great prestige as a learned and edifying account of church history from its beginnings down to Constantine's reunification of the empire just before the Council of Nicaea. When Rufinus's bishop asked him to translate it into Latin, he produced an abridged version and continuation (to the year 395) that smoothed away the stylistic and doctrinal infelicities of the original and presented the imperial endorsement of Nicene Christianity as the victory of grace amid the vicissitudes of human events. It was immensely popular, the continuation, it seems, appearing in Greek translation as well.[2]

The learned and fervently Eunomian layman Philostorgius, born in Cappadocia around 368, heartily detested such historiography, as may be imagined. The remnants of his writing show a lively intellectual curiosity encouraged by his sectarian creed, whose God is not the hidden deity of Gnosticism but one whose very substance can be known by human reason directed aright. He obviously drank deeply from the libraries, museums, and archives of Constantinople, his Dissimilarian spectacles bringing into focus a picture of the century preceding that was very unlike the one painted by Rufinus, with whom his own narrative, when he came to write it, was indeed in frequent argument.[3]

Their accounts do share the same central conviction: that the people of God, in the Old and New Testaments, is one people, with one history.

---

2. Rufinus's text is in Eduard Schwartz and Theodor Mommsen, eds., *Die Kirchengeschichte* (vol. 2.2. of *Eusebius Werke*; Berlin: Akademie-Verlag, 1908). For a translation of the continuation, see my *The Church History of Rufinus of Aquileia: Books 10 and 11* (New York: Oxford University Press, 1997), with bibliography.

3. Whether Philostorgius read Rufinus in the original, rather than in a Greek version of his work, is another matter. His translation of *alma Roma* as "glorious Rome" (2.9, 9a) makes one wonder how well he knew Latin, fond though he may have been of sprinkling his text with translations of technical terms from it. The relationship of Rufinus's continuation of Eusebius to the Greek text that closely parallels it is controversial; for a review of the debate, see my *Church History of Rufinus*, xiii–xvii.

But for Philostorgius's sect, the Council of Nicaea of 325 was but one in a series of attacks upon the true monotheistic faith delivered to the saints of old and repeatedly assailed by a polytheistic paganism that excelled in clever disguises. A creed that spoke of more than one co-eternal Person and of the begetting of one by the other endangered the unitary and impassible character of the true God. Moreover, an empire that sanctioned such a creed had fallen into apostasy.

Philostorgius cannot have imagined that the empire would ever welcome the publication of his views, but he may have hoped that the new university founded in Constantinople in 425 by Theodosius II would include some circles in which his revisionist account might be read with sympathy. It appeared sometime between 425 and 433, in twelve books bound in two volumes, its proper period the years from 320 to 425; but he apparently introduced this period with an account of the opening of the assault upon the monotheistic faith and worship of God's people drawn from the books of Maccabees. Alexander the Great seems to have fascinated him—he read widely in his biography (cf. 3.6)—but he remains for him always the ominous figure standing at the beginning of 1 Maccabees whose conquests brought the Jews that Hellenistic culture and its alluring polytheism that seduced so many of them from their covenantal faith and so bitterly divided their community long before any external pressure was brought upon them to apostasize. That pressure did come, of course, and he records it (1.1), and so the two weapons that, in his view, polytheism uses against monotheism, seduction and persecution, are introduced at the outset as the chief temptations experienced throughout the history of God's people.

The beleaguered faithful minority of monotheistic Jews is for Philostorgius the abiding image of the true church in his own history. That its enemy had enjoyed success he would have thought evident from the appearance of those groups of apparently polytheistic Christians now usually referred to as "gnostics"; they were in full vigor throughout the fourth and fifth centuries and, as we have seen, had often managed to join monotheistic Christian churches while retaining and promoting their own views. Modern scholarship may argue about the true origins and doctrines of Gnosticism, but in the period under consideration Catholics and "Arians" alike thought of it in the way in which Irenaeus and his successors had taught them: as paganism thinly disguised, its multiple and mutable deities begotten one from the other in activities utterly foreign to the impassible character ascribed to God in mainline Christianity. The music wafting from the gnostic shrine may have been played in an ecclesiastical key, but as far as they were concerned, the theme was straight out of Hesiod's *Theogony*, however Valentinus and his kind might have tried to trick it out.

If and how the gnostics of the fourth and fifth centuries used the Creed of Nicaea to advance their cause is unknown, but certainly Philostorgius views the "Arian" crisis that so deeply marks his period as at bottom the continuing struggle of the true faith against polytheistic paganism, in the guise of Gnosticism, which has wormed its way into the very life of the church and persuaded the civil power to sanction a revision of the Creed of Nicaea that must have seemed to him outright tritheism. Thus he portrays Aetius, the defender of the true faith, as fighting his first battle, after he finishes his education, not with a Catholic but with a Borborian, a member of that most disreputable of gnostic sects. He is so roundly defeated in debate that he comes close to despair, but he is rescued by a vision and upon recovery goes on to dispute with a Manichee, this time winning a resounding victory (3.15). His subsequent debates with those whom every Eunomian would have regarded as in effect exponents of the Nicene doctrine—however indignantly they would have rejected the label—he wins with absurd ease, now that he has honed his weapons against the real enemy. Of Marcellus and Photinus, by contrast, he says not a word; the real danger of the consubstantialist doctrine did not, for him, lie in a monarchian direction.

Philostorgius in fact groups into one "homoousian" party all those Christians who opposed Eunomianism (in the same way as those of Nicene sympathies liked to call "Arian" anyone who rejected the term "consubstantial" as used in the Creed of Nicaea). The reason is that the Eunomians regarded their own doctrine as the only effective defense against Gnosticism; those who professed the "homoeousian" or even the "homoean" creeds were fooling themselves if they thought that they had really rejected the consubstantialist faith. He includes in his own party, on the other hand, not only those who, like Eusebius of Nicomedia, offer signal resistance to the acceptance of the Creed of Nicaea and to its dread champion, Athanasius, but all Christians as well who retain intact the pure, original apostolic monotheism. That faith remained, in his apocalyptic view, uncorrupted where it lay beyond the pale of Roman authority (2.5, 6; 3.5).

Such is the central drama of our author's history: the enduring contest between the true monotheistic faith of God's people and the pagan forces arrayed against it. Gnosticism is always the silent partner in the debates between Nicene and Eunomian Christians, the real foe against whom Aetius fought the battle that nearly led to his death. And there is some evidence that this view comes from Eunomius himself.[4]

---

4. See Richard P. Vaggione, *Eunomius, The Extant Works: Text and Translation* (Oxford: Clarendon, 1987), 110–11.

Suppression and Survival of Philostorgius's History

This being the tenor of Philostorgius's history, it is not surprising that the government that championed the Nicene faith would seek to suppress it, seeing that it had previously ordered the burning of the works of Eunomius, one of the great heroes of his tale. A few copies did survive the censorship, however, one of which the ninth-century patriarch Photius found in his library in Constantinople and epitomized. Others also borrowed from Philostorgius, most extensively the author of the *Artemii Passio* (Artemius being the legendary martyr under Julian the Apostate),[5] and so, despite the eventual disappearance of the original text, it is possible to form some idea of what it contained by reviewing the epitome and the other references. An invaluable aid to this is Joseph Bidez's masterful edition, in which all the relevant pieces have been edited and furnished with an introduction that is indispensable to all studies of the historian.[6]

Character and Themes of Philostorgius's History

However much Philostorgius may have abhorred the religion of the pagans, he was by no means insensitive to the beauties of their culture. He followed Herodotus's lead in historiography, embroidering his narrative with learned excursions into geography and natural history and in general cultivating a style that would recommend him to his readers. The style was no empty show. His immersion in the scholarly resources offered by Constantinople has preserved for us, even in the abridgement of its original work, traditions that are otherwise unknown or that add perspective to matters related elsewhere.[7] If his sect taught him, in the strongest contrast to Gnosticism, that God's very substance can be known, then all the more can his will be known, and for Philostorgius the events of history, of nature, and of human endeavor, reveal that will. Calamities are, for him, always cautionary; he takes pains, for instance, to demonstrate logically that earthquakes cannot result from natural forces and must therefore come from the divine power acting immediately upon matter

---

5. An English translation of the *Artemii Passio* by Mark Vermes, with notes by Samuel N. C. Lieu, is available in *From Constantine to Julian: Pagan and Byzantine Views: A Source History* (ed. Samuel N. C. Lieu and Dominic Montserrat; London: Routledge, 1996).

6. Joseph Bidez, *Philostorgius, Kirchengeschichte: Mit dem Leben des Lucian von Antiochien und den Fragmenten eines arianischen Historiographen* (3rd ed.; rev. by Friedhelm Winkelmann; GCS; Berlin: Akademie-Verlag, 1981).

7. For an appreciation, see ibid., cix–cxii, cxxiv–cxl.

(12.10). He also makes sure that we hear in profuse detail of the ghastly ill-nesses that invariably befall apostates. Even in abridgement, his narrative of the emperors Constantine I and Julian reveals the same conviction. Both receive remarkable graces: Constantine the revelation of the heavenly cross leading to his conversion and military victories, and Julian the friendship and instruction of none other than Aetius himself. But Constantine turns against the faith he has miraculously received, bullying the bishops at the Council of Nicaea into promulgating a polytheistic creed, and his life thereafter becomes one of murderous intrigue within his own family in which he himself finally perishes. The whole horrid tale is crowned by the pagan worship offered to his statue that he erected in Constantinople—Philostorgius's deft comment on where he thought the Creed of Nicaea really tended.[8]

Constantine's belated repentance after the council (2.1) does him no good, then, just as Julian's benevolence toward Aetius does not save him from a bloody and premature death, and one may wonder if the story in 2 Macc 9 of Antiochus Epiphanes, whose agonizing and dishonorable death follows hard upon his fruitless repentance, was not the model at work here. It is extremely unfortunate that we no longer have the original text of Philostorgius's account of Julian. The idea that the Apostate modeled himself upon Alexander the Great is one that he would have found in Julian's own contemporaries, and, given our author's evident fascination with the Maccabees, this identification must have been richly suggestive to him. Even so, there were some awkward elements in Julian's biography that sorted oddly with the tenor of his history, to say the least: the singular benevolence he showed toward Aetius, which furnished the environment in which the Eunomians achieved their independence, and the singular hatred he showed toward Athanasius, which validated the latter's long-standing claim that his persecutors were unchristian. How he worked with this material we do not know; the epitome simply tells us that he did in fact speak freely of the first element. He must somehow have fitted it into the biography that, after Constantine's, is the second great sign from God in his history, with its extended narrative of the trial and execution of the fervently antipagan Arte-mius, the blasting of the Apostate's favorite shrine at Daphne and of his plans to restore the Jewish temple, and his miserable death in a foreign land.

If, under Philostorgius's nimble pen, not only natural wonders but the very lives of the emperors become portentous, one can understand his fond-ness for apocalyptic literature, in which he was deeply versed.[9] He seems not to have predicted an imminent end of the world, however; if he had, then surely his hostile epitomizer would not have foregone the satisfaction of

---

8. Ibid., cxxv–cxxvi.
9. Ibid., cxiii–cxxi.

saying so.[10] It is natural that he would have meant his work for the consola-
tion of his own sect, but he seems also to have written for the wider public.
He lived in a time when the state was showing itself ever more hostile to his
sect, but also to polytheistic paganism and to Gnosticism, so the trend of its
history cannot have seemed to him utterly hopeless. Theodosius II's reputation for learning and encouragement of scholarship would have suggested a
chance to signal a challenge to, not merely a denunciation of, his government.
That he ends his history on the note of peace and political unity, achieved
after great effort, indicates that such was his intention.

Philostorgius, then, is advancing a cause, and he does so with a zest
hardly muffled by his epitomizer. It is well to remember this when one reads
his narrative, especially since it becomes evident that he intends to counter
wherever possible the pro-Nicene story told by Rufinus of Aquileia in his continuation of Eusebius's church history. Here he sets himself a difficult task, for
Rufinus is a master storyteller; no one who has read, for instance, his account
of Athanasius's trial at the Synod of Tyre will soon forget the courtroom scene
in which his enemies are so dramatically confounded. But of course Philostorgius must try, Athanasius being one of the chief villains of his piece, and it
is really no discredit to his narrative powers that his revision has failed to supplant Rufinus's account. Those powers are better displayed elsewhere, as for
instance in his account of Athanasius's episcopal election—as alluring a piece
of tendentious narrative as one may hope to find, judging from those later
historians who repeat it with such uncritical zest. And the lyrical quality of
his central story of the rise and fall of Julian the Apostate is clearly discernible
even through the partial glimpses of it that the sources allow.

Critical readers, then, will remember the character of the history before
them: dissidence does not, after all, somehow guarantee objectivity. The angle
of the illumination that Philostorgius throws upon events that his opponents
might have preferred to leave in darkness must not be left out of account,
however grateful we ought to be that he has afforded us any sight of them
at all. Readers will also remember that what they have is not the original,
although Photius is usually a careful, if hostile, epitomizer, and his editorial
glosses can usually be detected (his inexplicable lapse at 7.12 is commented
on in the notes).

Notes on the Edition

The translation is from Joseph Bidez's edition mentioned above, except
for the extracts from the Syriac chronicles in appendix 7, which have been

---

10. Ibid., cxxi.

translated from the original rather than from the Latin translation of them offered by the editor. In all other instances, Bidez's text is the one translated, even where more recent editions of the same texts have been published since his edition first appeared, as is the case for instance with the *Artemii Passio* and the *Life of Constantine* in the Codex Angelicus 22.[11]

Bidez edited Photius's epitome in such a way that references to Philostorgius from other sources are mustered under the book and chapter of the epitome to which they seem parallel. His numbering of the sections has been reproduced throughout, but to it has been added the sectional numbering of Opitz's edition of the Codex Angelicus *Life of Constantine*.

To the twelve books of the epitome Bidez added seven appendices (*Anhänge*). The first two offer additional parts of the *Artemii Passio*. The third is a different *Martyrdom of Artemius*, independent of Philostorgius and used by the author of the *Artemii Passio* as a source in addition to him. The fourth is an extract from the beginning of a hagiography that pretends (falsely) to be drawn partly from Philostorgius. The fifth offers further material from the Codex Angelicus *Life of Constantine* about the final war between Constantine and Licinius. The sixth contains a life of Lucian of Antioch drawn not from Philostorgius but from the same source used by him. The seventh, finally, offers material drawn from the anonymous homoean historian of the later fourth century whom Philostorgius, among others, laid under tribute. Further sectional numbering has been added in the appendices where it seemed convenient (along with Opitz's numbering mentioned above).

The last part of the translation, titled "Supplement," is of those parts of the *Life of Constantine* drawn from Philostorgius but discovered after Bidez had published his original edition in 1913. They were published in the subsequent editions in the *Berichtigungen und Nachträge* section.

Notes on the Translation

The translation avoids mere transliteration where possible; thus *homoousios* is rendered "consubstantial" or "consubstantialist doctrine," *heteroousios* "other in substance," and so on, except where the context requires that the similarity of the Greek words to one another be brought out. The wordplays developed in the controversies of the time cannot be reproduced in translation, however; thus, for example, the name of our historian's hero, "Eunomios,"

---

11. The *Artemii Passio* has been edited by Bonifatius Kotter, ed., *Opera homiletica et hagiographica* (vol. 5 of *Die Schriften des Johannes von Damaskos*; PTS 29; Berlin: de Gruyter, 1988), 185–245. For the *Life of Constantine*, see Hans-Georg Opitz, "Die Vita Constantini des Codex Angelicus 22," *Byzantion* 9 (1934): 535–93.

suggests someone law-abiding or concerned with good order, but he soon received the epithet "Anomoios," which means literally "unlike," because of his doctrine that the Son is unlike God (if not unlike the Father). "Anomoios" was then at times perhaps deliberately misspelled "Anomios" or "lawless" by those wanting to suggest what they considered the tendency of his thought. Proper names are spelled as far as possible according to the way in which they usually appear in modern English dictionaries, histories, and atlases.

Ἕλλην and Ἑλληνικός are usually translated "pagan" rather than "Greek," that being their evident meaning here as in other Christian authors of the time, except where the reference is clearly ethnic or geographical. Τύραννος is usually translated "usurper" rather than "tyrant," except where it clearly refers to the personal qualities of some ruler. The technical Latin terms that Philostorgius transliterates (as he likes to do) are reproduced in their Latin form, in order to suggest the tone of the original.

When the same word or words are found in two independent sources drawing from the same part of Philostorgius, the editor prints them in angular typeface to mark them as identifiably what the historian originally wrote; they are also marked in the translation by boldface.

Our history of course often speaks of its leading characters in association with their followers or parties; on the proper translation of οἱ περὶ τὸν δεῖνα, see Timothy D. Barnes, *Athanasius and Constantius: Theology and Politics in the Constantinian Empire* (Cambridge: Harvard University Press, 1993), 248 n. 22.

In closing, special thanks are owed to Dr. John Fitzgerald, General Editor of the Society of Biblical Literature's Writings from the Greco-Roman World series, for his patient and tactful assistance with the preparation of the translation, to Dr. William Adler and Dr. Everett Ferguson for reviewing, correcting, and improving the manuscript in very many places, and to Dr. Sebastian Brock for assistance with the Syriac chronicles. Any faults that remain are entirely those of the translator.

And a final, and quite inadequate, acknowledgment of Joseph Bidez's work should be added to the many that have been paid him since his edition first appeared. It has been repeatedly and justly acclaimed as a masterpiece of erudition and scholarly judgment; the wealth of material offered in its introduction and textual apparatus can only be hinted at by the notes to the translation.

Prologue 1

On the History of Philostorgius, the Eunomian from Cappadocia

This hist'ry have I finished with the help of God's wise grace;
Diverse yet true the things of which it tells.

On the Same

Twelve letters form Philostorgius's fair name,
Hence these he followed when he wrote his books,
The first put first, and then sequentially;
The books' first letters thus compose his name.
[*Palatine Anthology* 9.193–194]

[Photius, *Bibliotheca* codex 40].[1] There was read what purports to be a church history by Philostorgius, of the Arian faith.

---

1. The modern critical edition of Photius's *Bibliotheca* is that of René Henry, ed. and trans., *Photius: Bibliothèque* (9 vols.; Paris: Belles Lettres, 1959–91). Codex 40 is in 1:23–25. However, the translation is, as usual, from Bidez's text (which does not differ significantly from Henry's).

Photius says in Codex 40 that he found Philostorgius's history bound into two volumes, and then he tells us what the second epigram just cited does: that the initial letters of the books spell out their author's name. As Bidez remarks (*Philostorgius,* xcix–ci), Photius will hardly have noticed this on his own; he must have read the epigram. Further, if, as seems likely, he did not hit upon the epigram by chance, then we may suppose that he found it at the beginning of the second volume and that that is why he tells us about the acrostic at that point in his abstract. If that is so, then, Bidez conjectures, the first epigram will have stood at the beginning of the entire history and served to introduce it.

The epigrams' style and knowledge of the acrostic show that they were composed by Philostorgius himself or by a friend. The same may be said of the title above them, which announces the author's birthplace and the proper name of his sect: "Euno-

The history runs counter to nearly all the church historians. It exalts all those of Arian sympathies, and heaps scorn on the orthodox, so that his history is not so much a history as it is a eulogy of the heretics, and undisguised criticism and condemnation of the orthodox.

His style is elegant, with poetical turns of speech that are neither excessive nor awkward. The figurative language is charming and pleasant in its very expressiveness. Sometimes, however, he uses such far-fetched and quite extraordinary expressions that he falls into absurdities and nonsense. His language is variously embellished, and to such a degree as to produce in the listener an impression that is unclear and not always pleasing. He does often embellish his account with fitting maxims, however.

His history goes from the beginning of Arius's sectarian activities down to the recall of Aetius the most impious. This Aetius was deposed from the diaconate by his fellow sectarians because his impiety surpassed even theirs, as our own author relates despite himself, but he was recalled by the most impious Julian and received in a kindly way. His history runs to six sections in one volume to reach this point in time.

The man is a liar, quite capable of writing sheer fantasy.

He exalts especially Aetius and Eunomius for their teaching, making the absurd claim that they alone cleared the rubble of time[2] from orthodox doctrine, and likewise Eusebius of Nicomedia, whom he calls "the Great," Theophilus the Indian, and several others for their marvels and their lives. But he criticizes in particular Acacius, the bishop of Caesarea in Palestine, for his supreme craftiness and invincible cunning, by means of which, he says, he got the better of everyone else, both those supposedly his doctrinal allies who had some grievance against him and those of opposing religious views.

This much I read, and then a little later in another volume I read another six books of his, so that his subject matter in its entirety takes up twelve books. Their initials when put together spell out the author's name, "Philostorgius."

---

mian," not "Arian" (Bidez, *Philostorgius*, xcix). Philostorgius's determination to have his doctrinal allegiance known runs throughout his history, into which he wove his own name by acrostic, as though to make it impossible to erase by simple removal of the title. The epigram's Ionic dialect, together with the opening word (ἱστορίην) inevitably suggest Herodotus, so the reader is not surprised to find our author's excursions into geography and natural history.

2. Aetius refers to his opponents as "Temporists" (Χρονῖται: Epiphanius, *Pan.* 76.11.1), perhaps since he thought that their doctrine of the sharing of essence between the Father and the Son implied change and thus time; see L. R. Wickham, "The *Syntagmation* of Aetius the Anomean," *JTS* 19 (1968): 550. For another view, see Raoul Mortley, *From Word to Silence* (Theophaneia 30–31; 2 vols.; Bonn: Hanstein, 1986), 2:129.

They go down to the time of Theodosius the Younger, stopping at the year when Theodosius entrusted the government of Rome, upon the death of Honorius, to his nephew Valentinian the Younger, the son of Placidia and Constantius.

However he may rage against the orthodox, our Philostorgius nonetheless does not venture to attack Gregory the theologian but unwillingly acknowledges his learning. He does try to criticize Basil the Great but simply increases his glory by doing so, since the very evidence of the facts compels him to acknowledge the force and beauty of the language of his discourses. And yet the coward refers to him as brash and inexperienced in debate, since, he says, he ventured to oppose Eunomius's writings.

Prologue 2
Epitome of the Church History of Philostorgius Made by the Patriarch Photius

His history takes up twelve books, the initial letters of the respective books forming his name when put together. He begins with the "strife," as he calls it, between Arius and Alexander, which he describes as the origin of the sect. He goes down to the proclamation of Valentinian (the son of Placidia and Constantius) as emperor and the suppression of the usurper John.

The history is not so much a history as it is his eulogy of the sectarians as well as slander and criticism of the orthodox.

Book 1

1. He says he has no idea who the author of Maccabees is.[1] He regards the first book as worthy of acceptance, however, since its narrative agrees with the prophecies of Daniel and because it relates with such care how the wickedness of men brought the affairs of the Jews to their worst state, and how the virtue of men restored them again, and then they took fresh strength against the enemy and the temple was purified of pagan defilements. The second book, he says, does not give evidence of the same author; it is rather a summary of what Jason of Cyrene wrote in five books recounting the war waged by Judas Maccabeus against Antiochus Epiphanes and his son, surnamed Eupator.[2] The third book he rejects, calling it bizarre and quite unlike the first in content. As for the fourth book, he too acknowledges that it was written by Josephus and says that it is not so much history as eulogy in what it relates of Eleazar and the seven Maccabean boys.

1a [*Suda*, Φ 527]. Philostorgius says that ... described Jewish events at greater length than did Phlegon; Phlegon and Dio mentioned them briefly and parenthetically to their main topic.[3] For [the first author] shows not the slightest concern for making piety or the other virtues attractive, just as they do not. Quite the contrary; Josephus seems to go out of his way to avoid offending the pagans.

2. While Philostorgius praises Eusebius, "son of Pamphilus," in other respects, including what pertains to his history, he says that he erred in ortho-

---

1. Philostorgius took a special interest in the story of the Maccabees: a beleaguered minority upholding the true monotheist faith against overwhelming odds (see Richard P. Vaggione, *Eunomius of Cyzicus and the Nicene Revolution* [Oxford: Clarendon, 2000], 44).

2. On Jason of Cyrene, see 2 Macc 2:23. What came to be called 4 Maccabees was ascribed to Josephus by Eusebius (*Hist. eccl.* 3.10.6) and Jerome (*Vir. ill.* 13).

3. Phlegon of Tralles, that ardent antiquarian, may have mentioned events in Jewish history in his *Olympiads*; their fragments do not contain any. See William Hansen, *Phlegon of Tralles' Book of Marvels* (Exeter: University of Exeter Press, 1996), 1–22. Cassius Dio's Roman history, which goes down to 229 C.E. in eighty books, mentions Jewish affairs mainly in 65.4.1–7.2 and 69.12.1–14.3.

doxy. His error, says the impious wretch, was that he considered the divinity to be unknowable and incomprehensible, and he says that he erred in other like ways. He too states that Eusebius brought his own history to an end with the succession of the sons of Constantine the Great.[4]

3. The impious fellow says that the votes for the archbishopric were in favor of Arius, who preferred Alexander to himself and managed to have them transferred to him.[5]

4. He says that there was a presbyter, Alexander, who was surnamed Baucalis because the bulge of superfluous flesh accumulated on his back gave him the shape of an earthenware jug, which the Alexandrians call locally a *baukalē*.[6] He ranked second after Arius and was behind the quarrel between Bishop Alexander and Arius on account of which the consubstantialist doctrine was devised.[7]

5. Constantius, the father of Constantine the Great, was, he says, proclaimed emperor of Upper Galatia, where the so-called Alps are found, because of his bravery.[8] Those regions are hard to approach and enter. Galatia is nowadays called "Gaul." Constantius died in that Britain which is called Albion. The youth Constantine reached him there while he was ill, having unexpectedly escaped Diocletian's plot, saw to his burial, and succeeded to his realm.[9]

6. He agrees with the others that the reason for the conversion of Constantine the Great from paganism to Christianity was the victory over Maxentius, in which **the sign of the cross** appeared in the east extending to a

---

4. Eusebius's *Historia ecclesiastica* ends with Licinius's defeat; his *Vita Constantini* ends with the succession of Constantine's sons.

5. On Alexander's election, see Epiphanius, *Pan.* 68.3.5; 69.11.4–6; Rufinus, *Hist. eccl.* 10.1; Socrates 1.5.1; Theodoret, *Hist. eccl.* 1.2.8–9. Alexander in 313 succeeded Achillas, who had succeeded Peter Martyr. Philostorgius, if Photius represents him accurately, is the only one to tell this story. Theodoret says that Arius's jealousy was aroused by Alexander's election.

6. *Baucalis* was an Alexandrian word for a drinking vessel (Athenaeus 11.784b). Epiphanius says it was the name of Arius's church (*Pan.* 68.4.2; 69.1.2; 69.2.4).

7. An Alexandrian presbyter named Alexander subscribed the letter of protest of the Alexandrian clergy to the Mareotic Commission (Athanasius, *C. Ar.* 73.5).

8. Constantius's brave military deeds are celebrated in *Pan. Lat.* VI (VII) 5–6; VIII (V) 2.1, 6–9, 12–21; VII (VI) 4.2–4; XII (IX) 25.1–2. Philostorgius uses "Alps" (Ἄλπεις) in the sense of "mountain passes" (cf. 3.24), as in the Latin *alpis*. His reference to Gaul as "Galatia" is an example of his fondness for giving places their classical names (see Bidez, *Philostorgius*, cxli).

9. On Diocletian's plot against Constantine, his escape, and his reunion with his father, see S II and the notes thereto.

great distance and formed of a brilliant radiance. It was encircled by stars like a rainbow that were arranged as letters forming the Latin words: "**With this conquer!**"

6a [*AP* 45: Artemius addresses Julian]. (Constantine) was favorably disposed to Christ, who had called him from heaven, when he fought the bitterly contested battle against Maxentius.[10] He showed him **the sign of the cross brilliantly radiant above the sun at midday,** the starry letters spelling out for him in Latin the victory in the battle.[11] [We ourselves were present at the battle, saw the sign, and read the letters. The whole camp saw it too, and there are many witnesses of it in your court, should you care to inquire.][12]

7. Even before the Council of Nicaea, he says, Alexander of Alexandria went to Nicomedia, met there with Hosius of Cordova and the bishops with him, and arranged that the Son should be acknowledged as consubstantial to the Father by conciliar decree and that Arius should be excommunicated.[13]

---

10. For the battle against Maxentius, see *Anon. Val.* 12; *Pan. Lat.* XII (IX) 3.3, 5–18; IV (X) 28.1–30.1; Eusebius, *Vit. Const.* 1.37–38; Lactantius, *Mort.* 44; Zosimus 2.15–16. S IV says there was no battle, Maxentius's army surrendering without bloodshed (but see 248 n. 31 below).

11. On the luminous sign of the cross, see Eusebius, *Vit. Const.* 1.28; S IV; *Chron. pasch.* a. 311; Rufinus/Eusebius, *Hist. eccl.* 9.1.1; *Bios* 335.24–26. *Pan. Lat.* IV (X) 14 and 29.1 (a. 321) speaks of a heavenly army with fiery soldiers coming to Constantine's aid. Lactantius, *Mort.* 44.5, says that Constantine was warned in a dream to put "God's heavenly sign" on his shields; he obeyed by marking them with "the letter X sideways, its top part bent around." The cross as a battle-standard was later to protect him in his war with Licinius (A5.21). On the question of Constantine's religious conversion, see Thomas G. Elliott, "Constantine's Conversion: Do We Really Need It?" *Phoenix* 41 (1987): 420–38; idem, "Constantine's Early Religious Development," *JRH* 15 (1989): 283–91; idem, "Constantine's Explanation of His Career," *Byzantion* 62 (1992): 212–34.

12. The square brackets at the end of 1.6a reproduce those in Bidez's text; they mark his suspicion that the *AP* might have drawn from Eusebius, *Vit. Const.* 1.28, at this point. But with Bidez's edition of the new material on the life of Constantine ("Fragments nouveaux de Philostorge sur la vie de Constantin," *Byzantion* 10 [1935]: 403–37), his suspicion vanished (see 435 n. 42).

13. Constantine sent Hosius of Cordova to Alexander of Alexandria and Arius with a letter urging them to settle their differences: Eusebius, *Vit. Const.* 2.63–73; Socrates 1.7.1; Theodoret, *Hist. eccl.* 1.7.1. Hosius attended the Synod of Alexandria of 324/5 (Athanasius, *C. Ar.* 74.4) and presided at the Synod of Antioch of 325 (Hans-Georg Opitz, ed., *Urkunden zur Geschichte des arianischen Streites, 318–328* [vol. 3.1 of *Athanasius Werke*; Berlin: de Gruyter, 1934–35], 18.1 and 19.1). See also Benjamin H. Cowper, *Syriac Miscellanies* (London: Williams & Norgate, 1861), 1–7; and *PO* 7:546–47.

7a [Opitz, *Vit. Const.* 27–28].[14] Arius and his associates took the round-about way through Palestine, Phoenicia, the rest of Syria,[15] Cilicia, and the remaining provinces that lay on their route to Bithynia and the emperor (whom they were eager to inform of what had taken place when they arrived, bringing with them the bishops' resolutions and testimonies); they had decided to visit all of them, taking a circular route, and had thus added a considerable time to the journey by so doing. Alexander meanwhile sailed by the fastest route from Alexandria to the Propontis and Nicomedia. Upon his arrival he conferred with Hosius of Cordova and his associates and persuaded them to support his views and endorse the consubstantialist doctrine, draw-ing them to his side with his quite reasonable remarks.

He used the following sort of words in informing all of them of Arius's blasphemy and perversity: "It is a dangerous business, my friends, to show favor unreservedly to those around one, especially when it comes to those who seem the friendliest, a dangerous business requiring great caution. For honors that exceed what suits men's station do not incline most of those upon whom they are bestowed to goodwill toward those who bestow them but embolden them rather to act insolently toward them.[16] And even though this sort of thing is not to be endured, yet endured it I have! What has made it bearable is that Arius in his supreme wickedness thinks that there still remains room for him to advance his evil, as though his malice had not yet reached its full measure. But he will not escape unpunished, let him be clear about that! Nor will he find joy in what his boldness has attempted against me. For he will come to realize that old men too have the mettle to requite injury. Let him then be excommunicated by us all, let our common anathema be issued, and let Arius be held in abhorrence along with all those whom the unclean demon has separated and driven from this sacred church."

Seeing that the bishops had many different views at the time, the emperor Constantine decided to summon a council of all the bishops to Nicaea and to put an end to their mutual bickering.

---

14. On the relationship of the *Vita Constantini* to Philostorgius, see 239 n. 1, first paragraph. The corresponding section numbers of Opitz's edition of this *Vita* are inserted at the relevant places in the translation (which, however, continues to follow Bidez's text); see Opitz, "De Vita Constantini."

15. "The rest of Syria" means Syria Coele (in contrast to Euphratensis; see also 3.8 and 11.8).

16. The danger of bestowing honors on the undeserving is a commonplace; see Cassius Dio 77.5.1.

8. A short time later the council was held in Nicaea. Among the other high priests of God in attendance were **Basileus, the** bishop **of Amaseia,** and **Meletius of Sebastopolis.**

8a [Nicetas, *Thes.* 5.7]. Philostorgius says in the first book of his history that those of Arian views were the following.[17] From Upper Libya: Sentianus of Boreum, Dachius of Berenice, Secundus of Teuchira, Zopyrus of Barce, another Secundus of Ptolemais, and Theonas of Marmarica. From Thebes in Egypt: Melitius. From Palestine: Patrophilus of Scythopolis and Eusebius of Caesarea, or "son of Pamphilus," as he was surnamed. From Phoenicia: Paulinus of Tyre and Amphion of Sidon. From Cilicia: Narcissus of Irenopolis, Athanasius of Anazarbus, and Tarcondimatus of Aegae. From Cappadocia: Leontius, Longianus, and Eulalius. From Pontus: **Basileus of Amaseia and Meletius of Sebastopolis.** From Bithynia: Theognis of Nicaea, Maris of Chalcedon, and Eusebius of Nicomedia, **surnamed "the Great,"** a disciple of the martyr Lucian conspicuous above all for his virtue, on account of which he received his surname.[18]

9. Even he acknowledges that they all agreed with the definition of faith in Nicaea, apart from Secundus of Ptolemais, whom Theonas of Marmarica followed. The remaining group of Arian leaders, namely, Eusebius of Nicomedia, whom he exalts with the title "Great," Theognis of Nicaea, Maris of Chalcedon, and the rest of the gang went over to the council. They did so deceitfully, he adds, and they concealed the term *homoiousion* in the word *homoousion*.[19] Nonetheless, they undertook to agree to the conciliar decrees,

---

17. This list of Arius's supporters at the Council of Nicaea is not reliable. Basileus of Amaseia had been executed ca. 320 by Licinius for abetting Constantine's alliance against him with Tiridates of Armenia. See Ernst Honigmann, *Patristic Studies* (Studi e Testi 173; Vatican City: Biblioteca apostolica vaticana, 1953), 6–27 ("Basileus of Amasea"); Vaggione, *Eunomius of Cyzicus,* 61 n. 159. His name is found neither in Heinrich Gelzer, Heinrich Hilgenfeld, and Otto Cuntz, *Patrum nicaenorum nomina Latine, Graece, Coptice, Syriace, Arabice, Armeniace* (Leipzig: Teubner, 1898), nor in Ernst Honigmann, "La liste originale des Pères de Nicée," *Byzantion* 14 (1939): 44–48. Rufinus (*Hist. eccl.* 10.5) says there were seventeen Arian sympathizers, six of whom chose exile with Arius.

18. On the martyr Lucian, see A6; Eusebius, *Hist. eccl.* 8.13.2, 9.6.3; Rufinus/Eusebius, *Hist. eccl.* 9.9; Epiphanius, *Pan.* 43.1.1; 69.5.2; 69.6.7; 76.3.5; Jerome, *Vir. ill.* 77; Sozomen 3.5.9; Gustave Bardy, *Recherches sur S. Lucien d'Antioche et son école* (Paris: Beauchesne, 1936).

19. The concealment of the word *homoiousios* under the other word refers to the convention of the ancient subscription, which was never a bare signature, but always a complete sentence or sentences of some sort. Subscriptions to creeds often borrowed the convention of the contractual subscription in presenting a summary,

Constantina, the emperor's sister, having advised them to do so.[20]

9a [Opitz, *Vit. Const.* 28]. When Sunday arrived, they gathered, and each of them delivered his opinion. The emperor was in their midst, but he waited to see what the assembly would decide. Hosius of Cordova and Alexander and their associates had in readiness the document that everyone needed to subscribe.

The text of the document reads as follows: "The gloriously triumphant Constantine Augustus decreed that a council of the holy bishops of the holy catholic and apostolic church should meet in Nicaea, the capital of Bithynia."

"We believe in one God, the Father almighty, the maker of heaven and earth, of all things visible and invisible," and so on. "But the catholic and apostolic church anathematizes those who say that there was a time when he did not exist, and that he did not exist before he was begotten, and that he was produced from nothing that exists, or that he is from another substance or essence, or that the Son of God is created or subject to change or alteration."[21]

---

however vestigial, of the contents of the document subscribed. Philostorgius in 1.9 and 9a says, then, that those in charge of the council required at least some of its members to include the word *homoousios* in their subscriptions. Jerome bears this out when he says that the "Arians" at the council subscribed using the word *homoousios* (*Dialogus contra Luciferianos* 20). On the pressure applied to them to subscribe, see also Rufinus, *Hist. eccl.* 10.5; Socrates 1.14.3; Sozomen 3.19.3–4. Those not of their number were not required to subscribe in this way; the formula for the usual subscription reads (in its Latin version): "Ego ille episcopus illius civitatis et provinciae illius ita credo sicut supra scriptum est" (*EOMIA* volume 1, bottom of second column on unnumbered page following page marked "to face p. 152"). It seems in fact to have belonged to the powers of the council presidency of those times to decide who might or must subscribe with some doctrinal elaboration and in what terms; see my "Paulinus' Subscription to the *Tomus ad Antiochenos*," *JTS* NS 53 (2002): 53–74, esp. 63–64.

What our author means, then, is that the "Arian" leaders at Nicaea managed to write their subscriptions so carelessly that the extra iota in the key word escaped the attention of those in charge. Sozomen (2.21.6) reports a rumor that Eusebius and Theognis prevailed upon the custodian of the Nicene documents to let them erase their subscriptions and then began to deny the necessity of holding to the consubstantialist doctrine. Both stories may be discounted. Constantia's motive in urging the "Arians" to yield may have been that she feared her brother might revert to paganism if the Christian leaders remained at odds (cf. Sozomen 3.19).

20. "Constantina" is more correctly written "Constantia." Rufinus, *Hist. eccl.* 10.12, records her sympathy with Arianism. Cf. Socrates 1.25.1–5; Sozomen 2.27.2–4; Theodoret, *Hist. eccl.* 2.3.1–3.

21. For the original text of the Creed of Nicaea, see *DEC* 1:5. It may be noted that Constantine's order about subscribing the Creed, and its attendant anathemas, did not include bishops (the ἄλλοι τοῦ κλήρου can hardly have meant them).

Those mentioned above brought this document into the assembly and not only required that everyone endorse the statement; they confirmed the approval of each of them by having him subscribe. All those of the party of Arius were also present there. They of course did not accept the orthodox creed. Hence the emperor issued the following quite religious decision: that all whosoever would not assent to the common decree of the bishops, whether they were presbyters, deacons, or others of the clergy, should be punished by exile. Philumenus was the one charged with carrying out the decision; he had obtained from the emperor the rank that the Romans call *magister*.[22] He therefore presented the document to Arius and those with him, ordering them to choose which they preferred: to subscribe and avoid punishment or to refuse and go into exile. They chose to go into exile and down to the depths of perdition, as they deserved.[23]

9b [Photius, *Bibliotheca* codex 40 as above, p. 1]. (Philostorgius) exalts ... Eusebius of Nicomedia, whom he calls "the Great," for his marvels and his life.

9c [Nicetas, *Thes.* 5.8]. Philostorgius toward the end of the first book says that some of those who subscribed the creed in Nicaea put the word *homoousios* into their subscriptions straightforwardly. But Eusebius and company contrived a cunning blasphemy and wrote *homoiousios* instead of *homoousios,* the exceptions being Secundus and Theonas, who were exiled to Illyricum with Arius and the presbyters with him.

10. He says that as Secundus was leaving for exile, he said to Eusebius, "Eusebius, you subscribed in order to avoid exile! As God is my witness, you will have to suffer banishment on my account." And Eusebius was sent into exile three months after the council, as Secundus had foretold, having returned openly to his own heresy.[24]

---

22. On Philumenus, *magister* (*officiorum*?), cf. *PLRE* 1:699.

23. Rufinus (*Hist. eccl.* 10.5) says that of the seventeen "Arian" sympathizers, eleven agreed to subscribe and six went into exile (he does not say that they were bishops).

24. Eusebius of Nicomedia and Theognis received some dissident Alexandrians, and the emperor in punishment banished them three months after the council, which seems previously to have left them in (conditional?) possession of their sees (cf. Opitz, *Urkunden zur Geschichte,* 27; 28; 31.2). Is the change of heart undergone by Eusebius, Theognis, and Maris in 2.1a and 2.1b connected with their dealings with these Alexandrians?

BOOK 2

1. Our mendacious Cacostorgius[1] says that following the general council and the unconcealed return to heresy of those associated with Eusebius, the emperor Constantine exacted punishment from them for having subscribed the word *homoousios* while holding other views, and he recalled Secundus and his associates. He also, so he says, sent letters everywhere disparaging the term *homoousios* and endorsing *heteroousios* ["other in substance"].[2] Alexander of Alexandria subscribed the letters, and thus he was brought to accord with Arius and company. But when fear of the emperor had waned, Alexander returned to his own doctrine, and Arius,[3] along with those who shared his views, once again separated from him and from the church.

1a [Opitz, *Vit. Const.* 34]. Eusebius, the bishop of Nicomedia, who had been quite won over to the heteroousian heresy, went to Chalcedon and took counsel with Theognis about matters that needed to be decided. They also met with Maris.[4] The three of them were sitting together in a portico of the church discussing the issues at hand and babbling on about their sect, finding themselves in disagreement, when suddenly there was a great earthquake at the place where they were, and there alone.[5] And intense darkness fell at about the third hour of the day, causing sheer terror.

1b [Nicetas, *Thes.* 5.8]. At the start of the second book, (Philostorgius) says that Eusebius, Theognis, and Maris repented of having subscribed at all,

---

1. If "Philostorgius" is from *philostorgos,* meaning "affectionate," then "Cacostorgius" should mean something like "evil-loving."

2. As for the terms "consubstantial" or "other in substance," neither is mentioned anywhere in Constantine's surviving letters.

3. Arius was recalled by Constantine on 27 November 327 and invited to court, where he presented a profession of faith (which may be found in Opitz, *Urkunden zur Geschichte,* 30; Constantine's letter of invitation to him is in *Urkunden zur Geschichte,* 29). He was restored to communion by a Council of Nicomedia in 327 or 328.

4. Maris was not banished with Eusebius and Theognis; cf. Sozomen 2.21.8.

5. This is the first, but hardly the last, mention of an earthquake; they are, Philostorgius teaches, caused directly by God (12.10) and are an infallible sign of divine anger.

went to the emperor, and said, "We acted impiously, your majesty, in subscribing the heresy from fear of you." Angered, he banished them to Gaul, which is western Galatia, and ordered that Arius and his companions be restored to their own cities.

2. Once Arius left the church, he says, **he wrote songs for sailing, grinding,** traveling, and so on, set them to the music he thought suitable to each, and through the pleasure given by the music stole away the simpler folk for his own heresy.[6]

2a [Nicetas, *Thes.* 5.8]. When Arius had left the most religious assembly and was excluded by the orthodox everywhere and no longer had any way to speak to the crowds and teach about the current issues, he proceeded **to write** some psalms to the best of his ability, as well as **songs for sailing and grinding** and the kind used by travelers when they are driving asses.

3. While he idolizes Arius for his battle with God that he wages against the Son, he says that he gets tangled in nonsense when he repeatedly presents God as unknowable, incomprehensible, and inconceivable.[7] And he is not such only for human beings, which might be a lesser evil; he is such for none other than the only begotten Son of God as well. He adds that it was not just Arius who was taken with this absurdity at the time, but most of that group as well. The exceptions were Secundus and Theonas and the disciples of the martyr Lucian, namely, Leontius, Antony, and Eusebius of Nicomedia; the rest of the heretical band fell for the doctrine described.[8]

------

6. On Arius's songs, see Athanasius, *Decr.* 16.3; *Dion.* 6; *Apol. sec.* 1.2; 1.5–7; 2.37; *Syn.* 15 (which says that it was after Arius left the church that he composed songs). It is unlikely that these songs were ever part of his *Thalia* (see Bardy, *Recherches sur Lucien d'Antioche,* 248–49).

7. On Arius's teaching that God is unknowable, see Athanasius, *Syn.* 15.3; *C. Ar.* 1.6 (the Father is invisible to the Son); *Ep. Aeg. Lib.* 12 (the Son knows neither the Father exactly nor even his own essence). See Rowan D. Williams, "The Quest of the Historical Thalia," in *Arianism: Historical and Theological Reassessments* (ed. Robert C. Gregg; Cambridge: Philadelphia Patristic Foundation, 1985), 1–35, esp. 25. Philostorgius gives evidence of a split among "Arians": those who found his teaching on divine unknowability appealing, and who might eventually have felt growing sympathy for the theology of the Cappadocian fathers; and those who tended toward "neo-Arianism."

8. On Eusebius, see Bardy, *Recherches sur Lucien d'Antioche,* 296–315; and Colm Luibheid, "The Arianism of Eusebius of Nicomedia," *ITQ* 43 (1976): 3–23. There is nothing in what remains of his writings to support Philostorgius's contention that he disagreed with Arius about God's knowability, and in fact his declaration that the Son's origin is indescribable and incomprehensible, both to human beings and to those above them (Opitz, *Urkunden zur Geschichte,* 8.3), suggests otherwise. His

4. Constantine, he says, did away with his own son Priscus after being taken in by his **stepmother's** slander. She in turn was caught in adultery with a *cursor* ["courier"], and he ordered her suffocated in the heat of a bath. Constantine not long afterwards paid the penalty for executing the boy when he was poisoned to death by his brothers while staying in Nicomedia.[9]

---

high standing with Philostorgius will have come from his association with Lucian the martyr and from his stout resistance to Athanasius and to the consubstantialist doctrine. It should be remembered that Photius, in his abstract in *Bibliotheca* Codex 40, contrasts the kind of adulation Philostorgius offers to Eusebius (for his life and manners) and to Aetius and Eunomius (for their doctrine). Philostorgius's own view, that God's essence is fully knowable, comes from his Eunomian masters (see the introduction above, "'Consubstantial' in Creed and Doctrine after Constantine").

9. "Priscus" is found as the anagram of "Crispus" in various sources. He was born ca. 305 to Minervina, who seems to have been Constantine's first wife, although this is disputed; *Pan. Lat.* VII (VI) 4.1, at any rate, refers to their union as a marriage (*Epit. Caes.* 41.4 and Zosimus 2.20.2 refer to Minervina as a concubine). In 307 Constantine married Fausta, the daughter of the emperor Maximian (not Maxentius, contrary to what Philostorgius says), as part of a political alliance, Minervina having died or been repudiated. Fausta bore him Constantine II, Constantius II, Constantina (or "Constantia"), Constans, and Helena. Crispus had an excellent character (Eusebius, *Hist. eccl.* 10.9.6; Eutropius 10.6.3) and was an accomplished general (*Pan. Lat.* IV ([X] 36.3–37.2) who defeated Licinius's navy in his father's war with him (*Anon. Val.* 23; 26–27). But two years later he was suddenly put to death, on his father's orders, at Pola in Istria, a fate to which his stepmother followed him the same year. It was also in 326 that a series of laws about the sanctity of marriage issued from Constantine's chancery: *Cod. theod.* 9.7.1 and 9.7.2 concerning adultery (3 February and 25 April, respectively), *Cod. theod.* 9.8.1 regarding seduction (4 April), and *Cod. justin.* 5.26 (14 June) forbidding married men from keeping concubines.

All of this left wide room for speculation among the ancient authors, as it has also among the moderns; see Aurelius Victor 41.11 and Eutropius 10.6.3. *Epit. Caes.* 41.11–12 says that Crispus died at Fausta's request, Fausta in turn being executed to console Helena. Zosimus 2.29.2 says, like Philostorgius, that Crispus was killed on suspicion of an illicit relationship with Fausta, who was herself stifled in a hot bath. Patrick Guthrie ("The Execution of Crispus," *Phoenix* 20 [1966]: 325–31) speculates that Constantine wanted to rid himself of his illegitimate son in order to make way for the eventual succession of his legitimate heirs, whose very lives might some day be endangered if their popular older half-brother succeeded to power. J. Rougé ("Fausta, femme de Constantin: criminelle ou victime," *Cahiers d'Histoire* 25 [1980]: 3–17) accepts Crispus's legitimacy and wonders if his stepmother plotted to get rid of him and of Licinius's son and others, who stood in the way of the succession of her own sons. Hans A. Pohlsander ("Crispus: Brilliant Career and Tragic End," *Historia* 33 [1984]: 79–106) reviews the evidence more cautiously, although he does think that

4a [Opitz, *Vit. Const.* 35–36]. Crispus, the oldest of Constantine's sons, born to him from Maxentius's daughter, was governing under his father (with the rank of Caesar) and distinguishing himself by his military exploits, when in the very flower of life, the year after the Council of Nicaea, he died, to use the most general verb. Now those who are full of heresy and impiety <say that> his life was brought to an end by his father; since their words are so marked by falsehood, it would be only right to omit them. But since I am making every effort to set down all the views expressed by those of old, it seems good to add this one to the present work, not to confirm but to refute those who like to speak falsehood. For they say that his **stepmother** Fausta was behind his murder, on account of her infatuation. Having fallen in love with the youth and being completely swept away by her feeling, she first tried to allure him by saying various things to get him to make love to her. But he showed complete resistance to her suggestions and would not let them even be mentioned, making it evident that he would never be persuaded. By now inflamed with desire and not knowing what would become of her, she proceeded to plot against the one she desired, turning her love to hatred. Angered at not having her desire fulfilled, she found a cure for her passion in the killing of her desired one and eagerly satisfied her longing with his murder. Thus she persuaded her own husband to kill his own son, making her illness his as well and pouring forth against him a varied and deceitful stream of words. Anger at what his wife told him forestalled any reflection on his part, and not pausing to examine the facts, he became a **Theseus** to his son; just as the latter killed **Hippolytus**, born to him from Hippolyte the Amazon, when **Phaedra** slandered him, so he slew Crispus when his wife accused him, his inner sense of judgment so shaken that he was unwilling even to exchange a word with him.

But justice did not shut its eyes to the act of passion, and a fitting punishment awaited the stepmother. She once again yielded to desire, this time for one of the emperor's couriers, whom the Romans call *cursores,* was caught in the act, and was put to death by her husband. He told her eunuchs in secret that when she went to the bath, they were to prolong the time she spent there—supposedly getting her treatment—whether she liked it or not, and were to relieve each other in shifts until she fainted from the stifling heat. Then they were to carry her out breathing her last, expending themselves to

---

the testimony of the ancient sources makes a link between the deaths of Crispus and Fausta probable. What they say about the kind of misdeeds they allegedly committed is another matter. Julian, at any rate, is anxious to protect Fausta from the sort of accusation found here (*Or.* 1.9B–C). How she was executed is not known; John Chrysostom says her husband tied her up naked on the mountains and left her for the beasts (*Hom. Phil.* 15: PG 62:318A–B).

ensure that her death was due not to intrigue but to an accident in the bath. Thus the punishment would be administered, and the way it was done would dispel the infamy attaching to guilt.

This, then, was the result of the wrong she had done the youth. But I do not know if that liar Philostorgius is telling the truth in what he says here against the devout and gloriously triumphant Constantine....

4b [*AP* 43: Julian speaks]. Constantine, as you yourself know, was the most gullible of men, stupid and senseless, and so made innovations in the cult, annulled the Roman customs, and turned away to Christianity; it was because he was afraid of his unholy acts and because the gods led him astray as one accursed and unworthy of their cult, drenched as he was with his own relatives' blood.[10] For he killed his brothers, who had done nothing wrong, along with his wife Fausta and his son Priscus, that good and worthy man. Abhorring these impious deeds, the gods led him astray and made him wander far indeed from their sacred and all-holy cult, and wiped out his accursed and abominable seed and his whole family from the human race.

[*AP* 45: Artemius answers]. Since you have derided the blessed Constantine, the noblest of emperors, and his family, calling him an enemy of your gods, insane, murderous, and drenched with his relatives' blood, I shall reply, in his defense, to your charges, that it was rather your father Constantius and his brothers who were behind the wrongdoing; they prepared the **lethal drug** for him and brought about his death, even though he had done them no wrong.[11] He for his part acted with perfect justice in putting his wife Fausta to death, since she had imitated the **Phaedra** of old in slandering his son Priscus and claiming that he was infatuated with her and had tried to violate her, just as Phaedra had done to **Theseus's son Hippolytus**. He requited his son, since he was his father, and indeed he did so according to the laws of nature. Later, however, when he had learned the truth, he put her to death too, passing upon her the fairest of sentences.

---

10. On the interpretation of Constantine's conversion to Christianity as motivated by guilt for the executions, see François Paschoud, *Cinq études sur Zosime* (Paris: Belles Lettres, 1975), 24–62 ("Zosime 2,29 et la version païenne de la conversion de Constantin"). Julian had already put this story out in *Caesares* 336A–B, but, as Paschoud (61–62) and Pohlsander (163) point out, Constantine's actions suggest otherwise: his generosity to the church after his victory over Maxentius shows that the real reason for his devotion to Christ was his sense of gratitude for Christ's help in the battle, while his baptism was a step he put off until just before his death.

11. On Constantine being poisoned by his brothers, see 2.16, 2.16a, and 32 n. 44.

5. He says that around this time Ulfila[12] brought over into Roman territory a great number of people from the Scythians beyond the Danube (of old the Scythians were called Getae, but now they are called Goths); they had been driven from their homeland because of their faith.[13] The nation was [he says] converted to Christianity in the following way. During the reign of Valerian and Gallienus, a great company of the Scythians from beyond the Danube crossed into Roman territory and overran much of Europe.[14] Crossing into Asia as well, they attacked Galatia and Cappadocia, took many captives, among whom there were members of the clergy, and returned home laden with booty. But the faithful throng of captives, in associating with the barbarians, converted not a few of them to the faith and brought them over from paganism to Christianity. Among the captives were Ulfila's forebears, who were of Cappadocian stock, from a village called Sadagolthina near the city of Parnassus. Ulfila himself was leader of the faithful who had gone into exile, having become their first bishop. He was appointed in the following way. During Constantine's reign he was sent on embassy with others by the nation's ruler (the barbarian nations there were indeed subject to the emperor) and was ordained [bishop] of the Christians in the land of the Goths by Eusebius and the bishops with him.[15] He looked after their various interests, invented

---

12. On various renditions of the Gothic bishop's name, see Ernst A. Ebbinghaus, "Ulfila(s) or Wulfila," *Historische Sprachforschung* 104 (1991): 236–38. On Ulfila's life, see Herwig Wolfram, *History of the Goths* (trans. Thomas J. Dunlap; Berkeley and Los Angeles: University of California Press, 1988), 75–85, and Knut Schäferdiek, "Die Anfänge des Christentums bei den Goten und der sog. gotische Arianismus," *ZKG* 112 (2001): 295–310. He was born ca. 311; his native place is noticed by S. Salaville, "Un ancien bourg de Cappadoce: Sadagolthina," *Echos d'Orient* 15 (1912): 61–63. His ancestors were carried off by Danubian Goths in 257.

13. Philostorgius follows the fashion of his day in identifying the Scythians, Getae, and Goths (cf. Isidore, *Etym.* 9.2.89; *Hist. Goth.* 66), three peoples originally of course quite distinct. He also, like his contemporaries, presents the barbarians of his time as the descendants of those mentioned in classical works; another example is in 9.17.

14. By "Europe," Philstorgius here means Thracian Europe, the Roman province. He can also use "Europe" in the sense of the continent and shift blithely from one meaning to the next without warning, as in 11.7 and 11.8.

15. On the date of his consecration as bishop, see Timothy D. Barnes, "The Consecration of Ulfila," *JTS* 41 (1990): 541–45. Barnes puts the date at 336, on the occasion of the Council of Constantinople of that year; the Gothic embassy would have been organized as part of Constantine's tricennalian celebration. Barnes's date is disputed by Hagith Sivan, "Ulfila's Own Conversion," *HTR* 89 (1996): 373–86, who notes that there is no mention of a Gothic delegation to the tricennalia and thinks

an alphabet just for them,[16] and translated all of the Scriptures into their language, except for the books of Kings, since these contain the history of the wars and the nation was warlike and needed its aggressiveness curbed rather than kindled. These books do have the power to do that, being held as they

---

that 337, the year of Constantine's death, is more likely, since the accession of a new emperor was often the occasion of visits by foreign delegations anxious to secure the continuation of old relationships. Ulfila would then have been consecrated between 337 and 341, but only after subscribing to Arianism: the price of admission to an imperial audience demanded of all delegations by Constantius's ecclesiastical advisers. It may be noted, however, that Philostorgius's report squares with what Eusebius says about embassies sent to Constantine after his conquest of "Scythia" in 332 (*Vit. Const.* 4.5; also *Anon. Val.* 31–32; Aurelius Victor 41.13; Eutropius 10.7.1; Jerome, *Chron.* 332). Ulfila, as a Christian, would naturally have formed part of a delegation to a Christian ruler. Most recently Schäferdiek ("Die Anfänge des Christentums," 299) has accepted Barnes's date of 336.

The question of the form of Christianity in which Ulfila was catechized, or in which he may have been indoctrinated before his consecration, is hard to answer. He is said to have been a Nicene adherent who later went over to Arianism (Socrates 2.41.23; 4.33.6–7; Sozomen 4.24.1; 6.37.6–12; Theodoret, *Hist. eccl.* 4.37.3–5). The idea of his allegiance to Nicaea may come simply from his supposed association with Theophilus, the Gothic bishop who subscribed the Creed of Nicaea—as, for that matter, did Eusebius of Nicomedia, Ulfila's consecrator (cf. Knut Schäferdiek, "Das gotische Christentum im vierten Jahrhundert," in *Triuwe: Studien zur Sprachgeschichte und Literaturwissenschaft* [ed. Karl-Friedrich Kraft, Eva-Maria Lill, and Ute Schwab; Heidelberg: Heidelberger Verlagsanstalt, 1992], 19–50, esp. 31–42). Ulfila subscribed the homoean creed of Constantinople of 360 and remained true to his homoean profession to the end of his life; it may be found in the *Dissertatio Maximini* 44–52; 63 (cf. Roger Gryson, ed., *Scolies ariennes sur le Concile d'Aquilée* [SC 267; Paris: Cerf, 1980]). At what point in his life one may speak of his "conversion" to "Arianism" remains unclear.

It is also uncertain when he returned as bishop to his native land. In 348, at all events, he was among those expelled in the persecution of Christians by Aoric, Athanaric's father. His group settled in Moesia, near Nicopolis, and there he remained until his death ca. 383, acting probably as "chorepiscopus" to the Goths there, rather than as bishop of Nicopolis. It was probably at this time that he wrote most of his theological works, as well as did his translation of the Bible (see Wolfram, *History of the Goths*, 80–84). On the Gothic settlement, see Velizar Velkov, "Wulfila und die *Gothi minores* in Moesien," *Klio* 71 (1989): 525–27; also Jordanes, *Getica* 115 and 267.

16. On Ulfila's invention of an alphabet and instruction of the Goths in writing, see Jordanes, *Getica* 267; *Passio S. Nicetae Gothi* 3 (PG 115:708A); J. Cathey, "Vom Analphabetentum zum Schreiber," in *Verschriftung und Verschriftlichung: Aspekte des Medienwechsels in verschiedenen Kulturen und Epochen* (ed. Christine Ehler and Ursula Schaefer; Tübingen: Narr, 1998), 88–98.

are in the highest esteem and capable of attuning the faithful to the worship of God.

The emperor settled this emigrant people in the region of Moesia, each individual where he liked. Ulfila he held in the highest esteem, going so far as to refer to him often as "the Moses of our time." Our author exalts him to the skies, describing him and those under him as an adherent of his own sectarian views.[17]

6. Our heretic says that all of the Indians of the interior[18] who had learned to revere Christ from the teaching of the apostle Bartholomew held to the doctrine of "other in substance." He also relates how Theophilus the Indian, who embraced that doctrine, journeyed to their country and gave a full account of their belief.[19] Now those belonging to this Indian people were of old called "Sabaeans," from their capital, Saba', while nowadays they are known as "Himyarites."[20]

6a [Scholion to Theodoret, *Hist. eccl.* 2.28.3 codex L f. 103v]. This is, it seems, the Theophilus surnamed "the Indian" by Philostorgius.[21]

7. He says that Eusebius, Maris, and Theognis, who were allowed to return by order of the emperor Constantine **after a full three years** had elapsed, published a sectarian creed and sent it out everywhere in order to overthrow the Council in Nicaea. They also removed and **excommunicated**

---

17. Despite what the last sentence of the chapter says, there is nothing particularly "Eunomian" about Ulfila's creed, which is of the usual homoean sort. But by the fifth century, the Goths were by far the largest group of monotheistic Christians to have rejected the Theodosian theological settlement (perhaps out of loyalty to Demophilus of Constantinople), and Ulfila was, understandably, regarded as chief among the founding spirits of their Christianity. It is these later developments that influenced the tale of his own religious history, as it was told on either side of the Arian divide

18. "The Indians of the interior" (τοὺς ἐνδοτάτω Ἰνδούς) should mean the people of the Indian subcontinent, in contrast to other peoples of, e.g., Arabia or Ethiopia, of whom the term "Indian" might also be used. Other examples of Philostorgius's geographical usages, however, suggest caution. On Bartholomew and India, see *Passion of Bartholomew* (in J. K. Elliott, ed., *The Apocryphal New Testament: A Collection of Apocryphal Christian Literature in an English Translation.* [Oxford: Clarendon, 1993], 519); Eusebius, *Hist. eccl.* 5.10.3; Rufinus, *Hist. eccl.* 10.9; Jerome, *Vir. ill.* 36.

19. Theophilus's adventures among the "Indians" are further recounted in 3.4, 3.4a, and 3.5.

20. "Saba'" (biblical "Sheba") was the name of the kingdom, not of its capital. The Himyarites were the inhabitants of Himyar, modern Yemen.

21. This section refers to Theodoret, *Hist. eccl.* 2.28.3, where it is said that a Theophilus came under provisional excommunication at the Council of Constantinople of 360 for refusing to condemn Aetius.

Alexander of Alexandria for having recanted and returned to the consubstantialist doctrine, as well as Eustathius of Antioch, whom they charged with sexual intercourse with a girl and indulgence in lustful pleasure; the emperor punished him by banishing him to the west.[22] He says that this unlawful synod numbered **250** members in all and that Nicomedia was the site of its lawless deeds.[23]

7a [Nicetas, *Thes.* 5.8–9]. But [Constantine], **after a full three years** had elapsed, decreed that Eusebius and his fellows should return as well. And what they did upon returning from Gaul was to summon a council of **250** bishops to Nicomedia and **excommunicate** Alexander and everyone else who preached the consubstantialist doctrine.

7b [Nicetas, *Thes.* 5.9]. They ordained some Arian to replace Eustathius.[24] [Theodore] of Mopsuestia, along with Socrates and Sozomen, says he was called Euphronius. Theodoret, however, and Theophanes the chronicler give his name as Eulalius. Philostorgius alone, in the second book of his history, says that they transferred Paulinus from Tyre to Antioch.

8. He spouts a lot of nonsense about his fellow sectarian Agapetus, the former soldier who was ordained presbyter by those of like mind with him

---

22. On the exile of Eusebius and company, see 1.10; 2.1; 2.1b; Sozomen 2.32.7–8. On their return, see Socrates 1.14; Sozomen 2.16. On Alexander's "recantation," see 2.1. On Eustathius's deposition, see Eusebius, *Vit. Const.* 3.59–62; Jerome, *Vir. ill.* 85; Socrates 1.24.1–5; Sozomen 2.19; Theodoret, *Hist. eccl.* 1.21 (on a trumped-up charge of fornication); Athanasius, *H. Ar.* 4 (for having insulted Helena). Socrates says he was convicted of Sabellianism but finds his source unsatisfactory; Sozomen, that he was deposed on grounds of immorality, although the common opinion is that doctrinal differences were the real cause. Henry Chadwick ("The Fall of Eustathius of Antioch," *JTS* 49 [1948]: 27–35) places his deposition at the Council of Antioch of 326, while Eusebius of Nicomedia and Theognis were still in exile; their supporters seized upon Eustathius's insult to Helena to turn the emperor against him. R. P. C. Hanson ("The Fate of Eustathius of Antioch," *ZKG* 95 [1984]: 171–79), thinks 326 is too early, since it does not allow enough time for him to gain the group of devoted followers who continued on for so long (if he had succeeded Philogonius only in 324). His later reputation also suggests that he was not deposed for immorality. Hanson puts his deposition in 328 or 329, upon the initiative of Eusebius of Caesarea.

23. The Council of Nicomedia mentioned here met soon after Arius's recantation, in November or early December of 327. Eusebius and Theognis were rehabilitated in early 328. Apart from Philostorgius, there is no record that it published a creed.

24. On the succession to Eustathius, see Socrates 2.9.5; Sozomen 2.19.6; Theodoret, *Hist. eccl.* 1.22.1; Theophanes 43B. Philostorgius 3.15 says that Paulinus was succeeded by Eulalius. Jerome, *Chron.* 328, gives the list after Eustathius as: Eulalius, Eusebius, Eufronius, Placillus, Stefanus, Leontius, etc.

and later became bishop of Synnada. He says that he raised **the dead** and expelled and eliminated many other calamities, and worked other marvels as well, and caused many of the pagans to convert to Christianity.

8a [*Suda*, A 156 Agapetus]. Bishop of Synnada; Eusebius, "son of Pamphilus," praises him highly, recording his extraordinary marvels, as the instances when he moved mountains and rivers and raised **the dead**. He says that Maximinus wanted to kill him for being a Christian when he was a soldier because he learned of the boundless admiration aroused by his deeds in so many people.[25]

9. He says that Constantine, **in the twenty**-eighth **year of his reign**, transformed Byzantium into Constantinople and went around **its perimeter on foot marking it off, carrying his spear in his hand**.[26] Now those **following** him thought that the area was being extended **further than** it ought, so one of them **went up** to him and asked, **"How much farther, my lord?"** He **answered quite plainly, "Until the one who is in front of me stops,"** thus making it evident that he was being guided by some heavenly power who was teaching him what to do. In founding the city he gave it the name "**Alma Roma**," which in the Roman **language means "[Rome the] glorious**."[27] He

---

25. Cf. *Vita Agapeti* in Athanasios Papadopoulos-Kerameus, ed., *Varia Graeca Sacra* (St. Petersburg: Kirshbauma, 1909), 114–29; Socrates 7.3; *Synax.* 473.4; Honigmann, *Patristic Studies*, 35 (Agapetus's alleged confession under Licinius). The *Vita* says that he was reared in a monastery and enrolled unwillingly in the army by Licinius; Constantine released him from service after he had healed one of his servants. He was able to move inconvenient rocks, rivers, and ridges by prayer and raised the dead on more than one occasion.

26. Cf. A7.7, 7a, 7c, 8b; Eusebius, *Vit. Const.* 3.48–49; *Anon. Val.* 30; Socrates 1.16; Sozomen 2.3.5–6; Zosimus 2.30–32.1; 2.35; Nicephorus, *Hist. eccl.* 8.4 (PG 146.20C–D); *Chron. pasch.* P285A; 287A; Zonaras 13.3.11; *Bios* 334.21–337.22; Theophanes 42B; *SOC* 2:3.10; François Paschoud, ed. and trans., *Zosime: Histoire Nouvelle* (3 vols. in 5 parts; Paris: Belles Lettres, 1971–89), 1:225. On Constantine's project, see Cyril A. Mango, "The Development of Constantinople as an Urban Centre," in idem, *Studies on Constantinople* (Aldershot: Variorum, 1993), 117–36 (first article in the collection). Work on transforming Byzantium began in 324. It was dedicated on 11 May 330. Philostorgius's story, that God had inspired the emperor to found the city, echoes Constantine's own conviction about the foundation of the "urbis quam aeterno nomine Deo iubente donavimus" (*Cod. theod.* 13.5.7 [a. 334]). Constantine's wall, thrown across the neck of the peninsula from the Sea of Marmora to the Golden Horn, trebled the size of the older city within the walls of Septimius Severus, as archeology has shown; see Gilbert Dagron, *Naissance d'une capitale: Constantinople et ses institutions de 330 à 451* (Paris: Presses universitaires de France, 1974), 35.

27. "Alma Roma" actually means something like "Foster Rome."

established a **senate,** provided a quite generous **allowance of grain to be distributed to the inhabitants,** and lavished upon it **every other adornment of civic life, so that its fame might rival that of elder Rome.**[28]

9a [Opitz, *Vit. Const.* 37]. Constantine, having now reached **the twenty-fifth year of his reign,** the consuls that year being Gallienus and Symmachus, decided to found a great city to be a memorial to posterity of his glorious reign.

He therefore made his way to Thrace, then at the height of its prosperity, and learning that Byzantium was ideally situated with respect to land and sea, he settled there. He divided the neck of the peninsula (the region is a peninsula) by throwing a wall across it from sea to sea, enclosing the suburbs and the neighboring ridges within it, with the result that the former city became a small part of the city being founded because of its extent. For he began at the place where the great porphyry column bearing his statue now stands,[29] and when he had completed this work of his skill and power, the whole of it spread to the sea on either side and over the land between.

Now I myself have heard the following from the oldest and most important sources. When Constantine, in the course of **determining** where the gates of the wall would be, was leading his **retinue** over the distance to which **the enclosure** was to extend, he proceeded **on foot** with **his spear in hand.** But when he had crossed the first ridge, gone on to the second, crossed it as well and continued on, it seemed to those following that he was **measuring off** a **greater** distance than was proper. So <one> of those in a position to speak freely to him **went up to him** and asked, "**How much farther, my lord?**" He **answered quite plainly,** "**Until the one who is in front of me stops.**" Thus it is clear that there seemed to be an angel going in front and indicating the measurements, since the project of founding the city was entirely pleasing to God, no less than that of Jerusalem of old. And indeed he was in the act of establishing here as well a public table of faith. Constantine therefore continued on for as long as the visible apparition did, and when it stopped, dissolved, and disappeared, he went up to the spot, planted his spear, and said plainly, "Thus far." It was where the main gates of the city are today.

---

28. On the food allowances, see Zosimus 2.32.1; Socrates 2.13.5.

29. On the porphyry column and statue, cf. 2.17 and A7.7a; Garth Fowden, "Constantine's Porphyry Column: The Earliest Literary Allusion," *JRS* 81 (1991): 119–31; Cyril A. Mango, "Constantine's Column," in *Studies on Constantinople,* 1–6 (third article), and "Constantine's Porphyry Column and the Chapel of St. Constantine," *Studies on Constantinople,* 103–10 (fourth article). Buried beneath the column were believed to be the baskets of leftover fragments of bread from the miracle of feeding the multitude in the Gospel and Noah's axe with which he built the ark (*Bios* 337.7–22).

In founding the city he called it "Rome the **Glorious**," which in the **language** of the Italians is "**Alma Roma**," the name he gave it. And he established a **senate** in it, **provided** a lavish **allowance of grain to be distributed to the inhabitants, and bestowed upon it every other adornment of civic life, so that its fame might rival that of elder Rome.**

10. He says that at the death of Alexander, the archbishop of this city, Eusebius of Nicomedia, moved to the archiepiscopal throne of the newly founded city.[30]

11. Our impious tool of falsehood says that when Alexander of Alexandria had died and the votes [for his successor] were divided among several different people, a certain amount of time being spent on this, the divine Athanasius broke into the church of Dionysius in the late afternoon, found two Egyptian bishops, shut the doors and barred them firmly with the help of his supporters, and in this way received ordination.[31] Those ordaining resisted vigorously, but when the violence offered them proved too much for their will and their strength, Athanasius got what he wanted. The other assembly of bishops that was there condemned him for this reason. But when Athanasius had secured his position, he sent the emperor an announcement of his elevation to the archbishopric that was made to seem as though it had come from the city itself.[32] The emperor, thinking that the letter had been

---

30. For "Eusebius ... moved to," reading μεταστῆναι instead of μεταστῆσαι, as the reviser suggests. Cf. Theodoret, *Hist. eccl.* 1.19.1–2; Alexander Monachus, *Invent. s. crucis* (PG 87:4065A9).

31. On Athanasius's election, see Epiphanius, *Pan.* 68.7.2–4; 69.11.4–6; Gregory of Nazianzus, *Or.* 21; Socrates 1.23.3; *Apophthegmata Patrum* 78. On complaints about his consecration, see Athanasius, *C. Ar.* 6.4 (ordained secretly after a minority nomination); *Festal Index* 3 (accused of being too young); Sozomen 2.17.4 (seven bishops broke their oath to ordain only the majority candidate). One should also consider that what Athanasius is reported to have said to the Council of Tyre later in this chapter, that he had refused to accept consecration from its members, may contain the kernel of truth that he had refused to acknowledge the power to ordain of those bishops gathered for the election whom he considered schismatical and had excluded them from his consecration.

32. Philostorgius's charge that Athanasius forged a letter to the emperor from the city council seems unfounded, given his enduring popularity among the Alexandrians, who were doubtless relieved to get one of their own as bishop, rather than one of the despised outlanders attending the turbulent election council. Athanasius, in fact, would hardly have needed to apply any pressure of his own to get himself nominated and consecrated, and then accepted by the other bishops; the traditional Alexandrian antipathy to outsiders would have generated enough energy for all of that (see Gon-

written by the city council, endorsed his possession of the throne.[33]

Later when he found out what had happened, he sent him to Tyre in Phoenicia to give an account to the synod there of what he had done.[34] Athanasius yielded to the imperial threats only with reluctance, and when he did give in and go to Tyre, he did not present himself in court. What he did do was hire a prostitute, whose bulging stomach betrayed her licentiousness,

---

zalo Fernández Hernández, "La elección episcopal de Atanasio de Alejandría según Filostorgio," *Gerión* 3 [1985]: 226–27).

33. An adequate commentary on this passage would run to a monograph. Alexander died in 328, so Athanasius's was the first episcopal election in Alexandria after the Council of Nicaea, whose canon 4 provided that a bishop should be ordained, or at least approved, by all the bishops of his province. The council had also set out directions for the reintegration of the Melitian clergy into the Catholic Church (Opitz, *Urkunden zur Geschichte,* 23.7–8), but the plan had not been executed, so that at Alexander's death, tensions between Catholics and Melitians, as between Catholics and Arians, were still running high (Alexander had refused to receive Arius back into communion). In addition, the council, by including Libya and Pentapolis, in canon 6, in the territory ascribed to the bishop of Alexandria, had in effect confirmed (or established?) the electoral right of the bishops of those places, so notable as seedbeds of dissent.

One can imagine, then, the tensions among the crowd gathered to participate in, or try to influence, the election of Alexander's successor. But it has also been suggested that this was the first election in which the suffragans of Alexandria arrived, armed with the freshly forged canon 4 of Nicaea, to wrest from the Alexandrian presbyters their traditional privilege of electing and ordaining one of their own number; see Fernández Hernández, "La elección episcopal de Atanasio," 211–29 (228 n. 25 for earlier literature on the privilege, which is referred to by Jerome, *Ep.* 146.1.6).

Modern commentaries on this passage often fail to take into account these complications and sometimes seem to engage in special pleading for or against the doctrine of apostolic succession. Cf. William G. Rusch, "À la recherche de l'Athanase historique," in *Politique et théologie chez Athanase d'Alexandrie* (ed. Charles Kannengiesser; Paris: Beauchesne, 1974),161–77; Duane W.-H. Arnold, *The Early Episcopal Career of Athanasius of Alexandria* (Notre Dame, Ind.: University of Notre Dame Press, 1991), 25–62, 89–99.

34. On the Council of Tyre, see Eusebius, *Vit. Const.* 4.41–42; Athanasius, *C. Ar.* 71–86; *P. Lond.* 1914 (in H. Idris Bell, *Jews and Christians in Egypt* [London: British Museum, 1924], 53–71); Epiphanius, *Pan.* 68.8–9; Ammianus 15.7.7–8; Rufinus, *Hist. eccl.* 10.17–18; Socrates 1.28–32; Sozomen 2.25; Theodoret, *Hist. eccl.* 1.29–31. Despite the impression given by Philostorgius (or Photius), the council did not meet until 335 (it was presided over by Eusebius of Caesarea, to whom Philostorgius refers). But his remark about Athanasius's reluctance to attend is quite what Athanasius himself says (*C. Ar.* 71.2). He was summoned on charges of crimes of violence against dissident clergy and their property.

and loosed her upon Eusebius, who was supposed to be president of the synod there.[35] His idea was that in the confusion and uproar that her accusation would doubtless provoke, he could slip away from court and avoid being tried.

Now the account given by our champion of falsehood of the way in which the plot was uncovered is the same as the one given by the orthodox of how the tart hired to attack the great Athanasius was convicted. For when Eusebius asked the prostitute if she knew her seducer, she insisted that she certainly did. When he asked as well if he was among the present company, she replied, "What are you saying, my lord! I am not so mad as to charge men such as these with addiction to lust!" And with that the truth began to be uncovered and the plot revealed. Eusebius was shown to be beyond all reproach, while Athanasius, instead of avoiding conviction, found himself doubly condemned, the charge of vicious slander being added to that of unholy ordination. Thus the sentence of deposition was unanimously pronounced against him. But he grew even more shameless, claiming that it was out of hatred that the council members had brought about his deposition and laid their charges, because he had refused to accept ordination to the archiepiscopal office from their hands.

The emperor therefore again bade another council to examine Athanasius's case. They collected other charges as well: they added to the accusations that he had loaded the confessor Callinicus, bishop of Pelusium, with iron shackles and thrust him into prison and had not left off mistreating him until he died.[36] Not only that, but the hand of Arsenius was produced at this time, and the business of the Mareotis and Ischyras and the sacred cup was brought

---

35. Our author's retelling of the story of the prostitute at the council exemplifies his underlying theme: the revision of the church history of Rufinus of Aquileia (and of Gelasius of Caesarea, until the death of Arius?). He sets himself an impossible task at this point, however, and Rufinus's earlier stories of Athanasius at the council, whether of unmasking the prostitute's falsehood by tricking her into identifying his presbyter as himself or of dramatically producing in court his supposed victim Arsenius, whose hand he had been accused of severing, in good health and perfect possession of both hands, while his judges stared aghast at the "hand of glory" lying ominously upon the evidence table, have remained in secure possession of the chroniclers' imagination.

36. Callinicus of Pelusium was one of the Melitians who had sought relief from the emperor from Alexander's persecution but had again fallen out of favor with Athanasius, whom he suspected of having broken a sacred vessel and whose communion he therefore refused. The accusation of imprisonment and torture was precisely that leveled at Athanasius during the council by Callinicus himself, whatever Philostorgius may say about his death (or be made to say by Photius). Cf. Epiphanius, *Pan.* 68.5.3; Athanasius, *Festal Letters* 4.5; *C. Ar.* 60.2; Sozomen 2.25.3–4.

up, and other matters of the sort, for which the synod excommunicated him and appointed Gregory of Cappadocia to replace him.[37] Such are the fables that our deceitful Cacostorgius spins about Saint Athanasius.[38]

11a [Opitz, *Vit. Const.* 49]. When the great Athanasius had been ordained, the emperor Constantine the Great rejoiced when he received the decree of the city and wrote to the Alexandrians in the following vein: "Upon reading the decree that you sent concerning the appointment of the bishop and learning that the matter has proceeded to the satisfaction of all of you and that the man is thus welcomed by all of you unanimously, I rejoice as well (how could I not?), and I declare that what you have chosen by your common decree is valid and confirmed."

12. He says that Helena, the mother of the emperor Constantine, built a city on the mouth of the **bay of Nicomedia** and called it Helenopolis.[39] **The**

---

37. On Arsenius and his hand, see Athanasius, *C. Ar.* 8.5; 63.4; 65.1–4; 72.2; Epiphanius, *Pan.* 68.10.1–2; Rufinus, *Hist. eccl.* 10.16–18; Socrates 1.29; Sozomen 2.25.8, 10. Ischyras was a Mareotic presbyter, the validity of whose ordination had been called into question; Athanasius was accused of authorizing violence against his person and his church property (cf. Athanasius, *C. Ar.* 11–17).

38. Despite Philostorgius, there was no second council to examine Athanasius at this time; the above charges were examined at the same Council of Tyre, which sent a commission of inquiry to the Mareotis to look into the accusations. Athanasius thereupon fled to Constantinople and persuaded the emperor to hear his case personally. Constantine's summons to the council was answered by a committee of six of its members, who upon arrival ignored the previous charges against Athanasius and simply accused him of threatening to interrupt the grain shipments from Egypt to the capital city. Athanasius protested, the hearing grew warm, and in the end the bishop lost his temper and his case and was banished to Trier (cf. Athanasius, *C. Ar.* 9; 86–87; Epiphanius, *Pan.* 68.9.5–6).

There is no record of the council appointing anyone to replace Athanasius, although one Pistus afterward put forward a claim to be bishop of Alexandria (Athanasius, *Ep. encycl.* 6); the circumstances of his appointment are obscure. After Constantine's death in 337, his oldest son announced the restoration of Athanasius, who returned to Alexandria on 23 November. But he was deposed again by the Council of Antioch of 338/9 (on charges of violence and improper resumption of his see). The council appointed Gregory the Cappadocian to replace him, an attempt was made to arrest him, and he escaped and sailed to Italy on 16 April 339. On Gregory's appointment, see Athanasius, *C. Ar.* 29.3; *H. Ar.* 10; Socrates 2.10.1; Sozomen 3.5.3–4; Theodoret, *Hist. eccl.* 2.4.3. On his misconduct, see Athanasius, *H. Ar.* 13–14.

39. Constantine refounded Drepanum as Helenopolis; in addition to its association with Lucian, Helena had been born there (Procopius, *Aed.* 5.2.1). Cf. Ammianus 26.8.1; A6.16–20; A7.4, 7.4a–c; Jerome, *Chron.* 327; Socrates 1.17.1; *Chron. pasch.* P283D; Theophanes 41B; Jan W. Drijvers, *Helena Augusta: The Mother of Constantine*

place meant so much to her simply because it was there that **the martyr Lucian** had been borne to his burial by a dolphin after his death by martyrdom.

12a [Opitz, *Vit. Const.* 52]. Constantine held his mother in such high honor that he founded a city named after her; it is on the right side <of the> **bay** <of> **Nicomedia. The place meant so much to her simply because of its association with Lucian,** the famous **martyr** of Christ.

13. He says that when the martyr Lucian was about to die and the reign of oppression was allowing neither church nor altar, and what is more his fetters and injuries did not permit him even to move, he offered the awe-inspiring sacrifice while he was lying on his own chest;[40] in this way he partook of the unblemished offering and bade the others share in it. The sacred rite was performed in the prison; the holy choir that surrounded him, as though he had already died, took the form of a church and shielded the proceedings from impious eyes.

14. He records many who were disciples of this martyr, among them Eusebius of Nicomedia, Maris of Chalcedon, Theognis of Nicaea, Leontius, who later became bishop of Antioch, Antony of Tarsus in Cilicia, Menophantus, Noominius, and Eudoxius. He also mentions Alexander and Asterius the Cappadocian, who he says yielded to the violence of the tyrants and went over to paganism but later made good their lapse; their teacher contributed to their repentance.[41]

---

the Great and the Legend of Her Finding of the True Cross (Brill Studies in Intellectual History 27; Leiden: Brill, 1992), 9–12, 35, 38.

40. "Offered … while he was lying on his own chest": ἐν τῷ οἰκείῳ στέρνῳ ἀνακείμενον τὴν φρικτὴν θυσίαν τελεσάμενον. But something is amiss: οἰκείῳ does not suit, and *Passio Luciani* 14 (appendix 6) twice says it was the offertory gifts that were lying on Lucian's chest, adding that he lifted his eyes to heaven during the service. Correct ἀνακείμενον to ἀνακειμένην, and the picture rights itself at once, the offering now lying on the matryr's chest.

41. On Lucian's disciples, see Bardy, *Recherches sur Lucien d'Antioche,* 185–216. Of those listed, Menophantus was bishop of Ephesus; "Noominius" should perhaps be read "Numenius." 1.9c and 2.3 add Secundus of Ptolemais and Theonas of Marmarica as unswervingly faithful to true doctrine. The "Eudoxius" here is probably not he of Germanicia; see Bardy, *Recherches sur Lucien d'Antioche,* 194. The list here is not complete, for Athanasius of Anazarbus is added to it in 3.15. On Theognis of Nicaea, see Bardy, *Recherches sur Lucien d'Antioche,* 210–14. His doctrine that God is Father even before begetting the Son is shared by Asterius (Athanasius, *Syn.* 19.2; Markus Vinzent, *Asterius von Kappadokien: Die theologischen Fragmente* [Leiden: Brill, 1993], 181–82), in contrast to Arius, who held that God is not a father before "begetting" (Thomas A.

15. He says that of the aforementioned Antony and Leontius preserved their heresy intact, while Eusebius, Maris, and Theognis were carried away by the Council of Nicaea, although they recovered from this change.[42] Maris, however, once recovered fell into yet another absurdity, and not only he but Theognis as well. The latter thinks that God is a father even before begetting the Son, because he has the power to beget. Asterius as well, he says, perverted the doctrine, affirming in his writings and letters that the Son is an exact image of the Father's substance.[43]

16. He writes that when Constantine **had reached the thirty-second year**

Kopecek, *A History of Neo-Arianism* [Cambridge: Philadelphia Patristic Foundation, 1979], 31–32).

42. The phrase "[preserved their] heresy" translates ἀσέβειαν; perhaps read εὐσέβειαν: "orthodoxy." "They recovered from this change": ἀνενεχθῆναι δὲ τῆς μεταβολῆς. It has been suggested to read τῇ μεταβολῇ (Bidez, *Philostorgius*, 347), but the following words ἐκεῖθεν ἀνενεχθέντα suggest that the preceding genitive is correct.

43. On Asterius's doctrine, see Bardy, *Recherches sur Lucien d'Antioche*, 328–57; Maurice Wiles, "Asterius: A New Chapter in the History of Arianism," in *Arianism: Historical and Theological Reassessments* (ed. R. C. Gregg; Cambridge, Mass.: Philadelphia Patristic Foundation, 1985), 111–51; Vinzent, *Asterius von Kappadokien*; idem, "Gottes Wesen, Logos, Weisheit und Kraft bei Asterius von Kappadokien und Markell von Ankyra," *VC* 47 (1993): 170–191; idem, "Die Gegner im Schreiben Markells von Ankyra an Julius von Rom," *ZKG* 105 (1994): 285–328. What one makes of Asterius depends to some extent on whether one accepts the ascription to him of the commentaries edited by Marcel Richard, *Asterii Sophistae commentariorum in psalmos quae supersunt* (Oslo: Brøgger, 1956). Recent scholarship doubts the authorship; see Wolfram Kinzig, *In Search of Asterius: Studies on the Authorship of the Homilies on the Psalms* (Göttingen: Vandenhoeck & Ruprecht, 1990), reviewed by Karl-Heinz Uthemann, *VC* 45 (1991): 194–203. Kinzig's reply is in "Asterius Sophista oder Asterius Ignotus," *VC* 45 (1991): 388–98. Philostorgius is quite right in ascribing to Asterius the view that the Son is an exact image of the Father's substance: ἀπαράλλακτον εἰκόνα τῆς τοῦ πατρὸς οὐσίας. Epiphanius *(Pan.* 72.6.1) quotes him likewise: the only-begotten Word and firstborn of every creature is the οὐσίας τε καὶ βουλῆς καὶ δυνάμεως καὶ δόξης ἀπαράλλακτον εἰκόνα of the Father. The importance of his doctrine is clearly implied by Athanasius's treatment of him. Despite what Philostorgius says, however, Wiles doubts that Asterius changed what was primitive Arianism. If he had, would not Athanasius have said so? For the Eunomians, the very notion of an image of God's ingenerate substance was a contradiction, and Philostorgius resented Asterius for expounding a doctrine that (as he thought) had encouraged the homoeans to come round to the confession of "like in substance" (cf. 4.4). "It seems at least possible that Philostorgius may have created an early Arianism in the image of his own later neo-Arianism, and then

of his reign, he was **poisoned** to death by **his brothers** in Nicomedia.[44] As
the end drew near and he became aware of the **plot,** he drew up a will that
demanded that his **murderers** be punished; he ordered that the first of his
sons to arrive should execute it, for fear lest they too should come to the same
end at their hands, and he gave the will to Eusebius of Nicomedia. Eusebius,

---

found Asterius lacking by that imaginary standard" (Wiles, "Asterius: A New Chapter," 113).

The fragments that remain of Asterius's writings do not reveal clearly how he coordinated his doctrines of the image, on the one hand, and of ingenerateness as God's exclusive characteristic, on the other (cf. Vinzent, *Asterius von Kappadokien,* 63–71). It is ironic that the term "exact image" was coined by none other than Alexander of Alexandria and taken up by Athanasius and Basil of Caesarea (see Raniero Cantalamessa, "Cristo 'Immagine di Dio,'" *Rivista di storia e letteratura religiosa* 16 [1980]: 345–48). "Ingenerateness," by contrast, became the Eunomian watchword. Small wonder, then, that Vinzent judges that Asterius was more influential than Arius himself on later "Arianism" (*Asterius von Kappadokien,* 31–32).

Philostorgius evidently thinks of Lucian (d. 312) as a witness to true Christian doctrine, which was later perverted by some of those supposedly his followers. One's opinion on Lucian's views will largely depend on how closely one connects him with the Creed of the Council of Antioch of 341, since the few fragments of his that remain (collected in Martin J. Routh, *Reliquiae Sacrae* [5 vols.; Oxford: Clarendon, 1846], 4:3–10) do not suffice to allow any inference about doctrinal influence on "Arianism" of any variety. The fact that the creed draws upon Asterius, who according to Philostorgius had corrupted Lucian's doctrine, makes its connection with the martyr improbable; see Hans Christof Brennecke, "Lukian von Antiochien in der Geschichte des arianischen Streites," in *Logos: Festschrift für Luise Abramowski* (ed. Hans Christof Brennecke, Ernst Ludwig Grasmück, and Christoph Markschies; BZNW 67; Berlin: de Gruyter, 1993), 187–88. Bardy, *Recherches sur Lucien d'Antioche,* 85–132, thinks otherwise. See also J. N. D. Kelly, *Early Christian Creeds* (London: Longman, 1972), 271.

The "Lucianists," then, if not students of the martyr's doctrine, may be understood as that group of homoeans from Asia Minor and Syria who encouraged his cult, which was centered on his burial place in Drepanum, situated in the province of which Eusebius of Nicomedia was metropolitan (Arius, from elsewhere, is not included by Philostorgius among the Lucianists, however much he may have claimed membership [Opitz, *Urkunden zur Geschichte,* 1.5]). The martyr's shrine enhanced the standing of Eusebius and his circle, and the latter's famous resistance to the consubstantialist doctrine made it easy to transfer to Lucian that brand of Christian monotheism that would have its systematic exposition in Aetius and Eunomius (Brennecke, "Lukian von Antiochien," 184–88). Such appears to be the history of doctrine still faintly visible beneath Photius's epitome.

44. The story of Constantine's poisoning by his brothers is also mentioned in 2.4 and 2.4b and told as well in Cedrenus 297A, Zonaras 13.4.26, and *Bios* 654.4.

however, suspected that the emperor's brothers might look for the will and want to find out what it contained, so he placed the document in the dead man's hand and hid it in the folds of his robe. And when they came looking for it, as he had thought they would, he acknowledged that he had indeed received it but had put it back into his hands. Then later he removed the document and handed it over to his son Constantius, who arrived before the others and who wasted little time in executing his father's orders.[45]

16a [*AP 7*]. The Christ-loving emperor Constantine advanced to the **thirty**-first **year of his reign** and **arrived at the thirty-second**, when he learned that the Persians were preparing for war against him.[46] He therefore arose from his own city and made his way as far as Nicomedia in Bithynia. There he died from a **plot** hatched by his **brothers**, who **administered poison** to him, a death foretold by a comet, they say.[47] Constantine's brothers on his father's side were Dalmatius, Hannibalianus, and Constantius. For he was the only son his father Constans had from Helena while he was still in private life, while from Theodora, the daughter of Maximian, surnamed Herculius, he had other sons, the aforementioned Dalmatius, Hannibalianus, and Constantius.[48] Constantine honored them with the titles of "Caesar" and *nobilissimus*.

---

45. The allusion in 2.4b to Constantine killing his brothers is picked up here with the story of his will, which made its executor an executioner. Rufinus (*Hist. eccl.* 10.12) tells of Constantine entrusting his will to an Arian presbyter, but there the testament simply bequeaths the empire to his successors; nothing is said about vengeance. However, his intentions about the disposition of his realm, whether put into testamentary form or not, are clearly revealed in the measures he took during his life in appointing as Caesars his sons Constantine (with Crispus) in 317, Constantius in 324, Constans in 333, and his nephew Dalmatius, son of his half-brother of the same name, in 335. The territories their father eventually assigned them to administer are those given in 2.16b, with Dalmatius given the lower Danube (cf. A. H. M. Jones, *The Later Roman Empire, 284–602: A Social, Economic, and Administrative Survey* [2 vols.; Oxford: Blackwell, 1964], 1:84–85), a division perhaps reminiscent of the former Tetrarchy. On the titles Constantine gave his half-brothers, cf. S II 5; Zosimus 2.39.2; Paschoud, *Zosime*, 1:246.

46. On the impending Persian campaign, see Eusebius, *Vit. Const.* 4.55–57.

47. On Constantine's death, see *Vit. Const.* 4.61–64; A7.13, 13a, d, e; Theophanes 50B; *Chron. pasch.* P286C; Aurelius Victor 41.16; Malalas 13.14. He died on 22 May 337. The comet is mentioned in Aurelius Victor and Eutropius 10.8.2.

48. Constantine I's father, Constantius I (referred to as "Constans" in 2.16a), was of modest origins and rose through the ranks of the army, Constantine being born to him ca. 275 from Helena, who was of even humbler background. The description of her here accords with that elsewhere: *Anon. Val.* 2 (*Helena matre vilissima*); Ambrose, *De obitu Theodosii* 42 (*stabularia*); Eutropius 10.2.2; cf. Drijvers, *Helena Augusta*, 15–

One of them, Constantius, had as sons Gallus and Julian from his wedded wife; Julian was surnamed "the Apostate" because he renounced Christ and went over to pagan worship.

[*AP* 41: Julian speaks]. You know ... that our family is especially suited to rule. For my father Constantius was born to my grandfather Constans from Theodora, Maximian's daughter. Constantine, however, was born to him from Helena, a common woman no better than a harlot, and that while he had not yet become Caesar but was still of private station. Constantine, then,

---

17; Bill Leadbetter, "The Illegitimacy of Constantine and the Birth of the Tetrarchy," in *Constantine: History, Historiography, and Legend* (ed. Samuel S. Lieu and Dominic Montserrat; London: Routledge, 1998), 78–85.

The statement that he was not yet Caesar at Constantine's birth is certainly true, but that he was still of private station then seems unlikely, given that he was praetorian prefect in 289 and had had to work his way up the ranks. *Bios* 308.4–5, 15–17 says that he was a tribune when he met Helena; that squares with his career in *Anon. Val.* 1: "protector primum, inde tribunus, postea praeses Dalmatiarum fuit." But his ascent into the higher circles of the Tetrarchy apparently entailed his repudiation of Helena and marriage to Theodora, daughter or stepdaughter of Maximian, the western Augustus, which probably took place before 289. He became Caesar in 293. Theodora bore him six children, the three sons among whom, Constantine's half-brothers, are listed in 2.16a.

Shortly after Constantine's death, most of the descendants of his stepmother Theodora were massacred by the army, including two of his half-brothers and the Caesar Dalmatius. Despite what Julian is made to say in 2.16a about both of his uncles being killed, in his *Ep. ad Ath.* 270C–D, he speaks instead of the murder of his father (Julius Constantius) and of an uncle, presumably Dalmatius (Socrates 3.1.6 does not mention Hannibalianus as one of the victims).

The motive for the slaughter seems to have been the desire of the army to exclude from power anyone not descended from Constantine himself. The story of the poisoning of Constantine by his brothers, and of the will, seems designed to absolve Constantius II of all blame for the deaths of his relatives (cf. Giuseppe Zecchini, "Filostorgio," in *Metodologie della ricerca sulla tarda antichità* [ed. Antonio Garzya; Naples: D'Auria, 1989], 581). Modern scholarship usually discounts it (although see Michael DiMaio and Duane W.-H. Arnold, "*Per Vim, Per Caedem, Per Bellum*: A Study of Murder and Ecclesiastical Politics in the Year 337 A.D.," *Byzantion* 62 [1992]: 158–211, for an imaginative reconstruction). There is, however, insufficient evidence that Constantius himself was directly responsible for the massacre (cf. Joe W. Leedom, "Constantius II: Three Revisions," *Byzantion* 48 [1978]: 132–45), although it has been asked if he did all he could to restrain the soldiers. Cf. Gregory of Nazianzus, *Or.* 4.21; Ammianus 21.16.8; Athanasius, *H. Ar.* 69.1; Libanius, *Or.* 18.31; Jerome, *Chron.* 338; Eutropius 10.9.1; *Epit. Caes.* 41.18; Zosimus 2.40; Theophylact 7 (PG 126:161B); Paschoud, *Zosime*, 1:246–47.

seized power in his arrogance and unjustly put to death my father and both his brothers.

16b [Opitz, *Vit. Const.* 64]. Constantine in the twenty-eighth year of his reign proclaimed his youngest son Constans Caesar and placed him between his two brothers, giving him Italy. For he had honored his oldest son Constantine with the rank of Caesar in the twelfth year of his reign, setting him over Upper Gaul; Constantius as well he had invested with the title of Caesar in the nineteenth year of his reign, bidding him govern the east.

17. Our enemy of God accuses the Christians of worshiping with sacrifices the image of Constantine set up upon the porphyry column, of paying homage to it with lamp-lighting and incense or praying to it as to a god, and of offering it supplications to avert calamities.[49]

18. He says that when Constantine the Great had died and those languishing everywhere in exile received permission to return, Athanasius too arrived in Alexandria from Gaul. Learning that Gregory had died,[50] he made his way just as he was straight from the ship to the church and resumed the throne, having no regard for those who had excommunicated him.

---

49. See 25 n. 29. On the homage paid to Constantine's statue (with lighted candles), cf. *Chron. pasch.* P285A–C. The porphyry column on which it was set was brought from Rome; it was later thought that the statue on top of it had been imported from elsewhere (Leo Grammaticus 87.13–18). It held a spear in its right hand and in its left a globe, and it wore a crown of seven rays. The image was perhaps deliberately ambiguous, being normal in imperial representation, but also suggestive of the sun-god or Mithras. The statue was feted yearly with hymns, acclamations, and a procession in a ceremony that perhaps only gradually assumed an undisguisedly Christian character. See *SOC* 1:Hesychias, 41; *SOC* 2:2.49; 2:1.45; 2:1.57; 2:2.45; Averil Cameron and Judith Herrin, *Constantinople in the Early Eighth Century: The Parastaseis Syntomoi Chronikai* (Leiden: Brill, 1984), 242–45.

50. See the second paragraph in 29 n. 38. Gregory had not only not died but had not yet even been appointed. Constantine II's letter to the church of Alexandria announcing Athanasius's return is dated 17 June 337; cf. Athanasius, *C. Ar.* 87.3–7; *H. Ar.* 8.1.

BOOK 3

1. He says that Constantine, the oldest of Constantine's sons, plotted against his brother Constans, whose generals engaged him in battle. He perished, and his portion of the realm was annexed to Constans'.[1]

1a [*AP* 8]. Constantine the Great was scarcely dead when the Roman empire was divided into three realms; it was his sons Constantine, Constantius, and Constans who divided it up.[2] **To the oldest**, Constantine, were allotted Upper **Gaul**, the regions beyond the Alps, **the British Isles**, and the territory as far as **the western ocean**. To Constans as the **youngest** went Lower Gaul or **Italy and Rome itself**. Constantius, the second-born of Constantine's sons, who was then engaged in the affairs of the east in the struggle with the Persians, received the eastern portion. He made Byzantium, renamed Constantinople and New Rome, into an imperial capital and made tributary to his realm and government all the territory from Illyricum to the Propontis **that was subject** to the Romans, as well as Syria, Palestine, Mesopotamia, Egypt, and all the islands.

[*AP* 9]. As was said, when there were three emperors, each of whom was governing his own portion, the oldest of them, Constantine, arose from

---

1. What let to the quarrel between Constantine II and Constans, and to the death of the former in 340, is not completely clear. The older brother seems to have treated the younger as subject to him, while Constans chafed under this and disobeyed, until finally Constantine demanded a formal division of their territory, which he had regarded as a common realm, claiming Italy and Africa as his by right. But when he invaded Italy, he was ambushed and killed near Aquileia, his body being thrown into the Alsa River. Cf. A7.13a and A7.14; Julian, *Or.* 2.94B–D; *Consul. const.* 340; Aurelius Victor, 41.22; *Epit. Caes.* 41.22; Eutropius 10.9.2; Jerome, *Chron.* 340; Rufinus, *Hist. eccl.* 10.16; Socrates 2.5; Sozomen 3.2.10; Zosimus 2.41; Zonaras 13.5.7–13; *Comp. chron.* 53.24–54.3; Cedrenus 297B–C; J.-R. Palanque, "Collégialité et partages dans l'empire romain aux IVe et Ve siècles," *Revue des études anciennes* 46 (1944): 54–58; Paschoud, *Zosime,* 1:245, 248.

2. Constantine's three surviving sons (see the last two paragraphs to 34 n. 48) were proclaimed Augusti and proceeded to a threefold division of the realm at a conference in Pannonia in the autumn of 337.

his own territory, went up to the region inherited by his youngest brother while he was away on a journey to Rome, and attempted an injustice against him. He laid a charge against him in his absence, to the effect that their territories had not been divided properly and that he had appropriated most of the realm belonging to him. But the generals and guardians of the country appointed by Constans said that they could make no change, great or small, without his consent and decision, for that would be wrong. So he prepared for war and took up arms against someone who had done no wrong, but in the battle it was Constantine who fell, and in his desire for the portion belonging to others he lost even what had seemed to be his sure possession.

[*AP* 10]. His people's sympathies therefore went over to Constans, and the entire western realm became subject to him, although he had never desired it; but such was the judgment of God, who said, "Do not move your ancestral boundaries or seize your neighbor's furrow."[3] For those who act wickedly against their neighbors bring ruin upon themselves, drawing God's justice upon them. Constans therefore ruled over the entire western realm, joining the two inheritances together and making both portions one realm.

2. He heaps praise upon Constantius and says that he built the church in Constantinople that is justly called "**the great**." In addition, he brought **the apostle Andrew over from Achaia** to the church that he **had built** and that is called after the apostles in common. Next to it he erected his father's **tomb. Not only that; he also translated the evangelist Luke from Achaia** to the same sacred precinct. The apostle **Timothy as well** he likewise brought over **from Ephesus in Ionia** to that same renowned and august house.[4]

---

3. The quotation about "ancestral boundaries" is from Deut 19:14. Cf also Prov 22:28; 23:10.

4. The "great church" is Hagia Sophia. It is disputed whether Constantine or Constantius laid its foundations; cf. Dagron, *Naissance d'une capitale*, 397–99. It was dedicated on 15 February 360, burned down on 20 June 404, was rebuilt and rededicated on 10 October 415, was burned down again during the riots on 15 January 532, and was completely rebuilt by Justinian. Cf. A7.31.2; Jerome, *Chron.* 360; Socrates 2.16.16; 2.43.11; *Chron. pasch.* P293D; 294B–C; Cedrenus 298D; Zonaras 14.6.19, 30; *Vita Pauli* in Photius, *Bibliotheca* Codex 257.475b27–28. As 3.2a notes, Hagia Sophia was next to the senate building in the Augusteum (see Raymond Janin, *Constantinople Byzantine: Développement urbain et répertoire topographique* [Paris: Institut français d'études byzantines, 1964], 155).

Contrary to 3.2, it was Constantine who built the Church of the Holy Apostles in Constantinople. He planned it, in fact, to be his sepulchre, his tomb in the center flanked by the apostles' coffins on either side amid the splendor of light and gold (Eusebius, *Vit. Const.* 4.58–60). He was in fact buried there (*Vit. Const.* 4.70), but, as 3.2 indicates, Constantius (doubtless prompted by his episcopal advisers) had other

2a [*AP* 17]. Our historian writes about Constantius and the martyr [Artemius] that not only could it be said of Constantius that he was eagerly attentive to divine matters, even if, led astray by Eusebius, the heretical and most godless bishop of Nicomedia, he went over to the Arian sect; but he was also in other respects moderate, particularly careful about decency, and outstanding in his exercise of self-restraint in diet and in other respects. He also had a very great concern for the churches, eager as he was to far outdo his father by his efforts in this regard. He constructed the great church next to the senate in his father's city right from its foundations.[5] To honor his father's **tomb**, he **built** a great church as a place of worship there, **translating the apostle Andrew from Achaia**, as I said, and placing him there. **Not only that, he also** brought over **the evangelist Luke from Achaia and Timothy from Ephesus in Ionia**.

3. He says that when Constantius learned that Athanasius had resumed the throne of Alexandria, he drove him from Alexandria and ordered that George from Cappadocia be ordained in his place. Athanasius, fearing both the threats and the plot to kill him, made his way back to the western emperor.[6]

---

ideas about how his father's position in the church should be represented and built the mausoleum for him by the church. Hence the importance of renewing the significance of the church by translating to it the relics of Andrew, Luke, and Timothy (cf. A1.16–18; A3.16; Simeon Metaphrastes, *Commentarius in divum Lucam* 10 [PG 115:1137C]). The translations took place in 356/7. The church was dedicated in 370 (see Dagron, *Naissance d'une capitale*, 401–5).

5. The portrait of Constantius as of sound character but deceived by unscrupulous bishops is shared by Epiphanius (*Pan.* 69.12.5–7) and Rufinus (*Hist. eccl.* 10.16). Ammianus takes a dimmer view (21.16.18).

6. On the chronology, see the second paragraph of 29 n. 38 and 35 n. 50. After Athanasius fled to Italy in 339, he managed to interest Julius of Rome and the emperor Constans in his case, and the Council of Sardica in 343 cleared and restored him, although he could not return to his see until October 346, after Constans had made forceful representations to his brother on his behalf (Gregory in Alexandria had conveniently died the year before). A council of Antioch of 349 or 352 appointed the infamous George of Cappadocia to replace him, but George could not enter Alexandria until a year after Athanasius had left it to escape arrest in February 356. Cf. Rufinus, *Hist. eccl.* 10.20; Theodoret, *Hist. eccl.* 2.14; Socrates 2.14; Sozomen 3.7.9 (he repeats Socrates' mistake about Gregory being removed from Alexandria).

Athanasius did not leave Egypt in 356 but remained in hiding there, so that the account in 3.3 suits rather the year 339, with the common confusion of "Gregory" and "George." Athanasius's adventures are continued in 3.12.

4. He says that Constantius sent an embassy to the people called of old **Sabaeans and now** known as **Himyarites**. The people is descended **from Abraham through Keturah**. Their country is called Great Arabia and Fortunate Arabia by the Greeks. It borders on the outer ocean. Its capital is Saba', from where the queen set out to journey to Solomon.[7] The people practice the custom of **circumcision** on the eighth day [after birth]. They also **sacrifice to the sun, the moon, and the local demons**. There are quite a few Jews living among them.

Constantius, then, sent an embassy to them with the purpose of converting them to the **true faith**. He planned **to win over** the leader **of the people** by the magnificence and number of his **gifts**, and hence to find an opportunity to plant the seeds of faith in him.[8] He also asked that it might be granted to build a church for the Romans who traveled there and for whoever of the local people might convert to the faith. He gave the embassy a generous amount for the cost of construction.

Theophilus the Indian was among the leaders of this embassy. Long before, when he was quite young, during the reign of Constantine, the previous emperor, he had been sent to the Romans as a hostage by the people known as Divaeans. The island they inhabit is called Diva, and they too are among those known as Indians. Now Theophilus, during the considerable time he spent living among the Romans, formed his character to the highest degree of virtue and his beliefs in accordance with orthodoxy, choosing to live in celibacy. He even entered the ranks of the deacons, Eusebius laying upon him his priestly hands, but this happened earlier. When he undertook the embassy, he received the dignity of bishop from those who shared his beliefs.

Now Constantius fitted out the embassy magnificently and with the utmost splendor, sending with it all of two hundred of the finest breed of

---

7. See further 2.6 and 22 nn. 18–20. For Abraham and Keturah, see Gen 25:1–4. Sheba was Abraham's grandson by Keturah. For the queen's visit to Solomon, see 1 Kgs 10:1–10.

8. "Plant the seeds of faith in him" translates the reading αὐτῷ instead of αὐτοῦ. On the embassy, see Albrecht Dihle, "L'embassade de Théophile l'Indien ré-examinée," in *L'Arabie préislamique et son environnement historique et culturel: Actes du Colloque de Strasbourg, 24–27 juin 1987* (ed. Toufic Fahd; Leiden: Brill, 1989), 461–68; and Gianfranco Fiaccadori, "Teofilo Indiano," *Studi classici e orientali* 33 (1983): 295–331; 34 (1984): 271–308. The embassy was sent during the 350s, perhaps ca. 356. Fiaccadori identifies "Diva" as the Maldives. Dihle finds the description of Theophilus's mission here similar to Rufinus's account of the establishment of diplomatic relations of Rome with Aksum (*Hist. eccl.* 10.9–10): the purpose was to encourage trade and so to build churches for the Christians among the merchants. Philostorgius's own mission to revise Rufinus does not, of course, mean that his narrative is to be discounted.

horses from Cappadocia conveyed on ships designed as cavalry transports, as well as many other gifts calculated to strike wonder at their sumptuousness and to enchant the beholder.

Upon reaching the Sabaeans, Theophilus tried to persuade their ruler to worship Christ and renounce pagan error. Now the Jews in their usual way <tried to counter him?>, but when Theophilus with his marvelous works showed on more than one occasion how invincible the Christian faith is, the opposition was reduced, however unwillingly, to utter silence. His embassy was successful; the ruler of the nation was converted to the faith in all sincerity, and he built not one but three churches in his country.[9] He did so not from the imperial funds brought by the embassy but from what he himself eagerly donated; so struck was he by Theophilus's works that he was anxious to rival his zeal. He put up one of the churches in the capital itself of the whole nation, called Tapharon.[10] Another was located in what was the Roman market center, toward the outer ocean. The place is called Aden, and it is where voyagers from Roman territory were accustomed to put in. The third church was in the other part of the country, where there is a well-known Persian market center at the mouth of the Persian Gulf there.

4a [Simeon Metaphrastes, *Martyrium Arethae* 1]. A Hebrew named Dhū-Nuwās was also ruler of Arabia Felix, the Saba' of old now called Himyar.... He maintained [the custom of] **circumcision** among all his subjects, some of whom practiced Judaism, while others were quite pagan in their ways, **sacrificing to the sun, the moon, and the demons**, which they venerated with statues and monuments according to **local** custom.[11]

---

9. The ruler converted to Christianity was Ta'ran Yuhan'im. Since the Christians in Persia were looked upon with suspicion by their king, as likely partisans of the Christian emperor of Rome, the gift of a church on his part was a political as well as a religious commitment. He probably maintained good relations with the Christians as long as relations with Rome remained favorable. It is hard to say how much Theophilus's mission changed the political and ecclesiastical situation on the Red Sea coast and when it was that Sassanid predominance was restored. Sapor II eventually reestablished Sassanid power in Arabia after Julian's death in 363 (cf. Dihle, "L'ambassade de Théophile," 467).

10. Tapharon is biblical Shephar, classical Sapphar or Saphar, modern Zaphar. The Persian market center was in Hormuz. The three churches, then, were located in the capital and in two coastal centers, just where the resident aliens lived.

11. 3.4a is Simeon Metaphrastes, *Martyrium Arethae* (PG 115:1249A). The martyrdom is set in the time of the emperor Justin. For commentary, see *DHGE* 3:1650–53. Dhū-Nuwās converted to Judaism and ruled Himyar from 523 to 525. He rebelled against the Christian Abyssinian vicegerent whose administration had been established by the Abyssinian expedition of 518, which had subjected Himyar to the

[*Martyrium Arethae* 2]. There [was] a populous city named Nedshran sub-ject to the Himyarite, which had already long ago come to a knowledge of the truth and accepted the **true faith**. This happened when Constantius, the son of Constantine the Great, sent an embassy to the **Sabaeans, the people now known as Himyarites,** who are **descended from Abraham through Keturah.** He **won over** the king **of that nation by gifts,** built churches, and sent out as head of those united in the true faith one Theophilus, a man who had chosen to **live** in celibacy, possessed the virtues of the moral and active life to a high degree, and was superior to all his contemporaries. The Jews opposed [the embassy] and persuaded the barbarian not to be ready to admit such a stranger into his realm or to make innovations in religion unless Theophilus first worked some sign, and only then allow him to enter the city, as is their wont as unbelievers to demand frequent signs. Encouraged by the divine promises that signs would accompany those who believe, he agreed [to their demand] unhesitatingly and showed great power in working the wonders requested.[12]

4b [Photius, *Bibliotheca* codex 40]. [Philostorgius] exalts … Theophilus the Indian … for his marvels and his life.

5. Theophilus, then, having settled the various matters with the Himy-arites as far as was possible in each case, as opportunity allowed, and having consecrated the churches and decorated them as best he could, sailed off to the island of Diva, which, as has been said, was his homeland. From there he went on to the rest of the Indian country, where he corrected much that was not being done by them in a lawful way.[13] They would, for instance, listen to the gospel readings while seated, and they did other things not permitted by divine law.[14] When, however, he had amended each of these matters with a view to their reverence and love of God, he confirmed the church's teaching. For, says our heretic, they had no need of instruction to correct their worship, since they had held to the doctrine of "other in substance" unfailingly from the beginning.[15]

Aksumite kings. The Christians, suspected of loyalty to the Christian Aksumite rulers, were put to death in large numbers.

12. For "signs would accompany those who believe," see Mark 16:17.

13. "The rest of the Indian country": Malabar (Fiaccadori, "Teofilo Indiano," 33:328; 34:271). The route taken by Theophilus to Himyar, the Maldives, and Malabar was that usual to the merchants of the time.

14. On standing while the gospel is read, see Caesarius of Arles, *Sermo* 13.3; *Constitutiones Apostolorum* 2.57.8; Sozomen 7.19.6; Joseph A. Jungmann, *The Mass of the Roman Rite* (trans. Francis A. Brunner; New York: Benziger, 1951), 1:448–49 (refs. to both eastern and western customs).

15. Notice how careful Philostorgius is to inform us that Theophilus had no need to correct the doctrine that he found among the Indians and that they had received

6. From there in Great Arabia he set sail for the land of those Ethiopians who are called Aksumites and who live along the nearest shores of the Red Sea, the whole of which is fashioned by the ocean as it forms a gulf here.[16] The Red Sea, which extends to a great distance, divides into two gulfs. One of them touches Egypt <at> Clysma, where it terminates and is called by the name of the place. Through it the Israelites of old, fleeing from the Egyptians, crossed the gulf dry-shod.[17] The other branch touches Palestine at the city called Elath since ancient times.[18] The Aksumites possess the regions on the Red Sea to the left of those <sailing in?> from the outside. They receive their name from their capital, which is Aksum. Nearer than these Aksumites, however, are the Syrians, who sojourn toward the east, by the outer ocean, and who are called "Syrians" even by the local people. It was Alexander the Macedonian who removed them from Syria and settled them there next to them.[19] They still speak their ancestral language. They are all quite dark, burned as they are by the bright sun. Xylocassia is found in abundance there, along with cassia, cyclamen, and cinnamon, and lots of elephants too.

Theophilus did not get as far as them, but he did reach the Aksumites, took care of matters there, and then returned to the Roman Empire. He was shown great **honor** by the emperor upon his return, although he did not receive a city of his own as his see; he was rather looked upon by his co-religionists as a **common** object of veneration because of his **virtue**.

6a [*Suda,* Θ 197 Theophilus]. Upon his return from India he resided in Antioch. He had no church of his own separately but belonged to all in **common** and might freely visit all the churches as though they were his own, the emperor bestowing every mark of the highest **honor** and respect upon

---

from the apostle Bartholomew (2.6); he regards his Eunomian monotheism as the true heir of the apostolic teaching, which it preserves by the doctrine of "other in substance." Thus he can present Bartholomew himself as preaching this doctrine (2.6).

16. "From there in Great Arabia": Fiaccadori ("Teofilo Indiano," 34:290–91) notes the gap in the story, Theophilus suddenly finding himself back in Arabia from Malabar; he holds Photius responsible. On Aksum and its conversion to Christianity, see Rufinus, *Hist. eccl.* 10.9–10; Socrates 1.19; Sozomen 2.24; Theodoret, *Hist. eccl.* 1.23; Heinzgerd Brakmann, "Axomis," *RAC* Supplement 1:5/6 (1992): 718–810, esp. 745–47. On trade between Rome and Aksum, see Eusebius, *Vit. Const.* 4.7.1; *Cod. theod.* 12.12.2 (356).

17. On Clysma as the place where the Israelites crossed the sea, see Eusebius, *Onomasticon* 44.3 (where it is treated as a common noun: διὰ τοῦ κλύσματος: "through the surf").

18. Elath = Aila.

19. On the Syrians resettled by Alexander, see Arrian, *Anabasis* 7.19.5 (Alexander's plans for settling the seaboard of the Persian Gulf and the offshore islands).

him. So did everyone in his charge; they welcomed him with the utmost warmth and were astonished at the greatness of his **virtue**. For the man was greater than words can describe; he was like an image of the apostles. It is in fact said of him that he once revived a dead Jewish woman in Antioch. Thalassius says so, and he is one of those who spent a great deal of time in the man's company and is the last person to be suspected of lying about such matters. And he has many contemporaries who back him up.

7. The Persian Gulf, which is formed by the ocean as it enters there, is huge and is encircled by many nations. The Tigris is one of the enormous rivers that empty their streams into it at its mouth. The Tigris seems to have its source in the east, south of the Caspian Sea in Corduena, and it flows past Syria, but when it arrives in the region of Susa, the Euphrates joins its current to it, and so it boils onward, swollen now to a great size. Hence they say it is called "Tigris" after the animal. But before it descends to the sea, it divides into two great rivers, and then it empties into the Persian Gulf from these two mouths at its end, which are divided from each other. It thus cuts off a considerable area of ground in between, making of it an island that is both of the river and of the sea; it is inhabited by a people called the Mesenes.[20]

8. As for the Euphrates River, it appears to take its rise in Armenia, where Mount Ararat is. The mountain is still called by that name by the Armenians. It is where, according to scripture, the ark came to rest, and they say that considerable remnants of its wood and nails are still preserved there.[21] From there the Euphrates starts as a small stream at first, growing ever larger as it advances and sharing its name with the many rivers that empty into it. It makes its way through Greater and Lesser Armenia and then proceeds on, dividing first the Syria that is properly called Euphratensis and then also the rest of Syria. Having passed through this region, and the remaining part [of Syria], and having broken up the lands through which it passes into a series of convolutions of every sort with its crooked course, it draws near to Arabia. There its way takes it in a circle opposite the Red Sea as it loops around a wide region, after which it turns toward the Caecias wind, midway between north and east. It then heads toward the Tigris River, although it cannot join its whole self to it, but wasting part of itself on the way, it empties the remainder of itself into the Tigris quite near Susa, this remainder being a mighty stream quite capable of carrying ships. There it also abandons its name and flows

---

20. On 3.7–11, see Nicephorus 9.19. On the inhabitants of Mesene, see Franz Heinrich Weissbach, "Mesene," PW 15.1:1082–95.

21. On the resting place and remains of the ark, see Josephus, *Ant.* 1.90–95; Eusebius, *Onomasticon* 2.23–4.25, and *Praeparatio Evangelica* 9.11; Epiphanius, *Pan.* 18.3.3.

with the Tigris down to the Persian Gulf. The land between these two rivers, the Tigris and Euphrates, is called Mesopotamia.[22]

9. Where the Tigris and Euphrates seem to take their rise has been described. But the truest account is given by our sacred scripture, when it says that their source is in Paradise.[23] Deriving from there their first supply of water, they proceed for a distance, probably flowing above ground. Then when they reach the great, sand-choked desert, they are gulped down deep, never stopping on their downward course until they come right to the impervious, rocky layer of ground that is there. Since the floor there stops them from descending farther, their waters now gather together, and, as they continually accumulate, their quantity and power force them straight forward. As these rivers travel underground, however, the surrounding earth absorbs a considerable amount of them, so that they arrive at the places where they issue forth reduced and weakened.[24]

Now there is no reason to doubt that they travel a great distance in the interior of the earth. There are many other streams everywhere, some of them quite large and powerful, which take their course underground. This is evident, for one can hear the loud noise they make, full of a confused rushing sound. Not only that, but when people have dug wells above them and have pierced a short way into the hard underlying rock, from beneath which the stream then boiled violently upwards, they have only with difficulty been hoisted back up by those standing on the edge of the well, and the stream that followed became a watercourse untroubled by any drought because of the ever-flowing spring from which it came. For the ineffable wisdom of God has fashioned the courses of streams, some of them invisible and some visible, to be like veins furnishing what is necessary. For thus sang the prophet

---

22. On the derivation of "Tigris," see Eusebius, *Onomasticon* 164.7–10. On the courses of the Tigris and Euphrates, see Pliny, *Nat.* 5.83–90; Anonymus in Dionysius of Byzantium, *De Bospori navigatione* (ed. Carl Wescher; Paris: Typographeum publicum, 1874), 122.

23. On the Tigris and Euphrates issuing from Paradise, see Gen 2:10-14; Geographer of Ravenna in Otto Cuntz and Joseph Schnetz, eds., *Itineraria romana* (2 vols.; Leipzig: Teubner, 1929–40), 2:1.8.

24. On the underground course of the two rivers, see Epiphanius, *Ancoratus* 58. Ammianus 23.6.15 and Justinus 42.3 also refer to the Tigris diving underground and reappearing (Justinus says 25,000 stadia later). Pseudo-Caesarius, *Quaestiones et Responsiones* 166, and Theodoret, *Quaestiones in Octateuchum (Genesim)* 29, explain that the reason the two flow underground for so long after leaving Paradise is to prevent the curious from following them upstream to the Garden. On the force of the river-water flowing underground from Paradise, see Philo, *QG* 1.12.

David: "He has founded it upon the seas and established it upon the rivers."[25] So he has, as it were, stored away the seas in [the earth's] great gulfs and has strengthened its foundations so that it may support the great bulk and multitude of the things it contains. And to the rivers he gives always an unfailing outlet through their ingenious structures, providing a place for the weight of the water to take its course in the channels and depressions of the lands that lead from the higher levels to the lower.

10. Resorting to conjecture, he states that Paradise lies in the eastern equinox, first because it is evident that almost all the regions to the south are inhabited, all the way to the outer sea.[26] At that distance this sea is burned by the sun, which strikes it with its rays from directly above, and this is what is called the equator. Another reason is that the river now called the Hyphasis, which scripture names the Pishon and which itself rises in Paradise, seems rather to flow south from the northern parts of the east and to empty into the ocean there opposite the island of Taprobane.[27] Along the banks of this river is found what is called the *caryophyllon,* whether that be a fruit or a flower.[28] The local people think that it is from a tree descended from those in Paradise. Now in fact the land above them is completely a desert, quite barren. But the fact that the river bears the flower shows that this river flows above ground for its entire length, without ever going under. Otherwise it would not be able to bear what germinates from there. And there is another sign of the linkage of earth with Paradise: they say that someone taken with a violent fever recovers at once after bathing in the river.[29]

But because the Tigris and Euphrates go under and come up again, they cannot bring anything from there, as the Hyphasis does. Neither for that matter can the Nile.[30] For indeed the inspired words of Moses say that it too

---

25. "He founded it upon the seas" (Ps 23:2).

26. On Paradise being in the East, see Gen 2:8; Louis Ginzberg, *Legends of the Jews* (7 vols.; Philadelphia: Jewish Publication Society, 1909–38), 1:11, 5:13; Philo, *QG* 1.7. Anastasius of Sinai, *Quæstio extra ordinem* 127 (PG 89:780), places it near India.

27. Taprobane is Sri Lanka.

28. The *caryophyllon* is the gillyflower or clove and was imported from India (Pliny, *Nat.* 12.30).

29. Marvelous nuts from Paradise were also on sale in Clysma in Egypt, where the merchant ships from India put in; see *Antonini Placentini Itinerarium* 41 (in Paul Geyer, ed., *Itineraria et alia geographica* [CCSL 175; Turnhout: Brepols, 1965]). Contrary to Philostorgius, Pseudo-Caesarius speaks of the Euphrates bringing down fruits and leaves from Paradise in its stream.

30. The ancient theories about the sources of the Nile are reviewed by Alan Lloyd, *Herodotus, Book II: Commentary 1–98* (EPRO 43; Leiden: Brill, 1976), 107–11: it rises far to the west, or in India, or from Ocean, or from beyond Ocean in "counter-earth,"

flows from there; he calls it the Gihon.[31] Among the pagans it was known as the Egyptian River.[32] One may infer that, taking its rise in Paradise, it passes underground before reaching inhabited country. It then passes under the Indian Ocean, circles about it, as one may conjecture (can any human being be certain about this?), makes its way beneath all of the intervening land as far as the Red Sea, passes under that as well, and issues forth on its other side beneath the so-called Mountain of the Moon. In this mountain it is said to form two great springs, at a good distance apart, that burst upwards from below. It flows through Ethiopia and then makes its way to Egypt by spilling down through towering rocks.

11. He says that the whole region toward the rising sun and in the south, even though excessively torrid, contains the mightiest and greatest things that earth and sea can nourish.[33] The most gigantic whales, for instance, live in this sea, and they have often been seen to surface by those who sail the ocean there. The land too contains elephants of the most enormous size, along with the so-called "bull-elephants," whose species is in all respects that of a huge ox, but with the hide and color of an elephant, and one might almost say the size as well. In fact, I once saw the animal when it was brought to Roman parts, and I describe what I saw. There are also serpents in those parts as thick as beams and up to fifteen fathoms in length; I have in fact even seen their skins that had been brought to Roman parts. The animal called the unicorn is also found there; it has a serpent's head but a crooked

---

or in the Ethiopian mountains. That it flowed underground for part of its course was evidently often assumed. The circular courses of subterranean rivers was an ancient notion (cf. Plato, *Phaedo* 112d–113c). In Ptolemy, the Mountain of the Moon supplies the snow for the Nile's sources (*Geographica* 1.17.5). Herodotus 2.28 speaks of two mountains, between which lie the springs of the Nile, from which it blusters forth; perhaps Philostorgius combines the last two traditions. Ammianus too knows a story about the Nile issuing from a mountain (22.15.8). Cf. also Eusebius, *Onomasticon* 60.3–4; Strabo 1.2.22, 29; Arrian, *Anabasis* 5.6.5; Seneca, *Naturales quaestiones* 4.2.3–5; Aristides, *Or.* 36.47–57.

31. Jewish tradition identified the Gihon with the Nile and the Pishon with the Ganges (Ginsberg, *Legends of the Jews,* 1:70 and 5:91–92; Josephus, *Ant.* 1.38–39; Philo, *QG* 1.12–13). Philostorgius seems alone in identifying the Pishon with the Hyphasis or Hypasis, which an ancient geographical error placed in the region of the Ganges (Adolf Kiessling, "Hypasis," PW 9.1:234).

32. For the Nile called the Egyptian River, see Strabo as above and 15.1.16; Ammianus 22.15.3.

33. It was commonly assumed that Indian animals were super-sized (Solinus, *Collectanea Rerum Memorabilium* 52.33–45; Pliny, *Nat.* 9.4–7) and that more animals are bred there because of the sun's power (Diodorus of Sicily 2.51.3–4).

horn that is not very large. Its entire chin is covered with a beard. Its long throat, lifted on high, is most like a serpent's coil. The rest of the body resembles rather a deer, but with the feet of a lion. One may see an image of it in Constantinople.[34]

The giraffe is another species found there.[35] It is in all respects a huge deer, but its body resembles a camel's in height. Its neck, however, which it carries high and erect, is of great length, out of proportion to the rest of the body. In addition, its whole coat, from the top of its head to the bottom of its feet, most resembles a leopard's by its spottedness, and its forefeet are higher than those behind. There is also found there the so-called goat-ape, a kind of ape. There are countless kinds of apes. There are, for instance, the bear-apes to be found there and lion-apes and dog-faced baboons and many other species of animals with which the form of an ape is found combined. The evidence for this is in the many examples that have been brought to our parts. There is, for instance, the so-called pan, whose head is goat-faced and goat-horned, and which is goat-legged from the flanks down, while the stomach, chest, and hands are simply those of an ape.[36] The king of India sent it to Constantius.[37] The animal lived for a while, shut up in a wickerwork cage because of its fierceness. When it died, its keepers stuffed it in order to give people something unusual to look at and brought it safe and sound all the way to Constantinople. For my part, I believe the pagans of old saw this animal and, struck by how odd it looked, gave it the status of a god, accustomed as they were to divinize strange things, as they did, for instance, with the satyr as well.[38] That is also an ape, with a red face, swift movements, and a tail.

---

34. Cedrenus as well mentions seeing images of "bull-elephants" and unicorns in Constantinople (322C). For the description of the former animal, see *Aristophanis Historiae Animalium Epitome* II 132 (in *Excerptorum Constantini De natura animalium libri duo : Aristophanis Historiae animalium epitome* [ed. Spyridon P. Lambros; Supplementum Aristotelicum 1.1; 2 vols.; Berlin: Reimer, 1885], 2:132). On the huge snakes, see Solinus 52.33. But our author's description of the unicorn seems to be unique; cf. Odell Shepard, *The Lore of the Unicorn* (London: Unwin, 1930).

35. On the giraffe, see Cedrenus above; Pliny, *Nat.* 8.6.9; Heliodorus, *Aethiopica* 10.27.

36. On the pan, see Cedrenus above. Paul of Thebes once met one in the desert and had a brief chat with it, but the creature was not inclined to say much; cf. Jerome, *Vita S. Pauli, primi eremitae* 8.

37. "Sent it to Constantius" translates Κωνσταντίῳ. The editor suggests that the true reading may be Κωνσταντίνῳ, referring to Eusebius's account of an embassy from India that presented exotic animals to Constantine (*Vit. Const.* 4.50).

38. On the satyr, see Pliny, *Nat.* 7.24; 8.216; Solinus 27.60.

Still another kind of ape is the sphinx; I describe it as I saw it.[39] All of its body is hairy, like other apes, except for the chest to the throat, which is bare. It has a woman's breasts, with a slight red swelling like grains of millet encircling all the bare part of its body and enhancing its appearance greatly, since it goes well with the human-like color in the middle. Its face is rather rounded, giving it the shape of a woman's. Its voice is somewhat human but is inarticulate, resembling that of someone muttering quickly and unintelligibly, and as it were with an air of anger and annoyance; it is in the lower range of high pitch. The animal is terribly fierce and mischievous and not easily tamed. It is my opinion that it was brought to Thebes in Boeotia of old, that it probably leaped upon some of those who flocked to see it and injured their faces, and that Oedipus, thinking it terrible that his fellow-countrymen had been wounded, killed the beast and became renowned for it. The fable, in adorning him with courage, refashioned the beast into something with wings because of its high leaps and fitted it with a woman's chest and a lion's body. The woman's chest was because of its exposed nakedness and its similarity to a woman's appearance; the lion's body was due to its ferocity and because for the most part it rests upon its four feet. The myth bestowed speech upon the beast because of the human quality of its voice but made it speak in riddles because what it uttered was unintelligible. There is nothing surprising in this. The pagans have had the habit of fashioning all sorts of other things in the form of fables.

The same country also contains the most enormous wild asses, whose coat is strangely variegated, with white and black splashes of color all jumbled together; they form stripes reaching from the spine to the flanks and abdomen, where they separate and wrap about each other in swirls to produce a strange and remarkable intricacy and variety.[40] In addition, that famous bird the phoenix is found in those parts. Not only that, but we know that the parrot comes from there, of all birds the most talkative and best mimic of human language,

---

39. On the sphinx, see Agatharchides, frg. 73 (in Karl Müller, ed., *Geographi graeci minores* [3 vols. Paris: Didot, 1855–61], 1:159); Diodorus of Sicily 3.35.4; Pliny, *Nat* 8.72 ("fusco pilo, mammis in pectore geminis"); Solinus 27.59 ("villosae comis, mammis prominulis ac profundis, dociles ad feritatis oblivionem"). It was common enough in antiquity to rationalize the story of Oedipus and the Sphinx, although usually it was along the lines of Oedipus defeating a woman brigand or pirate; cf. Palaephatus 8; Phanodemus, *FGH* 325E5bis; Pausanias 9.26.2; *Scholia vetera in Hesiodi Theogoniam* 326 (ed. Lamberto Di Gregorio; Milan: Vita e pensiero, 1975]). In Psellus, the Sphinx represents composite human nature, spiritual and material (in Jean François Boissonade, ed., *Tzetzae Allegoriae Iliadis* [Paris: Dumont, 1851], 355–62).

40. The zebra described by our author seems to be "Grévy's Zebra," larger than the more common kind and with a different pattern of striping; cf. D'Arcy W. Thompson, "The Greek for a Zebra," *The Classical Review* 57 (1943): 103–4.

and the many-colored and speckled birds that some call "garamantes," after the nation that exports most of them.[41] And there are a great number of other clearly extraordinary creatures, the full tale of which is beyond this account.

Gold too of the purest variety is produced there; something like strands of gold grow naturally from the ground there and lie one upon the other, showing clearly the origin of the gold.[42] The fruits are also quite large and beautiful, and their kernels are famous as well. Not only that, but the whole region of the Himyarites as far as the Red Sea yields fruit twice a year, so that they named the land "Fortunate Arabia." And in general the whole land toward the rising sun is far superior to the others in every way, while Paradise, being the best and purest part of the entire east, having the freshest and fairest airs and being irrigated by the clearest waters, obviously is incomparably superior in every respect to every land under the sun, washed as it is by the outer sea toward the rising of the sun.

12. Athanasius, he says, having reached the western emperor and bribed those influential with him with bounteous gifts, especially Eustathius, who held the office of *comes privatarum*,[43] as it is called, and was high in the emperor's confidence, managed to get a letter [sent] to Constantius that ran as follows: "Athanasius has reached us and has proved that the see of Alexandria belongs to him. Let him therefore receive it from you, or else he will acquire it by force of my arms."[44] Constantius, when he had received the letter, called together the bishops to hear their advice and was told by them that it was better to avoid war with his brother than to deliver Alexandria from Athanasius's tyranny. He therefore allowed him to resume the see and summoned George to him by letter.[45] He in turn made his way to Cappadocia,

---

41. On parrots, see Pliny, *Nat.* 10.117; Aelian, *Nat. an.* 16.2, 15. The Garamantes were Libyan Berbers centered on Garama; for their trade with Rome, see Erwin M. Ruprechtsberger, *Die Garamanten: Geschichte und Kultur eines Libyschen Volkes in der Sahara* (Mainz: von Zabern, 1997), 74–75.

42. On the abundance of gold, see Gen 2:12. Posidonius says that "white gold" (mixed with silver) sprouts from the ground in the northwest corner of Lusitania (Strabo 3.2.9).

43. On Eustathius, *comes rei privatae* (attested in office 15 May 345), see *PLRE* 1:310–11; Timothy D. Barnes, *Athanasius and Constantius: Theology and Politics in the Constantinian Empire* (Cambridge: Harvard University Press, 1993), 89–90.

44. There are different versions of his letter to his brother in Socrates 2.22.5 and Theodoret, *Hist. eccl.* 2.8.55–56. Athanasius was in fact charged with setting Constans against his brother: Athanasius, *Apol. Const.* 2–5.

45. The usual confusion between "George" and "Gregory" seems to be at work here (see 39 n. 6). There was no "Arian" bishop in Alexandria when Athanasius returned, Gregory having died there the year before. As for George, he had but a short

his homeland, and there spent his time looking after his own concerns. As for Athanasius, he made his way through the cities with now greater arrogance, speaking with the bishops he encountered and urging them to accept the consubstantialist doctrine.[46] None of them agreed except Aetius, the bishop of Palestine, who had been denounced for fornication and, hoping to conceal his disgrace by yielding to Athanasius, defected to his doctrine.[47] But he paid a very heavy penalty when his genitals putrefied and swarmed with worms, and thus he died. Maximus, the bishop of Jerusalem, also went over to Athanasius's doctrine, even though Maximian's persecution had made him a martyr, one of his eyes having been gouged out for the faith.[48] And Athanasius seduced many others to his doctrine in a short time.[49]

13. He says that Flavian of Antioch, having gathered together a crowd of monks, was the first to cry, "Glory be to the Father and to the Son and to the Holy Spirit!" For some of those before him had said, "Glory be to the Father through the Son in the Holy Spirit," this being the more popular acclamation, while others had said, "Glory be to the Father and to the Son in the Holy Spirit."[50]

---

time to enjoy his see, when he finally managed to take possession of it, before he was thrown out by Athanasius's supporters on 2 October 358 (Athanasius, *HA* 6). He returned on 26 November 361 (*HA* 7), just in time to get lynched.

46. Socrates 2.24 records Athanasius's triumphant progress from Antioch to Alexandria fifteen years earlier. His "arrogance" may refer to his performance of illicit ordinations on the way (2.24.8).

47. Aetius of Lydda, a staunch Arian if ever there was one (cf. Opitz, *Urkunden zur Geschichte*, 1.3; Theodoret, *Hist. eccl.* 1.5.5; 5.7.1), earned Philostorgius's ire by participating in the council called by Maximus of Jerusalem to rehabilitate Athanasius during his homeward journey (Athanasius, *C. Ar.* 57; Socrates 2.24.1–3). That Aetius could be called a partisan of the Nicene doctrine testifies to Athanasius's success in identifying his cause with that of orthodoxy; resistance to his claim was vigorous in the east at the time but would have to yield at last to the decisive intervention of Julian the Apostate, who singled out Athanasius from among all the bishops for persecution. To side with Athanasius, then, was, for Philostorgius, to affirm the Nicene Creed. Aetius then suffers the first of the cautionary deaths that our author loves to recount and of which Julian's reign will furnish him so many examples.

48. On Maximian's persecution, see 4.4a; Rufinus, *Hist. eccl.* 10.4; *AASS* Maii II 9 F; on the gouging out of Maximus's eye, see Rufinus, *Hist. eccl.* 10.18.

49. On the chronology, see the second paragraph of 29 n. 38, 35 n. 50. The narrative in 3.12 fits the time of Athanasius's flight to Italy in 339, his subsequent rehabilitation by the Council of Sardica, and his return in 346 after Constans threatened to supply him with a military escort, if necessary.

50. On different forms of the doxology heard in Antioch at the time, see Theodoret, *Hist. eccl.* 2.24.3; Sozomen 3.20.8. Bishop Leontius used to suffer from convenient

14. He says that even if those of Arius's school differed in their views from those favoring the consubstantialist doctrine,[51] still they shared with them in prayers, hymns, deliberations, and almost everything else except for the sacred sacrifice. But when Aetius came on the scene and initiated dissension in these matters as well, the members of his sect broke off all ties, friendships, and customs that had joined them to those of differing beliefs and set up a party that stood in the most marked opposition to them.[52]

15. Aetius's native place was [Antioch?] in Coele **Syria. His father was one of those whose life in the service went rather badly,** and, having died in those circumstances, our author says that the one in power at the time confiscated his property. The young Aetius and his mother were reduced to **dire** poverty, and for this reason he turned to goldsmithy so that his mother and he might have some way to survive.[53]

<But> when he had plied his trade sufficiently, his **gifts of mind** made him **turn** to the **intellectual** disciplines, and he **became a disciple** at first of **Paulinus,** who had transferred from the see of **Tyre** to that of **Antioch.**[54] But upon the death of his mother, for whose sake in particular Aetius had taken up

---

fits of coughing during the doxology, and the lay ascetics Flavian and Diodore, Nicene partisans who opposed his patronage of Aetius, taught the people the enormously popular antiphonal singing of the Psalms, to which, one may guess, the doxology was attached (see Theodoret, *Hist. eccl.* 2.24.7–11).

51. On divisions among the later "Arians," see Epiphanius, *Pan.* 73.23.2–8; 73.27.5–8; Rufinus, *Hist. eccl.* 10.26 (Epiphanius thinks the divisions were not, at bottom, doctrinal).

52. Philostorgius thus introduces us to Aetius as entering upon a scene of ecclesiastical unruliness in Antioch and of working to segregate from it that true Christian monotheism represented by his creed. But he (or Photius) is speaking proleptically here, since the picture of Aetius the schismatic cannot be squared with that of the Aetius who is fully integrated into the life of the Antiochene church as deacon and catechist (3.17). A separate Eunomian church will not be established until the time of Julian the Apostate, but the seeds were there: Aetius was convinced that Arius had perjured himself when he swore to Constantine, upon his return from exile, that he agreed with the Council of Nicaea, and he was determined to clarify church doctrine by methods of exposition that other "Arians" found overly reliant on logical distinction (cf. Socrates 2.35; Sozomen 4.12.1–2). Socrates says that it was in fact they who expelled him from their fellowship, but he pretended to have decided not to communicate with them on account of Arius's perjury.

53. Aetius was born ca. 313. On his early life and education, see Gregory of Nyssa, *Eun.* 1.42–44; Epiphanius, *Pan.* 76.2.1–2; Nicetas, *Thes.* 5.30; Vaggione, *Eunomius of Cyzicus,* 14–24.

54. Paulinus became bishop of Antioch in 327 or 328; he was a staunch ally of Arius (1.8a; Opitz, *Urkunden zur Geschichte,* 1.3; 8). The succession of bishops in

the art that gives to gold its varied shapes, he thenceforward went over completely to the **study** of the **intellectual disciplines** and soon became known for bettering most people in debate. This aroused <not> a little jealousy.

As long as Paulinus was alive, however, the jealousy remained idle. But six months later when he died and **Eulalius succeeded to the throne,** the jealousy returned in full force and caused Eulalius **to drive** Aetius from Antioch. He **made his way to Anazarbus** in Cilicia, where he again practiced his trade to earn a living, while continuing to debate with those he met.[55] Now a certain grammarian who admired his talent decided to share his art with him, so Aetius moved in with him and worked for him at menial tasks. And while he willingly taught him grammar, there came a time when Aetius demonstrated publicly that his teacher had misinterpreted the sacred scriptures, covering him with shame at his ignorance of such matters; his reward was to be turned out of his benefactor's house. After his rejection he fell in with Athanasius, who had been one of the disciples of the martyr Lucian but was now bishop of Anazarbus. When he had read the Evangelists with him and worked his way through each one of them with him, he went to Tarsus, to Antony, who was himself one of Lucian's disciples. He spent some considerable time with him learning from him about the letters of the apostle; Antony held the office of presbyter. But when Antony became bishop and could not spare the time to polish Aetius's education, he returned to Antioch to become Leontius's disciple.[56] Leontius was then a presbyter, and he too had been taught by Lucian; Leontius expounded the prophets to him, especially Ezekiel.

But from there as well he was once again driven by envy, according to Philostorgius's ravings; it would be nearer the truth to say that it was his unbridled tongue and his heretical views. So he proceeded from there to Cilicia. And a Borborian engaged him in debate concerning his own doctrine and utterly defeated him, at which he sank so low in spirits that he thought life not worth living, since he had seen falsehood prevail over truth. But when Aetius was in this mood, a vision came to him, so our author blathers, that dissi-

---

Antioch for this period is remarkably hard to establish; see Vaggione, *Eunomius of Cyzicus,* 18 n. 32; *DHGE* 3:698–701.

55. Aetius went to Anazarbus around 327–329. Its bishop, Athanasius, had defended Arius for saying that the Son of God is a creature (Opitz, *Urkunden zur Geschichte,* 11).

56. Vaggione (*Eunomius of Cyzicus,* 21) puts Aetius's return to Antioch in the mid 330s. His study of the Bible in the order of Gospels, Epistles, and Prophets seems to have followed a definite plan, perhaps that of Lucian of Antioch himself. His conviction about God's knowability may have come through Antony and Leontius from Asterius (Kopecek, *History of Neo-Arianism,* 71, 73).

pated his dejection and showed him in signs the invincibility of the wisdom that would now be his. From then on it was given to Aetius to be defeated by no one in debate.[57] Shortly thereafter, in fact, one Aphthonius, a leader of the Manichaean maniacs who was held in high renown by many for his wisdom and prowess in speech, tangled with him in Alexandria in Egypt, for Aetius, drawn by his reputation, came from Antioch to meet him.[58] When they came to grips with each other, no lengthy debate ensued, for Aetius reduced Aphthonius to silence and brought him down from great fame to great shame. So dejected was he by his unexpected defeat that he fell gravely ill and in the end died; his body did not survive the blow more than seven days. Aetius for his part defeated his opponents in debate **thoroughly** wherever he went and won a brilliant victory.

He then studied medicine in order to be able to cure sicknesses of the body as well as of the soul.[59] Sopolis was his instructor in this field, a man second to none in this art. Aetius excelled in medicine and **healed** those in need without charge. And if he ever lacked for necessities, he would go to one of his fellow craftsmen by night, so as not to be taken away from higher pursuits by day, and quickly execute whatever work needed the goldsmith's hand, thus earning from his fellow craftsman what he needed to live on. This took place during the time of Constantius, when Theophilus had returned from India and was living in Antioch.

---

57. The key to Philostorgius's understanding of Aetius is in the story of his defeat by the Borborian (a member of a radically antinomian gnostic sect) and his recovery and subsequent victory over the Manichee in debate. Aetius's real foe, for our author, is Christian polytheism of every kind, whether (as he thought) undisguised in Gnosticism or cleverly masked, as in the consubstantialist doctrine; it is against the confession of multiple and mutable deities, whether explicit or otherwise, that Aetius, and later Eunomius, range the weapons of their doctrine.

58. Tradition lists an Aphthonius among Mani's chief exponents (Photius, *Contra Manichaeos* 1.14 [PG 102:41B]); cf. Vaggione, *Eunomius of Cyzicus*, 24 n. 67. Death from disappointment in debate is not uncommon in Philostorgius: Basil of Caesarea suffers the same fate (8.12), and of course Aetius himself narrowly escapes it after taking on the Borborian.

59. Contrary to Philostorgius, Gregory of Nyssa says that Aetius studied medicine before taking up theological questions and that it was in fact in gatherings of his fellow physicians that he heard Arius's teachings hotly debated; he read up on Aristotle in order to fit himself to participate in the disputations more successfully (*Eun.* 1.42–44). This seems a more probable order of education, philosophy being keenly discussed in medical circles in antiquity. See Jonathan Barnes, "Pyrrhonism, Belief, and Causation. Observations on the Scepticism of Sextus Empiricus," *ANRW* 2.36.4:2611–17.

15a [Nicetas, *Thes.* 5.30]. That Aetius was a goldsmith is attested as well by Philostorgius, his fellow sectarian, who says in the third book of his history, "**Turning** therefore **to goldsmithy,** Aetius **became a highly skilled craftsman in gold.**"

15b [*Suda*, A 571 Aetius]. From Antioch in **Syria,** he was a teacher of Eunomius and born of poor commoners. **His father, one of those whose life in the service went ill,** died while he was quite young. Finding himself **in dire** straits, **he turned to goldsmithy** and **became highly skilled in it.** But since his **gifts of mind** were inclined toward higher **studies, he turned** to the **intellectual disciplines.** Indeed, he kept company with **Paulinus,** who had just come **to Antioch** from **Tyre.** He was still his **disciple** in the time of Constantine, showing clearly enough his great **prowess** in heresy when debating with those of differing views. By now most people found him insupportable. And when Paulinus died and **Eulalius succeeded to the throne** as the twenty-third after the apostles, many of those who had been defeated by Aetius and who considered it terrible to be **soundly** beaten by a craftsman, and a youngster at that, got together and **drove** him from Antioch. After his ejection **he went to Anazarbus.** He now very quickly showed enormous ability, his accomplishments always outmatching the opportunities given him. He never left off **refuting** some people and **curing** others in every different way, going about dressed shabbily and making his living however he could.

16. Aetius, he says, held a debate with Basil of Ancyra, Eustathius of Sebaste, and their party about the term "consubstantial," reducing them to utter silence by his **refutation** and incurring thereby their undying hatred, or so runs the fable our author spins.[60]

17. He says that Leontius, who, as was stated earlier, was a presbyter and Aetius's teacher, when made bishop of Antioch ordained his disciple to the diaconate and allowed him to teach church doctrine in church. Aetius avoided diaconal work and set about teaching. But when he had spent what he judged

---

60. As Bidez (*Philostorgius*, cxxiv) notes, Philostorgius labels as supporters of the consubstantialist doctrine anyone who rejects Eunomius's "other in substance" teaching, since he believes there is no middle ground between the two. The doctrine of "like in substance" expounded by Basil and Eustathius cannot, he thinks, be logically distinguished from "consubstantial" and therefore from the polytheism engaged in the preceding chapter. He makes this clear in 10.3.

Vaggione (*Eunomius of Cyzicus*, 160 n. 47) doubts that 3.16 is a doublet of the incident in 4.12 (against Kopecek, *History of Neo-Arianism*, 106–8), but he assumes that τοῖς περὶ means the party of Basil and Eustathius, not the two themselves. On the translation of οἱ περὶ τὸν δεῖνα, see Barnes, *Athanasius and Constantius*, 248 n. 22.

sufficient time in teaching sacred doctrine, he went back to Alexandria. For Athanasius was now proving a mighty champion of the consubstantialist doctrine there, and someone was needed to challenge him.[61]

18. He says that Flavian and Paulinus, who later shared the see of Antioch, were deposed by the aforesaid Leontius for disagreeing with his doctrine.[62] They had followed Eustathius <into> exile. He preserved from any loss of integrity due to the events of the time the discharge of his sacred responsibilities toward Antioch, or rather toward the orthodox faith as a whole.[63]

19. When Secundus and Serras chose Aetius for the episcopacy, he did not accept it, says our author, since he did not consider that they exercised the priesthood with integrity due to their fellowship with those who believed in the consubstantialist doctrine.

20. Eunomius, he says, came to Antioch from Cappadocia upon learning of the wisdom of Aetius and associated himself with Secundus. He in turn introduced him to Aetius, who was then staying in Alexandria. And they stayed together, the one teaching and the other studying the sacred sciences.

20a [Photius, *Bibliotheca* codex 40]. He exalts Aetius and Eunomius in particular for their teaching, making the absurd claim that they alone cleared the rubble of time from orthodox teaching.[64]

---

61. On Leontius's ordination of Aetius to the diaconate, see Athanasius, *Syn.* 38.4; Theodoret, *Hist. eccl.* 2.24.6–8; Socrates 2.23.5; 2.37.7. Epiphanius (*Pan.* 73.38.3; 76.1.1, 8) wrongly has him ordained by George of Alexandria. He was probably ordained early in 346 (Kopecek, *History of Neo-Arianism*, 96 n. 1). Kopecek (98–102) notes that Philostorgius and Theodoret, *Hist. eccl.* 2.24.7–11, have the same general chronology: a controversy over the form of the doxology at Antioch, followed by another one over Aetius's ordination, followed in turn by his giving up diaconal ministry but continuing in some other church work (Socrates 2.37.10 also implies Aetius's suspension from the diaconate). Kopecek conjectures that Leontius ordained Aetius to counter Flavian and Diodore indirectly, whereupon the two threatened to complain to the west. The emperor Constans having shown himself willing to intervene in church matters outside his own realm, and the scandal over Bishop Stephen having hardly subsided, Leontius felt he had to degrade Aetius.

62. The notice about Leontius deposing Flavian and Paulinus is wrong: Flavian was a layman at the time, and Paulinus, the leader of the Eustathians in Antioch, was not even in communion with Leontius (Sozomen 3.20.6; Theodoret, *Hist. eccl.* 1.22.2), nor, for that matter, with Flavian, although Philostorgius, as we have seen, likes to put homoeousians and homoousians in the same boat.

63. Regarding Leontius's practical care of the church of Antioch, see *Chron. pasch.* P289C.

64. On "rubble of time," see 2 n. 2.

21. Our heretic does not blush to say that he composed a eulogy upon Eunomius.[65]

22. Constans, he says, lost his life in the usurpation of Magnentius because of his zeal for Athanasius.[66] When he died, Constantius was in Edessa in Mesopotamia (where the Persian war[67] required his presence), so their eldest sister Constantia[68] (the widow of Hannibalianus), fearing that the usurper Magnentius might proceed to take over everything, appointed Vetranio, one of the generals, as Caesar. She was regarded as having the power to do this because the father of all of them, while still alive, had crowned her with a diadem and named her Augusta. When Constantius **learned of this,** he immediately sent a diadem to Vetranio and confirmed his imperial rank. Then he set out for the west in battle array against Magnentius, intending to ally himself with Vetranio, but since the latter showed signs of rebelling, he seized Vetranio and divested him of the imperial robe. He did him no further harm, however, but even **invited him to share his table** and then sent him off to Prusa in Bithynia, ordering that he be provided for in magnificent abundance and taking care that he should want for nothing that could contribute to the well-being of someone in private life.[69]

---

65. Eunomius met Aetius ca. 348–350 while he "was still young, perhaps in his early twenties.… [Aetius] was at least twenty years older" (Vaggione, *Eunomius of Cyzicus*, 29).

66. Magnentius's usurpation took place in January of 350. Constans was killed, and Magnentius began sounding out possible dissidents in the other half of the empire, among them Athanasius (*Apol. Const.* 6–10). On Magnentius's uprising, see A7.24.2; Eutropius 10.9.3; Aurelius Victor 41.23–24; *Epit. Caes.* 41.22–24; Zosimus 2.42.

67. On the war with Persia (which Constantius had inherited from his father), see Libanius, *Or.* 18.206–211; Julian, *Or.* 1.18B–19A; 20B–30A; 47C; 2.62B–67B; 74B; Themistius, *Or.* 4.57b; Zosimus 2.43.

68. Constantine I had given his daughter Constantina (here written "Constantia") as wife to Hannibalianus (*Anon. Val.* 35).

69. On Vetranio, see A7.24.6–7; A7.24f–h. He was proclaimed Caesar on 1 March 350 in Naissus, Constantina investing him with the purple robe (*Chron. pasch.* P291C–D). The signs of rebellion mentioned by Philostorgius refer to his occupation of the passes separating his forces from Constantius's (cf. 3.24). He also sent a delegation to Magnentius (Zosimus 2.44.2), and both the usurper and he sent envoys to Constantius urging him to accept the situation and be satisfied with a primacy of honor (Petrus Patricius, *Excerpta de Legationibus* 14; Zonaras 13.7.15–28). In Julian's representation of the episode, Vetranio certainly came to terms with Magnentius (*Or.* 1.30B–33C), having been persuaded by his young men to do so (*Or.* 2.76C). See also *Epit. Caes.* 41.25; Zosimus 2.43.1; Athanasius, *H. Ar.* 50.1; Eutropius 10.10.2–11.1.

23. He says that Sapor, king of Persia, sent an expedition against Nisibis and besieged it.[70] But he had to return in failure and unexpected shame, since Jacob, the bishop of the city, instructed the citizens about what to do and furnished an invincible defense for the city with his intercession with God.

24. The "Alps," both those called the Julian and the Succan, are narrow passes with huge mountains on either side pressing so closely in upon one space that they nearly shut it up.[71] These passes are like the defiles in Thermopylae, but the Julian Alps separate Gaul and Italy from Illyricum, while the Succan run between Dacia and Thrace. It was when Vetranio hastened to occupy them that he made Constantius suspect that he was planning to rebel.

25. While Constantius was making ready for war against the usurper Magnentius, he heard that Persia was moving heavy forces against the east, so he was forced to appoint Gallus to the rank of Caesar and send him against them. **Gallus was his cousin, for Gallus's father Constantius was the brother of Constantine the Great,** who was the father of Constantius and his brothers.[72]

26. Constantius, then, was victorious over the usurper, and at that very time **the sign of the cross** appeared; it was **enormous, and its stunning rays outshone the daylight. It appeared in Jerusalem most visibly around the third hour of the day, on the Feast called Pentecost.** That God-sent image

---

Vetranio's soldiers may have been bribed by Constantius to switch sides; see Bruno Bleckmann, "Constantia, Vetranio, und Gallus Caesar," *Chiron* 24 (1994): 53.

He offered no resistance to Constantius's arrival in his territory, at any rate, and in 351 the surrender of the imperial tokens took place in Naissus (Jerome, *Chron.* 351). For other descriptions of the scene, see A7.24.6–7; A7.24f; Julian, *Or.* 1.30D; 31A–32A; 2.76D–77C; Themistius, *Or.* 2.37A–C; Zosimus 2.44.2–4; Socrates 2.28.16–20. All the ancient sources agree that he retired in honor and comfort, which, given Constantius's usual brusque way with anyone he even remotely suspected of duplicity, suggests that his earlier negotiations with Magnentius may have been managed by Constantius himself to buy time.

70. On the siege of Nisibis, see 216 n. 38. The sieges of the years 337 and 350 are confused in 3.23; Bishop Jacob was there for the first only (the same confusion is found in the account in Theodoret, *Hist. eccl.* 2.30).

71. See 8 n. 8 on the meaning Philostorgius attaches to "Alps." The Succan Pass was on the road from Belgrade to Constantinople, between Sardica and Philippopolis (E. Oberhummer, "Succi," PW 4A.1:513–14).

72. On Gallus's appointment (in Sirmium on 15 March 351), see A7.25, 7.25a, b; Julian, *Or.* 1.45A–B; *Consul. const.* 351; Athanasius, *Festal Index* 24; Eutropius 10.12.2; Aurelius Victor 42.9; *Epit. Caes.* 42.1; Zosimus 2.45.1–2; Socrates 2.28.21; Sozomen 4.4.4; *Chron. pasch.* P292A–B; Zonaras 13.8.3–4. Gallus was Julian's brother; his father, Julius Constantius, was Constantine's half-brother.

was seen **extending from the place called Calvary all the way to the Mount of Olives,** with a great **rainbow** completely encircling it like a **crown.** The rainbow signified the goodwill of the one crucified and taken up, while the crown represented the emperor's victory. Nor was that brilliant and worshipful vision invisible to those in the camp, but being clearly seen, it cast Magnentius and those with him into helpless fear, devoted as they were to the worship of demons,[73] while it gave Constantius and his men boundless courage. Defeated in the first encounter, Magnentius then **recovered** a little, but in the second battle was resoundingly beaten, losing almost all his forces.[74] He fled to Lyons, and there the first thing he did was to kill his own brother as though out of kindness, in order to save him from mistreatment at the hands of the enemy, and then he did the same for anyone else there who was close to him. Finally, he put his sword beneath himself and ran himself through from front to back, and thus died, his usurpation having lasted not even four years.[75]

22a–26a [*AP* 10]. Not long afterwards Constans in turn, in giving himself up **to** revels, drunkenness, and **unnatural love** affairs, was putting the whole state at risk with his negligence and demeaning the majesty of the realm.[76]

---

73. On Magnentius's worship of demons, see Zonaras 13.8.12 (his use of magic to ensure victory). His coinage, however, does not support the view that he was pagan; cf. Lodovico Laffranchi, "Commento numismatico alla storia dell'imperatore Magnenzio e del suo tempo," *Atti e memorie dell'Istituto italiano di numismatica* 6 (1930): 134–205; Pierre Bastien, *Le monnayage de Magnence, 350-353* (Wetteren, Belgium: Éditions cultura, 1964).

74. On the war with Magnentius, see A7.25, 7.27, and 27a. The first battle was fought on 28 September 351 near Mursa. The fortunes of battle swayed back and forth, with enormous losses on either side (Eutropius 10.12; *Epit. Caes.* 42.4–8; Socrates 2.32.2). On Magnentius's victory (recovery), see Paschoud, *Zosime*, 1:256–57; Julian, *Or.* 1.35A–40C; 48BC; 2.55C–62A; 71C–73C; 97B–D; Aurelius Victor 42.10; Zosimus 2.45–53; Socrates 2.32; Zonaras 13.8.5–9.8. Constantius was able to enlist the barbarians against the usurper (Libanius, *Or.* 18.33; Socrates 3.1.26; Zosimus 2.53.3).

75. Magnentius decided on suicide when he discovered that his own bodyguard had decided to hand him over to Constantius and had surrounded his quarters on the pretext of guarding him; he killed all the relatives and friends with him, but his brother Desiderius survived his wounds (Zonaras 13.9.2–4). He died at Lyons on 10 August 353 by running himself through with his sword (*Epit. Caes.* 42.6). His other brother Decentius was in Sens and was preparing to go to his aid when he heard of his death; he hanged himself on 18 August (*Epit. Caes.* 42.8; Zonaras 13.9.6; Zosimus 2.54.2; Jerome, *Chron.* 353; Zeev Rubin, "Pagan Propaganda during the Usurpation of Magnentius," *Scripta Classica Israelica* 17 [1998]: 124–41).

76. For "was putting the whole state … of the realm" (Bidez, *Philostorgius*, 49.25), if, instead of διεπέττευε, διεῖπε is read, and instead of ἐξορχούμενος, ἐκμειῶν (cf. Bidez, *Philostorgius*, 348), the resulting translation would be: "was negligent in his

He was himself therefore **the victim of a plot** hatched by Magnentius, one of the generals, and lost his life and his realm together. When he had fallen, Magnentius came to power, with Nepotianus[77] and Vetranio sharing in the usurpation.

[*AP* 11]. **Learning of this** from his sister's letters, Constantius left the east, came to the west, engaged both of them in battle, and won decisively, Vetranio having gone over to his side. This was when **the sign of the cross, so enormous in size and** wholly terrible in appearance as to **outshine the daylight with its stunning rays, appeared in Jerusalem particularly around the third hour of the day, on** the **Feast called Pentecost. It extended from the** place **called Calvary to the Mount** of Olives, **from where** the Savior was taken up.[78]

Constantius, then, possessed the entire realm, the only one of the sons of Constantine the Great who remained. [12] Gazing upon the greatness of the realm he felt dizzy, since he was only human and had no one from his family to support him (he had no children, and none of his brothers was left), and he feared that some other usurper might rise up against his realm. He therefore thought about taking one of his relatives as sharer and supporter of his realm. And that is what he did, appointing Gallus, Julian's brother, as Caesar. **Gallus was** his **cousin** on his father's side, **since Constantius, the father of Gallus** and Julian, **was the brother of Constantine the Great.** He appointed him to this rank in Sirmium, giving him as his wife his own sister Constantia as surety of his fidelity and reliability and assigning him officials whom he himself appointed (he did not let him make the appointments himself, Caesar though he was); they were Thalassius,[79] whom he sent as praetorian prefect, and Montius, who had charge of official business with the title of *quaestor,* as such men are customarily called; he also raised him to patrician rank.

27. He says that Basil and Eustathius and their group fabricated some absurd accusations against Aetius out of their hostility to him and used them

---

government of the state in general and was setting at nought the majesty of the realm." Eutropius 10.9.3 says of Constans that he started well but soon turned "ad graviora vitia." Aurelius Victor 41.24 specifies pederasty.

77. Nepotianus was the son of Constantine I's half-sister Eutropia; he seized power in Rome on 3 June 350 and was defeated and killed on 30 June (Aurelius Victor 42.6–8; *Epit. Caes.* 42.3; Eutropius 10.11.2; Zosimus 2.43.2–4).

78. On the heavenly cross, see A7.25; Ernest Bihain, "L'épître de Cyrille de Jérusalem à Constance sur la vision de la croix (*BHG* 413)," *Byzantion* 43 (1973): 264–96; Socrates 2.28.22; Sozomen 4.5; Theophanes 63B; *Chron. pasch.* P292B–C.

79. Thalassius was praetorian prefect of the east from 351, but before going there to join Gallus he went on campaign with Constantius against Magnentius. Ammianus 14.1.10 says he treated Gallus high-handedly and thus made his temper even worse.

to anger Gallus. He accordingly, because he trusted bishops and was moved to anger, ordered Aetius to be interrogated and both his legs to be broken. But Leontius, the bishop of Antioch, reported to the Caesar that the contrary was true to what had been charged, and so the sentence of condemnation was lifted. Gallus had an interview with Aetius not long afterward and extended his friendship to him. He was often sent to Julian, especially when his brother learned that he was defecting to paganism; he was sent in order to save him from false worship if at all possible. Gallus in addition made Aetius a teacher of the sacred sciences.[80]

28. Gallus's courage having won him the highest distinction in the conflict with the Persians, those who delight in making accusations inflamed the emperor's jealousy, and when the Persian war was brought to an end by the Caesar's valor, Constantius sent Domitian, who was what is called a praetorian prefect, **charging** him to hinder in secret Gallus's excursions from Antioch; he intended in this way to detract from his reputation for courage and for civic concern. Domitian, however, carried out none of his orders with moderation but displayed arrogance in attitude and deed, nor **when he arrived in Antioch,** where Gallus was staying, did he even deign to visit him. For which reason, and for other contributing causes, he planned to put the insolent man to death, and he summoned Montius to second his decision. But he with supreme arrogance replied, "You have no authority even to appoint a comptroller! How could you kill a **praetorian prefect?**" At which Gallus's wife Constantia, furious at the contempt thus shown to Gallus, who was Caesar and husband of an Augusta (she had received this title from her father), herself hauled Montius over to the men-at-arms and handed him over, so that they took him by the fastest way to Domitian, whom they dragged from his throne, and, **tying ropes to the feet of them both,** put those evil men to an evil death. This was done quickly and with Gallus's approval.

28a [*AP* 12]. Gallus, since he had been sent at that time by Constantius, had charge of things in the east. No sooner had the Persians found out about him than they were in dread of him, having learned how young and energetic he was, and they no longer took the field against the Romans. He was in Antioch in Syria, while Constantius took care of matters in the west. It was at that time especially that the Roman Empire was completely at peace, since it

---

80. Theophilus the Indian became enamored of Aetius's theology and introduced him to Gallus around 351 (Kopecek, *History of Neo-Arianism*, 108–12). Basil and Eustathius's hostility to Aetius may have arisen from his earlier defeat of them in debate (3.16). On Gallus's friendship with Aetius, see Sozomen 3.15.8. On his attempts to keep Julian faithful to Christianity, see Julian, *Ep.* 82 (ed. Wright, LCL). Julian mentions his old acquaintance with Aetius in *Ep.* 46.404C.

was guarded by both men. And so things stood. [13] But Gallus, when he had put on the Caesar's purple robe and had now begun to climb the first steps to rule, did not retain the same attitude and loyalty that he had shown to Constantius but became **overbearing,** ungovernable, and implacable in **anger.**[81] Imprudent in his purposes and inconsistent in his plans, he disdained and transgressed the terms of the agreement he had made with Constantius; highhanded in the way he set about his business, he was quite insufferably arrogant in his execution of it. Consider the officials whom Constantius had sent with him to supervise official and public affairs, namely, the **praetorian prefect** Domitian (for Thalassius had died) and the *quaestor* Montius: because they did not obey and second his absurd and uncontrollable impulses, he ordered the soldiers **to tie ropes to** their **feet,** commanded them **to be dragged** to **the square,** and killed them both, men of eminent worth who had proven to be above all acquisitiveness and greed. The bishop of the city gave them a proper burial out of respect for their outstanding virtue.[82]

---

81. Ammianus 14.1.1 also mentions the presumption and arrogance Gallus showed when appointed Caesar, as well as his neglect of his agreement with Constantius ("ultra terminos potestatis delatae procurrens"). He refused to listen to Thalassius's warnings and advice but acted with "uncontrollable impetuosity" (14.1.10; cf. also 22.14.2 on his obstinacy in pursuing impractical and imprudent plans against advice). Julian himself acknowledged that his brother could not keep his temper (*Ep. ad Ath.* 272C). The report that the Persians feared his energy is echoed in Zosimus 3.1.1.

82. Thalassius having died in office, his successor Domitian arrived in Antioch "with the usual pomp" and disdained to call on Gallus, who then ordered his arrest (Ammianus 14.7.9–12). Montius addressed the household troops and countermanded the order, whereupon Gallus angrily told them to stand by him. They dragged Montius along the ground by ropes to Gallus's headquarters, where they threw Domitian downstairs, bound him with ropes as well, dragged the pair through the city, and threw them into the river (Ammianus 14.7.12–16). The story about Constantina's part in this fits what Ammianus says about her energetic cruelty ably seconding Gallus's own proclivities (14.1.1–8, 7.4, 9.3). The description of these in *AP* 13 (ταῖς παραλόγοις αὐτοῦ καὶ ἀκαθέκτοις ὁρμαῖς) squares with Ammianus 14.1.10: "irrevocabili impetu [ferebatur]."

As Ammianus shows, the bishop Leontius had to fish the bodies out of the Orontes River to bury them; his act, one of considerable courage in the circumstances, shows that Domitian and Montius were Christians and, as it was an indirect insult to Gallus, suggests a division between the bishop's party and that of Aetius, Gallus's favorite; cf. David Woods, "Three Notes on Aspects of the Arian Controversy c. 354–367 CE," *JTS* 44 (1993): 604–10.

BOOK 4

1. When Constantius **learned** what had happened to Montius and Dome-
tian, he was furious and sent for **Gallus.**[1] **Gallus** sensed that the **summons
boded no good, but,** fearing that to refuse it would mean **war,** he obeyed
the order. Constantia **set out before him,** since she was anxious **to meet
her brother first and intercede with him for her husband.** But when she
reached **Bithynia,** death brought an end both to her journey and her life. For
this reason Gallus became even more afraid, **but he did not** alter his initial
decision. Theophilus the Indian set out with him. **But when** he had reached
Noricum, Barbatio, a man with the rank of **general, was sent there** from
Milan, where Constantius was staying, with the purpose of **stripping** Gallus
of the purple and **banishing him** to **one of the islands of Dalmatia.** But
Theophilus, who was there, did not allow the deed to be done. For at the time
when Gallus was appointed Caesar, it was he who had acted as mediator of
the oaths taken between Constantius and him that established their pact of
mutual friendship and good faith and who was the guarantor of their good
relations. When Constantius, however, learned that Theophilus was proving
to be a hindrance, he ordered him to be banished and Gallus **to be reduced to
the station of a private person** and sent to the island to be kept under guard.
But **the eunuch** Eusebius, who had achieved [promotion to] **the rank of
praepositus,** continued **with the others of his party** to inflame Constantius's
wrath against Gallus, since they feared that respect for his oaths or for his
family relationship might cause him to recall the Caesar from exile, and once
the latter had escaped the peril he was in, he would bring those evil men to an
evil end. And thus their cajolery resulted in **men being sent to do away with**

---

1. On the episode, see A7.28, 28b, d; Jerome, *Chron.* 354; Eutropius 10.13;
Ammianus 14.11.1–24; Zosimus 2.55.2–3; Socrates 2.34.1–4; Sozomen 4.7.6–7; Zonaras 13.9.16–20; *Chron. pasch.* P2920–293A. The *protector domesticus* Herculanus
reported to Constantius what Gallus and his wife had done (Ammianus 14.10.2). The
emperor urged Constantina to come to meet him, but on the way she died at a way
station called, according to Ammianus, Caeni Gallicani (14.11.6).

Gallus.[2] But before **the deed** had been done, Constantius repented and **sent others** to prevent the murder. Eusebius's party, though, saw to it secretly that they did **not** reach the island or show anyone the order **rescinding** the death sentence **until** the condemned man had been put to death by the sword. And **it happened** as they desired.[3] This was why Julian, when afterwards he was invested with empire, exacted retribution from Eusebius and his party for the crime done to his brother.[4]

1a [*AP* 14]. Constantius learned very quickly about what had happened, so he summoned **Gallus to himself. He,** realizing that **the summons boded no good, but** reflecting further that if he were unwilling to obey he would have to take up arms and go to **war** against Constantius forthwith, chose rather the way of peace. And **sending** his wife **ahead** in order to soften Constantius, he set off by himself to face the danger. Constantia, then, **set out before him,** since she was eager **to meet her brother first and intercede with him for her husband** not to treat him harshly. Journeying with great haste, however, she fell sick while on the way, and having reached **Bithynia,** she died there in a way station called Gallicanum. Gallus for his part took this other unexpected turn of events as a great blow to him, **but** he continued on **nonetheless without** altering his plans. **But when** he reached a city of **Noricum** called Poetovio, **the general Barbatio was sent there** from **Milan,** where Constantius was staying at the time. He **stripped** Gallus **of the purple,** reduced him **to the station of a private person,** and banished him to **an island of Dalmatia.**

[*AP* 15]. When Gallus had been brought to the island, those behind the whole movement against him, especially **the eunuch** Eusebius, who held **the rank of** *praepositus,* **with the others of his party,** persuaded Constantius to get rid of him as soon as possible. He let himself be persuaded and sent men to kill him. But while they were already on the way, Constantius's mood changed once again **to** clemency, and **he sent** swift messengers with another letter **rescinding the sentence against** Gallus. Eusebius and his party, however, **persuaded** the official who had been sent **not** to present himself with

---

2. The eunuch Eusebius was *praepositus cubiculi* (Ammianus 14.10.5). For his influence on Constantius's decisions about Gallus, see Ammianus 14.11.2; Julian, *Ep. ad Ath.* 272D; Libanius, *Or.* 18.152.

3. Gallus was taken to an island near Pola in Histria, where Eusebius took part in the interrogation about his executions in Antioch. He was then beheaded and mutilated without a trial at the end of 354 (Ammianus 14.11.20–23; Julian, *Ep. ad Ath.* 271A, 271B; Libanius, *Or.* 12.35; Paschoud, *Zosime,* 1:263). Julian supports the story that Constantius repented of his death sentence (*Ep. ad Ath.* 270D).

4. On Julian's punishment of Eusebius, see 6.6a–7a; Ammianus 22.3.12.

the letter **until** he had learned that Gallus **had been killed.** This **is what happened,** and Gallus met his end.

2. Constantius, though, **reflected** on how heavy the burden **of government** was and how **he could not** bear **it alone, so he summoned Gallus's brother Julian from Ionia and** appointed **him Caesar,**[5] **betrothing his** own **sister Helena to him** as his wife, and **sent** him **to watch over Gaul,** for things there were in a state of chaos.[6]

2a [*AP* 15]. Constantius feared for the state, thinking that he **would not be able** to govern **the** whole **empire by himself** and knowing in addition that the Gauls were extremely easy to arouse whenever they became eager to support usurpation, due to their physical strength and mental inconstancy. He thus regretted that he had killed Gallus and, **reckoning** that it would be far safer to share his rule with one of his own kin than with someone not related and not of his family, **he summoned Gallus's brother Julian** from **Ionia** and appointed him **Caesar** in Milan, giving his own **sister Helena to him** as his wife and taking oaths with him. He then **sent** him to **Gaul to watch over** the realm there.

3. **Constantius himself** went **to Sirmium and stayed there.**

It was at that time that he brought back from exile the bishop of Rome, Liberius, who was eagerly requested by the Romans, and gave him to those who were asking for him.[7] He also says that Liberius too at this time sub-

---

5. On Julian's appointment, see A7.28, 28a–d; Julian, *Ep. ad Ath.* 274B–278A; Ammianus 15.8; Libanius, *Or.* 12.38–41; 13.20–22; 18.31–32; Zosimus 3.1.1–2.2; Eutropius 10.14.1; Aurelius Victor 42.17; *Epit. Caes.* 42.12; Eunapius, *Vit. soph.* 476; *Comp. chron.* 56.8–11.

6. On the chaos in Gaul, see Julian, *Ep. ad Ath.* 277D. That Constantius had it in mind in sending Julian there, see Aurelius Victor 42.17: "ne quid apud Gallos natura praecipites novaretur."

7. Liberius had been elected during the campaign against Magnentius, after which Constantius pressed him to join the eastern bishops in condemning Athanasius. Liberius resisted, calling for a council to treat of faith and order, but the emperor's representatives at the Councils of Arles of 353 and of Milan of 355 insisted that the question of Athanasius's canonical standing be treated independently of doctrinal issues, and he was condemned at both, Liberius's own delegates yielding at Arles. Brought to Milan in 355, Liberius still refused to subscribe the synodical sentence and was banished to Beroea in Thrace (cf. Ammianus 15.7.6–10). The Roman clergy soon broke their oath not to accept another bishop while he was alive (Jerome, *Chron.* 349; *Collectio Avellana* 1.2), and his archdeacon Felix was consecrated by three court bishops, including the powerful Acacius of Caesarea (Jerome, *Vir. ill.* 98). Exile wore down Liberius's resistance, and in 357 he gave in, subscribing both Athanasius's condemnation and some creed; on the question of which formula it was, see Hans

scribed against the consubstantialist doctrine, and against Athanasius to boot, as did Bishop Hosius,[8] a council having met there and drawn them into unanimity. Once they had subscribed, Hosius [he says] returned to his bishopric of Cordova and governed his see, while Liberius did likewise in the church of Rome. As for Felix, who had been made bishop of Rome in the meantime, he retired, keeping the title of bishop but not governing any church.[9]

3a [*AP* 15]. **Constantius himself** made his way to Illyricum and **stayed in Sirmium.** [16]. But hearing that the barbarians beyond the Danube were planning to attack the Roman Empire, he left Sirmium and made his way to the Danube.[10] He spent some considerable time near the [river] bank, and once the barbarian tribes had settled down, he took the road again for Thrace.

3b [*Cairo Codex* 86, f.280r, referring to the following text in Socrates 2.31.4: Since he (Hosius) refused his assent, they beat the old man and racked him, forcing him thereby to assent and subscribe the texts published at that

---

Christof Brennecke, *Hilarius von Poitiers und die Bischofsopposition gegen Konstantius II* (Berlin: de Gruyter, 1984), 273–97. It was probably the so-called "First Creed of Sirmium," a clearly anti-Arian profession but one that does not contain the word "consubstantial" (see Kelly, *Early Christian Creeds,* 281–82). When Philostorgius says that he contradicted the consubstantialist doctrine, what he means, as usual, is that he subscribed against Athanasius. On Liberius's fall, see Athanasius, *C. Ar.* 89.3; *H. Ar.* 41.3; Hilary, *Frag. hist.* B VII 7–11; *Collectio Avellana* 1.3; Jerome, *Vir. ill.* 97; Socrates 2.37.91–94; Sozomen 4.11.12; 4.15. The noble ladies of Rome begged Constantius for his return (Rufinus, *Hist. eccl.* 10.28; Theodoret, *Hist. eccl.* 2.17).

8. Hosius had reached a great old age when this controversy erupted, having been born ca. 256; he apparently subscribed the document, often called the "Second Creed of Sirmium," which outlaws the word "substance" in the creed and which was published in 357 by a group of bishops whom Philostorgius in 4.3 (not alone among the ancient sources) assumes was a council (see Barnes, *Athanasius and Constantius,* 138–39; 231–32). The "creed" was welcomed in Antioch by the newly arrived Eudoxius (see 67 n. 11), but Hosius's collapse would echo far down the annals of church history; cf. Athanasius, *C. Ar.* 89.3–4 (which mentions the blows to which he was subjected); *Apol. de fuga* 5; *H. Ar.* 42–45; Socrates 2.31.1–4; Sulpicius Severus, *Chronicorum Libri duo* 2.40.5; *Collectio Avellana* 2.32–39; *EOMIA* 1:541–42. He did not long survive his rough treatment, dying ca. 357/8. His subscription to such an anti-Nicene declaration sent a shock through the churches in east and west and galvanized Basil of Ancyra and George of Laodicea into organizing the "homoeousian" front that plays such a part in the subsequent events narrated in Philostorgius.

9. Felix was forced by Liberius's supporters to leave the city, but he stayed nearby, insisting on his position until the end, which came on 22 November 365, on his property near Portus (cf. Theodoret, *Hist. eccl.* 2.17.7).

10. The military campaign in 4.3a was against the Sarmatians and Quadi in 358 (Ammianus 17.12–13).

time (in Sirmium)]. Philostorgius says the same thing about Hosius, except that he does not add the business about blows and force.

4. He says that when Leontius, the bishop of Antioch, died, those who shared the same views brought Eudoxius over from Germanicia and installed him on the throne.[11] He was Arian in outlook, although Asterius's letters had brought him round to the doctrine of "like in substance."[12] His fellow sectarians, however, brought him back to the doctrine of "other in substance." Philostorgius, in describing Eudoxius as mild and decent in his manner and in every respect capable, shows himself quite out of order when he then accuses him of cowardice. He adds that **Arabissus in Lesser Armenia** was the native city of **his father** (who was called **Caesarius**). His father, **even though he had given in to his desires** with women, nonetheless achieved **martyrdom,** persevering in the contest until death, which conferred on him purification from his defilements and **crowns** of victory.

4a [*Suda*, E 3428 Eudoxius]. Bishop of Antioch, from **Arabissus in Lesser Armenia. His father Caesarius** achieved the **crown** of martyrdom in the reign of Maximian, **even though** he had earlier **given in to his desires for pleasure.** But he wanted to wash away those first stains with the blood of **martyrdom.** What happened is that they drove six great nails through each of his feet and delivered him over to the fire. And when in his yearning for the flames he succumbed to death immediately, his relatives removed his corpse, which was still half-burned and intact, and buried it on a property called Subil.

5. He says that Eudoxius advanced Eunomius to the diaconate but that the latter did not accept the office until the former had returned to full doctrinal accuracy.

6. He says that Basil of Ancyra took it hard when Eudoxius was appointed to Antioch, since he himself had had his eye on the see.

7. He says that Constantius's wife was subject to fits of hysteria,[13] and

---

11. When Leontius died in 357, Eudoxius managed to obtain from Constantius some sort of permission to assist with the pastoral needs in Antioch, and before the emperor knew it, he had transformed it into imperial approval to succeed to the see (Socrates 2.37.7–9; Sozomen 4.12.3–4; Theodoret, *Hist. eccl.* 2.25.1–2; 2.26.1; *Haer. fab.* 4.2). It is unclear how Eudoxius ever managed to win back Constantius's confidence after this trick and after intervening for Aetius and Eunomius. Hans Christof Brennecke conjectures that he must have found a way of distancing himself from the other two and that that was why Philostorgius treats him with such dislike (*Studien zur Geschichte der Homöer* [Tübingen: Mohr Siebeck, 1988], 58).

12. On Asterius, see 31–32 n. 43.

13. On Eusebia's hysteria, see Cedrenus 302C and Zonaras 13.11.29–30; she eventually died of it. We find her portrayed in 7.6a probably at the Synod of Sirmium of 358 referred to in 4.8.

since he was so deeply devoted to her, he was forced to recall Theophilus from exile, for the latter was reputed to be able to cure sicknesses by divine power. When he arrived, he asked forgiveness for the sins he had committed against him and besought him to cure his wife. Nor did he fail of his request, so our author says. For Theophilus laid his propitiatory hands upon the woman and removed the sickness from her.

8. He says that Basil took with him Eustathius of Sebaste and some other bishops and brought to the emperor accusations against Aetius especially, and also against Eudoxius, making up various charges against them, including that of being privy to and participants in Gallus's revolt, and he implicated Theophilus as well in the charges. The emperor believed him, especially because of the women (for Basil and his associates had won them over to his side).[14] He punished Theophilus by banishing him to Heraclea in Pontus, while Eudoxius had to withdraw from Antioch and live on his own property. Aetius and some others of their group he handed over to the authority of those who had accused them. Now Basil and his party held a disputation about the faith right in the emperor's presence; during it the doctrine that the Son is like the Father in every way was clearly stated, but in none of what was said was there any mention of "substance," not even of the word itself.[15] And they bent every effort to have this doctrine ratified by conciliar decree and subscription.

---

14. Basil and Eustathius had led the Synod of Ancyra earlier that year (358) in drafting its protest against the "Second Creed of Sirmium" (see 66 n. 8) and had headed its delegation to Constantius, whom they persuaded to call the synod in Sirmium referred to in n. 13. Philostorgius thinks Basil had his way with the emperor because he won over the women at court and worked on his suspicious nature; certainly if the words in 7.6a between Eusebia and the imperious Leontius of Tripolis, one of Basil's chief foes, occurred at this council, then the women would have needed little urging to support the homoeousians (see Woods, "Three Notes," 610–16).

On the Synod of Ancyra that published the homoeousian profession, see Epiphanius, *Pan.* 73.2–12; Sozomen 4.13–14; Theodoret, *Hist. eccl.* 2.25.3–4. The success of its delegation to Constantius may be judged by his remarkable letter to the church in Antioch in which he condemns Aetius, dismisses Eudoxius's claim to the see, and professes his own faith in homoeousian language (Sozomen 4.14). He makes it clear that his displeasure with Aetius is chiefly on account of his doctrine, whatever Philostorgius says, although suspicions about his closeness to Gallus also played a part in one of his exiles, whether at this time or following the Council of Constantinople of 360 (Sozomen 5.5.9).

15. It is hard to date the disputation referred to here, but it sounds like the conference of bishops held in Sirmium in 359 to plan the double council of Seleucia and Ariminum. The conference recommended proposing a creed that omitted all mention of "substance," and Basil, who by this time had lost the emperor's confidence (see

Now shortly afterwards, when news of what Basil had done reached Antioch, Eunomius was ordained deacon and sent on embassy to Constantius to get the decrees revoked, but he was caught by Basil and company while on the way and banished to Midaeum, a city of Phrygia. As for Aetius, who had been handed over to Basil and company, he was exiled to Pepuza in Phrygia, while Eudoxius withdrew to his native Armenia. Others too were sent into the exile decreed for them by Basil and company; they numbered seventy in all.[16]

9. When Basil and company had done all this, they went about everywhere and had the consubstantialist doctrine ratified. They persuaded many and even brought Macedonius of Constantinople over to their view, although previously he had been favorably disposed to Eunomius and his group. They did the same with many other bishops, winning some of them over with words and applying a combination of force and persuasion to others.[17]

10. He says that Patrophilus of Scythopolis, Narcissus of Irenopolis, and some others with them traveled to Singidunum and told Constantius what Basil had been up to. Astonished and deeply grieved, he ordered those condemned to return from exile and convoked two councils, one in Ariminum for those from the west and the other in Nicomedia for those from the east, from Libya, and from Thrace. The councils were to evaluate the statements made by each party. But the one in Nicomedia, so our heretic slanderously asserts, was cancelled by an earthquake, since most of those connected with it favored

---

n. 17 below), was among those accepting the formula (Sozomen 4.16.19–20; 4.22.6; Kopecek, *History of Neo-Arianism*, 176 n. 6).

16. Aetius's exile in Phrygia is placed by Theodoret (*Hist. eccl.* 2.27.12) after the Council of Constantinople. Contrary to Philostorgius, the emperor did not hand Aetius over to Basil; Basil removed him from the custody of the official charged with conducting him to his trial (Sozomen 4.24.5). But in general, Philostorgius's (or Photius's) summary of Basil's high-handed behavior echoes the charges laid against him at the council: banishments, imprisonments, torture, and false accusations directed against his enemies (Socrates 2.42.5; Sozomen 4.24.4–9).

17. On the struggle of the two parties against each other, see Epiphanius, *Pan.* 73.23.2–4. On Constantius's order of return of those exiled by Basil, see Sozomen 4.24.5. The emperor later blamed Basil for the churches' troubles, says Theodoret (*Hist. eccl.* 2.27.5). He had become convinced that the rifts in the church could be repaired only by a general council and called one to meet in Nicomedia in 358. But the city was destroyed by earthquake that summer, and in the intervening year Constantius, becoming disenchanted with Basil's methods of achieving a settlement, decided that a new creed would have to be promulgated, by separate councils in Ariminum and Seleucia, outlawing the use of the controversial word *ousia* ("substance") in statements of faith and thus in effect rescinding the Creed of Nicaea (Kelly, *Early Christian Creeds*, 289–91).

the consubstantialist doctrine; the shock brought down the church upon the heads of those who had already arrived and were meeting in it, fifteen in all, including the bishop of the city, Cecropius.[18] The one in Ariminum, numbering up to three hundred, rejected the word *ousia* for good, pronounced the Son to be like the Father according to the scriptures, and ratified the doctrine with the subscriptions of its members.[19]

11. Nicomedia having been overthrown by earthquake and fire and the flooding of the sea, as our author says, and many people having perished, the council convened in Seleucia, since Basil and company objected to Nicaea, while Tarsus was unacceptable to Eudoxius and Aetius and their group.[20]

---

18. On the earthquake in Nicomedia, see 7.30; 7.30a; Jerome, *Chron.* 358; *Consul. const.* 358. Sozomen (4.16.3–5) takes pains to refute Philostorgius's report of many bishops perishing in the church in Nicomedia when it collapsed; only two bishops, he says, died, and they were outside the church.

19. The Council of Ariminum met in July of 359; the sources suggest that over four hundred attended, rather than Philostorgius's three hundred. Due largely perhaps to Hilary of Poitier's correspondence from exile, the westerners now appreciated the importance of the Creed of Nicaea, and most of them refused to subscribe the new one. A minority of about eighty seceded, each side sending a delegation to court, as the councils had been instructed. Constantius refused to receive the majority delegates and wore them down through tedium and fear until they gave in and subscribed his creed on 10 October. When they returned to Ariminum, the majority refused them communion, but the praetorian prefect Flavius Taurus told the bishops they could not go home until they subscribed. The opposition gradually dwindled to twenty, who finally yielded when told they might formulate their subscriptions as they liked. The subscription of those times was, as noted, a complete sentence or sentences resuming the body of the agreement to which it was attached (see 11 n. 19). It was regarded as an authentic interpretation of it, as Valens of Mursa, one of the Arian leaders there, had been sharply reminded by the emperor himself when he had tried to omit a key phrase in his own subscription of the new creed the previous May (Epiphanius, *Pan.* 73.22.6). Thus the council fathers were told they might include in their subscriptions whatever they felt was lacking in the main body of the new creed. Valens himself wrote in his that the Son of God was not a creature like other creatures, the ambiguity of which was evidently not noticed by the others until later, when the rumor began spreading that they had subscribed an Arian creed. After they had authorized a new delegation to court, they were allowed to break up. See Hilary, *Frag. hist.* A V, VI, VIII, IX; B VIII; Athanasius, *Syn.* 8–11; Jerome, *Contra Luciferianos* 18; Augustine, *Contra Iulianum* 1.75; Sulpicius Severus, *Chronicorum Libri duo* 2.41; 2.43–44; Socrates 2.37; Sozomen 4.16–19; Theodoret, *Hist. eccl.* 2.18–21; *EOMIA* 1:541; Rufinus, *Hist. eccl.* 10.22.

20. On Basil's objection to meeting in Nicaea, see Sozomen 4.16.1. On the change of location to Tarsus and then Seleucia, see Socrates 2.39.4. For the proceedings, see

Now Basil and company contrived to divide the council, met by themselves, confirmed the doctrine of "like in substance," deposed their opponents, outlawed the doctrine of "other in substance," and took it upon themselves to ordain Anianus bishop of Antioch.[21] Eudoxius and Aetius and company, by contrast, ratified the doctrine of "other in substance" in writing and sent their document to every place.[22]

12. When the emperor learned what had happened, he ordered everyone to come to Constantinople, and in fact almost everyone from the west and the east and Libya gathered there.[23] Basil and Eustathius headed the group representing the doctrine of "like in substance," and they were supported by others

Athanasius, *Syn.* 12; Socrates 2.39–40; Sozomen 4.22; Sulpicius Severus, *Chronicorum Libri duo* 2.42; Theodoret, *Hist. eccl.* 2.26.4–11. It got underway later than the meeting in Ariminum amid scenes of unparalleled procedural confusion caused by contradictory directives from court (Socrates 2.39.13–14). On 28 September the majority, homoeousian in outlook, ratified the Second Creed of the Dedication Council, after the minority group of homoeans, led by Acacius of Caesarea, had withdrawn following protracted debate. When the minority returned (with the encouragement of the imperial commissioner) they proposed their own homoean creed (Kelly, *Early Christian Creeds,* 292), which was rejected by the other side, and, as at Ariminum, each party elected ten delegates to go to court to meet with those of the western council.

21. Anianus was ordained by the homoeousian party to replace the disgraced Eudoxius, but he was banished at once by the court (Epiphanius, *Pan.* 73.23.4; Socrates 2.40.46).

22. On the "anomoean" manifesto, see Kopecek, *History of Neo-Arianism*, 202–10. It is referred to in Theodoret, *Hist. eccl.* 2.27.6, and Basil, *De Spiritu Sancto* 2.4; Kopecek identifies it with the *Expositio Patricii et Aetii* in Athanasius, *HA* 13. The identification is not unobjectionable, as the *Expositio* insists that God's nature is unknowable, but of course the conviction that God's substance can be known is fundamental to Aetius's doctrine. How and when and why the manifesto was published is a matter of conjecture.

23. Philostorgius in 4.12 seems to confuse events at the Council of Seleucia with those immediately following, when Aetius was made to stand trial before high officials, and then before Constantius himself (see Vaggione, *Eunomius of Cyzicus,* 222 n. 136). Sozomen, at any rate, distinguishes between his trial for heresy (4.23.3–8) and the Council of Constantinople (4.24). Theodoret also has an account of a debate about faith in Constantius's presence, in which Aetius admits authorship of the anomoean profession and is banished forthwith (*Hist. eccl.* 2.27.4–21), but to coordinate his story with Philostorgius's is no simple matter. Aetius's trial may, at any rate, be placed in the autumn of 359, when the delegates from the twin councils, of Ariminum and Seleucia, were in Constantinople with the emperor for the negotiations on a compromise creed (despite what Philostorgius says, most of the council members had returned home).

there, including another Basil; still a deacon, he surpassed many others in eloquence, but he shrank from public debates because of his timidity. Aetius and Eunomius belonged to the group representing the doctrine of "other in substance"; superbly eloquent, they were both deacons. The bishops who filled the role of supporters were Maris and Eudoxius, who was then bishop of Antioch but later acceded to the throne of Constantinople, and none other than Acacius of Caesarea in Palestine, who pretended to share their views because of his grievance against Basil and company; the reason was that they held in honor Cyril, whom he had removed from his position as bishop of Jerusalem. Acacius, fearless in debate, had a knack for grasping the essential points at issue and expressing his understanding clearly, and thus it was he, and he alone, who drafted the letters of this council (and they are many).[24]

When each side presented itself for the debate about doctrine, Basil was spokesman for those who held the consubstantialist doctrine, while those favoring the doctrine of "other in substance" put forward Aetius to speak for them all, with Eunomius seconding him. When Basil and company saw that Aetius had been nominated to debate them, they feared his eloquence and said that those who were bishops should not dispute with a deacon about doctrine.[25] But their opponents countered by saying that the business at hand was not a judgment about rank but an examination of the truth, and so Basil and his circle agreed to the contest reluctantly. And, so our author says, they were so roundly defeated by Aetius's tongue that they not only acknowledged that the substance of the one begotten differs from that of the begetter and has nothing in common with it; they even confirmed their confession with their own subscriptions when Aetius requested this as well.[26]

---

24. On Acacius's astuteness in thought and speech, see Sozomen 4.23.2. It was he who had drafted the homoean creed read at the Council of Seleucia (Socrates 2.40.7, 18). He had installed Cyril in Jerusalem after removing Maximus (A7.25a). On his character, see Jean-Marie Leroux, "Acace, évêque de Césarée de Palestine (341–365)," in *Patres Apostolici, Historica, Liturgica, Ascetica et Monastica* (ed. Frank L. Cross; StPatr 8; TU 93. Berlin: Akademie-Verlag, 1966): 82–85.

25. Theodoret (*Hist. eccl.* 2.27.4) lists Basil of Ancyra and Eustathius, along with Silvanus of Tarsus and Eleusius of Cyzicus, as leaders of the party against Eudoxius. Philostorgius here repeats Eunomius's accusation that Basil of Caesarea was too timid to engage in the debate (Gregory of Nyssa, *Eun.* 1.78–79; cf. Stanislas Giet, "Saint Basile et le concile de Constantinople de 360," *JTS* 6 (1955): 94–9).

26. The idea that the substance of the begetter has nothing in common with the one begotten (since there cannot be more than one Ingenerate) is central to Aetius's doctrine; see Wickham, "The *Syntagmation* of Aetius the Anomean," 567. The subscriptions that Aetius is said to have obtained may be those appended to the minutes

When he learned what had happened, the emperor, who had allowed to ripen deep in his heart the accusation against Aetius that Basil had once planted, took the event as an excuse to let loose his anger. He therefore summoned both of them to an audience and asked Basil what the accusations were that he had against Aetius. He replied, "He teaches that the Son is unlike the Father." To this Aetius answered that he was so far from saying or thinking that the Son was unlike the Father that he even proclaimed that he was exactly alike. But Constantius seized upon the word "exactly," and not even waiting to find out in what sense he meant "exactly," he ordered Aetius to be turned out of the palace.[27] Later at the instigation of Acacius he was also sentenced to deposition, and it was not the orthodox alone who subscribed the decree of deposition, but those too who had most closely shared his doctrine, some of whom changed their views while others reluctantly dissembled in the name of expediency.[28] Now Constantius produced the document of the

---

of the meeting where the debate took place (on the subscription of minutes, see my "Paulinus' Subscription," 55 n. 9).

27. As noted, Philostorgius's account of Aetius's appearance before Constantius is hard to coordinate with the "parallel" story in Theodoret, *Hist. eccl.* 2.27.4–21, even though the latter source also says that the encounter led directly to Aetius's banishment following the accusation that he expounded the anomoean doctrine. Also difficult to understand is Constantius's reaction to Aetius's assurance that he taught that the Son is exactly (ἀπαραλλάκτως) like the Father. Perhaps the simplest explanation is that given by our author in 5.1: Aetius was condemned for contradicting himself. In his *Syntagmation* 3 and 33, he in fact denies that the Father and Son have an essence or nature that is ἀπαράλλακτον. But (if we may trust that Eunomius represented his master's doctrine accurately) he also held that the Son faithfully reflects the Father's will, and that may be what he meant to explain to the emperor (see Wickham, "The *Syntagmation* of Aetius the Anomean," 551). Constantius, however, must have been aware that the majority at the Council of Seleucia had endorsed the Second Creed of Antioch of 341, which describes the Son as the ἀπαράλλακτον εἰκόνα of the Father (Athanasius, *Syn.* 23.3), a creed that he was now pressing its delegates to discard in favor of one that said simply that the Son is like the Father according to the scriptures. It is understandable, then, that he would react strongly against any suggestion that another formula was being proposed (see Kopecek, *History of Neo-Arianism*, 351).

Another puzzle is to account for the distance that suddenly appears in this later episode between Aetius and Eunomius, who, far from sharing his master's fate, was actually approved by Constantius for appointment to the see of Cyzicus after the Council of Constantinople (5.3).

28. On Aetius's deposition (at the same council), see Theodoret, *Hist. eccl.* 2.27.13–16; Sozomen 4.25.5. The council's letter announcing his degradation for heresy is in Theodoret, *Hist. eccl.* 2.28.1–8.

westerners and ordered the others too who were present to subscribe it in person.[29] The document confessed the Son to be like the Father according to the scriptures. And there once again at the instigation of Acacius, whose thought was other than his speech, everyone subscribed, even those who earlier had championed the doctrine of "other in substance."

12a [Photius, *Bibliotheca* codex 40]. [Philostorgius] accuses especially Acacius, bishop of Caesarea in Palestine, of unequalled craft and supreme villainy, qualities with which, he says, he held everyone in his control, both those who apparently shared his views but held some grudge against him and those whose religious doctrines were contrary to his.

12b [Photius, *Bibliotheca* codex 40]. This Aetius was deposed from the diaconate by his own fellow sectarians because his heresy surpassed even theirs, as he himself [Philostorgius] relates, however reluctantly.

---

29. The "document of the westerners" is the final creed approved reluctantly at the Council of Ariminum and brought by its last group of delegates to the emperor: the court-appointed formula initially presented to the council and then revised under court supervision. Constantius insisted that the delegates of the Council of Seleucia subscribe it as well (Sozomen 4.23.8). They resisted at first, but the court could now represent them as recalcitrants hindering the work of church unity, and on the last day of the year they finally yielded and subscribed. As Philostorgius says, the creed confesses the similarity of the Son to the Father according to the scriptures and also outlaws the use of "substance" in describing their relationship.

Book 5

1. He says that afterwards Acacius deposed Basil and Eustathius and company from their sees, once he had persuaded the emperor and trumped up various charges against various persons.[1] He also deposed Macedonius, the bishop of Constantinople. Once Macedonius was gone, Eudoxius from Antioch was enthroned as his successor with Constantius's approval. Those deposed were also banished, Basil to Illyricum and the others each to a different place. Those sent into exile repudiated their own subscriptions that they had put to the Ariminum creed and once again announced their adherence, some to the consubstantialist doctrine and others to that of "like in substance." As for Aetius, deposed because he taught the doctrine of [the Son being] exactly [like the Father], which expressly contradicted his other sermons and writings, he was banished to Mopsuestia in Cilicia, almost all of his partisans and fellow sectarians having subscribed not only against him but against the creed he represented as well; some of them had changed their views, while others yielded to the currents of the times and put the emperor's will before what they considered to be the truth. Now Acacius, once he had removed and banished Basil and company because of his hostility to them and Aetius because of his heresy, returned to Caesarea and appointed high priests devoted to the consubstantialist doctrine to the widowed churches. He appointed Onesimus in Nicomedia to replace Cecropius, Athanasius in

---

1. 5.1 describes the actions taken by the Council of Constantinople of 360, as the parallel accounts show (Athanasius, *Syn.* 30; Socrates 2.41.5–43.16; Sozomen 4.24–25; Theodoret, *Hist. eccl.* 2.27–28). On the various depositions, see also A7.31; Basil, *Adversus Eunomium* 1.2; *Chron. pasch.* P294A. Zonaras (13.11.25–26) says that Constantius was also angry with Macedonius for having moved his father's body from the Church of the Apostles to the shrine of the martyr Acacius. Socrates (2.42.1–3) agrees that Acacius of Caesarea was the chief instigator of the depositions. On his hostility to Basil and his associates, see Epiphanius, *Pan.* 73.23.4. As for his attitude toward the term "consubstantial," it may be noted that he and two of those whom our author says he got consecrated at this time, Athanasius of Ancyra and Pelagius of Laodicea, endorsed the Creed of Nicaea at the Council of Antioch during Jovian's reign (Sozomen 6.4.6–11).

Ancyra to replace Basil, and another Acacius in Tarsus to replace Silvanus. As for Antioch, all the clergy there who had cooperated with Basil in his high-handed actions against Eudoxius and Aetius were expelled without a hearing.[2] [Acacius] also summoned Meletius from Sebaste in Armenia and enthroned him in place of Eudoxius, for Eudoxius had already gone to Constantinople. Now Meletius at first had followed the emperor's preference, professed the doctrine of "other in substance," and subscribed the westerners' document; but once enthroned in Antioch he became a doughty defender of the consubstantialist doctrine.[3] Acacius also ordained Pelagius in Laodicea. In short, wherever his power reached he displayed the greatest zeal in executing his plan to install the most fervent representatives of the consubstantialist doctrine in place of those who had been expelled.

2. He says that when the emperor learned from Acacius that Aetius was being treated in the friendliest possible way by Auxentius, the bishop of Mopsuestia, he ordered him to be banished to Amblada, where he could end his life in misery because of its barbarous and unfriendly inhabitants. But when Aetius, by his intercession with God, broke the intolerable drought and plague gripping the region, as our heretic falsely claims, the goodwill and reverence shown him by its inhabitants knew no bounds.[4]

2a [*Suda*, A 4450 Auxentius]. Bishop of Mopsuestia, he was among those who received the title of "confessor." He was among those who served with distinction under the emperor Licinius as one of his clerks, those in fact whom the Romans call *notarii*. His confession took the following form. In one of the halls of the imperial residence there was a spring of water surmounted by a statue of Dionysus, and a great vine that surrounded it cast a deep and welcome shade over the whole place. Once when Licinius went there accompanied by Auxentius and many others of his retinue, on the pretext of taking his ease, he glanced at the vine and saw a large bunch of grapes hanging from the branches, lovely to behold. He ordered Auxentius to cut it off, and so, suspecting nothing, he at once drew out his knife and cut the hanging bunch from its stem. Licinius then said to him, "Place the grapes at the feet of Dionysus." But he answered, "No, your majesty, for I am a Chris-

---

2. The phrase "were expelled without a hearing" translates ἐρήμην ἠλαύνοντο. There is no warrant for the reviser's suggested insertion of εἰς before ἐρήμην (compare 9.11: ἐρήμην αὐτοῦ κατεδικάσατο).

3. On Meletius's appointment to Antioch and his unexpected exposition of the consubstantialist doctrine, see 5.5; Epiphanius, *Pan.* 73.28; Socrates 2.44.1–4; Sozomen 4.28.3–8; Theodoret, *Hist. eccl.* 2.31.2–8. His inaugural homily is in Epiphanius, *Pan.* 73.29–33.

4. On Aetius's exile, see Epiphanius, *Pan.* 73.38.3; 76.2.4.

tian." Then Licinius said, "In that case resign from the service and be gone! You must do either the one or the other." Auxentius without hesitating took off his belt and gladly left the imperial residence just as he was.[5] Some time later the prelates made him bishop of Mopsuestia. Theodore, who was one of those educated in Athens, was his younger brother. He himself was some time later allotted the see of Tarsus.

Aetius at first took it upon himself to teach Eudoxius and the others worthy of the highest esteem, but once he had promoted Eunomius to the post of teacher, he used him for the most part instead of himself to teach the others, especially those requiring more advanced instruction. For he himself was best at setting forth principles, while the other was far more skillful at developing the principles set forth and interpreting them both clearly and sumptuously.[6]

3. He says that once Eustathius, Eusebius, and Eleusius and their party had been deposed, Maris and Eudoxius and their party ordained Eunomius bishop of Cyzicus with Constantius's approval.[7] Eunomius would not consent

---

5. On "Licinius … ease," see *Suda* A 2869. As Licinius's relationship with Constantine worsened, he became unfriendlier to his co-religionists; see Eusebius/Jerome, *Chron.* 320; Eusebius, *Hist. eccl.* 10.8.10; *Vit. Const.* 1.52 (he drove the Christians from his palace and dismissed officers unwilling to sacrifice to demons).

6. This comparison between Aetius and Eunomius is put again in similar terms in 8.18. On their relationship, see Athanasius, *Syn.* 38.4; Sozomen 4.13.2–3; Theodoret, *Hist. eccl.* 2.27.9, 13.

7. On Eunomius's consecration, see Basil, *Adversus Eunomium* 1.2; Gregory of Nyssa, *Eun.* 1.112; Socrates 4.7; Sozomen 4.25.6; Theodoret, *Hist. eccl.* 2.27.21; 2.29.2; *Haer. fab.* 4.3. One puzzle is, as noted, how Eunomius managed to distance himself sufficiently from Aetius to achieve acceptability; Theodoret (*Hist. eccl.* 2.29) and Sozomen (6.26.13) suggest that he concealed his real views for a time. Vaggione (*Eunomius of Cyzicus,* 226–29) thinks that he composed his *Apology* to distinguish himself from Aetius and clear himself before the Council of Constantinople; he succeeded partly because Eudoxius and company needed reliable men to replace those condemned by the council. Kopecek (*History of Neo-Arianism,* 358) suggests that Eudoxius was feeling guilty about abandoning Aetius and thus isolating Eunomius when his master was exiled, so he tried to make it up to him in this way.

Another puzzle is the time of Eunomius's consecration, which, Philostorgius implies, "must have taken place almost immediately [after Aetius's banishment], for we find him preaching in his own church a few days later on Epiphany (6 Jan.).... The 'Epiphany' in question must be that of 360, not 361, because the latter leaves too little time for Eunomius to be accused, summoned, and tried at the emperor's winter quarters in Antioch" (Vaggione, *Eunomius of Cyzicus,* 226 n. 167; cf. 6.2 and 6.4). Socrates (4.7) and Sozomen (6.26.13), however, place Eunomius's episcopate in Cyzicus in Valens's reign.

to the ordination before he had received their promise that Aetius would be released from his sentence of exile and deposition.[8] A period of three months was fixed for that.

4. He says that while Constantius usually was victorious in war, he suffered defeat in battle with the Persians because he had defiled his right hand with the blood of his own kin and had let himself be persuaded by Basil's accusations to banish Theophilus, Aetius, Serras, and their party.[9]

5. Our heretic says that Meletius of Antioch was banished to his native city of Melitine by Constantius when he himself was staying in Antioch, because he had perjured himself and because, while he went beyond all bounds in defending the consubstantialist doctrine, he feigned adherence to the doctrine of "other in substance."[10] [Constantius] summoned Euzoius, Arius's fellow sectarian, from Alexandria, ordered the bishops to lay hands on him, and appointed him bishop of Antioch.[11]

---

8. On the promise made about Aetius, see 7.5.

9. On Constantius's execution of his uncles, see 2.16; on the exiles, 4.8. Constantius never had much success fighting the Persians (Ammianus 20.11.32), and Julian knows of the rumor that he blamed his failure on his execution of his relatives (*Ep. ad Ath.* 271A).

10. On Meletius's appointment to Antioch, see 5.1. John Chrysostom says he did not last even thirty days in office; he became embroiled in disciplinary as well as doctrinal controversies (*De sancto Meletio Antiocheno* 1). On his banishment, see A7.33; Epiphanius, *Pan.* 73.34.1–3; Rufinus, *Hist. eccl.* 10.25; Jerome, *Chron.* 360; Socrates 2.44.5; Sozomen 4.28.9–10; Theodoret, *Hist. eccl.* 2.31.10; *Chron. pasch.* P296B.

11. On Euzoius's appointment, see Athanasius, *Syn.* 31.3; *HA* 7; Socrates, Sozomen, Theodoret as above; James D. Smith, "Reflections on Euzoius in Alexandria and Antioch," in *Critica et Philologica, Nachleben: First Two Centuries, Tertullian to Arnobius, Egypt before Nicaea, Athanasius and His Opponents* (ed. Maurice F. Wiles and Edward J. Yarnold; StPatr 36; Leuven: Peeters, 2001), 514–19.

BOOK 6

1. Some of the clergy of Cyzicus accused Eunomius to Eudoxius of teaching that the Son is unlike the Father; they did this by turning his doctrine of "unlike in substance" into a predication of the unlikeness of the Father to the Son.[1] They also said that he was changing the traditional customs and getting rid of those who refused to share in his heresy. The charges threw the church in Constantinople into turmoil; it was one of its presbyters, Hesychius, who stirred it up on purpose. So Eudoxius sent for Eunomius, who when he arrived accused Eudoxius of being slow and negligent in carrying out the promises he had made. The other replied that he was not ignoring them but that the uproar that he had occasioned had first to be settled. Thus Eunomius appeared before the clergy of Constantinople to defend himself, and he so won over those who had been protesting that he not only brought them round to the opposite point of view, but he even transformed them into fervent witnesses to his orthodoxy. For not only was he never caught teaching that the Son is unlike the Father in any of his discourses; he even openly declared that he taught his likeness according to the scriptures. He did not of course accept the doctrine of "like in substance," saying that it was equally blasphemous to teach that the Son is like the Father in substance and to regard him as not completely similar in accordance with those arguments that concern the Only Begotten God in relation to the Father who begot him without passion. Not

---

1. Theodoret's two accounts of what Eudoxius did about the charges against Eunomius, in *Hist. eccl.* 2.29.2–10 and *Haer. fab.* 4.3, differ notably from Philostorgius's and slightly from each other (in the latter he deposes Eunomius under imperial pressure); Sozomen 6.26.5–6 is closer to Philostorgius. Vaggione (*Eunomius of Cyzicus,* 230 n. 207, 231 n. 16) says that the protest against Eunomius must have come initially from the Cyzican clergy attending his consecration in Constantinople on 2 or 3 January 360 and that this is how the clergy of the capital got involved. But having cleared himself by his address to them (in which his favorite distinction between "God" and "Father" seems to have figured largely), he got leave to go on to his see, where his inaugural sermon on Epiphany, referred to in 6.2, upset the church so badly. For a different timetable, with Eunomius's hearing and sermon a year later, see Kopecek, *History of Neo-Arianism,* 392–405.

only did he win over the clergy in this way, but he produced in the whole church a great and delighted astonishment at his wisdom and orthodoxy by saying these very things. Eudoxius was so very pleased at this that he cried, "This is my defense to those who would examine me!" to the applause of the crowd for his apt and timely citation of holy writ.[2]

2. Our heretic says that Eunomius, hateful to God, addressed the crowd at Eudoxius's bidding on the Feast of Theophany, when more than ever they revealed their heresy and godlessness. For those accursed men did not shrink from joining Joseph to the Virgin after the ineffable nativity, nor did they show any fear in speaking even more shamelessly of the Son as the servant and minister of the Father, and the Spirit of the Son.[3]

Their style as well in these discourses lacks all oratorical grace; their unclearness, verbosity, and impure language render them decidedly disagreeable, ridiculous, and untidy and give evidence of the darkness, perplexity, and madness of the soul [that composed them].[4]

3. After his many words of praise for Eunomius, Eudoxius not only made no plans to fulfill his promises; he even tried to persuade him to subscribe both the deposition of Aetius and the creed of Ariminum, making out that their unlawful deed had been involuntary and a matter of expediency.[5] Eunomius got so upset at this that he subscribed neither but even left Cyzicus to them, first orally and then in writing, and went off to Cappadocia, his homeland.[6]

4. Acacius got angry at Eunomius for becoming bishop of Cyzicus, and he accused as well Eudoxius and company of ordaining bishop, without the others' consent, Aetius's disciple, a man eager to outdo his own master in his

---

2. Eudoxius's scriptural quotation is from 1 Cor 9:3.

3. On Eunomius's denial of Mary's perpetual virginity, see Pseudo-Chrysostom, *Opus imperfectum in Matthaeum* (PG 56:635–36); Vaggione, *Eunomius of Cyzicus,* 118 n. 251. He apparently thought that part of his pastoral duty was to clear out those traditions among his people that seemed contradicted by scripture (cf. Matt 1:25; 12:46–48; 13:55; Mark 3:31–32; Luke 8:19–20; John 2:12; 7:3, 5, 10); it may be recalled how Philostorgius speaks of Aetius and him as clearing the "rubble of time" from Christian doctrine (prologue 1). On Eunomius's view of the Son as the Father's minister, and the Holy Spirit as the Son's, see his *Apol.* 27.864CD.

4. For the comments on Eunomius's style, see Photius, *Bibliotheca* codex 138.

5. On Eudoxius's promise to Eunomius to have Aetius freed from exile, see 5.3. "Their" in this sentence and "them" in the following one appear to mean Eudoxius's circle.

6. Socrates (4.7.11) says that the people of Cyzicus expelled Eunomius for his heresy and that he returned to Eudoxius in Constantinople. Vaggione (*Eunomius of Cyzicus,* 231 n. 216) places his return to Cappadocia in perhaps April of 360.

vehement zeal for his sect. With his accusations he persuaded Constantius to summon Eunomius to Antioch. When he arrived he ordered him to make his defense before a conciliar court.[7] But when the court sought for his accuser, he was nowhere to be found. For Acacius was frightened (he had thought that his mere accusation to the emperor would suffice to bring his enemy into his power), so he remained completely silent. When Constantius learned this, therefore, he became suspicious of Acacius, thinking that he had made his accusation out of hostility rather than moral rectitude, and, ordering him to return at once to his own see, he reserved the examination of the issues to a larger council.

5. While Constantius was weighing these matters, he got wind of **Julian's revolt**.[8] He made his way at once to Constantinople, at the same time calling a **council** to meet in **Nicaea** to look into the doctrine of "other in substance." But when he reached **the place called Mopsucrenae,** he fell ill, and then, **having received baptism** from Euzoius, **he departed from life** and realm together, and from the councils that had promoted heresy.

5a [*AP* 19]. Constantius left Constantinople and took the road to Syria. When he reached the great city of Antioch, he stopped there to prepare for war against the Persians. But while he was staying in the city and getting the army ready, he received letters announcing **Julian's revolt.** Julian, as I

---

7. Vaggione (ibid.) dates the conciliar hearing to January or February of 361 and thinks that it was also at this time that Acacius complained about the welcome shown by Auxentius of Mopsuestia to Aetius (cf. 5.2), so that "the charges laid against Eunomius may have been part of a co-ordinated attack on master and pupil." Kopecek (*History of Neo-Arianism*, 407–10) connects the hearing with the council referred to in Athanasius, *Syn.* 31; Socrates 2.45.9–15.

8. On Julian's appointment as Caesar, see 4.2, 2a. His "revolt" refers to his proclamation as Augustus in Paris (February 360) by troops resisting Constantius's order to transfer them to the eastern frontier for the Persian campaign. See Julian, *Ep. ad Ath.* 284A–285D; Ammianus 20.4–5; Libanius, *Or.* 18.95–100; Eunapius, *Frag. hist.* 14.4; Gregory of Nazianzus, *Or.* 4.47. It is usually agreed that while Julian himself was not behind the proclamation, he did little to resist it and signaled his acceptance by granting the usual accession donative; see David F. Buck, "Eunapius on Julian's Acclamation as Augustus," *Ancient History Bulletin* 7 (1993): 73–80. Philostorgius thus shares Ammianus's view that Julian's accession was usurpation, in that his proclamation was not done in regular form; cf. Joachim Szidat, "Imperator legitime declaratus," in *Historia Testis: Mélanges d'épigraphie, d'histoire ancienne et de philologie offerts à Tadeusz Zawadzki* (ed. Marcel Piérart et Olivier Curty; Fribourg: Universitaires Fribourg, 1989), 174–88. His source for Julian's campaign against Constantius and then against the Persians is, however, the same as that used by Gregory of Nazianzus (see Bidez, *Philostorgius*, cxxxvi–cxxxvii).

explained earlier when I was giving an account of these matters, had been appointed Caesar in Gaul by Constantius for the protection of the west, but being no longer content to remain in the rank of Caesar, he put on the diadem and seized the higher office. And when he had taken over, he reflected not an instant further, nor did he think that he should delay, but intending to subject to himself then and there all of Europe[9] that belonged to the Roman Empire, he mustered the army, proceeded through the German territories to the Danube, secured the further bank, and drove through the regions adjoining it, eluding both prefects, the one named Taurus who had charge of Italy and the other, Florentius, who had charge of Illyricum.[10] But when he reached Pannonia,[11] he crossed the river to the other side and at once had in his power all the land of Illyricum, together with Italy and all the provinces out to the western ocean that belonged to the Roman Empire.[12]

[*AP* 20]. Constantius, when he learned of this from the letters, was shaken, as may be imagined, and was especially concerned about Constantinople, lest Julian should arrive there first and take possession of the city, as in fact he was planning; so he bent every effort to anticipate him. But while he was getting together the army, which was scattered throughout the cities of the east, and making it ready for the long journey, he sent word to the bishops to go as soon as possible to **Nicaea** and await him, for he planned to convene a second **council** there, the heretical Arians having incited him against the

---

9. In 6.5a, "Europe" means the continent; see 20 n. 14.

10. Florentius had been praetorian prefect of Gaul when he learned of Julian's proclamation as Augustus, had gone to meet Constantius in the east, and then had been appointed praetorian prefect of Illyricum. Taurus had been praetorian prefect of Italy and Africa since 355; he escaped to Illyricum at the news that Julian was on the march and together with his colleague fled to the east.

11. The phrase "reached Pannonia" translates κατὰ Παίονας ἐγένετο. Another possible reading is κατὰ πλείονος, which would yield "when he had gone further."

12. On Julian's maneuvers after being proclaimed Augustus, see Paschoud, *Zosime*, 2:86–97. Contrary to what Philostorgius says, negotiations between Constantius and him went on from the time of his proclamation all through the rest of 360, but by the end of the winter of 361 the break was final, with Constantius gathering his forces to march against him and inciting the barbarians to oppose him. Julian began moving in strength to meet him in the spring. The suggestion of swiftness conveyed in 6.5a does accurately characterize Julian's course at that time; he "rushed down like a torrent," says Libanius (*Or.* 18.111; also Ammianus 21.9.6; *Pan. Lat.* III [IX] 6.2; 7). He was probably already in Sirmium before summer, from there continuing on to Naissus. On Julian's march, see Julian, *Ep.* 8 (ed. Wright, LCL); *Pan. Lat.* III (IX) 6–9; Libanius, *Or.* 18.111–114; Ammianus 21.5.13–9.6; Zosimus 3.9–10; Sozomen 5.1.3–5.

consubstantialist doctrine. While he was crossing through Cilicia, however, and had reached **the place called Mopsucrenae,** he was stricken by a sudden illness and could go no further. Sensing that he was in a bad way and had not much longer to live, he summoned Euzoius, the bishop of Antioch, as quickly as he could and bade him baptize him. He lived just a short time after **having received baptism** and then **he departed from life** in that place, having reigned for forty years in all, half of them with his father and the rest alone.[13]

5b [*AP* 41: Julian speaks]. And ... Constantius ... murdered my brother Gallus, ... and he meant to do the same to us as well, except that we were saved by the providence of the gods. The gods prevented him, showing me openly their salvation.[14] Placing my confidence in them, **I renounced** Christianity and went over to the Greek way of life, since I knew well that the ancient way of life of the Greeks and Romans, with its fine customs and laws, included worship of those gods, belief in whom was grounded in reality.

6. As Constantius **was being borne** to his grave, Julian arrived and **went ahead** of the coffin, taking **the diadem from his head** and paying honor to **the man now dead** whose life he had meant to take when he went to war against him.[15]

7. When Julian seized the imperial throne, he recalled from exile Aetius as one who had been in trouble because of Gallus. He recalled not only him but the others as well who had been banished because of church doctrinal issues.[16]

---

13. Constantius re-entered Antioch at the beginning of August 361 and prepared to march against Julian. His death came on 3 November 361. See A7.32, 32a, b; Ammianus 21.15; Jerome, *Chron.* 361; Zonaras 13.11.10–12; *Chron. pasch.* P294D–295A; *Comp. chron.* 56.11–22. Gregory of Nazianzus (*Or.* 4.47) accuses Julian of causing Constantius's death, using one of his household servants.

14. For Constantius's execution of Gallus, see 4.1, 4.1a. During the massacre of Julian's relatives after Constantine's death, Julian himself was saved by Mark of Arethusa (A7.33g, h; Theophylact 10 [PG 126:165]). On Constantius's responsibility for the deaths of his relatives, see 34 n. 48, last paragraph. Julian had a dream foretelling Constantius's death (Ammianus 21.1.6, 2.2; 22.1.2; Libanius, *Or.* 18.118; Gregory of Nazianzus, *Or.* 4.47; Zosimus 3.9.5–6; Sozomen 5.1.8; Zonaras 13.11.9).

15. Julian went down to the harbor in Constantinople to await the arrival of Constantius's body by water and then, removing all of his imperial tokens except his cloak, took hold of the coffin with his hands (Libanius, *Or.* 18.120; cf also Zonaras 13.12.4). On the mourning of the army and the public, and the funeral procession, see Ammianus 21.15.4, 16.20; Gregory of Nazianzus, *Or.* 5.16–17. On the Church of the Apostles as Constantine's burial place, see 38 n. 4, second paragraph.

16. Julian's *Ep.* 15 (ed. Wright, LCL) to Aetius announced the remission of exile to all those banished by Constantius because of Christian disputes and invited him to

6a–7a [*AP* 20]. The army mourned Constantius, and having performed the customary rites in his regard and taken the usual measures for the preservation of his corpse, they placed him in a coffin. And putting him into a carriage, they bore him to Constantinople, each man following him with his own gear and in the same order in which the army had been mustered under its officers while he was still alive.

[*AP* 21]. Thus they reached Constantinople bringing the deceased. Julian, who had arrived from Illyricum, accompanied them; he was already in secure possession of the entire realm, since no one had dared oppose him after Constantius's death. **As they were bringing the deceased** to **the Church of the Apostles,** where they were to bury him **next to his father,** he led the bier, **having taken the diadem from his head.** But when they had buried him, he went off to the imperial residence, put on the diadem again, and took over the government, being now master of the entire Roman Empire. Now that Constantius was out of the picture, therefore, he gave free rein to his anger against whose who were left, especially those who from envy had brought about the death of Gallus. He lost no time in beheading the *praepositus* Eusebius, since it had seemed all along that the entire responsibility for Gallus's murder could be assigned to him and his accusations. He also sentenced Paul the Spaniard, one of the imperial clerks, to be burned, as one who had often displayed par-

---

visit him; see also *Ep.* 24.398D; Athanasius, *HA* 9; Epiphanius, *Pan.* 76.54.36; Rufinus, *Hist. eccl.* 10.28; Socrates 31.48; Sozomen 5.5.1; Theodoret, *Hist. eccl.* 3.4.1–2. Julian also gave him an estate on Mytilene (9.4) as a reward for his relationship with Gallus (see Vaggione, *Eunomius of Cyzicus*, 272).

Julian's accession was a turning point in the history of the Eunomian enterprise, and it is extremely unfortunate that we no longer have Philostorgius's original treatment of the episode. The paganism restored by the new emperor, with its multiple and mutable deities, was not only quite the opposite of what our author considered to be the true Christian monotheistic faith but was also, on his view, just where the Nicene profession of the consubstantial relationship of the Persons of the Trinity must lead. How, then, did he treat Julian's accession, and the singular favor he showed to the one whom Philostorgius regarded as the most effective opponent of his religious program? Was his reign presented as a salutary misfortune—a warning from God about where the doctrinal compromises made by people such as Acacius of Caesarea were heading? Our author had to face the double embarrassment of the Apostate's notable benevolence toward Aetius and equally notable malevolence toward Athanasius (Julian, *Ep.* 24 [ed. Wright, LCL]), the champion of a theology that, upon the Eunomian view, expounded a crypto-polytheism far more dangerous than open paganism. It is clear at least that he explained Julian's accession as punishment for Constantius's banishment of his hero (cf. 5.4), but how he then dealt with the paradoxical policies of this new Alexander is something that Photius's epitome does not reveal.

ticular hostility to Gallus in his actions. Both of these he sent to Chalcedon, where he exacted satisfaction from each. He also executed Gaudentius, commander of Africa, and some others who had wronged him, [22] but in these cases he sent letters to order their punishment.[17]

7b [Photius, *Bibliotheca* codex 40]. [Aetius] was recalled by that most impious man Julian (as our author [Philostorgius] relates) and was received cordially. And his [Philostorgius's] history, which comprises six books in one volume, goes as far as this time.

---

17. On Eusebius's maneuvers against Gallus, see 4.1. On Julian's convocation of a court of enquiry in Chalcedon, see his *Ep.* 13; Ammianus 22.3; Libanius, *Or.* 18.152–153; Gregory of Nazianzus, *Or.* 4.64. On Eusebius's condemnation to death by the judges, see Ammianus 22.3.12. Paul and Gaudentius had been Julian's enemies in Constantius's service (Julian, *Ep. ad Ath.* 282C). Paul had also been notorious for his accusations and executions of innocent people (Ammianus 14.5.6–9). On his death by burning, see Ammianus 22.3.11. Gaudentius had been sent by Constantius to Gaul to spy upon Julian and later had been sent to Africa to protect it from Julian (Ammianus 17.9.7; 21.7.2–5). On his execution, see Ammianus 22.11.1.

Book 7

1. Julian seized power and through **public proclamations** proclaimed complete **liberty to the pagans** to carry out all of their projects, in that way handing over the Christians to indescribable and unspeakable sufferings, since in every place the proponents of paganism subjected them to every kind of injury, to new sorts of torture, and to the most painful modes of death.[1]

1a [*AP* 48]. Julian had long harbored in his soul the **birth pangs** of the paganism conceived from his intercourse in Ionia with the philosophers of Maximus's circle,[2] but as long as his brother was still alive, and after him Constantius, he dared reveal nothing for fear of them.[3] Once they had passed away, however, and he was in power, he cast off all pretence and immediately **embraced paganism** with all his heart.

1b [*AP* 22]. When Julian had become master of the Roman Empire, as was said, his keenest desire was to restore paganism. He therefore sent **letters to every place** ordering that all haste and zeal should be applied to **rebuilding** the pagan temples and **altars**.[4]

---

1. On pagan attacks on Christians in Julian's time, see A7.33; 7.33a–h. Julian himself mentions them: *Misopogon* 357C and 361A; *Ep.* 41.438B (ed. Wright, LCL). See also Sozomen 7.21.1; *Chron. pasch.* P295C–D. For a survey of the ancient Christian sources, see Robert J. Penella, "Julian the Persecutor in Fifth Century Church Historians," *The Ancient World* 24 (1993): 31–43.

2. On Julian's indebtedness to Iamblichus for his philosophy, see his *Or.* 4.146A. On his relationship to Maximus of Ephesus, cf. Libanius, *Or.* 18.155–156; Eunapius, *Vit. soph.* 475; Rowland Smith, *Julian's Gods: Religion and Philosophy in the Thought and Action of Julian the Apostate* (London: Routledge, 1995), 29 and 186–87. He summoned him to court after becoming sole emperor (*Vit. soph.* 476–478).

3. On Gallus's attempts to keep Julian Christian, see 3.27.

4. On Julian's restoration of the pagan temples, see Libanius, *Or.* 18.126; John Chrysostom, *Bab. Jul.* 76 (ed. Schatkin, SC); Sozomen 5.3.1; Smith, *Julian's Gods*, xiv–xv; 207–18. Julian was a convinced polytheist, his Neoplatonism notwithstanding; he did not plan to establish a sort of pagan monotheist church, but he did aim from the outset to eliminate Christians from positions of influence.

1c [*AP* 35: Artemius speaks to Julian]. Know therefore that the strength and power of Christ is invincible and unconquerable. You yourself are certainly convinced of this from the **oracles that the physician and** *quaestor* **Oribasius** recently brought you from the Apollo in Delphi.[5] But I will repeat the oracle to you, whether you wish to hear it or not. It runs as follows:

Go tell the king the wondrous hall is fallen to the ground.
Now Phoebus has a cell no more, no laurel that foretells,
No talking spring; the water that once spoke is heard no more.[6]

---

5. Oribasius attended Julian at his death (see 7.15). 7.1c here confirms the notice in *Suda*, Δ 543 that he was Julian's *quaestor sacri palatii*, so the question about this in *PLRE* 1:653 may be regarded as answered. Cf. Silvano Faro, "Oribasio medico, quaestor di Giuliano l'Apostata," *Studi in onore di Cesare Sanfilippo* 7 (1987): 261–68.

6. The oracle is marked as spurious by Herbert W. Parke and Donald E. W. Wormell, *The Delphic Oracle* (2 vols.; Oxford: Blackwell, 1956), 2:194–95; and Joseph E. Fontenrose, *The Delphic Oracle: Its Responses and Operations, with a Catalogue of Responses* (Berkeley and Los Angeles: University of California Press, 1978), 56 and 353. The verses are also found in Cedrenus 304A. C. Maurice Bowra regards it as a "Christian fabrication" composed between 397 and 426 "to show the futility of Julian's belief in the Oracle" ("ΕΙΠΑΤΕ ΤΩΙ ΒΑΣΙΛΗΙ," *Hermes* 87 [1959]: 426–35, esp. 430, repr. with modifications in his *On Greek Margins* [Oxford: Clarendon, 1970], 233–52). Bernadette Cabouret agrees in "Julien et Delphes," *Revue des études anciennes* 99 (1997): 141–58. Timothy E. Gregory ("Julian and the Last Oracle at Delphi," *GRBS* 24 (1983): 355–66) thinks rather that the verses are a plea for help given to Oribasius by the priests at Delphi, if one supposes that the words "fallen to the ground" need not be taken literally. Georgios Fatouros ("ΕΙΠΑΤΕ ΤΩΙ ΒΑΣΙΛΗΙ," *Hermes* 124 [1996]: 367–74) says that the style of the verses differs so widely from that typical of an oracle that they cannot be regarded as even a forgery. He considers them to be rather an epigram composed by Oribasius to inform Julian that some oracle in Greece (perhaps at Delphi) was no longer functioning, Julian having sent him to report on its condition. The description of the ruin of the shrine was not meant literally but as a figure of its idle state. Philostorgius, Fatouros conjectures, was probably the Christian who hit upon the idea of transforming the epigram into an oracle.

On the oracle's site, see Pierre Amandry, "La ruine du temple d'Apollon à Delphes," *Académie royale de Belgique: Bulletin de la classe des lettres et des sciences morales et politiques* 75 (1989): 26–47. On the laurel and the water, see Auguste Bouché-Leclercq, *Histoire de la divination dans l'antiquité* (4 vols.; Paris: Leroux, 1879–82), 1:350 and 3:100–101. The spring water and the laurel (bay leaf) might "speak" in various ways, perhaps by putting the medium into a trance out of which the oracular spirit gave utterance. In one instance at least the oracle appeared written on the bay leaf after it was dipped in the water.

2. While George of Alexandria was presiding at a synod, he says, and compelling his co-religionists to subscribe the document against Aetius, the pagans burst in, seized him, inflicted gross mistreatment upon his body, and then handed him over to be burned.[7] Our heretical author even says that Athanasius was behind the deed.[8] Once George was slain, however, Athanasius resumed his own throne, the Alexandrians for their part welcoming him gladly.[9]

3. Concerning the image of our Savior that the faith of the woman with a hemorrhage had erected in thanksgiving to her benefactor: he relates that this monument **was put up** by the fountain inside the city together with other statues in order to furnish a pleasant sight to visitors.[10] Now an **herb grew up**

---

7. On George's lynching, see A7.33.1; 7.33a,b,d; Julian, *Ep.* 21 (ed Wright, LCL); Ammianus 22.11.8–10 (on Ammianus's source[s] for this episode, see Hans Christof Brennecke, "Christliche Quellen des Ammianus Marcellinus?" *Journal of Ancient Christianity* 1 [1997]: 226–50); Athanasius, *HA* 8; Epiphanius, *Pan.* 76.1.1–2; Gregory of Nazianzus, *Or.* 21.24; Socrates 3.2.10; Sozomen 5.7.2–3; Theophylact 13 (PG 126:169A); Matilde Caltabiano, "L'assassinio di Giorgio di Cappadocia (Alessandria, 361 d.C.)," *Quaderni Catanesi* 7 (1985): 17–59. On the chronology, see 39 n. 6 and 50 n. 45. After finally taking possession of his see under military escort on 24 February 357, a year after Athanasius had been forced to go into hiding and years after he had been elected to it, he was driven out again by the populace on 20 October 358, his indiscriminate rapaciousness having earned him the bitter hatred of Christian and pagan alike. He managed to return on 26 November 361, before news of Constantius's death had reached his city. The announcement of his death was made four days later, together with that of Julian's accession, and the populace at once seized George and hurried him off to prison. From there the pagans dragged him forth again on 24 December, butchered him, paraded him through the city on a camel, and then burned his body, mixing his ashes with those of animals lest the Christians recover them for use in instituting his cult as a martyr.

8. Philostorgius's connection of George's death with his condemnation of Aetius should be treated with reserve; his fondness for cautionary deaths is evident enough throughout his history. Socrates (3.3.1) and Sozomen (5.7.4) treat the story of the involvement of Athanasius's partisans in George's death as an unfounded rumor. The history of the incentives behind his execution is complex, however fervent the resentment that led to it; see Caltabiano, "L'assassinio di Giorgio," 31–59.

9. On the joy with which Athanasius was welcomed back, see Socrates 3.4.1; Sozomen 5.7.1.

10. On the image of "Christ" and the woman, see Ernst von Dobschütz, *Christusbilder: Untersuchungen zur christlichen Legende* (TU 18; Leipzig: Hinrichs, 1899), 197–205, 250*–73*. The story of the woman is in Mark 5:25–34; Matt 9:20–22; and Luke 8:43–48. Eusebius of Caesarea is the first to report the connection of the story with the image, without committing himself to the truth of the tradition (*Hist. eccl.*

by the **feet** of our Savior's image that was a remedy for all illnesses, especially consumption, and the reason for this was sought (for in the passage of time both the person portrayed and the reason for the monument had been forgotten; it stood in the open with nothing to cover it, and much of the body was buried in the dirt that kept falling upon it from higher ground especially in times of rain, the dirt covering the writing that explained each of the matters).[11] An inquiry was therefore instituted, the buried part was dug out, and the writing was found that told the whole story. But of the plant there was nothing to be seen after all that time, neither there nor elsewhere. The **statue** they moved **to the sacristy of the church** and paid it due honor; they neither worshiped nor adored it at all (it would have been unlawful to adore bronze or any other material). They rather showed their devotion to the One it represented by the sacred place in which they put it and the pleasure they took in visiting the place in order to see the sight it contained.

The pagans who lived in Paneas, when they were roused to impiety in Julian's time, tore the statue from its base, tied ropes to **its feet,** and **dragged** it down the main thoroughfare. While they were breaking up and scattering the rest of the body, some people who were grieved at what was happening managed secretly to take away the **head,** which had separated from the neck while being dragged along, and rescued it as best they could. He says that he himself saw the head.

It happens that Paneas was originally called Dan, a name it got from Dan, the son of Jacob, the **phylarch** of those who then inhabited the city.[12] It was

---

7.18). He speaks of bronze figures, in relief, of a woman and man (said to be Jesus), the woman in the pose of a suppliant, the man stretching out his hand to her. His description of the plant leaves it unclear whether it was real or part of the representation, but since he speaks of it as an antidote, it seems to have been real; otherwise, its medicinal virtue could hardly have been recognized, Eusebius speaking of it as a "strange kind of plant" (Dobschütz, *Christusbilder,* 201, thinks otherwise). He says the image stood at the gate of the woman's house. The sculpture is thought to have been meant to portray some pagan god of healing, not necessarily Asclepius (Dobschütz, *Christusbilder,* 198).

11. The development of the tradition can be seen in Rufinus's translation of Eusebius (*Hist. eccl.* 7.18.2): here the plant (obviously quite natural) acquires its healing powers if allowed to grow up from the bottom of the sculpture until it touches the hem of the robe. See also Giovan Domenico Mansi, ed. *Sacrorum conciliorum nova et amplissima collectio* (35 vols.; Florence: Zatta, 1759–98), 13:93D; Malalas 10.11–12; Sozomen 5.21.1–3.

12. Judges 18 tells how the Danites migrated to seek an inheritance for themselves, finally took and destroyed Laish, and, after rebuilding it, named it Dan.

later surnamed **Caesarea Philippi.** But the proponents of paganism erected a statue **of Pan** in it, and so it changed its name **to** Paneas.[13]

3a [*AP* 57]. There was also the **statue** of the Savior in the city of Paneas, a work of magnificent execution put up by the woman with the hemorrhage whom Christ healed, and erected on a notable site in the city; it was later recognized from the miraculous **herb that grew** there, so the Christians removed it and put it **in the sacristy of the church.** The pagans pulled it down, fastened ropes **to the feet, and dragged** it through the public square until it was broken up bit by bit and so destroyed. Only the **head** was left; that was seized by someone while the pagans were raising their clamor and speaking blasphemies and utterly disgraceful words against our Lord Jesus Christ, words such as no one had ever heard.

3b [Codex Vaticanus Gr. 96, f. 102r margin]. Concerning the Jordan, from Philostorgius's history: Right on the border of Palestine, just before the point where Phoenicia begins, lies the city formerly called Dan, from the tribe of Dan; this stems from the time when they alone of the whole people spent a long time wandering about, finally took possession of the regions there, and after difficulties settled there and built a city on the tops of their mountains that they called after their phylarch.[14] It was just within the boundary of Judea where it borders upon Phoenicia. Herod the Great later built it and renamed it **Caesarea Philippi.** It is now called Paneas; having erected the image of Pan in it, they changed the name of the city accordingly. There in Paneas is found one of the sources of the Jordan; there are two of them, and this one is still called Dan after the older name.[15] The other source, which is called Ior and

---

Eusebius says that Dan is a village four miles from Paneas on the road to Tyre and on the border of Judaea, where the Jordan appears (*Onomasticon* 76.6).

13. "Paneas" comes from *Paneion*, the shrine to Pan in the grotto at the source of the Jordan. The region was hellenized in the third century B.C.E. Augustus gave it to Herod in 20 B.C.E., and Herod in turn built a temple to Augustus there, the location taking on the name Paneas, which had been applied to the region as a whole. In 3 or 2 B.C.E. the tetrarch Philip built it into a city called Caesarea. From the second century its name was Caesarea Paneas, but from the fourth century we find it once again called simply Paneas (Emil Schürer, *The History of the Jewish People in the Age of Jesus Christ (175 B.C.–A.D. 135): A New English Version* (rev. and ed. Géza Vermès and Fergus Millar; 3 vols.; Edinburgh: T&T Clark, 1973–87], 2:169–71).

14. "Built a city on the tops of their mountains" translates πόλιν ἐπὶ τοῖς ἄκροις αὐτῶν ὄρεσι δειμάμενοι. It may be noted that πόλις means both an urban area enclosed by a wall and the territory it controls. The city of Caesarea Philippi itself was at the southwest foot of Mount Hermon.

15. On the tradition of the two sources of the Jordan, named Ior and Dan, see *Suda*, I 422; John Chrosostom, *In Jordanem fluvium* (Bernard de Montfaucon, ed.,

is about 160 stades distant from the first, springs from one of the peaks of the same mountain.[16] A river issues from each source, one of them called the Jorates, the other the Danites. Having made their way through the mountain, once they descend to the plain they join together **and form one** mighty **river,** the Jordan, in which both their waters and their names become mingled. It passes through the Lake of Tiberias, dividing it in two and flowing down its entire length with its own current until it passes out into the land on the other side, remaining always the same as it was; from there it flows through Palestine, and then the entire river empties into what is called the Dead Sea and vanishes.[17]

4. During the time when the proponents of paganism were everywhere behaving most wickedly against Christians, the following dastardly deed was done in Palestine by impious folk. They took **the bones of the prophet Elisha and of John the Baptist from their tombs** (both were buried there), mixed them together with the **bones of dumb** animals, **burned them** together to **ashes,** and scattered them **into the air.**[18] It also happened at times that when they arrested the proponents of Christianity, they placed them as sacrificial victims on the altars where fire had been kindled, and in their madness they proceeded to many other unspeakable deeds. Julian, when he learned of them, not only was not grieved but was especially gratified, since the ignominy of what was done attached to others, even though his was the will at work in their acts.[19]

Realizing, though, that this madness was furthering none of his plans (for the resolve of the Christian people was simply stiffening when it was under

---

Opera omnia quae exstant [13 vols.; Paris: Gaume, 1835–39], 10:778A); Jerome, *Commentariorum in Ezechielem libri XVI* 8.27.19. The Jordan actually has four sources, which become two streams, called in more recent times the Jordan and the Turan, before emptying into what was once Lake Huleh (mostly drained in the 1950s); see Henry O. Thompson, "Jordan River," *ABD* 3:955.

16. The phrase "[…springs from one of the peaks] of the same mountain" translates τοῦ αὐτοῦ … ὄρους. The word αὐτοῦ might simply mean "there," in which case the translation would be: "[one of the peaks] of the mountain there."

17. Josephus has the same account of the Lake of Tiberias being divided in two by the Jordan (*Bellum judaicum* 3.509, 515).

18. On pagan mistreatment of Christians, see A7.33.2–3, 7.33.c–h; Gregory of Nazianzus, *Or.* 5.29; Rufinus, *Hist. eccl.* 11.28; *Chron. pasch.* P295C; Theodoret, *Hist. eccl.* 3.7.2. Philostorgius (7.4, 7.4a) is the only author to mention the exhumation of Elisha.

19. On Julian's attitude toward the mistreatment, see Gregory of Nazianzus, *Or.* 4.61: he issued no order for the pagan attacks, but simply by not restraining them he made them public policy.

siege), he thought up the idea of kindling war between those bishops who had been banished on various charges and those who had replaced them in their sees. And so he gave either side full permission to do whatever it could to regroup and strengthen its position.[20] As a result, they fell upon each other, bringing great disgrace and criticism upon the faith, which was just what the Apostate wanted.

But his mischief did not end there. He also returned the clergy to the rolls of the city councils,[21] distributed **the churches' allowances** to those who served **demons,**[22] and persisted in doing everything he could to advance the cause of the demons and to ensure the destruction of the faith, or so he thought.

4a [AP 57]. In Sebaste, which was once called Samaria but is now a foundation of Herod surnamed Sebaste, they took **the bones of the prophet Elisha and of John the Baptist** from **their tombs,** mixed them together with the **bones of dumb** and unclean beings, **burned them,** and scattered the **ashes into the air.** [58]. As for Julian, that most lawless man, of all impious folk the most impious, when he heard of this he was glad and in his exultation at these events gave orders ... [continued in 7.9a].

4b [AP 31: Julian speaks]. You see ... how much nonsense ... he [the martyr] babbles against our religion from what he has gotten from **pagan learning?** By the golden-hued sun of this whole world, who is most dear to me, I will no longer stand for that most godless folk, the Christians, being educated in pagan **disciplines.** Just look at the great and unhappy nonsense that this dog has spouted in his account of the sacred men of philosophy from the education he got in the sacred **disciplines,** however lacking in system and method one may think it.[23]

---

20. Philostorgius by no means misrepresents either the intention behind, or the results of, Julian's amnesty of bishops in exile; see Ammianus 22.5.3–4; *Chron. pasch.* P296A–B; Sozomen 5.5.7.

21. On the restoration of Christian clergy to the city councils, see *Cod. theod.* 12.1.50, 13.1.4; Julian, *Ep.* 39 (ed. Wright, LCL); Libanius, *Or.* 18.148; Ammianus 25.4.21; Sozomen 5.5.2; Theodoret, *Hist. eccl.* 3.6.5. Service on the city councils was unpopular enough to have been made compulsory in the third and fourth centuries, although the reasons for this are not always easy to discover (Jones, *Later Roman Empire,* 739–57).

22. On Julian's transfer of the church's allowances to the temples, see John Chrysostom, *Bab. Jul.* 76; Sozomen 5.5.2; 6.3.4; Theodoret, *Hist. eccl.* 1.11.2–3; 3.6.5; 4.4.1.

23. Julian forbade school-teachers, but not students, to be Christian (*Ep.* 36). It may be thought, however, that he meant thereby to exclude Christians from advancement to positions of social influence, by making it practically impossible for them to attend school and yet retain their faith. Cf. A7.36c; Ammianus 22.10.7; 25.4.20;

4c [*AP* 22, immediately following 7.1b]. And all the **revenues** that Constantine the Great and his son Constantius assigned **to the churches** [Julian] took away and consecrated to the temples **of the demons**; instead of bishops, presbyters, and deacons, he appointed temple ministers, temple servants, sprinklers, sacrificers, basket-bearers, and all the other titles bestowed by this pagan foolishness. The impious Julian, then, did these and a great many other things in Constantinople.

[*AP* 23]. After this he sent out his mother's brother Julian as **governor,** or what is called "count" **of the east**; the latter had **renounced** the Christian religion in order to win his **favor** and showed great enthusiasm for paganism. He had his orders to injure and ruin the fortunes of the churches and to benefit and promote paganism everywhere and in every way. And when he arrived in Antioch, he tried to appear to outstrip his orders by his deeds. He removed from all of the churches [in addition to what had already been taken] all their valuables in silver, gold, and silk cloth that were left, and he also locked the churches so that no one could enter them to pray, putting bars and bolts on their portals. This, then, is what the governor of the east did in Antioch.[24]

[*AP* 24]. As for the emperor Julian, he stayed in Constantinople for some time longer, strengthening in it what he thought would most benefit the realm and planning and laboring to make paganism rise to greater heights.[25] He then left Constantinople and with the whole army took the road to Syria. Passing the entire way through Phrygia, he arrived at the last city of that region, named Iconium, where he turned off, leaving aside Isauria. Passing over Taurus, as it is called, he came to the cities of Cilicia, and drawing near to the way station in Issus, he camped there, following the example of Alexander of Macedonia.[26] For he too had waged war there in Issus with the Persian

---

Thomas M. Banchich, "Julian's School Laws. Cod. Theod. 13.5.5 and Ep. 42." *The Ancient World* 24 (1993): 5–14; D. Micalella, "Giuliano e la 'paideia,'" *Rudiae* 7 (1995): 245–52; Smith, *Julian's Gods*, 214; Jean Sirinelli, "Problèmes de la 'paideia,'" *Cahiers des études anciennes* 31 (1996): 135–46.

24. Julian appointed his uncle "count of the east" at the beginning of 362 (Ammianus 23.1.4). Sozomen 5.7.9 says that his hatred of Christians led him to acts of persecution that were contrary to Julian's intention. He collected the treasures of the church of Antioch and transferred them to the imperial residence and was anxious to lock up the churches (Sozomen 5.8.1–2). On the confiscation and closure, see also 7.8a.

25. Regarding "he stayed in Constantinople … strengthening in it," cf. Ammianus 22.9.2: "reliquit Constantinopolim incrementis maximis fultam." On Julian's journey to Antioch, see A3.2; Ammianus 22.9.2–14; Libanius, *Or.* 18.159–162 (he mentions Julian changing his route to escape ambush).

26. On Julian's imitation of Alexander, see 7.15a and 110 n. 71.

king Darius and had made the place famous by defeating him. From there he crossed the Gulf of Issus and came to the city of Tarsus, from where in turn he reached Antioch, fuming against the Christians and threatening to blot out their name once and for all.[27]

5.[28] He says that with matters taking this course, Eudoxius remembered the oaths and promises he had made to Eunomius about Aetius, and so he wrote to Euzoius in Antioch to summon a council that would lift the sentence of condemnation from Aetius.[29] Euzoius, however, did not agree to the request at all but singled out Eudoxius for special criticism for not taking the lead in doing what he was telling others to do. But when Eudoxius persisted in his request, then Euzoius too promised to do so.

6.[30] While Aetius and Eunomius were staying in Constantinople, Leontius of Tripolis went to them, along with Theodulus of Cheretapa, and Serras, Theophilus, and Heliodorus of both Libyas and their associates, and everyone

---

27. The editor suggests that the words "From there … Christians and" are taken from a source other than Philostorgius; see Bidez, *Philostorgius*, 83. In "threatening to blot out their name once and for all" (ἐπαπειλούμενος τὸ τούτων εἰς ἅπαν ἐξαλείφεν ὄνομα), read ἐξαλείφειν.

28. 7.5–6 and 8.2–4 are "partially overlapping accounts of what are apparently the same events" (Vaggione, *Eunomius of Cyzicus,* 274 n. 104). The paradoxical nature of Julian's reign continues to unfold in Philostorgius's historiography, as Aetius returns from exile, the special object of the benevolence of the very emperor to whom, in our author's view, his doctrine is most deeply and effectively opposed. Yet it is Julian's attitude toward Aetius that gives the Eunomians the liberty to establish their independence, as we shall see. That Eudoxius finds it convenient to recall his promise about Aetius at this juncture is hardly a surprise. Brennecke tries to defend Eudoxius from Philostorgius's portrayal of him as a political opportunist (*Studien zur Geschichte der Homöer,* 110–14), a desperate venture, given what the other sources say of him.

29. On the promises Eudoxius had made to Eunomius, see 5.3: Eumomius had refused to be ordained bishop of Cyzicus until the other had promised to release Aetius from deposition and exile. Eudoxius, now trying to avoid going back on his own condemnation, passes the job on to Euzoius (Brennecke, *Studien zur Geschichte der Homöer,* 110–11).

30. 7.6 describes what Kopecek calls "the first independent Neo-Arian synods" (*History of Neo-Arianism,* 416). It results in the formation of a Eunomian hierarchy, a sign of the gulf that Aetius and his followers now felt had opened between other Christians and themselves. Brennecke doubts the accuracy of the description of Eudoxius's behavior at this synod, since there is no evidence that he ever revoked Aetius's condemnation; he might have been forced by the political current of the day to provide facilities for the synod, but, had he attended it, he would never have played the ridiculous part Philostorgius assigns him (Brennecke, *Studien zur Geschichte der Homöer,* 112).

else who shared their views, those in fact who had refused to subscribe the condemnation of Aetius or the document of the westerners. They assembled and ordained Aetius; he and Eunomius were everything to them.[31] They also ordained other bishops, Eudoxius not only not dissenting but repeatedly signifying his approval of those to be ordained by Aetius and company. In the meantime, Euzoius too convened a council with about nine in attendance and revoked the measures long since passed against Aetius. He also revoked the six-month term after which Serras and company were to be punished by degradation from the priesthood unless they subscribed the deposition of Aetius and the western document.[32] When both measures had been taken, they prepared to send the documents to Eudoxius and his associates. But the devastating persecution unleashed against the Christians cut short this move.[33]

6a [*Suda*, Λ 254 Leontius]. Bishop of Tripolis in Lydia, his family came from the stock of those Moesians who had settled by the Danube and to whom Homer refers as hand-to-hand fighters.[34] That ill-minded Philostorgius associates himself in his book with this Leontius as a sharer in his Arian perversity. Leontius had one son, who showed little promise of turning out well, and so after prayer, they say, he had him put to death while he was still a youth, since he thought it best to bring his life to an end and to remove him from life's treacherous pitfalls before he committed some act of immorality. They used to call him a norm for the church. He was equally free with everyone in his attitude and quite outspoken. Once when a council was being held and Eusebia, Constantius's wife, was putting on airs and receiving the reverence of the bishops, he alone made little of her and stayed home.[35] She

31. Aetius was consecrated bishop in the summer of 362; on the event, see Epiphanius, *Pan.* 76.54.36. Euzoius's synod in Antioch met in the autumn of the same year.

32. For the six-month stay of deposition granted by the Council of Constantinople of 360 to those refusing to condemn Aetius, see Theodoret, *Hist. eccl.* 2.28.3–7. The "western document" is the homoean creed finally approved at the Council of Ariminum and endorsed by the Council of Constantinople.

33. The "persecution against the Christians" means the reprisals taken by Julian in Antioch after the burning of the shrine of Apollo on 22 October of that year, of which he suspected the Christians; see 7.8; 7.8a.

34. On Leontius of Tripolis, deposed by the Council of Seleucia, see Athanasius, *Syn.* 12.5; Epiphanius, *Pan.* 73.26.4; Socrates 2.40.43. The reference to Homer is in *Iliad* 13.5.

35. On the council mentioned here, see 68 n. 14, first paragraph. It must have met at some time during the marriage of Constantius and Eusebia and thus ca. 354–359. In this period, the Council of Sirmium of 358 is geographically more likely than that of Milan of 355, which it is doubtful Leontius attended (Woods, "Three Notes," 610–16). The portrait of Eusebia here squares with *Epit. Caes.* 42.40: "decoram quidem,

was annoyed at this and felt angry, and sent a message to him to complain and to coax him with promises, saying, "I will build a great church for you and furnish it lavishly if you visit me." But he replied, "If you should decide to do something like that, your majesty, then realize that you would be benefiting your own soul no less than me. But if you wished to receive a visit in a way that would maintain the respect due to bishops, then when I entered, you would come down at once from your lofty throne, advance to meet me respectfully, bow your head to my hands, and request my blessings. Then I myself would again be seated while you remained standing out of respect; you would be seated when I bade you by giving the signal. If you agreed to this, I would pay you a visit. Otherwise, you could not give gifts so many or so great that we would transgress the sacred law of the priesthood by surrendering the honor due to bishops."

When Eusebia received this reply, she grew furious and considered it insufferable that she should be addressed by Leontius in this way. Quite under the sway of anger, her womanish ill-temper and impulsive spirit gave vent to a continuous stream of threats, and, relating to her husband what had happened, she urged him to exact punishment for it. But he for his part praised the freedom of attitude Leontius had shown, calmed his wife's anger, and sent her back to the women's quarters.

And once while the emperor Constantius was seated before the bishops with the intention of governing the churches too, most of those present applauded and admired all that he said, declaring his words to be most excellent.[36] Leontius, however, remained silent. When the emperor asked him why he was the only one to say nothing, he replied, "I am surprised to find you taking charge of matters other than those for which you were appointed; you are to manage military and civil affairs, and here you are issuing orders to bishops about what pertains to bishops alone." The emperor, abashed, desisted from the attempt he had been making to impose his will in these matters. This is how frank Leontius was.

7. The Apostate did everything possible to make Valentinian, an officer who had charge of a military unit, abandon his faith (he held the rank of

---

verum per Adamantias et Gorgonias et alia importuna ministeria vexantem famam viri contra, quam feminis modestioribus mos est...."

36. The story about Constantius giving orders to the bishops is referred by Woods to the meeting in Constantinople in 359 of the delegates of the Council of Seleucia. Leontius would have been protesting against the emperor's decision to condemn Aetius, just as Eleusius of Cyzicus and Silvanus of Tarsus protested to Constantius at the same meeting that he was overstepping his authority (see Theodoret, *Hist. eccl.* 2.27.20; Woods, "Three Notes," 614–16).

count of the **so-called *Cornuti***[37]), but when he failed, he stripped him **of his rank** and banished him to Thebes in Egypt. They say that during the reign of Constantius, one of the so-called *silentiarii* saw him spewing fire from his mouth.[38] He saw him during the afternoon, when we usually take a nap after eating, and he told Constantius, since the latter had sent him to fetch Valentinian on some business, and so he witnessed the sight. The report made Constantius suspicious and afraid, but he caused the man no trouble; mastering his fear, he sent him to the fortresses of Mesopotamia to guard the places there and to repel the Persian attacks.[39]

8. Our author recounts in a way not much different than do the others the events concerning the martyr Babylas: how Julian mistreated the martyr's body, what the demons were forced to say, how Apollo's shrine was struck by lightning and burned to ashes along with its statue, and other marvels that were accomplished by human strength and by that which is above it.[40] He says that Saint Babylas was martyred with **three boys who were quite young and were brothers.** The reason for the martyrdom was as follows. When Babylas was **bishop of Antioch, some demon, they say,** put it into the head of

----

37. On the military division of the Cornuti, see Alfred Neumann, "Cornuti," PW 10Sup:133–34.

38. The "silentiaries" were palace ushers whose social standing rose steadily from the fourth through the sixth centuries as they increasingly enjoyed the confidence of those in the highest places; see Jones, *Later Roman Empire*, 571–72.

39. This is one of several stories in circulation about Julian's dismissal of Valentinian because of his Christianity: cf. Rufinus, *Hist. eccl.* 11.2; Sozomen 6.6.3–6; Theodoret, *Hist. eccl.* 3.16.1–3; Zonaras 13.15.4; Theophanes 79B; *Comp. chron.* 58.4–6; *Chron. pasch.* P297A (but compare 300C). What seems to be behind them is Valentinian's openly expressed repugnance to paganism and willingness to resign from the service rather than accept it (Ambrose, *De obitu Valentiniani* 55; Socrates 3.13.4; Sozomen as above). But Socrates makes it clear that Julian did not in fact dismiss him (4.1.8–10). Sozomen's story of his dismissal on the pretext of unprofessional conduct sounds like a confusion with the earlier episode in 357, when Valentinian, then a tribune, ran afoul of Barbatio, nominally Julian's infantry commander in Gaul, who got him cashiered by Constantius for misconduct (Ammianus 16.11.4–7). Philostorgius indicates that Valentinian was rehabilitated after Barbatio's exposure and execution in 359.

40. See A7.35; 7.35a; Sozomen 5.19–20; Theodoret, *Hist. eccl.* 3.10–12; Zonaras 13.12.35–43. On Babylas, see Margaret. A. Schatkin, ed., *Discours sur Babylas.* (SC 362; Paris: Cerf, 1990), 15–18, 59–60. All that can be said with certainty about Babylas is that he was a bishop of Antioch martyred around the middle of the third century; we are not sure under which emperor. Philostorgius's is one of the three most important versions of his *Passion* between John Chrysostom's account and that of Simeon Metaphrastes; the others are BHG 205 and BHL 889; for further details, see Schatkin, *Discours sur Babylas*, 49–50.

the Roman **emperor Numerian,** or, as some say, **Decius, to enter the church when it was full.** But the high priest of God **stood** in the entrance of the church and barred **the way in, saying** that he meant to do everything in his power **to prevent the wolf from** getting into **the flock. The emperor forsook** his idea **at once, whether because he feared a riot or for some other reason.** He **first** accused the bishop of **arrogance, and then he ordered** the holy man **to sacrifice to the demons,** since only that rite of expiation would lead to dismissal of the **charge** and afterwards to honor and glory. **But he** nobly resisted all that was put to him and was crowned with martyrdom.

8a [*AP* 49]. [Julian] set out for Daphne, the fairest quarter of Antioch. [51]. Julian set out for the suburb of Daphne, as we said, making ready to offer sacrifices to Apollo and hoping to receive oracles from him.[41] Daphne is a suburb of Antioch located in its higher regions and thickly shaded by groves of every sort. The neighborhood has trees and fruit in great abundance; it is a place where there is an incredible display of all sorts of trees, including cypresses, whose beauty, height, and size are incomparable. One finds streams of fresh water running everywhere, the springs that gush forth being of very great size, and it is from them that the city appears as among the best-watered of all. The area is also richly provided with splendid buildings for lodgings, baths, and other purposes, whose usefulness and elegance enhance it greatly. It had temples and statues of various demons as well, the most distinguished being Apollo's, to which devotion had been paid from time immemorial. For it was there, so the pagan myth pretends, that the incident took place with the virgin Daphne, whose name even today seems most closely connected with the place.[42]

[*AP* 52]. The statue of Apollo had been made in the following way.[43] The body was fashioned from a vine stock that was most skillfully adapted to form one coherent whole. The robe draped around it was all covered with

---

41. Julian often visited the shrine in Daphne (*Misopogon* 346B; 361D; Zonaras 13.12.35; Theophanes 76B; Cedrenus 306B). On the natural beauty of the place, see Libanius, *Or.* 11.235–237; 60.3–4; Sozomen 5.19.5–9; John Chrysostom, *Bab. Jul.* 68 (ed. Schatkin, SC). On the shrine, see Glanville Downey, *A History of Antioch in Syria: From Seleucus to the Arab Conquest* (Princeton: Princeton University Press, 1961), 82–86.

42. On the myth of Daphne fleeing from Apollo and being changed into a laurel, see Ovid, *Metamorphoses* 1.452–567; Plutarch, *Agis et Cleomenes* 9.2; and references in Schatkin, *Discours sur Babylas,* 181 n. 3. On its localization in the Antiochene suburb of Daphne, see Pausanias 8.20.2; John Chrysostom as above; Sozomen 5.19.6; Downey, *History of Antioch in Syria,* 83.

43. On Apollo's statue, see Libanius, *Or.* 60.9–11; Ammianus 22.13.1; Theodoret, *Hist. eccl.* 3.11.4; Malalas 10.9. It had been made by Bryaxis (Cedrenus 306B).

gold, and together with the exposed and ungilded parts of the body it shone with indescribable beauty. The statue was standing with a lyre in its hands as though conducting a choir, its hair and laurel crown shining with intermingled gold in a way designed to be most attractive to onlookers. The eyes were represented by two large stones, hyacinths, in honor of the Amyclean boy Hyacinth.[44] The beauty and size of the stones always gave the greatest luster to the statue, its makers having set them in a way that added immeasurably to its dignity, so as to draw into error as many as possible of those who would see it, enticing them by the supreme beauty of its appearance to worship it. And this in fact is what happened to Julian himself, who showed more devotion to it than to all the other idols, sacrificing to it thousands of animals of each kind.[45]

[*AP* 53]. But when he had done everything and tried everything to induce the idol to give an oracle and had failed, and both it and all the other idols there remained completely silent, he concluded that what was needed was the use of magic, or what the pagans call "holy work."[46] He therefore summoned one Eusebius, who had the greatest reputation among the pagans for his ability in this field, and ordered him to render the idol fully alive and active, omitting nothing that he might think necessary for this. But when Eusebius had tried all of his devices and had left nothing undone that had further occurred to him, and the idol remained silent in just the same and very natural way,

---

44. Hyacinth, whom Apollo loved, was buried in Amyclae (Pausanias 3.1.3; Lucian, *Dialogi deorum* 14).

45. The countless victims offered by Julian at the shrine are mentioned by John Chrysostom, *Bab. Jul.* 60; Zonaras 13.12.38.

46. On the silence of the oracle, see John Chrysostom, *Bab. Jul.* 60; 80; 81; *Bab.* 5 (ed. Schatkin, SC); Libanius, *Or.* 60.5; Ammianus 22.12.8; Rufinus, *Hist. eccl.* 10.36; Socrates 3.18; Sozomen 5.19.17–19; Theodoret, *Hist. eccl.* 3.10; Theophanes 76B; Zonaras 13.12.38–40. Julian himself mentions the silence in *Misopogon* 361C, where he says that the god had left the temple even before the fire and had signified as much to him when he first entered it. We cannot be sure quite what is meant here by the oracle remaining silent. As at Delphi, the water from the spring was thought to be infused with a mantic virtue, but how the virtue was expressed, whether for instance with the help of bay leaves or human mediums, is uncertain; see Bouché-Leclercq, *Histoire de la divination*, 3:267.

There is a suggestive resemblance between the structure of the present narrative and the earlier one about the anger of a pagan emperor upon the discovery that Apollo's oracular powers were being frustrated by the presence of Christians, the persecution he unleashed upon them, and his consequent perdition (Eusebius, *Vit. Const.* 2.50–54). The Eusebius summoned to work magic here cannot be identified. See also John Chrysostom, *Bab.* 5.

uttering nothing more than it had before, he was then asked by Julian what was above all the reason why it was silent, even though they had performed all of the usual rites in its regard. He replied that the truest reason why it and the other idols were silent was Babylas, who was buried there in Daphne: the gods **abhorred** his corpse and for that reason refused to visit their abodes. He said this because he did not want to tell the real reason, of which he was by no means unaware, namely, that it was obviously a higher power that had restrained the demons from acting, especially since the demon who played the part of Apollo had told him **clearly and explicitly,** so it is said, that he could give no reply because of Babylas.

[*AP* 54]. This Babylas is said to have been **bishop of Antioch. When the emperor Numerian** wanted **to enter** the Christian **church on a** feast day, **he stood before the doors** and prevented him from going in,

[*Suda*, B 10 Babylas]. **Bishop of Antioch, he is said to have stood before the doors of the church when it was full and some demon had made Numerian,** or as some say, **Decius,** eager **to enter it,** and prevented him,

[*AP* = *Suda*] **saying that he meant to do everything in his power to keep the wolf from getting in among the flock.**[47] **The emperor at once gave up the attempt to enter, whether because he feared the crowd might riot or for some other reason. But he resented the bishop's resistance, and when he had returned to the imperial residence, he had him brought in. First he charged him with arrogance in having blocked his way, and then he ordered him to sacrifice to the demons if he wished to escape the penalty stemming from the charge. Babylas, however, defended himself against the charge and rejected the proposal. Concerning the former, he said that it behooved him as shepherd to be zealous for his flock in every way; concerning the latter, he declared that he would not choose to abandon the God who really exists and sacrifice to murderous demons who go under false names. When the emperor saw that he would not obey, he ordered him to be bound with chains and shackles and taken off to be put to death by decapitation. As he was being led off to his death, he sang the following words from the psalm: "Return, my soul, to your rest, for the Lord has been good to you."**[48]

---

47. On the image of the wolf among the flock, see John 10:11–12.

48. Eusebius of Caesarea knows the story about the emperor rebuffed at the doors of the church and about Babylas's martyrdom, but he does not connect the two (cf. *Hist. eccl.* 6.29.4; 6.34; 6.39.4). Where they are connected, the emperor in question

[*AP* 55 = *Suda*]. They say that there were also three boys, quite young, who were brothers and were being reared by him; they were themselves arrested by the emperor, it is said, and since they too refused to sacrifice, even after every method had been attempted to force them, the emperor ordered them to be beheaded as well. When they arrived at the appointed place, Babylas put them in front of him and led them to the sword first, lest any of them shrink back from death out of fear. And while they were being decapitated, he recited the words, "Here am I, and the children God has given me."[49] Then he himself offered his neck to the sword, having charged those who would gather up **his body to bury the chains and shackles with him,** "that they may adorn me," he said, "where I lie." They lie with him still, it is said.[50]

[*AP* alone]. When Eusebius told him that Babylas was preventing the idols from giving oracles, Julian at once ordered those to whom it pertained to remove him from Daphne in his coffin (made from a large stone) and transfer him somewhere else far away, wherever they wanted. The city populace at once poured forth as though to some great event, surrounded the coffin, and began pulling it. The coffin, however, acting as though it were not being drawn by human beings but moved by a higher power, anticipated the eagerness of those who drew it on by the way it followed. For that very day they brought it more than fifty stades and placed it in what is called the "cemetery."[51] That is a building in front of the city where the bodies of many of the men of old are kept, including some indeed who were martyred for the faith. It was thus to that place that they brought the coffin then.

[*AP* 56]. As for Julian, he got ready a good many sacrifices and offerings, intending to go up to Daphne with them the next day with every hope now of

---

bears the guilt of the murder of some prince who was under his protection (see John Chrysostom, *Bab. Jul.* 23–33; A7.1; *Synax.* 11.9; Simeon Metaphrastes, *Certamen* 1). See also Jerome, *Chron.* 252; *Vir. ill.* 54; 62.

49. On the three boys with Babylas, see John Chrysostom, *In Juventinum et Maximinum martyres* 578A; Theodoret, *Hist. eccl.* 3.10.2; Simeon Metaphrastes, *Certamen* 7–17; *Antonini Placentini Itinerarium* 47. Gregory of Tours (*Historia Francorum* 1.30) gives their names as Urban, Prilidan, and Epolon. On the torture and persuasion applied to them, see Simeon Metaphrastes, *Certamen* 10–13; Simeon Metaphrastes (*Certamen* 16) confirms that Babylas put the three in front of him at the place of execution as his offering to God. His quotation is from Isa 8:18 and Heb 2:13.

50. On Babylas's request to be buried in his chains, see John Chrysostom, *Bab. Jul.* 61; *Homiliae in epistulam ad Ephesios* 9.2; Simeon Metaphrastes, *Certamen* 17.

51. On the "cemetery" in Antioch, see Evagrius, *Hist. eccl.* 1.16. Babylas had been buried there, before being translated to Daphne by Julian's brother Gallus precisely in order to stifle the oracle (Sozomen 5.19.12–14; John Chrysostom, *Bab. Jul.* 93).

receiving a response, if not from the others, then at least from Apollo. For all of his intense and eager expectation was fixed upon him, since the business at hand pertained to him more than to any other, given its connection with the oracular art and the fact that the region of Daphne was sacred to him; Julian thought it likely that he would be <more> powerful in his own place than any other demon. But Eusebius and the so-called priests and the crowd of temple ministers were in great discomfiture as they awaited the emperor and labored into the night around the idol, trying everything to ensure that when he arrived he might find that it spoke, since there was no longer any excuse for delay. But when the night was far advanced, suddenly fire fell from the sky and struck the temple; it spread at once to every part of it and burned it along with the idol and the offerings.[52] With everything enveloped in flames and fire shooting up high, a great cry went up at once around the temple and a tumult like none other. Many strove to battle the flames, but no one proved equal to the challenge. Some ran to the city to inform Julian, the governor of the east, while the rest of the crowd stood dazed, looking at the unbelievable disaster that had overtaken them. Now the fire spread nowhere else, even though there was so much wood growing so thickly there; it attacked and burned down only the temple with those inside, so that the idol and all the offerings were destroyed once and for all. Only a few of the buildings' foundations were left as a record of the incident; they still show **rather clearly** the mark of the fire **sent by God.**

[*AP* 57]. Julian, when he heard the full story, was filled with anger, and thinking that it would be awful if the Christians were to make a joke of what had happened, he immediately ordered them to be expelled from the great church, which was to be rendered completely **inaccessible** to them by locking it up tight; he also ordered all of the valuables to be confiscated.[53]

He gave **the pagans permission** as well to enter the Christian churches and to do whatever they liked. Once the impious tyrant Julian had issued these orders, there was no crime so enormous that it was not committed and no words so outrageous that they were not spoken, people in every city uttering the unspeakable with unbridled tongues against the Christian faith and

---

52. On the fire, see Julian, *Misopogon* 361B; Libanius, *Or.* 60; Ammianus 22.13; John Chrysostom, *Bab. Jul.* 93–94; 114; *De laudibus sancti Pauli apostoli* 4 (492D); *Expositio in Psalmum CX* 4 (271D); Theodoret, *Hist. eccl.* 3.11.4–5; Sozomen 5.20.5–6; Theophanes 77B; Zonaras 13.12.42.

53. On the locking of the church and confiscation of its valuables, see 7.4c; Ammianus 22.13.2; John Chrysostom, *In Juventinum et Maximinum martyres* 2 (581C and E); Jerome, *Chron.* 363; Theodoret, *Hist. eccl.* 3.11.5–12.1; Sozomen 5.20.5–6; Theophanes 77B; Zonaras 13.12.43.

blaspheming against our Lord and God Jesus Christ. In Sebaste ... [continued at 7.4a].[54]

9. The Apostate thought that he would prove **false** our Savior's prophecies that Jerusalem would be so completely overthrown that not even a **stone would be left** upon a **stone**[55]; not only, however, did he not succeed in his **attempt,** but he even provided unshakeable, if involuntary, confirmation of what the prophecies contained. What he did was to gather the Jews from **wherever** they were, provide them with **funds** and other assistance from his own resources, and bid them restore the temple. But the terrors **sent by God,** which defy all description, not only snuffed their enthusiasm but reduced the Jews and him to utter helplessness and shame. What happened is that **fire devoured** those who were daring to set to work, **an earthquake buried the site,** and still other folk were cut to pieces in other accidents, so that the arrogance that had thought to bring shame upon the words of the Lord ended up by proclaiming, despite itself, how impossible it was to taint such venerable prophecies with any hint of shame.[56]

---

54. The story of the oracle and the fire in the *Artemii Passio* reveals an astonishing (and uncharacteristic) lapse of attention on Photius's part. Here the oracle not only remains mute throughout but is blasted to rubble on the very night following the removal of the martyr's body. And a comparison of Philostorgius's source (the anonymous homoean historian in A7.35) with the source that in turn drew upon him (the *Artemii Passio*) shows that this must have been the order of events in the Eunomian's own history. But Photius claims, not once but twice, that according to Philostorgius the translation of Babylas was followed by the restoration of the oracle's speech (7.8 and 7.12). He is here summarizing, not some minor notice in his source that he might have carelessly misread, nor some heterodoxical pronouncement that he might have wanted to reduce to more orthodox proportions, but one of the most extended and dramatic narratives to meet his eyes: the divine fire falling upon the pagan emperor's favorite shrine while the most exhaustive efforts were being vainly expended to make it speak and reducing to ashes this central symbol of the pagan restoration then under way. That Photius, after reading this, can claim that, according to Philostorgius, the martyr's removal actually unstopped the oracle's mouth, just as the pagan sorcerer had promised, is most remarkable.

55. See Mark 13:2; Matt 24:2; Luke 19:44; 21:6.

56. See A7.36a; Julian, *Ep.* 51.398A; *Frag. Ep.* 11 (ed. Wright, LCL, 3:300); Ammianus 23.1.2–3; Cyril, *Catecheses* 15.15; Gregory of Nazianzus, *Or.* 5.3–4, 6–7; Ambrose, *Ep.* 1a (40).12; John Chrysostom, *Adversus Judaeos* 5.11; *Bab. Jul.* 119 (ed. Schatkin, SC); Rufinus, *Hist. eccl.* 10.38–40; Socrates 3.20; Sozomen 5.22.4–14; Theodoret, *Hist. eccl.* 3.20; Theophanes 80B; Zonaras 13.12.24–25; For the modern literature, see David P. Levenson, "The Ancient and Medieval Sources for the Emperor Julian's Attempt to Rebuild the Jerusalem Temple," *JSJ* 35 (2004): 409–60. The ancient Jewish sources do not explicitly mention the project. The other ancient

9a [*AP* 58]. Julian himself … gave orders for the restoration of the temple of the Jews in Jerusalem as well. He put the Christians out of the city and allowed the Jews to settle there, sending one Alypius to carry out zealously the work of rebuilding the temple.[57]

[*AP* 68]. As we said earlier, Julian the Apostate sent orders to Jerusalem to rebuild the temple of the Jews that Vespasian and his son Titus had destroyed and burned together with the city, just as Christ the Lord had foretold concerning it to his disciples, bearers of God's word: "Not a **stone will remain** upon a **stone** that will not be thrown down." The wicked man, then, in his desire to show that Christ's words were **false,** was above all **anxious** to rebuild the temple, and he ordered that the total cost of construction be paid **from public funds.** The God-killing Jews flocked together therefore and **set to work** with **great** joy and **were excavating** the foundation trench **with silver mattocks** and shovels and making ready **to lay** the **foundations,** when a terrific **storm** arose that **buried** the excavation site.[58] All during that night it lightened and thundered ceaselessly, until finally as day was approaching there was an **earthquake** in which many perished even of those who had stayed out of doors. And a **fire** that came **out of the excavated foundations** incinerated everyone who was there. There were also cities that collapsed, Nicopolis, Neapolis, Eleutheropolis, Gaza, and many others. Not only that, but the **colonnade** by the Jewish synagogue in **Aelia,** that is to say, Jerusalem, **fell down,** killing many of those mentioned earlier, and fire burst forth mysteriously and incinerated a great many Jews. Darkness also fell upon these places, while continuous earthquakes caused great damage in many cities.

10. Many of those who **raged** against the Christians and the faith **got their** just **deserts,** the clearest and most obvious example being Julian, the **governor of the east,** who was the uncle of Julian the Apostate on his mother's side, along with Felix, the state **treasurer,** and Elpidius, the chief of the imperial household (in the language of the Romans they are called *comites privatarum*).[59] These three were among those who **had denied** the **faith** in order to win the **emperor's favor.**

---

sources suggest that the work, part of Julian's restoration of old temples, had to be abandoned almost as soon as begun, because of natural disasters.

57. On Alypius of Antioch, see A7.36a.4; Ammianus 23.1.2; Rufinus, *Hist. eccl.* 10.38; *PLRE* 1:46–47.

58. The silver tools were used because of the prohibition against the use of iron in dressing the stones for the altar (Deut 27:5).

59. Philostorgius's fondness for dramatic deaths is well displayed in this section (see also 3.15 and 8.12). His history in fact brims over with cautionary catastrophes, very much in line with both the Jewish and the pagan traditions from which Chris-

In Felix's case, the largest of his inner blood-vessels burst for no apparent reason, sending blood spurting from his mouth and making him a horrible sight for onlookers. He did not last for even a day, but late in the evening, when his blood was gone, he sent forth his soul as well.

As for Julian, he was stricken by a painful and mysterious illness and lay flat for forty whole days, speechless and unconscious. Then, rallying a little, he bitterly denounced his own criminal arrogance, aware that he was now paying the penalty for it. And thus, having survived long enough to testify to his own wickedness and being afflicted with lesions of every sort in his stomach, he was torn apart from his own soul at last.

Elpidius, for his part, was found to have taken part in the usurpation of Procopius, who rebelled against Valens, even though he was caught later than the others; stripped of his property, he ended his days in prison, living in ignominy, detested by everyone, and known by the surname "Elpidius the sacrificer."

And someone else went with those just mentioned into the church that they were looting, carrying away the offerings, plundering the valuables, and thus insulting the one who was worshiped in them; what he did was to pull up his clothes and lewdly urinate on the altar.[60] But he immediately paid a heavy and grievous price, for the members by which he had offered the insult rotted away right into his innards, producing an unspeakable swarm of worms, and so he ended his life in a misery that is quite beyond description. And that is not all, for others who dared similar deeds paid penalties as great.

11. The Roman emperor Hadrian, surnamed Aelius, renamed Jerusalem **Aelia** after himself in order to separate and sever the Jewish people from it completely and ensure that not even its name would offer them an occasion to claim it as their native city.[61] For he feared their hotheadedness and reck-

---

tian historiography borrowed. Ghastly deaths from corruption and worms were regarded as a special punishment for godlessness; there are full references in Jacques Moreau, ed., *Lactantius: De la mort des persécuteurs* (SC 39; Paris: Cerf, 1954), 60–64. On the deaths of Felix and Julian, see A7.35; on Heron and Theotecnus, A7.36, 36a.1. Felix was *comes sacrarum largitionum* in 362; Julian had converted him to paganism (Libanius, *Or.* 14.36; cf. *PLRE* 1:332). Elpidius (Helpidius) was *comes rei privatae* in 362–363 (*PLRE* 1:415). Theodoret, *Hist. eccl.* 3.12.2–13.5, is close to Philostorgius. Ammianus confirms Felix's sudden death by hemorrhage: "Felice enim largitionum comite profluvio sanguinis repente extincto" (23.1.5). John Chrysostom likewise in *Expositio in Psalmum CX* 4 (271E); *Bab. Jul.* 92 (ed. Schatkin, SC).

60. Theodoret (*Hist. eccl.* 3.12.3) identifies Julian as the one who had desecrated the altar.

61. Hadrian emptied Jerusalem of its Jewish residents after the second Jewish-

lessness, thinking that, once assembled in the city on the pretext of offering worship, they might cause the Romans trouble.

12. He says that once the relics of the martyr Babylas had been translated, the pagan oracles, beginning with the one in Daphne, started giving predictions and responses, divine providence allowing them to speak but turning to utter shame the eagerness to honor them shown by their devotees. For the very means by which the pagans sought to make the demons prophesy, that they might exalt them the more, were the means by which divine providence forced them to show how powerless and erroneous they were, since it became quite clear that the oracles they produced were false and ineffectual. Thus when all the oracles together, each in turn, predicted that Julian, the emperor's uncle, would not die of his illness, at the very moment the prophecies were being read, the pitiful man died a wretched death.

13. He says that someone named Heron, from Thebes in Egypt, who ended up a bishop and then went over to paganism, was immediately attacked by a putrefying disease that consumed his entire body, making him a horror to everyone. With nowhere to turn, he lay in the streets receiving compassion from no one, since the Christians shunned him completely, while the pagans' fellowship extended only as far as their subjection of him to error. Heron thus died a bitter and utterly wretched death. There was someone else named Theotecnus who went over to paganism; all of his flesh suddenly rotted and became infested with worms, which consumed even his eyes. As he was dying he went mad and devoured his own tongue, and so he passed from bitter torments to punishments far heavier yet. God brought about many such wonders, exacting condign penalties from those who gave themselves to reckless impiety.

14. He says that when Julian ordered Jerusalem to be rebuilt so that he could **show** that the **Lord's predictions** about it were without effect, he brought about just the opposite to what he had intended. For in addition to the other extraordinary portents that fell upon his work and attacked it, there was the following. When the foundations were being made ready, one of the stones that were at the bottom of the basement was moved aside and revealed the entrance to a cavern built into the rock. As it was impossible to see what was inside because of the depth, those in charge of the work, wanting to know what was there, tied one of the workmen to a long rope and let him down. When he reached bottom, he found water standing knee-high in the cavern. Going all around feeling the walls, he discovered that the cavern was rectangular, but when he turned back and made his way to the center, he came upon

---

Roman war of 132–135; see Cassius Dio 69.12.1; Eusebius, *Hist. eccl.* 4.6.3–4; John Chrysostom, *Adversus Judaeos* 5.11 (645D).

a pillar sticking up slightly above the water. Putting his hand out to it, he found a book lying on it wrapped in the finest and purest sort of linen. Picking up the book just as he found it, he signaled the others to lift him up.

When he was back up, he showed them the book, which amazed everyone, especially because it appeared to be newly made and untouched and because it had been found in that place. Now the book, when opened at the very beginning, had the following in large letters (and this astonished the pagans and Jews even more): "In the beginning was the Word, and the Word was with God, and the Word was God."[62] In sum, the writing contained the entire Gospel proclaimed by the tongue of the virgin discile in speaking about God. It showed in fact, together with the other marvelous works displayed from heaven at that time, that the Lord's prediction about the temple remaining forever deserted would never prove false. For the book taught divinely that the one who foretold these things is God and the Maker of all things and thus proved that their work of construction was in vain, the divine and irrevocable decree having ordained that the destruction of the temple would be forever.[63]

Jerusalem was formerly called Jebus and was inhabited by members of the tribe of Benjamin until King David used Joab to capture it **by promising him high command.** He kept his promise to him when he received it, and he built a city in it that he made the capital of the entire Hebrew people.[64]

15. The Apostate, persuaded by the pagan oracles everywhere that his power would be invincible, set out on campaign against the Persians.[65] Now there was an **old man** who had left the Persian army, having been dismissed from it. He went after the Apostate on his march into Persia and got him trapped in remote wastelands and hopeless circumstances, in which most of

---

62. The quotation from the book found in the cavern is from John 1:1.

63. The "divine decree" is a reference to Dan 9:27; Mark 13:14; Matt 24:15; Luke 21:20.

64. Jebus, the earlier name for Jerusalem, is in Josh 15:8; 18:28; Judg 19:10–11; 1 Chr 11:4. On the Benjaminites as its inhabitants, see Josh 18:28; Judg 1:21; Eusebius, *Onomasticon* 106.3–5. On its capture by Joab and the promise David made to him, see 1 Chr 11:4–6; on David building the city, 1 Chr 11:8; Josephus, *Ant.* 7.63–68.

65. On Julian's Persian campaign, see A7.37–38a. He did a lot of questioning of oracles about it (Ammianus 22.12.7), many of which were favorable: Theophanes 81B; Eunapius, *Frag. hist.* 27; Gregory of Nazianzus, *Or.* 5.9, 25; Socrates 3.21.6; Theodoret, *Hist. eccl.* 3.21.1–4. There were also unfavorable ones: Ammianus 23.1.5–7; 23.2.6–8; 23.5.5; 23.5.10–14; *Epit. Caes.* 43.8; Malalas 13.19. On his disregarding the latter, see Marcel Meulder, "Julien l'Apostat contre les Parthes: un guerrier impie," *Byzantion* 61 (1991): 458–95.

the people perished, and thus rendered the soldiers a ready prey for his coun-trymen.[66]

The Persians drove against them, bringing with them their old allies, the Saracen lancers,[67] one of whom stretched out his **spear** toward Julian and **struck** him mightily in the abdomen. When he pulled out the point, excre-ment followed, drawn out along with blood. Then one of the bodyguards came up and lopped off the head of the **Saracen** who had struck him. Julian, **mortally** wounded, was quickly hoisted onto a shield by his staff and taken to his tent. And because the blow had been struck so suddenly, in an instant, and no one knew from where, it was commonly thought that the deed had been done by his own men.

As for the wretched Julian, **he took the blood** from his wound **in his hands and flung it** toward the sun, **saying** clearly to it, "Take your fill!"[68] Indeed, **he called** the other **gods** evil and murderous as well.

He was attended by the best of doctors, Oribasius, the Lydian from Sardis.[69] But the wound defied all attempts at healing, and in three days Julian departed from life, having worn the Caesar's robe for five years and the diadem after Constantius's death for two and a half years.[70]

Now our author says that he **flung his blood** at the sun and his reproaches **at his gods,** but most historians write that he hurled both at **our Lord Jesus Christ**, the true God.

15a [*AP* 69]. Julian departed from Antioch with his entire army and made his way to the land of Persia. And having captured the city of Ctesiphon, he decided to proceed from **that one great** deed to others greater still. But the utterly abominable man did not realize how deluded he was. For he had con-

---

66. On the old fugitive who leads Julian astray, see Festus, *Brev.* 28; Jerome, *Chron.* 363; Gregory of Nazianzus, *Or.* 5.11–12; Socrates 3.22.9; Sozomen 6.1.10–12; Malalas 13.22. John Chrysostom, without mentioning the Persian fugitive, speaks of the impassible terrain into which Julian got (*Bab. Jul.* 122 [ed. Schatkin, SC]).

67. On the Saracens as Persian allies in this battle, see Ammianus 25.1.3.

68. On Julian's cry, see Eunapius, *Frag. hist.* 24; 26; Sozomen 6.2.11; Malalas 13.23; *Chron. pasch.* P298B; Zonaras 13.13.30.

69. On Oribasius, see 7.1c; Eunapius, *Vit. soph.* 498–499; Lydus, *De mensibus* 4.118. He had helped Julian against Constantius (*Vit. soph.* 476); Julian's *Ep.* 4 (ed. Wright, LCL) is addressed to him; see also *Ep. ad Ath.* 277C.

70. On Julian's death (26 June 363), see Ammianus 25.3; Libanius, *Or.* 1.133; 18.268–269; 24.6; Gregory of Nazianzus, *Or.* 5.13; Rufinus, *Hist. eccl.* 10.37; Sozomen 6.1.13; Theodoret, *Hist. eccl.* 3.25.5–6; Zosimus 3.29.1; Lydus, *De mensibus* 4.118. For commentary, see Paschoud, *Zosime*, 2:203–8. On the rumor that he had been struck down by one of his own men, see Ammianus 25.6.6; Socrates 3.21.13; Sozomen 6.1.14. On the length of Julian's reign, see Socrates 3.21.18; Zonaras 13.13.22.

ceived a diabolical desire for idolatry and hoped that through his godless gods he would have a long reign, become a new Alexander,[71] get the better of the Persians, and wipe out the race and **name** of Christians for good, but he failed of his overweening purpose. For he met an **old** Persian who fooled him into thinking that he could take over the Persian kingdom and all its wealth without effort and who **brought** him with his whole army to the Carmanian Desert and into trackless lands, crevasses, **wastelands,** and **waterless places.** And when he had **worn** them **down with thirst and hunger** and killed off all their horses, the Persian **admitted** that he had led them astray on purpose in order to see that they perished and to keep his homeland from being ravaged by its bitterest foes. They chopped him up limb from limb on the spot and so put him to death, but then, as if they were not in enough **trouble,** they stumbled upon the Persian army without looking for it, a battle ensued, and Julian himself, while running **hither and yon** and **giving orders,** collided **with a spear,** one belonging to a soldier, some say. Others say it belonged to one of the **Saracens** with the Persians. But the Christian account, the true one, is ours as well: that it was Christ the Lord who was ranged against him. For a bent bow appeared suddenly from the air, and an arrow was loosed at him as at a target and, driving through his flanks, pierced clear **through his abdomen.**[72]

He **wailed** loudly and woefully, and he thought he saw **our Lord Jesus Christ** standing before him and laughing at him. Filled with darkness and madness, **he took** his own **blood in his hand** and **flung** it into the air, and about to expire, he cried aloud, "You have won, Christ! Have your fill, Galilean!" And thus he died a frightful, horrid death, reviling **at length his gods** as he departed from life.

---

71. On Julian as a new Alexander, see 7.4c; Libanius, *Or.* 18.260; Socrates 3.21.7; C. Franco, "L'immagine di Alessandro in Giuliano imperatore," *Studi classici e orientali* 46 (1997): 637–58. Julian was often compared to Alexander, a tradition that of course Philostorgius found particularly portentous (see introduction). Julian himself seems to have regarded Marcus Aurelius as the best model, even if Alexander exemplified military talent and Hellenic culture.

72. On the bent bow appearing in the air, see Socrates 3.21.4; Callistus, who accompanied Julian, wrote that he was struck down by a demon (ὑπὸ δαίμονος). On Christ's appearance to him, see Sozomen 6.2.10; Theodoret, *Hist. eccl.* 3.25.7; *AASS* Octobris X 45.

BOOK 8

1. On the day after the death of the Apostate, the army appointed Jovian emperor. He made **a thirty-year treaty with Persia** (since there was no other way **to be saved,** the entire army having been reduced to a tenth of itself[1]), in which **he ceded to it Nisibis and the fortresses** that the Romans had erected like a wall against the Persians as far as Armenia.[2]

Merobaudes and those with him brought Julian's body to Cilicia and buried him, not designedly but just by chance, opposite the grave that held the bones of Maximinus; their sepulchers were separated from one another only by a highway.[3]

1a [AP 70]. When the transgressor had fallen in the battle-ground between the armies, Jovian was proclaimed emperor by the camp. He made a peace **treaty with Persia,** handed over Nisibis **without** its inhabitants to the Persians, and departed from there, for the army was perishing from famine and disease.

2.[4] He says that while Euzoius and his circle did publish the document on behalf of Aetius and his teaching, they did not carry out what it entailed.

---

1. The statement that the Roman army had been reduced to a tenth of itself is contradicted by Ammianus 25.7.2, who describes it as "not much smaller" than when it had invaded (but see Lydus, *De mensibus* 4.118). It was famished, however (Ammianus 25.7.4).

2. On Jovian's accession and his deeply controversial treaty with Persia, see A7.39, 39a, b; Ammianus 25.5–9; Libanius, *Or.* 18.276–280; 24.8; Themistius, *Or.* 5.65a–66a; Gregory of Nazianzus, *Or.* 5.15–17; Festus, *Brev.* 29; Eutropius 10.17; Jerome, *Chron.* 364; John Chrysostom, *Bab. Jul.* 123 (ed. Schatkin, SC); Rufinus, *Hist. eccl.* 11.1; Zosimus 3.30–34; Theodoret, *Hist. eccl.* 4.1.1–2.3; Socrates 3.22.1–7; Sozomen 6.3.1–2.

3. On Flavius Merobaudes, see Timothy D. Barnes, "Patricii under Valentinian III," *Phoenix* 29 (1975): 155–70, esp. 159–62. Julian was buried outside Tarsus (Libanius, *Or.* 18.306; Ammianus 23.2.5; 25.9.12–13; 25.10.5; Zosimus 3.34.4). Maximinus Caesar had died in Tarsus (Eutropius 10.4.4; Aurelius Victor 41.1; *Epit. Caes.* 40.8).

4. 8.2–4 resumes the story of Eunomian affairs from 7.5–6; see 95 n. 28. There we find the work of Euzoius's council, which met to rehabilitate Aetius, interrupted by the persecution of Christians following the destruction of Apollo's shrine. Kopecek

So Aetius and Eunomius and company, who were in Constantinople, took matters at last into their own hands and arranged everything as they thought best, including the appointment of bishops.[5] Among them were Candidus and Arrian, who were put in charge of the churches in Lydia and Ionia, while Theodulus from Cheretapa became bishop of Palestine.[6] As for Constantinople (for a not inconsiderable multitude that had defected from Eudoxius and from some other sects had swelled the party of Aetius and Eunomius), they first ordained someone named Poemenius for their church there. That was what turned Eudoxius, who until then had cherished hopes of unification with them, into their decided adversary. And when Poemenius died shortly after, they ordained Florentius in his stead. They also ordained Thallus for Lesbos when its shepherd departed from life. They appointed Euphronius for Galatia-by-Pontus[7] and for Cappadocia, and Julian for Cilicia. But as for Antioch in Coele Syria, Theophilus the Indian arrived there on his own shortly after with a view chiefly to inciting Euzoius to carry out the decisions made about Aetius, but if he failed, then to lead those of the people there who embraced his doctrine. As for the two Libyas and those in Egypt who held to their views, they were entrusted to Serras, Stephen, Heliodorus, and company.

Philostorgius never tires of heaping praise upon all of these, proclaiming their eloquence and extolling their lives.

3. He mentions one of the bishops, Theodosius,[8] who was a fervent supporter of his sect, saying that he went off <after> the pleasures to be had from women and added other heretical ideas to the original doctrine, among which was that, while Christ was changeable in his own nature, he was raised to

---

(*History of Neo-Arianism*, 417–18) also conjectures that Euzoius was just as happy not to have to take the matter further, since Meletius had returned to Antioch in 362 as part of Julian's general amnesty of bishops and could have taken advantage of any support he showed for Aetius to strengthen his own position.

5. Vaggione (*Eunomius of Cyzicus,* 278 n. 104) places the ordinations in 8.2 in the winter or early spring of 362; they did not have Eudoxius's approval.

6. On Theodulus, deposed at the Council of Constantinople of 360, see Athanasius, *Syn.* 12.2, 5; Socrates 2.40.43.

7. Reference is made to "Galatia-by-Pontus" to distinguish it from the "Galatia" that is synonymous with "Gaul."

8. The Theodosius in 8.3 is he of Philadelphia in Lydia, also deposed at the council above; see Athanasius, *Syn.* 12.2, 5; Epiphanius, *Pan.* 73.26.5 (he subscribed the homoean creed at the Council of Seleucia); Socrates 2.40.43; Sulpicius Severus, *Chronicorum Libri duo* 2.42.6. His "view of Christ's changeability was fully in line with the position of early Arianism, [but] contradicted the Neo-Arian view" (Kopecek, *History of Neo-Arianism,* 420).

the state of immutability by his supreme cultivation of the virtues. He added that the deity neither speaks nor hears, for otherwise hands and ears would have to be made for him.[9] And, says our author, he made other such heretical statements.

4. Aetius came to Lydia to install Candidus and Arrian in the churches.[10] Now Theodosius, just mentioned, fearing that the lives of those men would be the condemnation of his own, began to feel hostile toward Aetius, even though he had previously refused to put his subscription to the document drafted against him. He made common cause with Phobus[11] (who was also one of those who had not chosen to condemn Aetius, and their long acquaintance and identically depraved styles of life had made them friends as well), and they in turn associated themselves with Auxidianus (who was a bishop just as they were) and plotted against Aetius and Candidus and company. They also gathered six other bishops, held a synod, and sent a letter with their unanimous approval to Eudoxius, Maris, and company.

The letter charged Aetius with unlawful ordination, especially since following his deposition from the diaconate he had jumped from his state of degradation to an even higher rank, even though those who had deposed him had not revoked their decree. It also rejected the ordination in Candidus's case as illegally performed without their common consent and said the same of the other ordinations carried out by Aetius and company.

Eudoxius was glad to receive the letter, and as for the oaths he had sworn to Eunomius, the letters to Euzoius, and his many and various promises, he paid no mind to any of them. He wrote instead to Theodosius and company to urge them to action, although he suggested they proceed against those who had performed the ordinations rather than those who had received them.[12]

5. The emperor Jovian restored the **churches** to their original good order, removing from them all the mistreatment to which the Apostate had subjected them. He also recalled those whom the latter had banished when they

---

9. Even granted the Mediterranean fondness for gesture with speech, "hands" (χεῖρες) hardly suits the argument, and one may suppose that χείλη ("lips"), or one of its inflections, was what was originally written.

10. Brennecke places the ordinations in 8.4 in Julian's time (*Studien zur Geschichte der Homöer,* 113 n. 24); Vaggione (*Eunomius of Cyzicus,* 281) thinks they may have taken place in the spring of 364. Philostorgius himself seems to have placed them after Julian's death, when the Eunomians lost their powerful patron and their opponents would have felt freer to express their hostility.

11. The "Phobus" here is probably Phoebus of Polychalandus; see Athanasius, *Syn.* 12.5; Epiphanius, *Pan.* 73.26.5; Socrates 2.40.45.

12. For Aetius's ordination, see 7.6. The reason for Eudoxius's hostility to the Eunomians is found in 8.2.

had not given up the faith, among them Valentinian, who was brought back from Thebes in Egypt.[13]

6. He says that Candidus and Arrian and company, being relatives of the emperor, went to visit him in Edessa and hindered Athanasius in his efforts to win the emperor over. The emperor, however, reserved the claims made by both parties for a common court of inquiry without giving a clear decision in favor of either side for the moment.[14]

6a [*AP* 70]. When [Jovian] arrived on Roman soil, he joined the sect of the Anomoeans or Eunomians.[15]

7. Eudoxius wrote to Euzoius against Candidus and Arrian. Euzoius was grieved and wrote back to him in association with Elpidius to criticize what had been decided and to urge rather that he refrain from involvement in that sort of resolution; at the same time he complained mildly about the long delay in carrying out the agreements made with Eunomius on Aetius's behalf.

8. The emperor Jovian set out for Constantinople, and **when he arrived** in **Ancyra** he gave one of his two sons, Varronian, who was quite young, the title *epiphanestatos* (in the language of the Romans this is *nobilissimus*). **From there** he went on with the army, with the severest sort of **winter weather** setting in. Many perished along the way, but he reached **Dadastana** with the rest.[16] **Turning aside at some way station** he took food and then lay down to sleep **in a house** that had just been **plastered**. A fire **having been lit** to **warm** the house, **dampness began to be given off** from the **freshly-coated walls.** It gradually crept in through his nostrils, stopped up

---

13. On Jovian's restoration of church allowances, see A7.40, 7.40a; Athanasius, *HA* 12; Rufinus, *Hist. eccl.* 11.1; Theodoret, *Hist. eccl.* 4.4; Sozomen 6.3.4–6; Malalas 13.27; John of Nikiu, *Chronicle* 81.3. Julian's banishment of Valentinian to Thebes is in 7.7; his recall in Sozomen 6.6.7.

14. Athanasius came off rather better than Philostorgius suggests in his meeting with Jovian, to whose side he made all speed as soon as he heard of Julian's death (Athanasius, *HA* 12; *Festal Index* 35; appendix to *Ep.* 56). On the sectarian petitions to Jovian, see Socrates 3.25.1–6. It is true that the emperor made no decisions about the Macedonians (3.25.4), but he showed clearly the esteem in which he held Meletius (3.25.8), and that of course put great pressure on the latter's rival in Antioch, Euzoius, whose attempt to distance himself from Eudoxius's measures against the new Eunomian bishops is recorded in 8.7; "the Neo-Arians were [Euzoius's] mainstay ... in Antioch; he could not very well alienate them" (Kopecek, *History of Neo-Arianism*, 422).

15. In 8.6a, "When ... arrived" translates ἐλθὼν δὲ αὐτός; see Bidez, *Philostorgius*, 353.

16. The phrase "he reached Dadastana with the rest" translates μετὰ τῶν ὑπολειφθέντων instead of μετὰ τοὺς ὑπολειφθέντας, "after the rest."

his respiratory passages, and **caused** the emperor **to choke** to death; he had reigned for nearly ten months.[17]

His body was brought to Constantinople, while the army arrived in **Nicaea** and there **proclaimed** Valentinian emperor when twelve **days** had passed. It was Datian the patrician who suggested the move in a letter from Galatia (he had been left there because of his age and the severity of the weather); he was joined in this action by the prefect Secundus, the general Arinthaeus, and Dagalaifus (the chief of the *domestici*).[18]

When the army **requested** the emperor, as he was being carried upon his shield during his proclamation, **to take a partner** in **government,** he motioned it to silence with his hand, and with a calm and regal air he said, "It was your vote that was the authority that made me, a private citizen, emperor, but henceforth **the consideration** and execution of **what is to be done** rests not with the subjects but with the ruler."[19]

Proceeding on to Constantinople, **he made his brother** Valens his **partner in government.** He took him along as far as Sirmium and then he set out for the west. While in Sirmium he divided with him the paraphernalia of government designed to dignify the ruler and provide him with services and attendance, and then he sent him off to Constantinople, entrusting to him

---

17. On Jovian's death, see A7.41, 41a; *Consul. const.* 364; Ammianus 25.10; Zosimus 3.35.4; Eutropius 10.17.3–18.2; *Epit. Caes.* 44.4; Jerome, *Chron.* 364; Socrates 3.26; Sozomen 6.6.1; Theodoret, *Hist. eccl.* 4.5. Philostorgius reports the common rumor of suffocation. Ammianus says the cause is unknown, although he mentions the rumor as one possibility (25.10.12–13). It was also said that he was poisoned (John Chrysostom, *Homiliae in epistulam ad Philippenses* 4.15.5 [PG 62:295]; Cedrenus 309A; Zonaras 13.14.10–13). He died on 17 February 364.

18. On Datian, see *PLRE* 1:243–44. Long a valued adviser to Constantius II, he was consul in 358 and patrician before 360. Saturninus Secundus Salutius was praetorian prefect of the east 361–365 and 365–367 (*PLRE* 1:814–17). Flavius Arinthaeus was a tribune in 355 and perhaps *comes rei militaris* in 363–364; he was a cavalry commander on Julian's Persian expedition (*PLRE* 1:102–3). Dagalaifus was *comes domesticorum* 361–363; Jovian promoted him to *magister equitum* 363–364. Philostorgius incorrectly gives his office at the time of Jovian's death (*PLRE* 1:239). On Valentinian's proclamation as emperor on 26 February 364, see Socrates 4.1.1–4; Zosimus 3.36. The importance of Secundus's part is suggested by *Chron. pasch.* P300C–D, P301A, and Malalas 13.28. See also Ammianus 26.4.3; *Consul. const.* 364; *Epit. Caes.* 45.3; Zonaras 13.14.14–18; 13.15.1–3; *Comp. chron.* 58.15–18.

19. Philostorgius's version of Valentinian's reply to the request for a co-ruler is echoed in Sozomen 6.6.8 and Theodoret, *Hist. eccl.* 4.6.2. Ammianus's version, in 26.2.6–10, is rather different: he asks for patience while he considers his choice. It fell upon the one Dagalaifus feared it might (26.4.1–3).

that part of the east that Constantius had ruled; he himself chose the other two parts in the west and ruled the entire Occident.[20] Not long afterwards he advanced his son Gratian, still a youth, to imperial office and formed him in his own ways.[21]

8a [*AP* 70]. **When he arrived in** the province of **Galatia**, there in **Dadastana, in some** district with that name, he died **suddenly.**

The people had no ruler for forty **days,**[22] until they arrived in **Nicaea** and **proclaimed** Valentinian [emperor]. Valentinian in turn proclaimed **his** own **brother** emperor on **25 February,** thirty-two days after he had begun to reign.

The bishops of the pure and orthodox faith met Valentinian, accordingly, and asked that a council be held.[23] He replied, "To me God has subjected

---

20. On the division of the realm between the brothers, see Ammianus 26.5.1–5; Zosimus 4.3.1; Paschoud, *Zosime,* 2:335–36. Valentinian gave Valens the prefecture of the east, retaining for himself Illyricum, Italy, Africa, and Gaul.

21. Gratian was proclaimed Augustus on 24 August 367 at Amiens; he was a little over eight years old. See A7.42, 42a; *Epit. Caes.* 45.4; Ammianus 27.6.4–15; Zosimus 4.12.2; Zonaras 13.15.8; *Comp. chron.* 58.18–20.

22. Compare the length of the interregnum in 8.8 and 8.8a: twelve days versus forty, respectively. The former figure is, of course, the right one. Valens was actually proclaimed on 28 March.

23. On the bishops' meeting with the emperor, and the subsequent Council of Lampsacus in 364 or 365, see Socrates 4.2.2–4; 4.4.1–3; Sozomen 6.7.1–10; Carl J. Hefele and Henri Leclercq, *Histoire des conciles d'après les documents originaux* (8 vols.; Paris: Letouzey, 1907–52), 1:974. Sozomen's version of Valentinian's answer is quite close to Philostorgius's (Socrates says the bishops approached Valens) and accurately reflects the emperor's church policy; cf. Ambrose, *Ep.* 75 [21] 2, 5. But the text of 8.8a, after his reply, is unsound. The words, "He said … corrupt" may have originally been a marginal notation. The name "Valens" further down may likewise have been absent from the original text, and "not long afterwards" (οὐ μετ' οὐ πολύ) is also suspicious (Kotter omits them in his edition, *Opera homiletica et hagiographica* [vol. 5 of *Die Schriften des Johannes von Damaskos*; PTS 29; Berlin: de Gruyter, 1988]). On the textual problems, see Bidez, *Philostorgius,* 110 and 353–54.

The Council of Lampsacus, in contrast to the confused report in 8.8a, annulled the decrees of the the Council of Constantinople of 360, endorsed the Creed of the Dedication Council of Antioch and the doctrine of the similarity in substance of the Son to the Father, and deposed Eudoxius and Acacius. Its members then asked Valens to confirm their measures, but he revered Eudoxius and announced that he required the bishops of his realm to be in communion with him; thus he effectively reestablished the homoean creed. The strange report of the alliance of Eudoxius and the Eunomians at the end of 8.8a is a further mark of the confusion of this section; one notices the contrast with 9.3–4.

the things of the world, while to you the churches. I therefore have nothing to do with the latter. Hold a council, then, wherever you wish." He said this, then, while he was still of orthodox views and not yet corrupt. The bishops gathered in Lampsacus (a city of the Hellespont) and drafted a summary of the orthodox doctrines of the faith. And setting out the creed of the martyr Lucian, they condemned the doctrine of "unlike."[24] They subscribed the creed published by the holy fathers in Nicaea and sent it to all the churches. But when the emperor Valens was drawn into the anomoean sect almost immediately afterwards, the bishops once again began to be harried and banished; Eudoxius along with Aetius, Eunomius, and the other sectarians representing the anomoean doctrine were behind this.

9. He says that Hypatia, Theon's daughter, practiced the **sciences** under her father's direction but became much better than her teacher, **especially at star-gazing,** and instructed many people in the sciences. Our heretic also says that during the reign of Theodosius the Younger the woman was **torn to pieces** by those championing the consubstantialist doctrine.[25]

? 9a [*Suda*, Υ 166 Hypatia]. She **was torn apart** by the Alexandrians and her body mocked and scattered throughout the whole city. She suffered this, some say, at the hands of Cyril because of envy of her superb expertise, **especially in astronomy.**

10. He records that it was in the reign of Valens and Valentinian that Philostorgius lived; he was supreme among physicians, and his sons were Philagrius and Posidonius.[26] He says he saw Posidonius, who was outstanding in the field of medicine. He adds, though, that he was unsound in maintaining that it is not demonic attack that makes people mad but that their disease is due to an unhealthy mixture of certain humors. For the power of demons, he

---

24. On Lucian, see the last two paragraphs of 32 n. 43. On his "creed," see Bardy, *Recherches sur Lucien d'Antioche*, 85–132.

25. On Hypatia, see the letters of Synesius of Cyrene addressed to or referring to her: listed in Antonio Garzya and Denis Roques, eds., *Synésios de Cyrène: Correspondance* (3 vols.; Collection des universités de France 397; Paris: Belles Lettres, 2000), 3:446; Socrates 7.15; Malalas 14.12; *Palatine Anthology* 9.400; Maria Dzielska, *Hypatia of Alexandria* (trans. F. Lyra; Cambridge: Harvard University Press, 1995), 111–17. The mob who lynched her in March of 415 was apparently not motivated by pro-Nicene fervor but by resentment of her friendship with the prefect Orestes and the suspicion that she was encouraging his resistance to "Cyril's attempts to encroach upon the sovereignty of the civil power" (104). The rumors that she was a sorceress working against Cyril were spread to justify the murder.

26. Nothing more is known about the physician Philostorgius than what our author says here.

said, in no way threatens human beings.[27] He also says that Magnus in Alexandria gained a good reputation in practicing the same art.[28]

11. Our heretic, however unintentionally, expresses admiration for the wisdom of Basil the Great and Gregory the theologian.[29] He calls Nazianzus "Nadiandus." As for Apollinaris of Laodicea, he prefers him to the other two **when it comes to** knowledge of **sacred scripture.** But he says that Basil **was more brilliant** than Apollinaris. **In comparison to the other two, however, the rhythm of Gregory's discourse was better suited to composition, and it could be said that his style was more powerful than Apollinaris's and more deliberate than Basil's.**

11a [*Suda*, A 3397 Apollinaris of Laodicea; B 150; Γ 450]. Philostorgius too mentions Apollinaris in his history, writing as follows.

Apollinaris flourished at that time in Laodicea in Syria, as did Basil in Caesarea in Cappadocia and Gregory in **Nadiandus,** which is a way station in that very same Cappadocia. These three men championed the consubstantialist doctrine at that time in opposition to that of "other in substance" and were so far superior to all the other leaders of that sect before and after until my own time that Athanasius must be reckoned a child in comparison to them. For they achieved perfect mastery of what are called the external disciplines and had a deep acquaintance with the sacred scriptures, being able both to read them and to cite them easily from memory, especially Apollinaris, who even knew Hebrew. Not only that, but each of them was quite a good writer in his own way; Apollinaris **was** by far **the best at the style suited to commentary,** while Basil **was most brilliant in panegyric. In comparison to the other two, however, the rhythm of Gregory's discourses was better suited to composition, and it could be said that his style was more powerful than Apollinaris's and more deliberate than Basil's.** As great as was their talent in speaking and writing, however, the people who saw these men found their personalities equally attractive. Thus the occasions on which they were seen and spoke, and the things they published in writing, all became the means by which they drew into fellowship with themselves those able to be caught more readily for whatever personal reason.

Thus writes Philostorgius the Arian about these men, in a cursory way.

11b [Nicetas, *Thes.* 5.38]. The heretic Philostorgius too, in the eighth book of his history, while praising this most heretical Eunomius, says that

---

27. On Posidonius's opposition to the theory that mental disturbances are caused by demons, see Aëtius of Amida, *Iatrica* 6.12.

28. On Magnus, see Eunapius, *Vit. soph.* 497–498; *Palatine Anthology* 11.281; Libanius, *Ep.* 147 (written in 388).

29. On the appreciations offered in 8.11, see Photius, *Bibliotheca* codex 137.

Apollinaris **was the best at the style suited to commentary,** while Basil **was most illustrious** only **for his oratory. In comparison to the other two in both areas, however, the rhythm of Gregory's discourses was better suited to composition, and it could be said that his style was more powerful than Apollinaris's and more deliberate than Basil's.**

11c [Psellus, *Logos pros Pothon* 6]. And even if someone named Philostorgius numbered [Gregory of Nazianzus] among the greats, saying that the **rhythm** of his **discourses** was **better** than the others', I took no pleasure at all in his saying so.[30]

12. He says that not only Basil the Great but Apollinaris too wrote in opposition to Eunomius's *Apologia.* Then when Eunomius in turn took on Basil **in five books** and the latter read the first one, **he became so dejected that he died.**[31] This is how much our author prefers falsehood to truth.

12a [Nicetas, *Thes.* 5.38]. Apollinaris and Basil both wrote in refutation of the *Apologia* that Eunomius had published. Gregory, however, (and this is the clearest sign of his intelligence) realized how modest his ability was in comparison to the other and held his peace, contenting himself with the refutation of some of Eunomius's propositions in his work *On the Son* in the guise of a rebuttal of the anomoeans.[32] As for Eunomius, he did not consider Apollinaris worth even a rebuttal (and in fact the latter's response to his writings had been feeble and negligent), but he did contradict Basil **in five books.**

---

30. "I took no pleasure" translates οὐ ... γέγηθα. Perhaps read γέγηθε: "*he* took no pleasure."

31. In 8.12, on the date and occasion of Eunomius's *Apologia* (or *Liber Apologeticus*), see Bernard Sesboüé, Georges-Matthieu de Durand, and Louis Doutreleau, eds., *Contre Eunome: Basile de Césareé* (SC 299, 305; 2 vols.; Paris: Cerf, 1982–83), 1:28–34. It was probably composed in 360 or 361, perhaps with a view to clearing himself of suspicions about his doctrine at the Council of Constantinople or with those considering him for the episcopacy. The text is presented in the edition above (2:234–98) and in Vaggione, *Eunomius, The Extant Works*, 34–74. Basil's reply, *Contra Eunomium,* is presented in Sesboüé, de Durand, and Doutreleau, *Contre Eunome.* The first part of Eunomius's response to Basil, the *Apologia Apologiae*, seems to have appeared in late 378, the occasion being the altered ecclesiastical situation with the accession of Theodosius I. Philostorgius's statement that it eventually ran to five books may be accepted. Basil did in fact die around that time (1 January 379), but we may treat our author's explanation of his demise with suitable reserve, as with the other dramatic deaths in 3.15 and 7.12. The work has perished, apart from the fragments preserved by Gregory of Nyssa in his own *Contra Eunomium* (see Vaggione, *Eunomius, The Extant Works,* 79–127). Apollinaris and the others who wrote against Eunomius are listed in Jerome, *Vir. ill.* 120.

32. Gregory's work *On the Son* is his *Or.* 29 and 30 (Περὶ Υἱοῦ).

And when Basil received the first two of these books to be published, **he was so cast down that he died.**

12b [Photius, *Bibliotheca* codex 40]. This Philostorgius, however much he may have fumed against the orthodox, did not dare to attack Gregory the theologian but acknowledged his education, however unwillingly. But he tried to tarnish the reputation of Basil the Great and only succeeded in showing how **brilliant** he was. For he was forced to acknowledge the power and beauty of the discourse in his **panegyrics** because they were so evident in the very works, but the coward calls him **arrogant** and inexperienced in works of disputation because, so he says, he dared set himself against Eunomius's writings.

13. He shamelessly tells the most obvious lies about the holy men just mentioned, Basil and Gregory, claiming that they said not that the Son had become a human being but that he had dwelt in a human being and that for this reason Apollinaris had parted company with them. But he criticizes the latter, although not for the reasons for which the orthodox found fault with him; he represents him, rather, as turning his attention to other endeavors. He does, however, say of him, as do the others, that he even denied the resurrection of the body.[33]

14. He says that what Apollinaris wrote against Porphyry is much better than Eusebius's efforts against him and also better than Methodius's writings on that subject.

15. He says, and I do not know where he gets the information, that Apollinaris was a bishop and that Novatus was of Phrygian stock.[34]

16. He records that Valentinian and Valens were from Cibalis.[35]

17. He says that among those holding to the consubstantialist doctrine, the most renowned was Theodore,[36] bishop of Heraclea in Thrace, along with

---

33. Denial of the resurrection is quite out of character for Apollinaris; see Hans Lietzmann, *Apollinaris von Laodicea und seine Schule: Texte und Untersuchungen* (Tübingen: Mohr Siebeck, 1904), 46. Jerome says the thirty books he wrote against Porphyry are regarded as among his best works (*Vir. ill.* 104). He also mentions with esteem Methodius's books against Porphyry (*Vir. ill.* 83; *Ep.* 48.13; 70.3).

34. "Novatus" is the form of Novatian's name commonly found in the Greek authors. He was probably of Roman stock, but the number of his followers in Phrygia may have suggested to Philostorgius a Phrygian ancestry.

35. "Cibalae" (in Pannonia) is the more usual form of the name. Cf. Ammianus 30.7.2; Zosimus 3.36.2; Libanius, *Or.* 20.25.

36. The company assembled by Philostorgius in 8.17 is actually made up of some of the most implacable opponents of the term "consubstantial." Theodore of Heraclea was pilloried at the Council of Sardica (Hilary, *Frag. hist.* B II 1.7.3). Athanasius lists him as among the principal heretics (*Ep. Aeg. Lib.* 7; *H. Ar.* 28.1; *Ep.* 47). He was a

George, who was of Alexandrian stock and had practiced the philosophical way of life and who was bishop of Laodicea in Syria.[37] Coming after them in time was Eustathius, an old man venerated by the people and persuasive,[38] and also Basil, and in addition Macedonius of Constantinople and Eleusius, bishop of Cyzicus. With them were Marathonius and Maximinus, presbyters of the church in Constantinople.[39]

18. In comparing Eunomius to Aetius, he says that Aetius was better at furnishing proofs and readier at replying to all points, for, he says, it was just as though he had everything all heaped together artlessly on the tip of his tongue. Eunomius, however, was superior in the clarity and elegance of his teaching, and especially in the way he suited it to his students.[40]

---

member of the Mareotic Commission investigating the charges against Athanasius (Athanasius, C. Ar. 72.4). Jerome, however, thinks highly of him (Vir. ill. 90).

37. Similarly, George of Laodicea detested the term "consubstantial" (Socrates 1.24.2). He had been excommunicated by Alexander of Alexandria and had helped the early Arians formulate their doctrines (Athanasius, Syn. 17.5–7; Apol. de fuga 26.4). He had been singled out as one of the chief heretics at the Council of Sardica (Hilary, Frag. hist. B II 1.7.3). But he was also set against Eudoxius's homoean doctrine (Sozomen 4.13.1–3) and was the leader of the homoeousians with Basil of Ancyra (Epiphanius, Pan. 73.1.5–6). His exposition of this faith is in Epiphanius, Pan. 73.12.1–22.4.

38. Eustathius is he of Sebaste; Sozomen also mentions his gifts of persuasion (3.14.36). He headed the Macedonian delegation in 365 to Liberius of Rome (Socrates 4.12).

39. Eleusius and Marathonius are mentioned together in Suda, E 813 as attracting crowds of followers by their asceticism rather than by their eloquence. Philostorgius himself gives witness to Eleusius's homoeousian convictions (9.13). All this suggests again that our author likes to assign to the consubstantialist camp anyone opposed to the Eunomian doctrine, which, he thinks, is the only effective alternative to what the other represents.

40. On the comparison of Aetius and Eunomius, see 5.2a.

BOOK 9

1. The ninth book of Philostorgius fabricates some incredible deeds for Aetius, Eunomius, and Leontius, and in addition for Candidus, Evagrius, Arrian, Florentius, and above all for Theophilus the Indian, and for some others as well whom this mad heresy portrays as among the more fervent souls.[1] And the one concocting these absurdities shows no awareness of how ridiculous they are.

2. He says that Moses punished Jannes and Jambres and company with sores and brought about the death of the mother of one of the two.[2]

3. He says that Valens, upon his return to Constantinople from Illyricum, showed that he held Eudoxius in high esteem.[3] And although Eudoxius especially could have fulfilled the promises made to Eunomius, he had no intention of doing so. Euzoius as well had the same opportunity of doing what he had done for them by means of the council in Antioch. But so completely had they both forgotten about these things that Euzoius turned to disparaging the men he had championed, remarking jestingly in church that Aetius and company were "sky-climbers" and insulting Theophilus by calling him

---

1. On Arrian, see 9.18. Theophilus was said to have raised a dead person to life (3.6a).

2. On Jannes and Jambres, see 2 Tim 3:8. The reference in 9.2 to "the mother of one of the two" presupposes that they are not brothers, contrary to what is found in the version of the apocryphon concerning them in *P. Chester Beatty XVI* (see Albert Pietersma, *The Apocryphon of Jannes and Jambres the Magicians* (Religions in the Graeco-Roman World 19; Leiden: Brill, 1994), 49. The text is quite fragmentary, but it appears that the mother perishes while trying to help the dying Jannes in some way. That Philostorgius mentions the mother rather than, as usual, the father (Balaam) shows that he knew the book directly, not just the traditions surrounding it (see Pietersma, *Apocryphon of Jannes and Jambres*, 108–9, 209, 217).

3. On Valens's esteem for Eudoxius, see Gregory of Nyssa, *Eun.* 1.60; Sozomen 6.7.9; Theodoret, *Hist. eccl.* 4.12.2–13.1. With Julian's death, the Eunomians had lost their imperial patron, and Eudoxius could freely express his hostility toward them (see 7.6 and 8.2–4). Euzoius now sided with him, because Valens had banished Meletius from Antioch, and he preferred to have the emperor's support (Kopecek, *History of Neo-Arianism*, 422–23).

an "Ethiopian."[4] Thus the struggles were not about orthodoxy and faith but about discrimination in color and race. As for Eudoxius, he made some disdainful remarks about them and said in church, "I do not call them heretics, which is what they would like to hear, so as not to lend countenance to their separation; but I do call them pests."

4. When Aetius and Eunomius and company had broken once and for all with Eudoxius and Euzoius and company, they left Constantinople to Florentius.[5] Aetius sailed off to Lesbos and lived there on a property near Mytilene, where he received with gracious speech those who came to see him. The property was a gift from the emperor Julian in token of his regard for him. As for Eunomius, he crossed to Chalcedon and dwelt there in a garden that was his own property by the sea-walls, and he showed no less concern for his visitors. Neither of them had charge of a church particularly assigned to him, but those who shared their views considered them fathers and guides of them all. Eunomius, in fact, did not even perform a liturgy from the time he left Cyzicus, nor for that matter for the rest of his life, even though none of the bishops of his sect would ever do anything pertaining to the affairs of the church without his approval.

5. When Valens reached the third year of his reign, he took the field against the Persians, on which occasion Procopius usurped power in Constantinople.[6] Procopius was related to Julian, and many there were who thought the realm should be his, and many a tongue conveyed the thought. For this reason when Jovian became emperor he escaped from Mesopotamia, fled with his wife, and remained in hiding, moving often from place to place

---

4. "Sky-climbers" (οὐρανοβάτας) is an example of the jokes often made of the Eunomians' claim to know God's very essence. Basil speaks sarcastically of them as "passing through heaven and all the powers transcendent" (*Adversus Eunomium* 1.13), while Gregory of Nazianzus places Eunomius "above the clouds" (*Or.* 27.9). See also Gregory of Nyssa, *Eun.* 1.60. As Euzoius here shows, Arius's original followers, who shared his views about God's incomprehensibility, joined in the fun. Theognis of Nicaea expressed himself likewise, if the text ascribed to him is sound, when he said that to speak rightly of the Father and the Son "super nubeculam est ambulare" (Bardy, *Recherches sur Lucien d'Antioche*, 212). The epithet applied by Euzoius to Aetius may involve a play on Ἀέτιος and ἀετός ("eagle"). See also Epiphanius, *Pan.* 76.54.17–24.

5. On the final break between Eudoxius and the Eunomians, see Socrates 4.13.1–2; 5.24.1–6; Sozomen 7.6.2; Theodoret, *Hist. eccl.* 2.29.10–12.

6. On Procopius's revolt, see Eunapius, *Frag. hist.* 31–32; *Vit. soph.* 479; Ammianus 26.5.8–9.11; Jerome, *Chron.* 366; *Consul. const.* 365; 366; Libanius, *Or.* 1.171; 19.15; 20.25–26; Themistius, *Or.* 7.91a–93c; Socrates 4.3; 4.5; Sozomen 6.8.1–3; Zosimus 4.4.2–4.8.4; Paschoud, *Zosime*, 2:340–49; Pio Grattarola, "L'usurpazione di Procopio e la fine dei Costantinidi," *Aevum* 60 (1986): 82–105.

in trying circumstances, until he had had enough of wandering about and, as our author puts it, staked everything on one last throw.[7] Making his way to Chalcedon, he hid himself on Eunomius's property outside the city while its owner was away. And from there he crossed over to the city and took control of the government without bloodshed.[8] Shortly afterwards, when he took the field against Valens, he was defeated by the treachery of his generals Gomoarius and Agilo, and fled to Nicaea.[9] He planned to move on from there on the following day but was arrested by Florentius, whom he had appointed commander of the city garrison, and led in fetters to Valens by the one who had arrested him. Procopius was beheaded after six months of usurpation, but Florentius was not saved by his own treachery; the soldiers delivered him to the flames from an old grudge, because while he was garrison commander of Nicaea under Procopius he had mistreated many of them who had sided with Valens.[10]

6. While Procopius was usurping power, Eunomius paid him a visit when he [Procopius] was staying in Cyzicus. His arrival brought about the release of those being kept in prison by him.[11] They were in prison for siding with Valens, and their relatives had compelled Eunomius to undertake the embassy. Once he had undertaken it and freed the men, he returned at once.

Around the same time, the person sent by Procopius to govern the island brought Aetius to trial because he had been accused by the locals of favoring Valens.[12] The accusation would have resulted in his execution if some-

---

7. Procopius was proclaimed emperor on 28 September 365, while Valens was away from Constantinople on campaign. The phrase "staked everything on one last throw" is the same expression used in Libanius, *Or.* 24.13; Ammianus 26.6.12. Valens had made himself unpopular in the city because of his exactions in preparation for the war with Persia, and, as Philostorgius suggests, dynastic loyalty swayed many toward the usurper.

8. The phrase "without bloodshed" resembles Ammianus 26.9.11: "quoad vixerat incruentus."

9. The treachery of Gomoarius refers to his desertion with his men to Valens at Thyatira in March or April of 366 (Ammianus 26.9.6). Agilo's treachery occurred at the subsequent battle at Nacolia in Phrygia, when he suddenly went over to Valens, many of his men following (Ammianus 26.9.7).

10. Florentius and the tribune Barchalba accompanied Procopius as he sought refuge afterwards but decided to try to save their own lives by delivering him up to Valens. All three were put to death (Ammianus 26.9.8–10), the usurper being executed on 27 May 366.

11. Ammianus 26.8.11 says that Procopius pardoned all his opponents in Cyzicus.

12. The "island" where Aetius was is Lesbos (cf. 9.4).

one influential with Procopius had not arrived on the scene at that moment and snatched Aetius from the sword. In addition, since the one dispatched by Procopius was related to Herrenian and Gerresian (they were brothers and had been with Eunomius[13] and been accused with him), he was quite forcible in the way he threatened the official who had condemned them, and having cancelled the sentence of death against them, he acquitted them of the charges.

As for Aetius, he took them with him and set off for Constantinople, where he stayed with Eunomius and Florentius. Shortly after, when he died, Eunomius closed his mouth, shut his eyes with his fingers, and performed the other last rites with his fellow sectarians in the most splendid fashion.[14]

7. While Eudoxius was staying in Marcianopolis with Valens,[15] the clergy in Constantinople voted to drive Aetius from the city.[16] When the latter reached Chalcedon, he wrote to Eudoxius and told him what had happened.[17] But not only was he not deflected from his course by the letter; he even showed that he was grieved that nothing worse had befallen him.

8. They accused Eunomius, he says, of having hidden Procopius on his own property while he was plotting the usurpation. He barely succeeded in evading the charges and the death they would have brought with them. He was, however, banished to Mauretania, the praetorian prefect Auxonius having ordered him into exile. But he was hurried forth during the winter.[18]

---

13. In "brothers who had been with Eunomius," "Eunomius" seems an error for "Aetius" (see Bidez, *Philostorgius*, 118).

14. Aetius was in his seventies at the time of his death (Vaggione, *Eunomius of Cyzicus*, 296).

15. On Valens in Marcianopolis, see A7.43, 43a; A7.44; Ammianus 27.5.5–6; Zosimus 4.10.3–4.11.1; Paschoud, *Zosime*, 2:351–52. He is attested there from 10 May 367 and was still there on 30 May. It was the capital of Moesia Secunda, and he went there to deal with the Goths who had supported Procopius. He used it as a base of operations and after wintering there had still not left it by 3 May 369.

16. "Aetius" is an error for "Eunomius" (see Vaggione, *Eunomius of Cyzicus*, 298 n. 225).

17. If Eunomius thought it worthwhile to seek Eudoxius's help in his trouble, the latter must have made friendly overtures to him during the usurpation of Procopius, the relative of Julian, Aetius's patron. That Procopius and Eunomius were on close terms is suggested as well by 9.5–6. The charge against Eunomius in 9.8 is thus understandable, as is Eudoxius's haste to distance himself from him then (see Kopecek, *History of Neo-Arianism*, 427–29).

18. "Hurried forth" translates ἠπείγετο rather than ἐπήγετο (see Bidez, *Philostorgius*, 119, 354). But the story of Eunomius's exile labors under the difficulty that Auxonius had no power to banish anyone to a place outside Valens's realm, such as

And when he reached Mursa in Illyricum, the bishop of which was someone who happened to be named Valens, he was given the warmest of welcomes and recalled from exile, Valens having gone with Domninus (the bishop of Marcianopolis) to see the emperor and informed him of his situation in moving terms.

The emperor was on the verge of having a meeting with Eunomius after his recall, but Eudoxius used his skills to prevent the audience. Afterwards, when he had gone to Nicaea to install a bishop there (Eugenius, its bishop, had died), he came to the end of his life before he could carry out his intention. And Demophilus was transferred from Beroea to Constantinople, the emperor Valens playing the part of a council in making this decision.[19]

9. He says that in Borissus (a village in Cappadocia Secunda) there lived a presbyter named Anysius who had four sons and one daughter named Eulampios;[20] she was the mother of the Philostorgius who wrote this history. Now her husband, named Carterius, revered the teaching of Eunomius. He persuaded his wife to change her allegiance to his doctrine, since she had been brought up by her father and mother to adhere to the consubstantialist doctrine. And she, once persuaded, brought her brothers around and then, one by one, her father too and the rest of her family.

10. He says that it was Theodore, the bishop of Heraclea, who had the chief part in installing Demophilus in Constantinople, for he was regarded as having the privilege of performing that priestly function.[21] As Demophi-

---

Mauretania, nor did he do so at any other time. In addition, the journey from Constantinople to Mauretania would not have taken Eunomius anywhere near Mursa, the place that Philostorgius says he reached. But again, Mursa is in Pannonia Secunda, outside Valens's territory. Thus Woods infers that what really happened was a bungled attempt by Auxonius to arrest Eunomius, not to banish him, and that Eunomius fled to a place outside the prefect's jurisdiction where he was sure of his welcome. Philostorgius described his flight as something amounting to banishment, and Photius carelessly misread his initial reference to Mursa and turned it into Μαυρουσίδα γῆν (Woods, "Three Notes," 616–19).

19. On Eudoxius's death (in 370) and Demophilus's succession, see Socrates 4.14.2–3; Sozomen 6.13.1; Theodoret, *Hist. eccl.* 5.40.8.

20. Other suggested spellings of "Eulampios" are "Eulampion" or "Eulampia." The conversion occurred during Valens's reign.

21. "Theodore" is a confusion of "Dorotheus." Sozomen 3.3.1 says that the bishops of Nicomedia and Heraclea had the right to consecrate their colleague in Constantinople because they were his neighbors. Zonaras 13.3.29, by contrast, grounds their right in the tradition of civil law, from the time when Byzantium was subject to Perinthus.

lus was being enthroned, however, many of the crowd in attendance shouted "worthless!" instead of "worthy!"[22]

11. Modestus succeeded Auxonius as prefect, and since he was unfriendly toward Eunomius, our author says, he convicted him, *in absentia,* of having thrown the churches and the cities into confusion, and he banished him to the island of Naxos.[23]

12. Caesarea was originally called Mazaca, a name derived from Mosoch, the ancestor of the Cappadocians. As time went on, the name was slightly altered to Mazaca.[24]

13. Eunomius having left Cyzicus, no bishop had yet been appointed in his stead, our author says.[25] Now Demophilus went there with Dorotheus and some others to install one, but he could get nowhere, because the people there who held to the formula of "like in substance," as they had been taught by Eleusius, were unswerving in their allegiance to the doctrine.[26] Once Demophilus and those with him had accepted what the people of Cyzicus demanded, however, and had anathematized Aetius and Eunomius (for such was the demand), and had proclaimed publicly, in speech and writing, that Eunomius was an anomoean, and had placed not only their creed but those as well who accepted their doctrines under one and the same curse, then they consented to the ordination, although they did not allow anyone

---

22. On the cry of "worthy" as part of the ceremony of episcopal enthronement, see Eusebius, *Hist. eccl.* 6.29.4; *Testament of Our Lord* 1.21. See also Plutarch, *Galba* 18.4 (the soldiers shout εἰ ἄξιος of Galba at a show after he becomes emperor). See also Vaggione, *Eunomius of Cyzicus,* 299 n. 235.

23. Modestus is attested as praetorian prefect from 1 August 369 to 2 November 377. Kopecek (*History of Neo-Arianism,* 430) guesses that Basil may have been behind his move against Eunomius, since Basil and the prefect were on friendly terms; this may be why Philostorgius dwells in 9.12 upon the notoriously pagan origins of Basil's see. "Naxos" renders Ναοξίαν.

24. On Mosoch, see Gen 10:2; on his connection with Caesarea, Josephus, *Ant.* 1.125; Sozomen 5.4.1; *Hieroclis Synecdemus* (ed. Burckhardt), 57. In "the name was slightly altered," here "the name" means either Mosoch's, or else the first Μάζακα should perhaps be corrected to something like Μόζοκα (see Bidez's apparatus).

25. On Eunomius's departure from Cyzicus, see 6.3. He spent his exile composing his reply to Basil's *Contra Eunomium* (Kopecek, *History of Neo-Arianism,* 431).

26. On the devotion of the people there to Eleusius, see Socrates 4.6.7. The phrase "the people there ... doctrine" renders the text with κρατύνοντας, as printed. But if κρατύνοντος or κρατύναντος is read (Bidez, *Philostorgius,* 120), then the translation would be: "because the people there were unswerving in their allegiance to the formula of 'like in substance,' as they had been taught by Eleusius, who maintained [or 'had established'] the doctrine."

to <under>go it other than the one whom they themselves had decided on. Now the one ordained began at once to preach clearly the consubstantialist doctrine.

14. Upon the death of Euzoius of Antioch, Dorotheus of Heraclea was transferred to his see.[27] Our author disparages Demophilus and Dorotheus, saying that the latter was the most boastful of men and that Demophilus was the most skilled at **fuddling and confusing everything,** especially church teachings.[28] So much so that once while preaching in Constantinople, he went so far as to say that the Lord's body, [when] mixed with the divinity, proceeded to lose all of its identity, in the same way as a pint of milk thrown into the vastness of the sea.

Thessalonica was Demophilus's native city, and the rest of his family was not undistinguished. But Demophilus performed many misdeeds against the so-called Eunomians.

14a [*Suda*, Δ 470 Demophilus]. Bishop of Constantinople, he was a man who in his rashness was capable of **mixing up everything together** in a disorderly rush like a wild torrent. His discourses are littered with rubbish, as one may see at least in the oration contained in his commentaries, which are still preserved; one would have thought he would have taken a little more care to get it right at least then, when what he said was being set down in written records. In them he utters much that is incoherent, and this is quite explicit in his books *The Father and the Son,* where he says:

"The Son has been engendered by the will of the only Father timelessly and directly, that he might be a minister and servant of the Father's counsels.

---

27. On the succession of Dorotheus, see Socrates 4.35.4; 5.3.2; Sozomen 6.37.17.

28. Kopecek (*History of Neo-Arianism*, 435–36) suggests that the criticism of Demophilus in this section arises from the severity with which he treated the Eunomians after his harrowing experience in Cyzicus, which had convinced him that their influence was threatening the peace of the church. To make matters worse, he seems (if the excerpt in 9.14a is any indication) to have learned his catechism from Asterius, whose doctrines Philostorgius detested (e.g., 4.4). Vinzent (*Asterius von Kappadokien,* 208 n. 25) characterizes the excerpt here as a summary of various of Asterius's texts. Reminiscent of him is the idea that the Son is a minister of creation, which cannot bear God's unmediated power (Vinzent, *Asterius von Kappadokien,* 94, 100, 203; also Athanasius, *Decr.* 8.1; *Apol. sec.* 2.24). It was a doctrine particularly abhorrent to Eunomius, since, as we see here, it suggested the Son's inferiority to the rest of creation; Eunomius, by contrast, laid stress upon the ontological superiority of the Son to created things (*Apol.* 15; Kopecek, *History of Neo-Arianism,* 436–39). Philostorgius, then, offers here a bit of genuine Eunomian criticism of the standard "Arianism" of his day.

For God foresaw that what he was about to make could not possibly <attain to?> the insuperable rank of the God who was to make them when they came to be (for either they would all have to become gods in conformity with the dignity of their Maker, and from being what they were they would be gods, or else they would have to be unmade when they were made, like wax brought to a hot fire). And thus the Son was produced as a mediator between the things that were to be and the God who begot him, in order that by associating himself in condescension with the things that come to be, he might accomplish the Father's plan. So he has become the mediator between God and us who have come to be through him."

He does not realize that in saying this he is making out that the God of the universe is weak and jealous and declaring the Son to be inferior to all creatures. For God would be weak, according to what Demophilus says, if after planning to do so, he was then unable to give existence to everything. Nor would he be free of envy if, while able to make all things gods, he appeared to be making sure that what was to come to be would not receive that dignity from him. As for the Son, there is not one of the creatures that could not be shown to be superior to him, if in fact he did not come to be for his own sake but for the purpose of and with a view to their creation. For surely everything that comes to be because of other things is necessarily of lesser value than the things for which it comes into existence. And he says a lot of other nonsense.

15. During Valens's reign, the pagan oracles delivered pebbles marked all over with letters to those who approached them; when **put together** the letters **seemed** to some **to spell** "Theodosius," while to others "Theodulus," "Theodore," or something similar. For the letters that were engraved went **as far as *delta*,** the demons, as usual, giving **ambiguous** responses for the destruction of those who believed in them and the avoidance of failure [in prediction]. Thus it happened that someone named Theodore was swept away by the deception and took the first steps toward usurpation, and quickly perished along with his followers. Valens exacted retribution not only from them but from a good many innocent folk as well, simply because their names began with those letters.[29]

16. Valentinian **died** after reigning for twelve years and left his son Gra-

---

29. On the episode, see A7.45; Eunapius, *Frag. hist.* 38–39; Ammianus 29.1–2; Zosimus 4.13–15; *Epit. Caes.* 48.3–4; Socrates 4.9; Sozomen 6.35; Zonaras 13.16.37–45 (a cock was made to peck at letters on which seeds had been placed); Cedrenus 313B–C. Theodore was a *secundicerius notariorum* (Paschoud, *Zosime*, 2:356). *Suda,* I 14 mentions someone else who perished after trying to discover who would succeed Valens.

tian as heir to the realm.[30] He also left two other children, a daughter Galla and Valentinian, who was about **four years** old and whom his mother Justina and the army in **Pannonia** immediately made **emperor.** Gratian, however, when he **found out about** the proclamation, did not approve of it, since it **had been made** without **his consent,** and he even **punished** some of those involved there in this illegal move.[31] He did, however, consent **to have** his brother as **emperor** and to take the place of a father for him.[32]

17. The Scythians **beyond the Danube** were driven out when the Huns **attacked** them, and **they crossed over** to **Roman** territory in friendship.[33] The Huns are those whom people of old called the Neuri; they dwelt by the

---

30. Valentinian died in Illyricum of a stroke on 17 November 375. Gratian was his son from his first wife, Macrina, whom he had divorced and then married Justina, the widow of the usurper Magnentius, in 370. Justina gave him Valentinian II and three daughters, Justa, Grata, and Galla (Zonaras 13.15.8–9). He had already had Gratian proclaimed Augustus in 367 in order to help secure the dynasty. Gratian, now sixteen, succeeded him in Trier. On 22 November, government ministers proclaimed Valentinian II Augustus in order to secure the loyalty of the Illyrian army. Valentinian, then four, and his mother were staying near Sirmium at the time. Valens and Gratian accepted the move, perhaps after some initial irritation. See A7.46, 46a, b; Ammianus 30.10; *Epit. Caes.* 45.10; Zosimus 4.19; Rufinus, *Hist. eccl.* 11.12; Socrates 4.31.7–8; Sozomen 6.36.5. Zecchini ("Filostorgio," 583) contrasts 9.16 with Ammianus 30.10.6, where the fear that Gratian might be angry with the proclamation is said to have proven baseless, and conjectures that Philostorgius is trying to put Gratian in an unfavorable light. It should be noticed, however, that Philostorgius is drawing from the anonymous homoean historian here (A7.46).

31. In "some of those involved there," "there" translates αὐτοῦ.

32. In "to have his brother as emperor" (βασιλεύοντα), perhaps συμβασιλεύοντα: "co-emperor."

33. In 376 the Goths of southern Russia asked to be received into the Roman Empire in order to escape the Huns. Valens agreed to accept them and to give them land in Thrace if they would serve in the army. In the autumn of the year they were ferried across the Danube, and a start was made in settling and enrolling them, but as winter came on, many of them were still in the transit camp. When provisions ran short, greedy officials began selling them into slavery in return for food. The remaining Ostrogoths, who had not yet gotten permission to cross into Roman territory, took advantage of the ensuing disturbances to cross the river. The last straw was the massacre of a Visigothic escort by a Roman officer; all the Goths rose in revolt and plundered Thrace. Valens met them at Adrianople on 9 August 378 and was routed in a battle that was indeed the "beginning of evil times" for the empire, as Rufinus puts it; two-thirds of the Roman army perished there, together with many officers and two *magistri militum* and the emperor himself. See A7.48–48b; Eunapius, *Frag. hist.* 41–43; *Epit. Caes.* 46.2; Ammianus 31.1–13; *Consul. const.* 378; Jerome, *Chron.*

Rhipaean Mountains, from which the Tanais flows down and empties into Lake Maeotis.[34]

The Scythians, when they had moved over, behaved reasonably at first toward the Romans but then turned to robbery and finally went to undeclared war. When Valens heard of this, he left Antioch, made his way to Constantinople, and from there headed to Thrace. But when he joined battle with the barbarians, he lost many men and turned to **headlong flight**.[35] Reduced to dire straits and utter helplessness, he and a **few followers hid** in one of the **buildings** containing hay that were in the fields. The barbarians did to the **building** what they did to everything else in their path: they burned it down, never suspecting that the emperor was inside.[36]

Thus he perished, and along with him the Roman Empire was shorn of its greatest and mightiest part. As for the barbarians, they freely **plundered** all of Thrace, with Fritigern at their head. Gratian grieved for his uncle and mourned over the disaster that had befallen the Romans. And he appointed Theodosius emperor and sent him to his uncle's realm.[37]

378; Rufinus, *Hist. eccl.* 11.13; Zosimus 4.20–24; Socrates 4.34–38; Sozomen 6.37–40; Theodoret, *Hist. eccl.* 4.12, 31–36; Malalas 13.35; *Comp. chron.* 60.27–61.14.

34. Our author's archaizing proclivity is well displayed here. The "Scythians" are of course Goths, and the Huns are identified with the Neuri of Herodotus 4.17 and 4.105; the culture of the time did not care much for new things, including new peoples on the stage of history. The geographical note at the end of 9.17 suggests the lengths to which the fashion went (see Bidez, *Philostorgius*, cxli; Zecchini, "Filostorgio," 593; 2.5 and 20 n. 13).

35. On our author's assessment of the scale of the disaster, see Noel Lenski, "Initium mali Romano imperio: Contemporary Reactions to the Battle of Adrianople," *TAPA* 127 (1997): 129–68. The Goths proceeded from Thrace into Macedonia and Illyricum; "the destruction was thus wide-spread in the Balkans and the terrors it brought spread well beyond these geographical boundaries" (Lenski, "Initium mali Romano imperio," 137). In the year after the battle, the panegyrics sounded hopeful that the Goths would be repaid in kind. But in 382 Valens's successor, Theodosius, was forced to deal with them and give them what they had demanded originally: land in Thrace and political autonomy. After that, the official rhetoric tended to magnify the disaster of Adrianople in order to justify the subsequent treaty (Lenski, "Initium mali Romano imperio," 142–44).

36. Two accounts of Valens's death appeared immediately after the battle: in one he just vanished, while in the other he was burned alive in some building (Lenski, "Initium mali Romano imperio," 152).

37. Gratian summoned Flavius Theodosius, a former general renowned for his military skill, from his Spanish estates, where he had been living since his father's execution in 376, and proclaimed him Augustus in Sirmium on 19 January 379. See Ammianus 31.15–16; *Consul. const.* 378–379; Rufinus, *Hist. eccl.* 11.14; Zosimus

Theodosius was a native of Spain, which is now called Hiberia, the River Hiberus, which runs through it, having evicted its previous name.[38]

18. Theodulus from Cheretapa having died (he had been bishop of Palestine), Eunomius and company ordained Carterius in his place. But he died soon after, so they appointed John to succeed him. Eunomius himself and Arrian and Euphronius traveled with him from Constantinople to the east in order to bring Julian there from Cilicia, to meet with Theophilus the Indian in Antioch and to arrange things elsewhere in the east.[39]

19. The emperor Theodosius met the barbarians at Sirmium (where he had gone right after his accession, the situation being urgent), defeated them in battle, and from there made a splendid progress to Constantinople.[40] He put the churches in the charge of those holding to the consubstantialist doctrine and drove the Arians and Eunomians from the city. Among them was Demophilus, who when expelled went to his own city, Beroea. Hypatius was banished from Nicaea and made his way to his native city of Cyrus in Syria. Dorotheus too was driven out of Antioch and went to Thrace, from where he had come. And others were scattered to various other places.[41]

4.24.3–4; Socrates 5.1–2; Sozomen 7.1.1–7.2.1; Theodoret, *Hist. eccl.* 5.4.9–5.6.3; Orosius 7.34; Theophanes 103B–104B; Zonaras 13.17.9–16; Adolf Lippold, "Theodosius I," PW 13Sup:837–961. Most of the sources say that the territory given to Theodosius corresponds exactly to Valens's old domain, although Sozomen 7.4.1 reports that he was given Illyricum as well. See Lippold, "Theodosius I," 13:842; Paschoud, *Zosime,* 2:386.

38. The Hiberus or Iberus is the Ebro.

39. After Valens's death, Gratian released the bishops his uncle had exiled (Socrates 5.2.1); Eunomius was thus able to return from Naxos (cf. 9.11) and deal with the changing ecclesiastical situation. For Theodulus, Euphronius, and Julian, see 8.2. For Arrian, see 9.1. Vaggione (*Eunomius of Cyzicus,* 318) wonders if the Carterius here is Philostorgius's father (cf. 9.9).

40. The same narrative pattern of a victory of Theodosius over the barbarians, followed by his entry into Constantinople, is found in Zosimus 4.25; Orosius 7.34.5–6; *Consul. const.* 380; Socrates 5.6; and Sozomen 7.4. Zosimus 4.33.1 refers to the magnificence of his entrance. Philostorgius is the only one to specify Sirmium as the place of victory, and there may be a confusion, for which perhaps Photius is responsible, with the notice of the place of Theodosius's accession.

41. On the expulsion of the groups mentioned from Constantinople, see Socrates 5.7 (which dates the event to 26 November 380); Sozomen 7.4–6; Malalas 13.37; Marcellinus, *Chron.* 380; *Cod. theod.* 16.1.2–3; 5.6. Theodosius made it clear in his enactments that his government would recognize as officially Christian only those churches that adhered to Nicene orthodoxy.

Book 10

1.[1] Dorotheus, then, was driven from Antioch, as has been said. But the presbyters of Antioch, Asterius and Crispin, and the rest of the clergy met together, the bishops of some of the neighboring cities being present as well, and sent to Eunomius and company to ask for their fellowship. They wrote back that they would accept them only if they revoked the condemnation of Aetius and his writings. They also demanded that they reform their lives, which were infected by some unworthy manners. The others, however, did not accept the condition then set forth and later even went on to revile Eunomius and company in church, calling them visionaries and empty-headed idiots for having demanded such things of them.

2. Our author accuses Arius, the leader of their heresy, of saying that **the God of the universe** is manifold and composed of many elements, for he does not claim that one may grasp how great God is but rather that how much each one grasps depends on how far one's **ability** extends. And he teaches that he is neither a substance nor a hypostasis nor any of the other things that he is called. He adds that the council in Ariminum and the one in Constantinople taught the same things, the latter declaring the generation of the Only Begotten to be quite unknowable to everyone and restricting knowledge of generation to that only of things that come to be.[2] This is also the council that condemned Aetius.

---

1. 10.1–4 justifies, on doctrinal and disciplinary grounds, the Eunomians' rejection of the homoeans' request for communion now that their bishops had been banished. The charge that Arius said that God is manifold is echoed by Ambrose, according to whom Arius believed in "plures ... et dissimiles potestates" (*De fide* 1.6). For his teaching about God's unknowability, see 2.3 and 16 n. 7.

2. "Restricting knowledge ... come to be" translates τῶν γινομένων μόνον τὴν γνῶσιν αὐτῆς περιστείλασα. Another possible reading is τῷ γειναμένῳ μόνῳ: "restricting knowledge of it to the one who begot him alone." This would fit better the Creed of Constantinople of 360 (see Kelly, *Early Christian Creeds,* 293). For Aetius's condemnation by this council, see 4.12.

3. The disciples of Arius divided into many sects in their explanations of the likeness of the Only Begotten to the Father.[3] Some of them said that each is God because of his foreknowledge, others because of his nature. Others again said that it is because each can create from nothing. But, he says, these doctrines, however they may seem to differ, amount to the same thing: that the Son is consubstantial to the Father. He also says that after these people became divided in their views, they went on to a great deal of other disgraceful behavior, buying and selling episcopacies and pursuing sinful corporeal pleasures.

4. He says that the Eunomians separated themselves so thoroughly from the sects just mentioned that they did not even accept their baptism or ordination. Now the Eunomians did not baptize with three immersions but with one, baptizing, so they said, into the Lord's death, which he underwent for us once, not twice or thrice.[4]

5. He says that the emperor Theodosius invested his son Arcadius, who was quite young, with imperial rank.[5] Not long afterwards the emperor Gratian was killed in Upper Gaul as a result of a plot by the usurper Maximus. Our author fabricates many slanders against Gratian,[6] going so far as to

---

3. On the "Arian" divisions, see Socrates 5.23; Sozomen 7.17.9–14; Theodoret, *Haer. fab.* 4.4. On Eunomius's reduction of all forms of Christianity save his own to the consubstantialist faith, see Vaggione, *Eunomius of Cyzicus,* 330 n. 110; Bidez, *Philostorgius,* cxxiv.

4. On baptism into the Lord's death, see Rom 6:3. On the Eunomian practice, see Didymus, *De Trinitate* 2.15; Theodoret, *Haer. fab.* 4.3; Mansi, *Sacrorum conciliorum,* 3:546C; Vaggione, *Eunomius of Cyzicus,* 332 n. 119. Socrates (5.24.6) and Sozomen (6.26.2–4) blame Eunomius's successors for the innovation here mentioned. Epiphanius (*Pan.* 76.54.32–34) accused Eunomius of baptizing his catechumens upside-down into the three names of his peculiar Trinity— an example of the kind of stories about the liturgies of his sect that Vaggione (*Eunomius of Cyzicus,* 332) thinks doubtful. He is inclined to accept the notice in 10.4, however, and thinks that the purpose of the liturgical change was to avoid suggesting that those referred to by the three names were equal or indistinguishable (see Vaggione, *Eunomius of Cyzicus,* 330–44).

5. For "invested," reading περιτίθεται instead of παρατίθεται. Arcadius was born ca. 377 and made Augustus on 19 January 383.

6. On Gratian's character, see Eunapius, *Frag. hist.* 57. He had many admirable qualities but lacked both interest in administration and advisers who could supply for his inexperience. He alienated the regular army by consorting with his barbarian auxiliaries and adopting their fashions. Moreover, his fiscal policies, including the withdrawal of financial support for the pagan cults, disaffected the nobility. Magnus Maximus seems to have been *comes Brittaniarum* at the time of his revolt in the spring or summer of 383. When Gratian marched against him, his troops abandoned him,

liken him to Nero.[7] His orthodoxy did not please him, it seems.[8]

6. The emperor Theodosius found some of the servants of his bed chamber favoring the doctrines of Eunomius, and he drove them from the palace. He also sent men to seize Eunomius and take him by the quickest way from Chalcedon, ordering them to banish him to Halmyris.[9] This is a place in the Moesia that is in Europe, in the region of the Danube.[10] When the Danube froze, however, Halmyris was captured by the barbarians who crossed over. And Eunomius was banished from there to Caesarea in Cappadocia, where he was an object of hatred to the people there because of the works he had composed against its bishop, Basil. But he was allowed to leave there and go to live on his own property, called Dacora.[11] Here Philostorgius says that he himself saw him when he [Philostorgius] was twenty years old and had gone to Constantinople. He praises Eunomius to the skies, saying that he was of incomparable intelligence and virtue. He also describes in the most flattering terms the appearance of his face and the rest of his features and likens to pearls the words from his mouth. Further on, however, he inadvertently

---

and he fled with his retinue to Lyons, pursued by Andragathius, the usurper's *magister equitum,* who in the end tricked him into attending a banquet apart from his bodyguard and assassinated him there; the date was 25 August. See Ambrose, *Enarrat. Ps.* 61.24–26; *Epit. Caes.* 47.7; Rufinus, *Hist. eccl.* 11.14; Zosimus 4.35; Socrates 5.11.2–9; Sozomen 7.13.8–9.

7. The comparison with Nero, that villain of the apocalyptic literature of which Philostorgius was so fond, indicates that the Eunomians never forgot that Gratian had initiated the measures against non-Nicene Christians that Theodosius took up (see Timothy D. Barnes, "The Collapse of the Homoeans in the East," in *Historica, Theologica et Philosophica, Critica et Philologica* [ed. Elizabeth A. Livingstone; StPatr 29; Leuven: Peeters, 1997], 3–16). The unleashing of his persecution, if understood as foretold in the appearance of the beast in Rev 13, would be seen as the signal for the appearance of those portentous calamaties that so crowd the remaining pages of our history.

8. For "did not please him," reading ἤρεσκεν instead of ἤρκεσεν.

9. On Eunomius's exile, see Socrates 5.20.4; Sozomen 7.17.1. They agree that the reason for it was the many converts he was making from his residence in Constantinople; cf. Theodosius's decree in *Cod. theod.* 17.5.17 against the *Eunomiani spadones.* Vaggione (*Eunomius of Cyzicus,* 356) places his exile in the summer of 389.

10. In the phrase "the Moesia that is in Europe," "Europe" means the continent (see 20 n. 14).

11. Jerome has Eunomius still living in Cappadocia in *Vir. ill.* 120. His exile marks a shift in attention in Philostorgius to the events in secular history, the stage upon which God's anger is displayed; see Alanna E. Nobbs, "Philostorgius's View of the Past," in *Reading the Past in Late Antiquity* (ed. Graeme Clarke et al.; Rushcutters Bay, NSW, Australia: Australian National University Press, 1990), 262.

acknowledges that he stammered, and he does not hesitate to glorify his stutter as highly polished speech. He also maintains that the leprous patches that had disfigured and spotted his face had actually adorned his body.[12] He extols all of his works, saying, however, that the letters are far superior to the rest.[13]

7. When Placidia[14] died, her husband, the emperor Theodosius, married Galla, the sister of the emperor Valentinian the Younger and the **daughter** of [Valentinian] **the Great,** born to him from Justina, who favored the teachings of Arius. It was Galla who bore Theodosius a daughter as well: Placidia.[15]

8. Theodosius joined Valentinian at Thessalonica and set out against the usurper Maximus. For the usurper, having taken over Gratian's realm, **planned** to add to it Valentinian's as well. Now the emperors sent against him, as commanders of their forces, Timasius, Richomer, Promotus, and Arbogast. But his attendants suddenly pulled him off **his throne,** stripped him of the imperial tokens, and **led** him to the emperors as a private person. And there Maximus was beheaded, having usurped power for five years in all.[16]

---

12. On Eunomius's leprosy, see Rufinus, *Hist. eccl.* 10.26; Jerome, *Commentariorum in Isaiam libri XVIII* 65.4–5. On heresy as leprosy, see Quodvultdeus, *Liber Promissionum* 2.6.10–11 (CCSL 60).

13. On the superiority of Eunomius's letters, see Photius, *Bibliotheca* codex 138 P98ª17–21 (Photius thinks their style as deplorable as that of his other works).

14. "Placidia" is probably to be corrected to "Placilla." Her real name is Aelia Flacilla. She married Theodosius ca. 376 and bore him Arcadius, Pulcheria (d. 385/6), and Honorius. She died in 386.

15. Justina had been forced by the Gothic incursion to move with her son from Sirmium to Milan, where they requested a church where their homoean court could worship. Gratian gave them one, only to return it to the Catholics following the promulgation of *Cod. theod.* 16.5.6 (January 381), which declared Nicene Catholicism the only legal religion and outlawed assemblies within cities of Photinians, Arians, and Eunomians. But with Gratian now dead, Justina began in 385 to press Ambrose to yield her a basilica, triggering the now famous drama that eventually gave the usurper Maximus an excuse to descend upon the young Valentinian's domain under the pretext of relieving the beleaguered bishop (Rufinus, *Hist. eccl.* 11.16; *Collectio Avellana* 39.3). The boy, his mother, and his sister Galla fled to Thessalonica in 387 to seek Theodosius's protection. The emperor, just widowed, married Galla late that year on the condition that she and her family adopt Catholicism. See Socrates 4.31.17–18; *Chron. pasch.* P304D; Zosimus 4.43–44; Paulus Diaconus, *Historia Romana* 12.7; Zonaras 13.18.17–18.

16. In the summer of 388 Theodosius began moving in strength through Upper Pannonia toward Aquileia, where Maximus was staying. Andragathius, his general, had fortified the Alpine passes, but then, persuaded that an attack by sea was imminent, he left the army in order to direct naval operations on the Adriatic. When

9. After the victory over Maximus and his progress to Rome,[17] the emperor was about to leave the city when a strange and unusual star appeared in the sky; it was to be the harbinger of great evils to afflict the world.[18] It shone forth for the first time at midnight by the morning star in what is called the Zodiac, large and not much inferior to the morning star in its flashing radiance.

Then there was a gathering of stars from everywhere that clustered around it (one might liken the sight to a swarm of bees englobing their leader). Whereupon, as though from the force of their mutual compression, all of their light blazed forth combined into one flame. The sight was just like that of a great, fearsome double-edged sword shining with a startling brilliance, all of the other stars having migrated so as to assume this shape, while that one alone that had been the first to be seen appeared underneath in the situation of the root or hilt of the whole form, and as though generating all the brightness of the star revealed, like the flame leaping up from the wick of a lamp. That was how strange the object was that appeared.[19]

Theodosius's forces came upon the leaderless army of the usurper, they brushed aside the Alpine defenses and fell upon the main body at Aquileia. The victory was not bloodless (despite what Rufinus pretends in *Hist. eccl.* 11.32), but it was quick (*Pan. Lat.* II [XII] 34.1–2), and Maximus was taken and executed on August 28. Cf. *Pan. Lat.* II (XII) 32.2–44.2; Zosimus 4.44–46; Theodoret, *Hist. eccl.* 5.15; Orosius 7.35.1–5; Rufinus, *Hist. eccl.* 11.17; *Epit. Caes.* 48.6; Socrates 5.12; 5.14; Sozomen 7.13.8–11; 7.14.5–7.

17. On Theodosius's progress to Rome (in 389), see *Consul. const.* 389; *Pan. Lat.* II (XII) 45–47; Socrates 5.14.3; Sozomen 7.14.7.

18. On the star, compare Marcellinus, *Chron.* 389: "Stella a septentrione gallicinio surgens et in modum luciferi ardens potius quam splendens apparuit." If Philostorgius's πλησίον τοῦ Ἑωσφόρου were read as παραπλήσιον, his description would come nearer to Marcellinus's "in modum luciferi." For 390, Marcellinus reports a "columna pendens ardensque" in the sky, as though it were unrelated to the star of the year before. See also Ernest W. Brooks and Jean-Baptiste Chabot, eds., *Chronica minora* (CSCO 1–6; 6 vols.; Paris: Typographeo Reipublicae, 1903–5), 1:648 (a. 381): "Terribile in caelo signum columnae per omnia simile apparuit."

19. On the sword-shape, see Pliny, *Nat.* 2.89: the ancients called a certain kind of comet *xiphias* because it tapered to a point. For what it portended, see 11.7. The sword-like shape seems to suggest the heavenly cross, the sign of God's favor to Constantine (1.6; 1.6a) and Constantius (3.26), now ominously inverted to gleam balefully down upon the empire that had banished the true faith. This is the crown upon Philostorgius's revision of Rufinus of Aquileia's history, which ends happily with Theodosius's final victory over a usurper just before his death. Our author wants us to know that the emperor's victory over Maximus was not to be understood as God's approval of his banishment of Eunomius.

And the movement of the star differed from every other course. It began its movement at the place where, as was said, it appeared, and at first it rose and set with the morning star. But then it drew apart little by little, ascending toward the north slowly and gradually and making its own way obliquely toward the left from the viewpoint of its observers. Its orbit, however, was the same as that of the other stars in whose courses it went. Now when it had finished its own journey after forty days, it pushed into the center of the Great Bear, and having appeared for the last time in its exact middle, there it went out. And that is not all, for our author describes many other strange things concerning this sword-shaped star.

10. Our author says that he pitted himself against Porphyry on behalf of Christianity.

11. During the time the sword-bearing star appeared, two human bodies were seen, one of which, in Syria, exceeded the usual human measure in size, while the other, in Egypt, was incredibly short. The Syrian was five cubits plus a span in size, although his feet did not correspond to the height of the rest of his body but were bent inward so as to make him bandy-legged. His name was Antony. The Egyptian, on the other hand, was so short that he made a pleasant sight mimicking the partridges in their cages, and the birds made a game of fighting with him. And what was yet stranger was that the man possessed intelligence; it was not impaired by his shortness. Nor was his voice uncouth, and his speech gave evidence of the nobility of his mind. Both of these people flourished during our author's time, and they did not die young; the tall one departed this life after his twenty-fifth year, while the short one reached nearly the same age.

Our author scatters throughout his history many other tales of marvels, some of which are contemporary with those just related, while others took place earlier.[20]

12. Philostorgius says that the Wednesday and Friday fast is not limited just to abstinence from meat but that the canons prescribe that no food is to be touched until evening.[21] He gives as an example one Eudoxius, a fellow sectarian but a presbyter in rank, although one who was deprived of his reproductive organs, saying of him, "He was so given to fasting that throughout the

---

20. On the influence exercised by apocalyptic literature on Philostorgius's narrative of natural wonders, see Bidez, *Philostorgius*, cxiii–cxxi; John O. Arendzen, "A New Syriac Text of the Apocalyptic Part of the 'Testament of the Lord,'" *JTS* 2 (1901): 401–16.

21. On various fasting customs, see *Did.* 8.1; *Const. ap.* 5.13, 15, 18–19; 7.23; *Apostolic Canons* 64; 69; Socrates 5.22.36–40; 7.22.3; Sozomen 7.19.9; Rudolph Eugen Arbesmann, "Fasttage," *RAC* 7.506–524.

whole year it was not just [on?] the [days] that by precept commemorate the Lord's passion...."[22]

---

22. On the lacuna at the end of 10.12, see Bidez, *Philostorgius*, 131.

<Book 11>

1.[1] ... sport with lions and bears, he [Valentinian] departed from life itself, from his realm, and from contests with beasts when he was in his twentieth year. Furthermore, he could not control his temper, which is the main reason he lost his life. For once when he was conversing with Arbogast in the palace, the words between them roused him to anger, so he made a move to draw a sword against the general.[2] But when he was prevented (for the man-at-arms whose sword he tried to draw stopped him), he tried to say something that would allay Arbogast's suspicions for the time being. His words, however, only served to transform Arbogast's suspicion into certainty. For when he asked the reason why Valentinian had attempted such a thing, the latter answered that he would do away with himself, since although he **was sovereign,** he could do nothing he **wanted.** Now Arbogast did not push the matter further at the time, but later in Vienne in Gaul, having noticed the emperor, who had eaten lunch and at midday in the deserted part of the imperial residence ... to the riverbank engaged in his usual idle pastimes.[3] He sent some of the guard against him. They laid violent hands upon the wretch and savagely strangled him to death,[4] none of the emperor's attendants being present, for it was the time for their lunch. Those, then, who had strangled him, in order to forestall an immediate search for those who had done the

---

1. On the lacuna at the beginning of 11.1, see Bidez, *Philostorgius,* 132.

2. Arbogast was a barbarian, perhaps of Frankish stock, who had risen to the position of *comes rei militaris* or perhaps *vicarius magistri militum* when Gratian sent him in 380 to help Theodosius against the Goths. Theodosius kept him and included him in his staff, perhaps with the rank of *magister militum,* in the campaign against Maximus in 388. Following the usurper's defeat, he was sent to Gaul to deal with his son, and he stayed in the west as Valentinian's guardian and regent.

3. The phrase "to the riverbank" translates the reading ἐπὶ τοῦ ποταμοῦ τὸ χεῖλος. On the textual corruption here, see Bidez, *Philostorgius,* 132 line 15, and apparatus *ad loc.*

4. "They laid violent hands upon the wretch and savagely strangled him to death" follows the translation of Edward Walford, *The Ecclesiastical History of Sozomen: Also the Ecclesiastical History of Philostorgius* (London: Bohn, 1855), 506.

deed, wrapped his handkerchief around his throat like a noose and hoisted him up from it as though he had hanged himself deliberately.[5]

2. Arbogast, when he had done away with Valentinian, realized that his family situation prevented him from becoming sovereign (his father had been a barbarian), so he made a certain Eugenius, a *magister* in rank and a pagan in conviction, Roman emperor.[6] When he learned of this, Theodosius crowned one of his two sons, Honorius, emperor and spent the whole winter preparing for war. And when spring arrived, he marched forth against the usurper, **taking the mountain passes** by betrayal **when he assaulted them.** He joined battle with the usurper by the river (it is called the Coldstream), and a **fierce struggle** ensued in which many fell on either side, but victory spurned the usurper and crowned the legitimate ruler. The usurper was seized and **beheaded.** As for Arbogast, he despaired of saving his life and killed himself **by falling on his sword.**[7] Afterwards the emperor went on to Milan, sent

---

5. The present episode took place in the spring of 392 in Vienne, by which time Arbogast certainly held the rank of *magister militum*; several sources say he assumed the title without permission. Valentinian died on 15 May, after a period of fruitlessly trying to assert himself in the government of his realm; he was twenty years old. The sources are divided on whether it was murder or suicide, and although the question can no longer be decided with absolute certainty, it may be noted that the young emperor had just sent to Ambrose to ask to be baptized. See Ambrose, *De obitu Valentiniani* 15; Jerome, *Ep.* 60.15; Rufinus, *Hist. eccl.* 11.15; Epiphanius, *De Mensuris et Ponderibus* 20; Orosius 7.35.10; Socrates 5.25.1–5; Sozomen 7.22.1–2; Zosimus 4.53–54; Gregory of Tours, *Historia Francorum* 2.9; John of Antioch, *Frag.* 187 (*FGH* 4:608–10); Paschoud, *Zosime*, 2:452–58.

6. Flavius Eugenius was *magister scrinii* when Arbogast elevated him on 22 August 392. His hopes for recognition by Theodosius were dashed when the latter crowned Honorius (reading περιτίθησι [στέφανον] rather than παρατίθησι) Augustus on 23 January 393. Christian though he was, or had been, he now sought support from the pagan senators, restoring the Altar of Victory in the senate house in Rome and promising to turn Ambrose's cathedral into a stable after defeating Theodosius.

7. Theodosius marched from Constantinople in May of 394; he found the pass over the Julian Alps apparently undefended until on 5 September, upon emerging from a defile in the valley of the Frigidus fluvius, he discovered the way ahead blocked by Arbogast's army and his retreat cut off by forces whom the latter had left in ambush at the top of the pass to seal it off. Theodosius lost the first engagement heavily, but during the following night the unit that had been left in ambush defected to him, and that is what Philostorgius will mean by ταῖς Ἄλπεσι προσβαλὼν ἐκράτησεν αὐτῶν προδοσίᾳ (see Paschoud, *Zosime*, 2:483–84). When the battle was renewed on 6 September, a violent wind sprang up and blew straight into the faces of the usurper's soldiers, disrupting their order and causing them to panic. Eugenius was captured and executed the same day; Arbogast committed suicide two days later. See Rufinus, *Hist.*

for his son Honorius, and handed over the entire west to him.[8] **But after his victory over** the usurper, he fell ill with dropsy and died, having reigned for sixteen years; his time as emperor taken as a whole saw him achieve great success in life.[9] "For it was following upon brilliant victories that he became sole ruler of the Roman Empire and could contemplate himself as father of two emperors to whom he could hand over a peaceful realm, and it was in this most happy state that he departed from life upon his own couch, this being, I ween, the reward for his fervent zeal against idols."[10]

These being the heretic's words about the most orthodox Theodosius, he does not blush to make fun of him for his lack of self-restraint and of **moderation in enjoyment of luxury,** which was, he writes, the reason why he fell victim to dropsy.[11]

3. In the east, Rufinus was the chief influence over Arcadius, while in the west Stilicho enjoyed that same position with Honorius. **Neither of them** refused to accord to either of the sons of Theodosius the robe and **name** of emperor, and both of them held the reins of government in act and speech, ruling the ruler with the title of under-officer. Neither of them, though, was content with the position he held under his emperor. Rufinus was scheming to transfer the very title of emperor to himself, while Stilicho was striving to

---

eccl. 11.32–33; Zosimus 4.53–58; Socrates 5.25; Sozomen 7.22.4–8; 7.24; Theodoret, *Hist. eccl.* 5.24; Orosius 7.35.11–19; Claudian, *Panegyricus de tertio consulatu Honorii Augusti* 63–105; *Epit. Caes.* 48.7; John of Antioch, *Frag.* 187 (*FGH* 4:608–10).

8. On the summons to Honorius, see Claudian, *Panegyricus de tertio consulatu Honorii Augusti* 109–141; Rufinus, *Hist. eccl.* 11.34; Zosimus 4.59; Paschoud, *Zosime,* 2:468.

9. Theodosius died in Milan on 17 January 395, having been made Augustus in January of 379. See Socrates 5.26; Sozomen 7.29.3–8.11; Hydatius, *Chron.* 395; *Epit. Caes.* 48.19–20.

10. His zeal against idolatry had been evidenced not only in his legislation but also in his battle against the usurper, whose army had marched under idolatrous standards and who had set up a great statue of Jupiter to overlook the field of combat; see Rafaelle Perrelli, "La vittoria 'cristiana' del Frigido," in *Pagani e cristiani da Giuliano l'Apostata al sacco di Roma* (ed. Franca Ela Consolino; Soveria Mannelli: Rubbettino, 1995), 257–65.

11. The contemporary assessments of Theodosius's character vary according to the ideology of those making them (see Paschoud, *Zosime,* 2:393–94). Philostorgius's remarks about his immoderateness are like those of the pagan Zosimus 4.28.1; 4.33; 4.50; both of them follow Eunapius, *Frag. hist.* 48–49. A different picture is offered, naturally, by *Pan. Lat.* II (XII) 13 but also by *Epit. Caes.* 48.18–19. Philostorgius's mixture of praise and blame is due to contrasting attitudes to Theodosius's measures against pagans, on the one hand, and anti-Nicene Christians, on the other. Like his contemporaries, he very easily assumed that heterodoxy and vice went hand in hand.

have it bestowed upon his own son Eucherius. Rufinus, however, was hacked to pieces on the so-called *tribunal* at the emperor's very feet by the swords of the soldiers brought back from Rome who had fought with Theodosius against the usurper; they had orders from Stilicho to do this, and they also did it because he had been caught sneering at them.[12] His life reached its end on the very day the paymasters[13] had all but invested him with the purple.

He says that Rufinus was tall and manly. One could see his intelligence by the movement of his eyes and his readiness of speech. Arcadius, by contrast, was short, slight of build, weakly, and **dark** in complexion. And his **dullness** of mind was evident in his speech and the way his eyes looked as they drooped sleepily downward beneath their drowsy lids. This is what fooled Rufinus, who thought that the sight alone would make the army glad to choose him as emperor and to get rid of Arcadius.[14]

So they cut off Rufinus's head, put a stone in its mouth, raised it up on a pole, and ran about with it everywhere. They cut off his right hand likewise and **carried it around** to the shops **of the city,** crying, "**Donations for Mr. Greedy!**"[15] And they collected a lot of gold with the request, for the onlookers eagerly gave their gold, as though viewing an agreeable spectacle.

Rufinus's desire for sovereignty, however, was terminated at this point. As for Stilicho, who had been plotting against Honorius, our author says, he and his fellow conspirators were slain by the army at a signal from the emperor.[16]

---

12. Rufinus had been praetorian prefect since 392; Theodosius had entrusted Arcadius to his care when he left for the war with Eugenius in 394, and the new emperor was barely eighteen at his accession. His brother Honorius, entrusted to Stilicho, was eleven. Eucherius was younger still, having been born in 389 from Serena, Theodosius I's niece. Rufinus was killed on 27 November 395 by the troops he was reviewing on their return from the campaign against Eugenius. One version of his assassination is that Stilicho got Gaïnas, their commander, to do the deed; the other is that the soldiers themselves took spontaneous revenge on him. It is no longer possible to decide which to prefer. See Claudian, *Eutr.* 2.130–256; 293–427; Zosimus 5.4; 5.7; John of Antioch, *Frag.* 190; Socrates 6.1.4–7; Sozomen 8.1.2–3; *Chron. pasch.* P306B.

13. "Paymasters" translates στρατολόγοι, a word of uncertain meaning. The apparatus *ad loc.* (Bidez, *Philostorgius*, 134), refers to Claudian, *Eutr.* 2.311–312, which presents Rufinus as buying the legions' loyalty with his gifts.

14. On Rufinus's intelligence, see Eunapius, *Frag. hist.* 63. On Arcadius, see Cedrenus 327C. On his dullness, see 11.6; Zosimus 5.14.1, 22.3, 24.2.

15. For Rufinus's head on a spear, see Claudian, *Eutr.* 2.433–435. For his amputated hand begging, see 2.436–439; see also Jerome, *Ep.* 60.16; Zosimus 5.7.6; Marcellinus, *Chron.* 395.

16. For the further adventures of Stilicho, see 12.1–2.

4. He says that Eutropius crept into the imperial residence after Rufinus; he was a eunuch born into slavery who had risen to the rank of *praepositus* but was not satisfied with his situation.[17] Since his castration had kept him from the purple, however, he persuaded the emperor to give him the titles of patrician and consul. And from then on the eunuch was father of the emperor, he who could not engender even an ordinary child.[18]

5. He says that Eutropius ordered Caesarius, Rufinus's successor, to transfer Eunomius from Dacora to Tyana in order to be guarded by the monks there.[19] For he envied him his fame and so would not even allow his corpse to be buried with that of his teacher, even though many people requested this repeatedly. He also had public edicts issued ordering his books destroyed.[20]

6. He says that the emperor Arcadius married Bauto's daughter after his father's death.[21] Bauto was of barbarian stock but had distinguished himself as a military commander in the west. The **woman** did not share her husband's **sluggishness** but was quite **forward** in the **barbarian manner**. She had by then borne Arcadius two daughters, Pulcheria and Arcadia, and later gave birth to Marina and a son, Theodosius, as well.[22] At the time, though, mother though she was of the two children, she was **wantonly insulted** by Eutropius, who went so far as to threaten her with speedy dismissal from the imperial residence. She went straight to her husband, just as she was, hugging a child in each arm. Wailing loudly and holding out the babies, she shed a torrent of

17. On Eutropius, see Eunapius, *Frag. hist.* 66; Zosimus 5.3; 5.8–14; 5.17–18.3; Sozomen 8.7.1; John Chrysostom, *Eutr.* (beginning); Claudian, *Eutr.* 1.8 and *passim*; Socrates 6.5.3. He was *praepositus sacri cubiculi* (imperial chamberlain).

18. On "father of the emperor," see Claudian, *Eutr.* 2.prologue.50; 2.68.

19. Eunomius was moved to Tyana in the spring or summer of 396. He died probably in the winter of 396–397.

20. See *Cod. theod.* 16.5.34 (4 March 398) for an edict against the Eunomian clergy and their books. Eutropius had arranged to have John Chrysostom brought to Constantinople and consecrated on 26 February 398; John took a strong line against the Eunomians.

21. Bauto's daughter was Eudoxia; the wedding was on 27 April 395. See Zosimus 5.3; *Chron. pasch.* P306A. On Bauto, see Zosimus 4.33.1–2; on Eudoxia, Zonaras 13.20.8–9; Cedrenus 334A; Zosimus 5.24.2.

22. On the names and birthdays of Eudoxia's children, see Kenneth G. Holum, *Theodosian Empresses: Women and Imperial Dominion in Late Antiquity* (Berkeley and Los Angeles: University of California Press, 1982), 53. "She had by then borne" means by the time in 399 when Eutropius fell. Pulcheria had indeed been born on 19 January of that year, but Arcadia was not to come along until the following year; it was Flaccilla who had been born in 397.

tears and behaved in general as a woman seething with passion does with her feminine arts to make her husband feel sorry for her.

Arcadius was stricken with pity for the children, now sobbing in concert with their mother, and his temper was roused. And then at last, in his anger and in the severity of the language to which it prompted him, Arcadius was an emperor. He immediately stripped Eutropius of all of his honor, took away his wealth, and banished him to the island of Cyprus.

Shortly afterwards, however, certain people handed in an accusation against him that when he was consul he had wrongly used decorations that were allowed to no one but the emperor alone, and he was **summoned** from Cyprus. A council was convened in the place called Pantichion (the prefect Aurelian and other high officials in the government examined the charges), and Eutropius was found guilty and beheaded.

This is what Philostorgius says about Eutropius. Others, however, have recorded other reasons for his **dismissal** from office, his banishment, and indeed for his death.[23]

7. "In my time," he says, "the loss of human life was so great that never did any age know the like since time began," this being what the sword-star had signified, he claims.[24] It was not just the army that was reduced, as of old in the previous wars, nor did the calamities occur in [only one] part of the earth. It was all the provinces that perished, all Europe that was brought to ruin, and no small part of Asia that was lost with it, along with much of Africa, especially the part subject to the Roman Empire. It was the barbarian sword that worked most of the ruin, but famine, plague, and hordes of savage beasts did their part, as well as horrible earthquakes that leveled cities and dwellings to their foundations and rendered the destruction quite inescapable. In some places the ground split open into chasms that furnished ready tombs for those who dwelt there, and there were deluges of water from the sky, and in other places fiery droughts, and lightning storms that inflicted on people a manifold and unbearable terror. Not only that, but hail larger than slingstones rained down in many places, for it was noted that what fell weighed up to eight "pounds." And the heavy snows and bitter cold that attacked those whom the other disasters had not already killed brought their lives to an end

---

23. On Eutropius's downfall, see John Chrysostom, *Eutr.* 4; Claudian, *Eutr.* 2.prologue.1–20, 52, 76; 2.21; *Cod. theod.* 9.40.17; Zosimus 5.18.1–2; Socrates 6.5.4–7; Sozomen 8.7.3–5. Other reasons suggested in the sources for Eutropius's downfall are his mismanagement of relations with the Ostrogothic leader Tribigild (Claudian, *Eutr.* 2) or the latter's demand that he be removed (Zosimus 5.17.4–5).

24. In this and the following chapter, Philostorgius unfolds the tale of the disasters, natural and otherwise, portended by the sword-star of 10.9 (see 139 nn. 18–19).

and clearly proclaimed the divine wrath. But to relate this in detail would be beyond all human ability.[25]

8. He says that those Huns who had subdued much of Scythia this side of the Danube and devastated it earlier later crossed the river when it was frozen, drove in masses into the Roman Empire, and, spreading throughout Thrace, plundered all of Europe. But the Huns who were toward the sunrise crossed the Don River, poured into the east, and burst through Greater Armenia into what is called Melitine. From there they attacked Euphratensis, drove as far as Coele Syria, and, overrunning Cilicia, slaughtered people beyond count.[26]

That was not all, for the Mazices and Austuriani (who live between Libya and the African people) laid waste Libya from their eastern marches, devastated no small part of Egypt, and did likewise when they attacked the Africans to the west.[27]

As if that were not enough, Tribigild, a Scythian by birth who was of those now surnamed "Goths" (the Scythian nationalities are quite numerous and diverse) and who had a barbarian force where he dwelt in Nacolea in Phrygia with the title of count, turned from friendship with Rome and became an enemy.[28] Starting with Nacolea itself, he captured most of the cities of Phrygia and wrought a great slaughter of the people. General Gaïnas (himself a barbarian), who was sent out against him, gave away victory, since he was planning to do the same to the Romans himself.[29] Trigibild, as though

---

25. On the natural disasters, see Matt 24:7; Luke 21.11; Claudian, *Eutr.* 2.24–46 (earthquakes, floods, fires, weird births, and a rain of blood in the year of Eutropius's consulship); Jerome, *Commentariorum in Ezechielem libri XVI* 5.17; 13.12–14; Brooks and Chabot, *Chronica minora*, 2:17 (a. 410), 64–66 (a. 396), 67 (a. 401), 68 (a. 404), 69–70 (a. 407–8), 70 (a. 409 and 412), 295, 402, 407–8; Socrates 6.19.5 (fall of large hail in Constantinople in 404).

26. On the Hunnish incursions across the Danube, see Jerome, *Ep.* 60.16; 77.8; Claudian, *In Rufinum* 2.26–53; Sozomen 8.25.1. "Europe" here must mean the province, in contrast to the meaning in 11.7. On the Hunnish invasion of Armenia and other parts of the East, see Socrates 6.1.7; Sozomen 8.1.2; Brooks and Chabot, *Chronica minora*, 2:136–37 (*Chronicon Miscellaneum ad Annum Domini 724 Pertinens*; see 205 n. 1 for this chronicle).

27. On the Austuriani, see Ammianus 26.4.5; 28.6.2; on the Mazices, Ammianus 29.5.17–19.

28. Tribigild commanded the Ostrogoths settled in Phrygia by Theodosius I. He rose against Rome in 399 when Eutropius withheld his donative. See Eunapius, *Frag. hist.* 75; Socrates 6.6; Sozomen 8.4; Zosimus 5.13–22; Claudian, *Eutr.* 2.174–473, 565–579.

29. Gaïnas, who had commanded the Gothic auxiliaries in the war against Eugenius and the troops returning from the west who slew Rufinus, engaged Tribigild

escaping from Gaïnas, came from there upon Pisidia and Pamphylia and utterly destroyed them. Then, having seen his force reduced through many hardships and Isaurian battles, he won through to the Hellespont, crossed over to Thrace, and shortly after perished. As for Gaïnas, after his treachery he returned to Constantinople in his general's guise and began thinking how he could take it over. But a heavenly armed force, which appeared and **frightened** those about to execute his plan, saved the city from capture and handed over to human justice those found out.[30] There ensued a great slaughter of them. Gaïnas was so frightened that as soon as night fell he gathered all he could, overpowered those at the gates, and got out of the city. And since Thrace had been devastated and could neither provide anything he needed nor bear further depredation, Gaïnas made his way to the Chersonese, planning to **cross over** to Asia on rafts.

When the emperor found out what his plan was, he sent against him General Fravitta, a Goth **by nationality and a pagan** by religion but loyal to the Romans and most able in warfare. While Gaïnas was sending his army ahead of him **on rafts** to make the crossing, he engaged the rafts with a naval force and easily slew all those sailing on them. As a result, Gaïnas despaired of his chances and fled to the northern parts of Thrace. Not long after, some Huns attacked and killed him, and his pickled head was brought to Constantinople.[31]

In addition to the calamities already mentioned, the Isaurians wreaked all sorts of havoc.[32] Toward the east they overran Cilicia and neighboring Syria, not just Coele Syria but the rest of Syria as well, going as far as Persia itself. They also struck north and west, attacking Pamphylia and devastating Lycia. They spread ruin over the island of Cyprus and took the Lycaonians and

---

in collusion rather than battle, in order to strengthen his position against the ascendancy of Eudoxia following Eutropius's downfall. He won concessions from Arcadius and entered Constantinople in a position of power before the end of 399 but could not hold his ground against the empress and the bishop. Tensions between his Gothic troops and the populace rose until he left the city and told his men to join him quietly, but at some point during the withdrawal a fight broke out, the city gates were shut, and the Goths trapped inside were massacred.

30. The heavenly force is referred to in Socrates 6.6.18–22; Sozomen 8.4.12–14. See also Synesius, *Aegyptii sive de providentia* 116 B–C.

31. On Gaïnas's leaving the city and Fravitta's pursuit, see Eunapius, *Frag. hist.* 79–82. After the disaster at the Chersonese, Gaïnas retreated across the Danube, where, on 23 December, he was slain by Uldin the Hun. See Marcellinus, *Chron.* 400–401.

32. On the Isaurian incursions, see Eunapius, *Frag. hist.* 86; John Chrysostom, *Ep.* 68; 69; Zosimus 5.25; Sozomen 8.25.1; Marcellinus, *Chron.* 405.

Pisidians captive. They forced most of the Cappadocians from their homes, daring to raid even into Pontus. And they, of all the barbarians, treated their captives the worst.

Book 12

1. Philostorgius speaks harshly of Stilicho on many points, adding that he was guilty of usurpation.[1] He also says that Olympius, one of the *magistri,* grabbed someone who was carrying a sword[2] in the palace to attack the emperor, wounding himself in the process but saving the emperor, and that he helped him do away with Stilicho, who was staying in Ravenna.

Others, however, say that it was not Olympius, but Olympiodorus, and that he did not defend the emperor but **plotted against** his benefactor Stilicho and falsely accused him of usurpation. They add that he was not a *magister* at the time but became one later, after Stilicho's unwarranted assassination, for which he received this rank as a reward. Not long afterwards, however, he too **was clubbed to death** and so paid the **penalty** for having **murdered** Stilicho.[3]

2. During the aforementioned time Alaric, a Goth by nationality, gathered a force in northern Thrace and attacked Greece and captured Athens and Macedonia and plundered neighboring Dalmatia. He also attacked Illyricum, crossed the Alps, and burst into Italy.[4] He had been summoned by Stili-

---

1. On this episode, see Zosimus 5.32–35; 5.44–46.1; Sozomen 9.4.7–8; Orosius 7.38.5; Brooks and Chabot, *Chronica minora,* 1:300 (a. 408); Cedrenus 335B–C; Theophanes 124B; Olympiodorus 2; 8.

2. The text of the passage "grabbed [someone] who was carrying a sword" may be defective; it has been translated as it stands.

3. The notice about Olympius and Olympiodorus has been garbled, whether by Photius or a later copyist; see Bidez, *Philostorgius,* 140; Barry Baldwin, "Olympiodorus of Thebes," *L'antiquité classique* 49 (1980): 228–29. Beneath the confusion there can still be detected the original gist: the contrast between what Philostorgius and the historian Olympiodorus say about Honorius's anti-German minister Olympius, who orchestrated the disaffection of the soldiers that brought about Stilicho's execution on 22 August 408. Olympius became Master of Offices thereafter, but his intransigence and incompetence led to his dismissal and flight to Dalmatia, where he was put to death in 412.

4. See Eunapius, *Frag. hist.* 65; Zosimus 5.5.5–8; 5.26; 5.29; Jerome, *Ep.* 60.16; Claudian, *In Rufinum* 2.187–191; Sozomen 8.25; 9.4. Alaric had commanded the Visigothic auxiliaries at the battle of the Frigidus (11.2); they had suffered heavy losses

cho while the latter was still alive, so our author says, he being the one who opened the Alpine gates to him as well. Stilicho indeed engineered every sort of plot against the emperor, nor was he deterred because he was his son-in-law,[5] but he even prepared a drug to make him sterile.[6] But he did not realize,

---

but afterwards had been dismissed to return home in Lower Moesia, and their yearly allowances stopped. Disgruntled, they rose in 395 and marched toward Constantinople and then to Macedonia and Thessaly. Near Larissa they met Stilicho leading the eastern soldiers back from the war with Eugenius, but before a decisive battle could be fought, Arcadius's ministers, who suspected Stilicho of seeking an opportunity to reinforce the claim of the western realm to jurisdiction over Illyricum, ordered him to dismiss his forces and return to Italy. The ever-loyal Stilicho obeyed, and Alaric and his army were free to march into Attica, capture the Piraeus, and force Athens to surrender. In 397, Stilicho brought an army to Greece that ousted the Goths from Arcadia, but he had to return to Italy to counter the rebellion of Gildo in Africa before he could deal Alaric a crushing blow. Once again unhindered, the latter devasted Epirus, until finally Arcadius's ministers recognized his position by naming him *magister militum per Illyricum,* thereby establishing him as a buffer to what they feared were Stilicho's designs on that region. It was perhaps with the understanding of those ministers that he invaded Italy at the end of 401; there he was twice defeated by Stilicho in 402 and had to withdraw. And in 405 Stilicho turned the tables on Constantinople by making his own arrangement with Alaric and having Honorius in his turn appoint him *magister militum per Illyricum,* following which the Goth withdrew to Epirus to await further instructions from Stilicho in connection with the latter's plan to transfer eastern Illyricum to Honorius's domain.

In the event, he had longer to wait than he liked, Stilicho's plan being deferred first by Radagaisus's invasion of Italy in 406 and then by Constantine's usurpation in 407. Tired of waiting, Alaric headed for Noricum at the beginning of 408 to demand payment for the time he had wasted in Epirus, gaining his way through the passes with an ease that Zosimus at least found suspicious (5.29.4) and that seems to echo a tradition that is also behind Philostorgius's accusation (found also in Orosius 7.38.2) that Stilicho let him in (see Paschoud, *Zosime,* 3:217).

5. Honorius was Stilicho's son-in-law by virtue of his marriages to his daughters: first Maria, in 398; then when she died childless in 407 or 408, Thermantia in 408. Philostorgius thus says that it was the emperor Honorius against whom Stilicho plotted. Zosimus 5.32.1, by contrast, records the rumor that it was Theodosius II whom Stilicho planned to replace with his son Eucherius. Both stories are unfounded. *Cod. theod.* 9.42.22 (22 November 408), which mentions a supposed collusion between Stilicho and Alaric, says nothing about a plot to enthrone Eucherius (see Paschoud, *Zosime,* 3:231). On the rumor, in addition to Zosimus above, see 11.3; Orosius 7.38.1; Jordanes, *Romana* 322; Sozomen 9.4.7.

6. On the story of Stilicho's drug, see Paschoud, *Zosime,* 3:209. Zosimus 5.28 says Stilicho's wife arranged to have Honorius made impotent because she thought her daughter too young for sexual relations at the time of her wedding. Philostorgius's

in his eagerness to proclaim his son Eucherius emperor unlawfully, that he was cutting off and destroying in advance his offspring that might legitimately succeed to the throne. And he says that Stilicho displayed his usurpation of power so openly and fearlessly that he even struck coins that lacked only his image.[7]

3. After Stilicho had been killed, the barbarians with him took his son and left immediately. And when they neared Rome, they let him seek refuge in one of the holy places offering asylum, while they ravaged the area around the city, both because they wanted to avenge Stilicho and because they were starving. But when Eucherius was slain on orders from Honorius that superseded the rights of asylum, the barbarians for this reason joined Alaric and incited him to war against the Romans.[8]

Alaric **made his way** quickly **to** Portus. This, the largest dockyard of Rome, includes three harbors and is the size of a small city. It is here that all the public food supply is stored as well, according to ancient custom. **Having taken Portus** easily, he besieged Rome and through starvation and other means subjected it completely. Alaric then, in accordance with the Romans'

---

comment on the story is to the effect that Stilicho might have seen one of his grandsons succeed Honorius, had he been patient.

7. Zecchini ("Filostorgio," 586–88) accepts our author's story of Stilicho minting unauthorized coins and says that he did so in order to pay for the troops he needed during the crises of 407–408. The claim that he did so in order to further his dynastic ambitions reflects the official version of the reason for his downfall: that he appropriated public funds for his own use (*Cod. theod.* 9.42.22).

8. When Honorius received the news of the death of his brother Arcadius on 1 May 408, he wanted to go to Constantinople to supervise the accession of his young nephew, Theodosius II, but was dissuaded by Stilicho, who wished to go there himself to achieve his dream of an administrative reunification of the two halves of the realm. Rumors quickly spread, however, that the real purpose of his visit was to enthrone his own son Eucherius, and the Roman troops at Ticinum, where Honorius had gone to send them off to Gaul, broke into a violent mutiny and killed many of the high officials among Stilicho's supporters. The latter refused to let the barbarian troops punish the mutineers, sought an interview with Honorius at Ravenna, was told that his arrest had been ordered, and took sanctuary in a church, but came out when promised his life. Then, however, he was told that Honorius had ordered his execution, to which he submitted, loyal to the end, ordering his men not to resist. The mutineers now turned to killing the families of the barbarian allies, who in response flocked to Alaric's standard. Stilicho's son Eucherius got away to Rome and took refuge in a church there but was dragged out and killed by emissaries from Honorius a few days before Alaric arrived in the late autumn of 408. See Zosimus 5.34.5; 5.35.3–4, 6; 5.37.4–6; Olympiodorus 6; Sozomen 9.4.8; Orosius 7.38.6.

choice (he permitted them this) **proclaimed** Attalus their **emperor.** He was of Ionian stock, pagan in religion, and prefect of the city.[9]

Afterwards, following the proclamation, he allowed the remnant of the Romans, those, that is, who had survived the starvation and the **cannibalism,** to get food for themselves from Portus. Then, taking Attalus, for whom he acted as general, **he marched to Ravenna against Honorius.**[10] Attalus ordered Honorius **to retire to private life** and to purchase the safety of the rest of his body by the amputation of its extremities.[11]

Sarus, however, to whom Honorius had given the generalship after

---

9. Alaric blockaded Rome, reducing it to a state in which it paid the heavy ransom he demanded and promised him a treaty. He withdrew to Etruria, but Honorius refused to honor the promise of a treaty or indeed to negotiate with the Goth at all. In 409, then, Alaric returned to Rome and by cutting off its grain supply from Portus forced the senate to agree to the proclamation of a rival emperor: the elderly city prefect Priscus Attalus, a pagan quickly baptized by an African bishop. See Zosimus 6.6.1–6.7.1; Olympiodorus 3; Socrates 7.10.4–5; Sozomen 9.8.1. Philostorgius alone of all the sources is reported to have said that Alaric allowed the Romans their choice in the matter, which is hardly true and is probably an instance of Photius's carelessness in epitomizing. Our author may have said something like Sozomen does: that Alaric had the senate proclaim Attalus.

10. On the report of cannibalism among the starving Romans, see Olympiodorus 4. On Attalus's "appointment" of Alaric as general, see Zosimus 6.7.2; Sozomen 9.8.2. On the march against Honorius, see Zosimus 6.7.6; Sozomen 9.8.4; Procopius, *Bella* 3.2.29.

11. On the demand for Honorius's retirement and mutilation, see Olympiodorus 13; Sozomen 9.8.5; Zosimus 6.8.1; Paschoud, *Zosime,* 3:249–50. Paschoud says that either Philostorgius himself errs in his report or has once again been misrepresented by Photius. What happened is that Jovius, Stilicho's old supporter who had succeeded Olympius and was acting as Honorius's legate in his negotiations with Attalus, received the latter's demand that Honorius retire to an isolated place, retaining the pomp of office without the power. Jovius accepted the demand with alacrity and in fact turned coat and added the suggestion that Honorius be mutilated. The latter was contemplating flight when four thousand troops arrived from the east in his support and, in addition, news reached him that his loyal governor in Africa had destroyed the expeditionary force sent there by Attalus to secure the grain shipments. Alaric now sought and received a promise of fresh negotiations from Honorius on condition that he depose Attalus, which he did in the summer of 410; the old man had in any case begun showing signs of an unsuitable independence of mind. But before the negotiations could begin, Alaric's camp was attacked by Sarus, and, suspecting the Romans of treachery, he marched on Rome once again and sacked it in August of 410.

Stilicho, met Alaric, beat him in battle, and chased him from Ravenna.[12] Alaric made his way to Portus and stripped Attalus of his imperial power; some say he was accused of being ill-disposed to him, while others say that it was because he planned to make a truce with Honorius and thought that he should first get rid of what was likely to be an obstacle. After that, Alaric returned to Ravenna and offered a truce but was rebuffed by the Sarus just mentioned, who said that someone liable to punishment for his recklessness was not worthy to be taken into friendship.

Alaric, angered at this, marched on Rome as an enemy a year after his previous attack on Portus. And thus it happened that all the magnificence of that glory and the renown of that might was decimated by the fire of the foreigner, the sword of the enemy, and captivity by the barbarian. And when the city was lying in ruins, Alaric plundered Campania, and there he fell ill and died.[13]

4. Now his **wife's brother**[14] ....

---

12. Philostorgius/Photius's notice about Sarus is once again garbled. The Gothic leader had helped Stilicho beat Radagaisus in 406; the following year Stilicho sent him against the usurper Constantine in Gaul, where he was this time unsuccessful. Zosimus 5.36.2 nonetheless criticizes Honorius for not doing precisely what 12.3 says he did: appointing Sarus to succeed Stilicho as *magister militum in praesenti* (see *PLRE* 2:978–9). On the whole episode, see Sozomen 9.8.9–11; 9.9.2–4; Zosimus 6.9–12; Olympiodorus 3; 13; Socrates 7.10.4; Jordanes, *Getica* 156–157; Procopius, *Bella* 3.2.14–27.

13. After the sack, Alaric led his forces south, taking with him Honorius's sister Galla Placidia and intending to invade Africa. But a storm wrecked his ships, and he had to withdraw north. At Consentia he took sick and died late in 410. He was succeeded by his brother-in-law Ataulf.

14. On the state of the text in 12.4–6, see Bidez, *Philostorgius*, 143–45. Galla Placidia remained with Ataulf when he passed into Gaul early in 412 and then continued north to force his company upon the latest usurper, the Gallo-Roman Jovinus. Jovinus disappointed him by naming his brother Sebastian emperor, so he struck a bargain with Honorius to put down the usurpation and then struck off Sebastian's head and sent it to Ravenna. Jovinus himself was put to death while under escort to the same place in the autumn of 413. Honorius's side of the agreement was to send provisions to the Goths in return for getting his sister back, but he was kept from fulfilling it by the revolt of Heraclian, the governor of Africa, who closed down the grain supplies and invaded Italy in 413. Ataulf, miffed, retained Placidia and thus entered into rivalry with Honorius's new *magister utriusque militiae*, Constantius, who himself desired to marry her and perhaps succeed his childless master. But at Narbo on 1 January 414 Placidia, perhaps following her own ambition and personal inclinations, married Ataulf, who in response to Constantius's naval blockade of Narbo proclaimed the durable Attalus emperor once again. The blockade, however, forced the Visigoths to

....

....

.... they were of Sauromatian barbarian stock, and [he?] who had sprung from iron was then joined to the race of
clay. And that is not all, but it [happened] also when again Ataulf was joined in
marriage to Placidia, since the substance of clay[15] ....

....

....

....

.... harboring the hope that he
himself might marry Placidia once he had vanquished Ataulf.[16] But not long
afterwards Ataulf, who had done many wicked deeds, was slain by one of his
own men in a fit of anger. Thereupon the barbarians made their peace with
Honorius, and having received provisions and part of Gaul for agriculture,
they handed over to the emperor his sister and Attalus.

5. Afterwards Rome recovered from these many calamities and people settled there.[17] The emperor visited it and encouraged its settlement with hand
and tongue. And ascending a dais, the first step of which he compelled Atta-
lus to bestride...

....

.... [he] cut off two **fingers of his right hand,** one of which ...... while the
other is called the forefinger. And he banished him[18] to the island of Lipara,
inflicting no further penalty, but even providing the necessities of life ......[19]

----

abandon the government and move to Spain, leaving Attalus to be captured, taken to
Ravenna, put on display and mutilated in Rome in 416, and then banished to Lipara.

Ataulf and his followers settled in Barcelona, and Placidia gave him a son, Theodosius, who died in infancy, Ataulf himself being murdered in the summer of 415 in a
feud. His successor, Sigeric, was in turn killed a week later, and the new king, Wallia,
was forced by the continuing blockade to come to terms with the Romans: Placidia in
return for provisions. Constantius at last had his prize, and on 1 January 417 he married his reluctant fiancée.

15. The words about iron and clay refer to Dan 2:31–45. Hydatius (*Chron.* 414)
also associates the marriage with Daniel's prophecy, but this time with Dan 11:6.
"Iron" was thought to mean the Roman empire (see Arendzen, "New Syriac Text,"
407).

16. On Placidia's adventures, see Stewart I. Oost, *Galla Placidia Augusta: A Biographical Essay* (Chicago: University of Chicago Press, 1968), 103–35.

17. On Rome's rapid recovery after its sack, see Olympiodorus 25.

18. For "he banished him," reading τοῦτον [φυγαδεύει] instead of τούτους.

19. On Honorius's treatment of Attalus, see Olympiodorus 13; Prosper Tiro,
Chron. 417; Orosius 7.42.9.

6. During the same time, Jovinus rose up ....
.... perished, and his brother Sebastian, who had his heart set on the same thing, paid the same penalty.[20] <But Heraclian>, who followed their example and whom fortune mocked even more, ended his life more honorably, it being clearly proclaimed by divine .... does not leave unadorned, nor approve of usurpers, but of those who support the legitimate emperor, with whom she herself is ranged.[21]

7. When Arcadius died, his very young son Theodosius was proclaimed successor to the eastern empire. His sister Pulcheria was with him, and she assisted with the imperial subscriptions and made sure they were in order.[22]

8. When Theodosius had reached adolescence, on the nineteenth of July at about the eighth hour, the sun was so completely eclipsed that stars appeared. And such a drought followed this event that there was everywhere an unusually high number of deaths of human beings and animals.

There appeared in the sky with the sun while in eclipse a cone-shaped light, which some out of ignorance called a comet. But it showed none of the features of a comet. For the light did not form a tail, nor was it at all like a star; rather, it resembled a great lamp-flame appearing on its own, with no star under it to form a wick for it. Its movement was also different. It began where the sun rises at the equinox, from there passed over the last star in the Bear's tail, and went on slowly westward. But when it had traversed the sky, it disappeared, having taken more than four months to make its journey.

---

20. On the rebellions in 12.6, see Jordanes, *Getica* 165; Orosius 7.42.6, 10–14; Olympiodorus 19; 23; Marcellinus, *Chron.* 412; Hydatius, *Chron.* 413; Prosper Tiro, *Chron.* 413; Malalas 13.48; Theophanes 127B; *Cod. theod.* 15.14.13.

21. In "with whom she herself is ranged," "she" may refer to divine providence or justice, if πρόνοια or δίκη stood in the lacuna.

22. Theodosius II was seven years old when his father Arcadius died in 408; Pulcheria was nine. Their mother Eudoxia had died in 404, and power had passed in 405 into the capable hands of the praetorian prefect Anthemius, who established enduring peaceful relations with Persia at the beginning of the reign of Yezdegerd I and a settlement with the troublesome adherents of John Chrysostom. Anthemius continued in office until 414, ensuring a peaceful transition at the death of Arcadius. It was in that year that the formidable Pulcheria, then just fifteen, was named Augusta and took over the supervision of her brother's education and control of the government (see Socrates 7.1.1; Sozomen 9.1; Theodoret, *Hist. eccl.* 5.36.2–3; *Chron. pasch.* P414; Marcellinus, *Chron.* 414; George Monachus, *Chron.* 611.5; Theophanes 156B). She could not convince Theodosius of the danger of subscribing documents unread (Zonaras 13.23.19–25) until finally, in exasperation, she placed in front of him a bill of sale of his own wife and then, when he had subscribed it with his usual carelessness, showed him what he had done (Leo Grammaticus 110.4–9; *Suda*, Π 2145).

The light sometimes stretched out to such a great length that at its apex it exceeded the proportions of a cone, while at other times it contracted to the measurements proper to that figure. And it had other portentous features that showed how it differed from the usual phenomena. It first appeared at midsummer and lasted until almost the end of autumn.[23]

This was, then, yet another sign of great wars and indescribable human slaughter. And the year following there began earthquakes that it would be hard to compare to those previous,[24] while along with the earthquakes a fire burst down from the sky that destroyed all hope of safety. It did not, however, cause the loss of human life, for the divine benevolence sent a strong wind that drove the fire from wherever it was and blew it into the sea. And then there was a strange sight to be seen: the waves on fire far and wide as though they were a thickly vegetated landscape, until the conflagration was completely quenched by the sea.

9. In many places, when the earthquakes occurred one could see the roofs of houses separate from each other with a great noise of crashing and clattering, so that the sky became plainly visible to those inside. And then after they had been separated so far apart, they came back together and were once again so closely joined as to leave no trace of what had happened. The same accident occurred in many places to the floors as well. What happened was that those living under the grain storage rooms were smothered when the grain poured down upon them through the floor structures. And afterwards the floor fit so tightly together again that no one could see from where the lethal grain had poured.

And other such unheard-of events occurred at the time, showing that they resulted not from natural causes, as the pagans foolishly suppose, but were the lashes of divine anger.

10. He tries in various ways to show that earthquakes are caused neither by floods of water, nor by blasts of wind shut up within the hollows of the

---

23. On the eclipse and the strange star, see Brooks and Chabot, *Chronica minora,* 1.300 (a. 418); Hydatius, *Chron.* 417; Marcellinus, *Chron.* 418. On the shape of the star, compare 10.9.

24. On the earthquakes, see Marcellinus, *Chron.* 419. In 12.10 Philostorgius lists the natural explanations of earthquakes in the same order as does Ammianus 17.7.11–12 (water pressure in the recesses of the earth, or subterranean winds that find no outlet, or excessive drought or rainfall that opens gaps in the earth to admit blasts of air from outside). They were the traditional ones (Aristotle, *Meteorologica* 2.7–8; Pliny, *Nat.* 2.192; Seneca, *Naturales quaestiones* 6.12.2). It is important to notice the trouble he takes to show that it is unreasonable to accept the natural explanations.

earth, nor even by any kind of shifting of the earth, but solely by the divine will for the correction and rebuke of sinners. He says that he maintains this because none of the elements just mentioned could cause such impressive phenomena by their natural power. At God's will, however, even the smallest raindrop or lightest snowflake falling upon Olympus in Macedonia, or any other of the largest mountains, would move it easily. And God is often found using these things to chastise people. The Red Sea, for instance, which he could easily have separated at one stroke, he first lashed and pushed together with a strong south wind, and thus separated, although the south wind has no such natural power; the supernal force used it in a marvelous way to accomplish its own will. And the rod that struck the rock made springs of water flow from it, and the stream of the Jordan healed leprosy,[25] although it was not their natures that enabled them to do so; it was rather their Maker, who has the great and ineluctable power to remake each created thing for whatever use he wants.

11. After the death of Eudoxius, who was head of the Eunomian assembly in Constantinople, Lucian, the son of Eunomius's sister, was appointed in his place. They say that he was addicted to the love of money and related vices and, fearing that he would have to pay the penalty for this, seceded from the rest of the Eunomian sect and set himself up as leader of his own party. He headed a not inconsiderable sect, since all those of infamous character and those given over to a variety of vices flocked to him.[26]

12. The emperor Honorius took General Constantius as his partner in rule because he was related to him, Placidia having already borne him a son, Valentinian, and Honorius conferred on him the rank of *nobilissimus*.[27] The images of Constantius were sent to the east, as was customarily done by those who had just acceded to the throne. Theodosius, however, did not approve of the appointment and did not accept them. Constantius was making ready to

---

25. On the parting of the Red Sea, see Exod 14:21; on the water from the rock, Num 20:11; on the Jordan healing leprosy, 2 Kgs 5:14.

26. See further Arendzen, "New Syriac Text," 406–9: the denunciation of "wicked pastors."

27. On Constantius and his marriage to Placidia, see 157–58 n. 14. She bore him two children, Honoria, born in 417 or 418, and Valentinian III, born on 2 July 419. Constantius was elevated to the rank of Augustus in 421 and died the same year. See Olympiodorus 34; Socrates 7.24.2; Sozomen 9.16.2; Procopius, *Bella* 3.3.4; Zonaras 13.21.9–10; Malalas 13.48–49; Theophanes 130B; Prosper Tiro, *Chron.* 418; 420; Marcellinus, *Chron.* 419; Brooks and Chabot, *Chronica minora*, 1:630, 656–57; Hydatius, *Chron.* 420–421; *Comp. chron.* 68.30–69.1.

go to war over the insult when death intervened and relieved him of his life and his cares after he had reigned for six months.[28]

13. In the tenth consulship of the emperor Theodosius and the thirteenth of Honorius, Honorius died of dropsy, and John usurped power and sent an embassy to Theodosius. The embassy was unsuccessful, and the legates were mistreated and were furthermore banished, each to a different part of the Propontis. Theodosius sent Placidia and Valentianian III to Thessalonica (after Constantius's death they had escaped to Byzantium), bestowed the rank of Caesar on his cousin there, and entrusted the campaign against the usurper to General Ardabur and his son Aspar.[29]

Bringing with them Placidia and Valentinian, they drove through Pannonia and Illyricum and took Salona, a city of Dalmatia, by storm. From there Ardabur proceeded against the usurper with a naval force. As for Aspar, he took the cavalry and, outrunning rumor in the swiftness of his onset, captured the great city of Aquileia, with Valentinian and Placidia in his company.

So he took possession of that great <city?> without trouble. As for Ardabur, a strong wind took him and blew him, along with two other triremes,

---

28. After Constantius's death, the relationship between Honorius and Placidia deteriorated to the point where she and her children withdrew to Constantinople in 323, the same year that Honorius died. As soon as news of this reached Theodosius, he sent a force to occupy Salona in Dalmatia (contrary to what 12.13 says about Ardabur taking the city on his way to put down the usurper; cf. Socrates 7.23.1). This move, together with his previous refusal to recognize Constantius as Augustus, may have suggested to western officials that he meant to become sole emperor over the entire realm, a possibility that was countered by the elevation in December of John, *primicerius notariorum* in Rome, to the imperial throne. When John's legates were mistreated by Theodosius, the usurper sent that rising star, his lieutenant Flavius Aetius, to get help from the Huns among whom he had once lived as a hostage and with whom he had maintained close ties. See Olympiodorus 41; 46; Gregory of Tours, *Historia Francorum* 2.8; Zonaras 13.21.17–18; Cedrenus 336B; Brooks and Chabot, *Chronica minora*, 1:630; Socrates 7.23–24; Procopius, *Bella* 3.3.5–9; Theophanes 149B–150B; Malalas 14.7; Marcellinus, *Chron.* 424–425; Hydatius, *Chron.* 424–425; Prosper Tiro, *Chron.* 423–424.

29. If Theodosius had had any thoughts of becoming sole emperor, he now abandoned them and in 424 belatedly recognized Constantius's title as Augustus and Placidia's as Augusta, raised Valentinian to the rank of Caesar, and sent his mother and him with Ardabur to Salona (already occupied by his forces). From there Ardabur proceeded by sea and Aspar by land. The latter quickly captured Aquileia, Aetius not yet having returned with his Huns, while Ardabur, who had been blown into the clutches of the usurper in Ravenna, took the advantage of his situation described in 12.13.

into the hands of the usurper, who however treated him kindly with a view to making a treaty. Ardabur took advantage of the great freedom he had <to suborn?> the usurper's retired officers,[30] who were already in the mood for this, and he consolidated a plot against him. He sent to his son Aspar to come as though to a victory assured. The latter arrived quickly on the scene with the cavalry, there was some sort of battle, John was captured when he was betrayed by his staff, and he was sent to Placidia and Valentinian in Aquileia. There his hand was cut off first and then his head; he had usurped power for a year and a half. And then Theodosius sent and proclaimed Valentinian emperor.

13a [Photius, *Bibliotheca* codex 40]. [Philostorgius] goes down to the time of Theodosius the Younger, stopping at the year when Theodosius entrusted the government of Rome, upon the death of Honorius, to his nephew Valentinian the Younger, the son of Placidia and Constantius.

14. Aetius, John the usurper's lieutenant, arrived three days after his death, leading as many as sixty thousand barbarian mercenaries. Battle was joined between him and Aspar's men, and great slaughter ensued of those on either side. Afterwards Aetius made peace with Placidia and Valentinian and received the title of count. The barbarians were persuaded to lay aside their anger and their arms with the assistance of gold, and having given hostages and accepted pledges, they retired to their own lands.[31]

---

30. The translation "<to suborn?> the usurper's retired officers" reflects ἀποστρατήγους <ὑπαγόμενος>. Perhaps read ὑποστρατήγους ("staff officers").

31. On 12.14, see Prosper Tiro, *Chron.* 425; Brooks and Chabot, *Chronica minora*, 1:658 (a. 425). On Philostorgius as a source for the story of Aetius, see Giuseppe Zecchini, *Aezio: L'ultima difesa dell'Occidente romano* (Rome: Bretschneider, 1983), 37–40. The Huns having been bought off, Aetius, about whom so much was to be heard in the years following, was given the rank of *comes et magister militum per Gallias* and sent off to deal with the Visigoths besieging Arles. On 23 October 425 Valentinian III was proclaimed Augustus in Rome by the representative of the emperor in Constantinople, thus stamping the western throne with the fateful claim of eastern primacy.

APPENDIX 1
BEGINNING OF THE *PASSION OF ARTEMIUS*
WITH PHILOSTORGIUS'S REMARKS ABOUT ARTEMIUS

Account or Narrative of the Martyrdom
of the Great, Holy, and Glorious Martyr and Wonder-Worker Artemius[1]
Gathered from the Church History of Philostorgius
and Certain Others
by John, a Monk of Rhodes[2]

---

1. The first two appendices give the opening part of the *Passion of Artemius*, in which its author mentions his sources, and then those sections of it that appear to draw in some way upon Philostorgius but that cannot be readily mustered within the framework of Photius's *Epitome*. On Artemius, see A7.36; Ammianus 17.11.5; 22.11.2, 3, 8; Athanasius, *Festal Index* 32; *S. Pachomii Vita Prima* 137–138; *Vita Tertia* 190; *De S. Pachomio Ep. Ammonis* 31; perhaps Julian, *Ep.* 21 (ed. Wright, LCL) 379A–B; *PLRE* 1:112; Jürgen Dummer, "Fl. Artemius dux Aegypti," *APF* 21 (1971): 121–44; Francesco S. Barcellona, "Martiri e confessori dell'età di Giuliano l'Apostata: dalla storia alla legenda," in *Pagani e cristiani da Giuliano l'Apostata al sacco di Roma* (ed. Franca Ela Consolino; Soveria Mannelli: Rubbettino, 1995), 53–83; Gabriele Marasco, "L'imperatore Giuliano e l'esecuzione di Fl. Artemio, *dux Aegypti*," *Prometheus* 23 (1997): 59–78. He was *dux Aegypti* in 360, which supports what is said in A1.8 about his close relationship with Constantius. In 362, however, he was arrested, tried, and executed on Julian's orders, although modern scholarship is not agreed on what grounds. The charges mentioned in the ancient Christian sources are zeal against paganism, including the destruction of pagan religious property, and implication in Gallus's death. The former, together with his persecution of Athanasius and his followers and his execution by the Apostate, apparently won him his credentials as a true anti-Nicene martyr in Philostorgius's eyes.

2. The *Artemii Passio* is usually credited to one John of Rhodes (of uncertain date: eighth or ninth century), although its most recent editor has put in a claim for John of Damascus (ca. 655–ca. 750); see Kotter, *Opera homiletica et hagiographica*, 185–245. The text here translated is, as usual, Bidez's; hence the "of Rhodes" in the subtitle (for which the manuscript support is quite slim; see Kotter, *Opera homiletica et hagiographica*, 185–87). On the writing, see Bidez, *Philostorgius*, xliv–lxviii; Kotter, *Opera*

1. As I set out to recount the manly deeds of the great and glorious martyr Artemius, the contest he underwent, and the nobility of his lineage when traced back to its origins, O divinely gathered sacred assembly, I invoke the martyr himself and the grace of the Spirit overshadowing him to aid and assist me in my discourse. And I appeal to you as well, as one who has need of your prayers, that what I set out to do may be free of difficulty and offense and that I may steer my narrative of his martyrdom and confession in the direction I have chosen.

And may no one criticize my endeavor on account of the first and ancient record of this marvelous and revered man. Its author wrote to the best of his ability and as the occasion required, things then being in a state of much bother and confusion. He was not himself someone who wrote with elegance and a practiced style but with simplicity and restraint; concerned only for the truth, he aimed to deliver his words in no particular way, having just touched with his fingertip the sacred discipline of rhetoric, as the proverb says, 2. just as I myself am not equal to recounting the narrative, even though my love for the martyr attracts and dominates my thoughts and forces me to speak. He is rather to be commended for the enthusiasm and faith he showed concerning the martyr, since he dared, even though artlessly, to undertake the narrative of his martyrdom, especially since the impious apostate Julian had ordered that no record or any other kind of description should be made of those martyred for Christ, just as the former emperors had prescribed, but that most of them should perish with no one to speak on their behalf.[3] This edict having been published everywhere, when those who confessed Christ were punished, none of the official record-keepers or so-called shorthand-writers hesitated to obey the order, that being their way. For the Apostate strove to obliterate the very renown of the martyrs. Only a very few folk hidden in dark and lightless places dared to attempt to compose accounts of these men, living as they did in fear of the sovereign's cruelty. Thus untold numbers of Christians perished throughout the world without being granted a hearing in the usual way. But the athletes of Christ suffered no harm from not being memorialized, since those whose names God inscribed in heaven had no need of human records. But enough of this subject.

---

homiletica et hagiographica, 185–201. Others were also at work on Artemius's legend, as appendices 3 and 7.36 show. Further, as the subtitle here suggests, he acquired a great reputation as a wonder-worker, especially of healings (see Virgil S. Crisafulli and John W. Nesbitt, *The Miracles of St. Artemios: A Collection of Miracle Stories by an Anonymous Author of Seventh Century Byzantium* [Leiden: Brill, 1997]).

3. The earlier martyrdom used by the author of *Artemii Passio* and mentioned by him here may be found in appendix 3.

3. As for me, O sacred assembly, Christ's people divinely gathered, holy nation and royal priesthood, when I had read so many works, and especially of authors writing about the lives and deeds of the emperors, and then those concerned with the history of the church, and had found the martyr's name ringing down through the passages, with everyone acknowledging him to be an illustrious and famous man, I did not think it right to consign these matters to oblivion but to bring them into the open and set them before you as those who love Christ and the martyrs, lest the excellent achievements of this divine martyr lie hidden with insufficient words to express them. I also wanted to delight your ears with the telling of this narrative and with the brave deeds of the martyr that have recently come to light.

4. Many historians, then, have mentioned this revered man: Eusebius, surnamed Pamphilou; Socrates, of the sect of Novatus; Philostorgius, himself of the sect of Eunomius; Theodoret; and several others.[4]

Of this group, Eusebius, who lived in the time of Constantine the Great and was well known and the most learned of the bishops of the time, says that the martyr was a member of the senate and one of the emperor's closest acquaintances and that he was most fervent in seeking to be first a companion, and then a friend, of his son Constantius. The blessed man apparently never ceased being Constantius's friend, giving evidence as he did of his wonderful character and great works.[5] As for Philostorgius, however fervent a supporter of Eunomius's sect he may have been, he yet exalts the martyr above all others, extolling the constancy and scrupulousness he showed in his actions and tracing the martyr's noble lineage from its origins, and all this even before he describes the contest of his martyrdom. I too will therefore begin the account of him as do the records of old.

5.[6] It was a time when idolatry had just come to an end and the error induced by demons squelched by the kindness of our great God and Savior Jesus Christ shown to the blessed and revered Constantine, the most splen-

---

4. The "several others" are perhaps those in A3.16–19.

5. Eusebius does not in fact mention Artemius at all. The information that he is said here to have given seems reliable, however; Artemius quite probably was close to Constantius, who would have needed someone he trusted in Egypt, given the continuing tensions there (see Dummer, "Fl. Artemius dux Aegypti," 140–41 n. 135). Bidez (*Philostorgius*, li–lii) conjectures that the inaccuracies found at the beginning of section 4 are due to John's use of some compilation of church history rather than the original historians themselves, the exception being Philostorgius, of whom the text of *AP* shows acquaintance at first hand.

6. Compare sections 5 and 6 with Theodoret, *Hist. eccl.* 1.2.

did and devout emperor, son of Constans[7] and of the blessed Helena, that
he might recall him from the vain error of idols [by?] showing him[8] the
life-giving cross in the sky, so that he might overcome the hostile, wicked
emperors through the influence and power of the precious cross, and that
the horn of the Christians, dear to God, might be lifted up when it had been
aided and increased by his zeal and faith. Thus the gospel of Christ filled the
whole world, all the altars of the idols and their statues and all of their temples
were destroyed, wherever they were on earth, and all of God's churches were
rebuilt that the previous impious emperors who hated Christ had burned to
the ground.[9]

6. When this had happened, the devil, who envies the good, could not
bear such a change in affairs, so he caused a tempest and upheaval through
his own toadies. Arius, that is, after whom this madness was named and who
was a presbyter of the church in Alexandria, upset it badly by introducing
a lawless doctrine full of every kind of blasphemy. With darkened mind he
said that the only begotten Son of God, who is before the ages, was a creature
and foreign to the substance of God the Father. For this reason, the Council
in Nicaea of the 318 fathers met and after deposing Arius declared that the
Son of God, our Lord Jesus Christ, was consubstantial to the Father. But these
matters are treated as well by the non-Christian histories, while several of our
own historians have described them with all detail and clarity. And this is not
the suitable time to dwell on them, since they would require a more detailed
treatment and investigation. What I will do next will be to relate how his life
came to an end. [There follows 2.16a.]

8 [just after 3.1a *AP* 8].[10] Now the great Artemius was with Constantius
on every occasion and for every affair, since he was the best of friends and a
fervent admirer of those who distinguished themselves in virtue and learn-

---

7. Constantine's father is also called "Constans" in 2.16a (*AP* 7 and 41).

8. The translation "recall him from the vain error of idols [by?] showing him"
reflects the reading ἀνεκαλέσατο διὰ τῆς instead of καὶ τῆς.

9. On the tradition that Constantine destroyed pagan temples, see A7.8; *AP*
33; Sozomen 2.5; *Bios* 324.16–19. The tradition has its roots in Eusebius's biography,
whose evidence in this matter is far from clear: compare *Vit. Const.* 2.44 and 45 with
2.56 and 60, and these passages again with 4.23 and 25. Julian's words, however, must
be taken as decisive: Constantine neglected the temples; it was his sons who destroyed
them (*Or.* 7.228B). This agrees with Libanius, *Or.* 30.6 and 62.8. The tradition that
Constantine destroyed the temples was encouraged by his son's antipagan policies as
well as by Constantine's removal of temple artifacts in order to adorn Constantinople
(Eusebius, *Vit. Const.* 3.52–58; Libanius, *Or.* 62.8; Zosimus 5.24.6).

10. Section 8 in appendix 1 corresponds to section 9 in PG 96:1260 and in Kotter's edition (*Opera homiletica et hagiographica*, 206).

ing and of the Christian faith. No one has left us any written record of his native place and family, save that the ancestors of the thrice-blessed man were both noble and great. Whence the following is also related of him, that he was the one ordered by Constantius to arrange the return of the all-holy relics of Christ's apostles Andrew, Luke, and Timothy, as our account will show as it proceeds.[11] I will relate all these things in proper order, setting them out chronologically and explaining them in all due detail.

16 [just after 4.3a]. When [Constantius] happened to be in Odrysian territory, where the emperor Hadrian had founded a city and thus given his name to the place, he found out from one of the bishops that the bodies of Christ's apostles Andrew and Luke were buried in Achaia: Andrew in Patrae and Luke in Thebes in Boeotia.[12]

When the emperor Constantius heard this, he rejoiced at the report and shouted aloud and said to those present, "Call Artemius here." When he came on the run, he said to him, "I congratulate you, most God-beloved of all men!" He replied, "May you rejoice in me in every way, your majesty, and may nothing trouble you ever!" The emperor went on, "Can you think of anything more wonderful, O best of friends, than the discovery of the bodies of Christ's apostles?" The great Artemius replied, "Who has revealed this treasure to us today, my lord, and where is he from?" Constantius said, "The bishop of Achaia, who is currently in charge [of the church] in Patrae. But go now, best of men, and have them brought back to Constantinople with all speed."[13]

17. When Artemius heard these words from the emperor, he made his way to where the apostles were in order to bring back their all-holy relics to Constantinople. [3.2a inserted here].

18. Artemius was an outstanding person and was the one assigned to see to their transportation. As a reward for this service, the emperor, at the bishops' request, put him in charge of Egypt.[14] This is what the author of the history says about the martyr, testifying about him that even before the contest of martyrdom he was respected by all because the excellence of the life he led was so obvious. Now as regards Luke, the eunuch Anatolius, one of the

---

11. On the translation to Constantinople of the relics of Andrew, Luke, and Timothy, see 3.2, 3.2a, and 38 n. 4; see also A3.16; *Consul. const.* 356; 357; Jerome, *Chron.* 356; 357; *Vir. ill.* 7; *Chron. pasch.* P295B.

12. On Hadrian and the Odrysian territory and the bishop who told Constantius about the relics, etc., see Simeon Metaphrastes, *Commentarius in divum Lucam* 10 (PG 115:1137C).

13. On the charge to Artemius to carry out the translation, see Zonaras 13.11.28; *Comp. chron.* 56.1–5; *Synax.* 147.47–49; 266.13–16; 412.16–22.

14. On Artemius's assignment to Egypt, see Theodoret, *Hist. eccl.* 3.18.1.

servants of the imperial chamber, who had himself experienced the effect of his holiness, gave the following account. Anatolius said that he had been in a bad way and that the illness had progressed to where it had baffled the doctors' skills. Now those who were bringing the coffin in which Luke was lying had sailed in, and it was just being borne from the sea to the church, and when he came up eagerly and helped the others carry it to the extent that his strength allowed, he was at once freed from his sickness and remained so for the rest of his life, which continued on for quite a few years.[15]

---

15. On the story about Anatolius, see Simeon Metaphrastes, *Commentarius in divum Lucam* 11.

Appendix 2

From the *Passion of Artemius*: Defense of Christianity against the Emperor Julian

26. The Apostate said, "You wicked man, who have no share in the benevolence of the gods, has Christ, whose short life began but yesterday in the time of Caesar Augustus, been made an eternal king by you today?" The martyr answered, "With respect to his humanity and the mystery of his inexpressible and ineffable dispensation or incarnation, that is indeed so, your majesty, since with respect to his divine generation before the ages, there is no time that will be found to precede it."

The Apostate, thinking that Christ's martyr was someone uneducated and untrained in pagan wisdom, spoke mockingly to him, "So, then, you wretch, your Christ has been begotten twice? If that is your boast, why, the pagans too have men of the highest wisdom, who have been begotten not just twice but even three times! Hermes, surnamed Trismegistos, was aware that he had come into the world three times, as his sacred and marvelous books relate, and for this reason he is called "Trismegistos."[1] Pythagoras likewise, who came later than he, was also born thrice, first as an Egyptian ship's captain, then as Euphorbus, the one mentioned by Homer, and finally as Pythagoras of Samos, Mnesarchus's son."[2]

---

1. On the origin of the epithet "Trismegistos" ("thrice-greatest"), see André-Jean Festugière, *La révélation d'Hermès Trismégiste* (4 vols.; Paris: Belles Lettres, 1950), 1:73–74 (it is the combination of the Greek superlative μέγιστος with the Coptic repetition of the adjective to indicate the superlative, hence μέγιστος repeated twice and then reduced to τρισμέγιστος). On the interpretation of "Trismegistos" as "thrice-born," see Arthur Darby Nock and André-Jean Festugière, *Corpus Hermeticum* (4 vols.; Paris: Belles Lettres, 1972), 4:148–49.

2. On the listing in the ancient sources of Pythagoras's successive rebirths, see Maria Timpanaro Cardini, *Pitagorici: testimonianze e frammenti* (3 vols.; Fiorenza: La Nuova Italia, 1958), 1:38–43; and Walter Burkert, *Lore and Science in Ancient Pythagoreanism* (trans. Edwin L. Minar Jr.; Cambridge: Harvard University Press, 1972),

27. The martyr laughed at this nonsense, or rather at the cleverness of the wise emperor and the absurdity of the pagans, but, suspecting that the tyrant was trying to make fun of Christ's generation by what he said, he replied to him with great severity and nobility:

"I should never have responded to you from the beginning, you vilest of men, nor granted you any answer in defense, but I said what I said because of the crowd that is here, since the greater part of it belongs to Christ's flock, and I shall now speak briefly out of a concern for their salvation. The prophets originally, many generations ago, foretold Christ, and there are many testimonies of his advent even in the oracles you have and the Sibylline writings.[3] The reason for his incarnation was the salvation and restoration of the human race from its lapse. For he came to the earth and drove out all illness and disease, and, what is still more incredible, he raised the malodorous dead with a single word; but most marvelous of all is that, having undergone the suffering of the cross for the world's salvation, he rose from the dead on the third day, as five hundred witnesses may tell,[4] even with soldiers guarding his tomb, so that one who wishes to contest his resurrection can find no way to do so. Having risen from the dead, he was seen by his disciples and stayed with them for no less than forty days, and while they were watching and looking on, he was taken up into the heavens, having sent out upon them the gift and power of the Holy Spirit. They spoke in foreign tongues as a result, without needing an interpreter. For the Holy Spirit spoke in them, so that they could foresee what was far off and prophesy the future. They went out and preached him everywhere, taking nothing along except his invisible power: they had neither shield nor spear nor sword, but naked, unarmed, and poor though they were, they captured the whole world, raising the dead, cleansing the leprous, and casting out demons. And who were they who did such things? Fishermen and unlettered folk ignorant of the world's wisdom.

28. "But those whom you mentioned in ridiculing Christ's generation, those wise men and theologians, as you have just referred to them, even if we were to admit that this nonsense were true, how did they benefit the world, or even a small or the least part of the world, by being begotten twice or three or four times? In the books of Hermes and Pythagoras, who ever raised the

---

138–41. Euphorbus is mentioned by Homer in *Iliad* 16.808–815, 850; 17.9–81; he was the son of Panthoös and Phrontis and was killed by Menelaus.

3. On the Sibylline prophecies of Christ, see Elliott, *Apocryphal New Testament*, 613–15; Johannes Geffcken, *Die Oracula Sibyllina* (GCS 8; Leipzig: Hinrichs, 1902), oracles of Christ's birth: 8.456–479; 12.28–33; of his return: 3.93–96; of his judgment: 2.241–244.

4. On the five hundred witnesses to Christ's resurrection, see 1 Cor 15:6.

dead or cleansed the leprous or expelled the demons whom you worship? As
for Hermes, whom you address as Trismegistos, he was an Egyptian man, and
having been brought up in Egyptian manners and having married a wife, he
produced children, the eldest of whom they call Tat, with whom he conversed
and to whom he dedicated his discourses. He also dedicated them to Asclepius of Epidaurus,[5] the originator, so you say, of the art of medicine and the
one to whom he explains his theology, which goes as follows:

"'To conceive of God is difficult, but to speak of him is impossible. For
he is of triple substance, an indescribable being and nature, having no likeness among mortals. But those whom human beings call gods have wrapped
themselves thickly in fable and error.'[6]

"And concerning the coming of Christ, he relates some obscure prophecy
that is not his own but that he derives from the theology of the Hebrews.[7]

"But why should Hermes' rotten, stinking words that you revere concern
me, when they have long since festered and decayed? Nor is it right to ask the
dead about the living, when one has the real witnesses in the divinely inspired
writings that foretold Christ's advent and divinity.

29. "As for Pythagoras, the founder of the Italian school, what great or
wonderful thing did he accomplish in his life, to which he was thrice born?
Was it that he went to Olympia, as you say, and showed his golden thigh to

---

5. On the genealogy of Hermes Trismegistos in the ancient sources, see Brian
P. Copenhaver, *Hermetica: The Greek Corpus Hermeticum and the Latin Asclepius in
a New English Translation, with Notes and Introduction* (Cambridge: Cambridge University Press, 1992), 133, 164–65 (Thoth-Agathodaimon-Hermes Trismegistos-Tat).
The Greeks identified Tat (= Thoth) with Hermes (Festugière, *La révélation d'Hermès
Trismégiste,* 1:67; Copenhaver, *Hermetica,* 93–94). The Hermetic discourses dedicated
to Tat are (in Nock and Festugière, *Corpus Hermeticum*) IIA, IV, V, XII, and XIII. The
discourse dedicated to Asclepius is in *Corp. herm.* 2.296–355.

6. On the quotation beginning "To conceive of God," see *Corp. herm.* 3.2–3;
4.129. "For he is of triple…" is not from the Hermetic literature; perhaps it origi-
nated as a marginal comment that the author of *AP* mistook for part of the original;
see Walter Scott, *Hermetica: The Ancient Greek and Latin Writings Which Contain
Religious or Philosophic Teachings Ascribed to Hermes Trismegistus* (4 vols.; Oxford:
Clarendon, 1936), 4:238.

7. In speaking of Hermes' prophecy of the advent of Christ, *AP* is retelling a tradition going back to Lactantius, who expounds passages from the Hermetic literature
that he thinks mention the double birth of God's Word: from the Father and from
his human mother (see Scott, *Hermetica,* 4:15–20). Lactantius's interpretation was
repeated by later Christian authors; see Paolo Siniscalco, "Ermete Trismegisto, profeta
pagano della rivelazione cristiana," *Atti della Accademia delle Scienze di Torino* 101
(1966–67): 83–113.

the judges of the games? Or that when he heard an ox bellowing as it was about to be sacrificed, he said, 'It has the soul of a man I dearly loved, and the wretch is speaking to me by bellowing?' Or that he made an eagle flying high up fall to the ground by incantation?[8]

"Such are the wonders worked by the thrice-born in Olympia, the thrice-miserable one maddened by his lust for glory and his hallucinations, who established the oath of the Tetraktys and called it the spring of ever-flowing nature and who worshiped the beans that caused his companions and him to perish when he was being pursued by the people of Tarentum. For when he refused to tread upon the place in which beans had been sown, he was slain there with his companions and disciples and [so] fell victim to his enemies.[9] Theano, his wife and disciple, when she refused to say why they did not eat beans, first had her tongue cut out and then lost her life with it.[10] 30. Behold the claims to superiority of your philosophers, the twice- and thrice-born, as you yourself have said in your speech; behold as well the miracles worked by my Christ for the salvation and restoration of the human race.

"Now Pythagoras and Hermes lead the souls of human beings down to the depths of Hades and perform certain transmigrations and reincarnations, transferring them sometimes into dumb animals and beasts and sometimes dragging the soul down into fish and plants and other cycles and revolutions,

---

8. On Pythagoras showing his golden thigh, see Aelian, *Varia Historia* 2.26; 4.17; Ammianus 22.16.21; Iamblichus, *VP* 28.135; Porphyry, *Vit. Pyth.* 28; Plutarch, *Numa* 8.5. The golden thigh was a sign of divinity (Burkert, *Lore and Science*, 159–60). On his recognition of a friend's voice in the cries of an animal, see Diogenes Laertius 8.36. On his bringing down of an eagle, see Iamblichus, *VP* 5.25; Porphyry, *Vit. Pyth.* 62; Plutarch, *Numa* 8.5. On the oath of the Tetraktys, see Iamblichus, *VP* 28.150; Kurt von Fritz, "Pythagoras," PW 24:200–203.

9. On Pythagoras's reverence for beans, see Diogenes Laertius 8.39–40. Iamblichus (*VP* 31.189–194) says that the tyrant Dionysius ambushed a group of Pythagoreans on the way from Tarentum to Metapontum (because they had rejected his friendship); they refused to cross a bean field in order to escape and so were all killed save two: Myllias of Croton and his wife Timycha of Lacedaemon. Myllias was ordered taken away when he declined to say why they had refused to tread on the beans, and Timycha was ordered to be tortured, but she bit off her tongue and spat it out at Dionysius in order to avoid speaking.

10. On Theano as Pythagoras' wife, see Diogenes Laertius, 8.42. Nonnus (*Historia* 18) says she was arrested by a tyrant to force her to reveal the secrets of her sect, but she avoided doing so in the same way as Timycha. See also Olympiodorus, *In Platonis Phaedonem commentaria* 1.8; Gregory of Nazianzus, *Or.* 4.70.

and driving it off.[11] But Christ, being true and eternal God, rendered the soul immortal and unageing by the divine spirit that was from the beginning and by his inbreathing, when he fashioned the first human being, as the divine and irreproachable books of Moses relate. And even when it fell with the body through disobedience and the deception of the serpent, destroyer of souls, he came to earth, and having lived with us and showed us the way of salvation through baptism and his resurrection from the dead, he led the soul back from the depths of Hades to the heavens. And when he comes back to judge the living and dead, he will raise up the bodies, join them to their souls, and render to each according to his deeds." [There follows 7.4b.]

34. The Apostate said, "But Constantine, you miserable wretches, abandoned the gods when he made innovations due to the wicked things he had learned, deceived as he was by you Galileans, since he lacked education and had no grounding either in Roman laws or Greek customs. I, on the other hand, having been highly educated in the Greek and Roman manner, you scoundrel, and well trained in the theologies of the men of old, Hermes, Orpheus, and Plato, and having become quite familiar with the Jewish scriptures and spurned their claptrap, order people once again to observe that most ancient custom and worship handed down by our ancestors, which is beloved of the gods, rather than to follow the follies of uneducated revolutionaries."[12]

41 [Julian speaks, continuation of 6.5b]. "...I renounced Christianity and went over to the Greek way of life, since I knew well that the most ancient way of life of the Greeks and Romans, with its fine customs and laws, included worship of those gods, belief in whom was grounded in reality. 42. For who can be of doubtful mind who sees the sun riding through the sky and the moon being drawn on a golden-railed chariot by a yoke of bulls? The one makes the daytime bright and rouses people to their work. The other illumines the night and beautifies the stars and with its unsleeping beams urges people to their sleep. Thus do the Greeks and Romans teach about the gods, Artemius, and not wrongly, but fittingly and with sound judgment. For what is there that is brighter than the sun? Or more radiant than the moon? What more delightful and comelier than the chorus of the stars? These are the beings the Greeks and Romans regard as divine and worship and upon whom they fix their hopes. They call the sun

---

11. On Hermes as the god of death and conductor of souls to the underworld, see S. Eitrem, "Hermes," PW 8.1:789–92. On Pythagoras as the divine traveler to the underworld and teacher of reincarnation, see Burkert, *Lore and Science,* 120–65.

12. On Julian's education in the pagan manner, see 7.1a. On his education in the sacred scriptures, see Cyril, *Contra Julianum imperatorem: Prooemium* (PG 76:508A).

Apollo, the moon Artemis, and the greatest stars, which they call planets and which occupy the seven heavenly spheres, they name Saturn, Jupiter, Mercury, Mars, and Venus. These govern the whole world, and by their powers the whole earth under heaven is administered. People therefore put up images of them that they revere and honor, at the same time making up certain fables for the fun of it. But they do not honor the images as gods, far from it! Only the simplest and most uncultured people suppose so. Those who embrace philosophy and investigate the divine realm carefully know to whom they accord honor and to whom the worship of the divine statues is extended."[13]

46 [Artemius speaks, after 1.6a]. "But why do I say these things? The prophets originally predicted Christ, as you yourself know quite well. The testimonies concerning his advent abound: among them are the prophecies from the gods you worship and the oracles, as well as the Sibylline books, and the poetry of Virgil the Roman that you call "bucolic."[14] Apollo himself, the soothsayer you so admire, uttered the following words about Christ. Responding to a question put by his ministers, he replied,

> O would that you had never asked me at my very end,
> Unhappy ministers of mine, about the holy god
> And spirit holding cluster-like all things in its embrace:
> The stars, the light, the rivers, Tartarus, the air and fire!
> This spirit drives me all unwilling from this very shrine.
> And now the day when I must yield my tripods[15] is at hand.
> O grieve for me, ye tripods, grieve: Apollo now departs;
> Departs: a mortal man who is from heaven forces me;
> He is the God who suffered, yet his godhead suffered not."[16]

---

13. Maximus of Tyre (*Dissertationes* 2.2; Hermann Hobein, ed., *Maximi Tyrii Philosophumena* [BSGRT; Leipzig: Teubner, 1910]) and Porphyry (in Eusebius, *Praeparatio evangelica* 3.7.1) explain that the images of gods are like the letters of an alphabet, conveying a meaning only to those who have learned the script. *Corp. herm.* 2.326, by contrast, claims that the statues of the gods are themselves alive and work wonders.

14. Constantine (in Eusebius, *Oratio Constantini imperatoris ad sanctorum coetum* 18–21) quotes both the Sibyl and Virgil's "Bucolics" concerning Christ's Advent (the Sibyl's verses speak of the coming judgment of a heavenly king).

15. On the use of the tripod in the oracle, see Parke and Wormell, *The Delphic Oracle,* 1:24–25; and Bouché-Leclercq, *Histoire de la divination dans l'antiquité,* 3:100–101. The tripod also represents the oracle in Eusebius, *Vit. Const.* 2.50.

16. On the oracle here cited, see Friedrich Dübner, "Miscellanea," *Revue de Philologie* 2 (1847): 240–42; Gustavus Wolff, *Porphyrii de philosophia ex oraculis hau-*

47. The Apostate replied, "Apparently you were not commander in Egypt, Artemius, but some sort of oracle-collector, or rather an altar-beggar or beggar-priest and gatherer of old and antiquated fables and myths of drunken crones." The martyr said, "Your supposition is not right, O emperor, and does no credit to your wisdom and virtue. What I am doing is taking my proofs from your gods and from the sciences dear to you, that you may learn the mystery of truth from what is familiar to you. And do not think that I take any pride in using pagan words (let not the oil of the sinner anoint my head!); it is rather that in my concern for the salvation of your soul, I leave no stone unturned in order to persuade you. But I fear that, just as Satan blinded the Adam of old, the first one to be made, through disobedience and eating from the tree, so he has stripped you, O emperor, of the faith of Christ in his envy of your salvation.

"But as for your calling the sun and moon gods, and the stars as well, I blush at this mark of ignorance, or rather foolishness. Did not Anaxagoras of Clazomenae, who was, after all, your teacher, say that the sun was a red-hot mass and that the stars were bodies like pumice-stones, completely lifeless and insensate?[17] How is it, then, that you yourself, best of emperors and most philosophical, address as gods the things that your teachers reject and discredit? For I know that you adhere to the school of Plato. Plato was a disciple of Socrates, Socrates of Archelaus, and Archelaus and Pericles of Anaxagoras. How is it, then, admirable sir, that you address these things as gods, that you venerate the sun above all and swear the imperial oath by him, filling your letters, discourses, and greetings with the words "by the sun."[18] But why continue in this vein? I will not deny my Christ, far be it! Nor will I embrace the foul impiety of the pagans. I hold to what I was taught and stand by the traditions of my forebears, which time will never overthrow,

---

rienda (Berlin: Springer, 1856), appendix 5.3; Karl Buresch, *Klaros: Untersuchungen zum Orakelwesen des späteren Altertums* (Lepizig: Teubner, 1889), 99–100, 130–31. The last line ("He is the God who suffered...") was not originally part of the oracle but the first line of a hymn to Christ that must have followed the oracle in some manuscript and was later added to it by a copyist (see Joseph Bidez, "Sur diverses citations, et notamment sur trois passages de Malalas retrouvés dans un texte hagiographique," *ByzZ* 11 (1902): 388–94; Scott, *Hermetica*, 4:241 n. 2.

17. On Anaxagoras's view of the sun and stars as hot stones, see Hermann Diels, ed., *Die Fragmente der Vorsokratiker: Griechisch und deutsch* (rev. Walther Kranz; 6th ed.; 3 vols.; Berlin: Weidmann, 1951–52), 59.A42.6 (2:16). On the philosophical succession from Anaxagoras, see Diogenes Laertius 2.16.

18. On the oath by the sun that Julian took, see, e.g., his *Or.* 7.222C; Philostorgius 7.4b (*AP* 31). On the report that the sun had presided at Julian's birth, see Eunapius, *Frag. hist.* 24; 26; Sozomen 6.2.11.

"'even if wisdom is found through utmost thought,'
to quote your poet Euripides."[19]

---

19. The quotation from Euripides is in *Bacchae* 203 (Richard Seaford, trans.,
Euripides: Bacchae [Westminster: Aris & Phillips, 1996], 79). Lines 201–203 in fact
recommend holding to ancestral traditions in religion.

Appendix 3

The Premetaphrastic Martyrdom of Artemius[1]
On the Twentieth of the Same Month
The Martyrdom of the Great, Holy, and Glorious Martyr and Wonder-Worker Artemius
Bless Us

[1] It took place in the reign of Julian, who was filled with great impiety and ungodliness against the orthodox confession of faith of the Christians and who restored the abominations and temples of the idols that the pious and most august Constantine, who had reigned in piety, had demolished and destroyed.[2]

[2] This Julian, who had become insane and made himself a house infested by the demon, went down to the province of Cilicia. Having wrought much havoc among the Christians in Tarsus and Aegae, he crossed the Gulf of Cilicia from there and went up to Antioch, behaving arrogantly toward

---

1. In the editor's title, "premetaphrastic" means antedating the tenth-century hagiographer Simeon Metaphrastes. The writing also antedates the *Artemii Passio,* the author of which refers to it as artless in style but lays it under heavy tribute (cf. A1.2 and 166 n. 3). On the text, see Bidez, *Philostorgius,* xlv–li, lxviii, 356–61; Albert Dufourcq, "Gestes d'Artemius," in idem, *Étude sur les gesta martyrum romains* (5 vols.; Paris: Fontemoing, 1900–1988), 5:183–90; Baudoin de Gaiffier, "Les martyrs Eugène et Macaire, morts en exil en Maurétanie," *AnBoll* 78 (1960): 38. The work may be dated between the beginning of the sixth century (when the translation of the relics mentioned in section 14 took place) and the composition of *AP* (Bidez, *Philostorgius,* 357; on the possible time of the composition of the latter, see 165 n. 2). It does not draw upon Philostorgius, so it can be used to identify those parts of *AP* that are not from Philostorgius as well. The section numbers in the translation are not in the critical text but have been added for the sake of convenience.

2. On Constantine's reputation as a destroyer of pagan temples, see A1.5 and 168 n. 9. On Julian's restoration of them, see 7.1b.

the Christians.[3] Eugenius and Macarius, the pious martyr-presbyters, were denounced to him.[4] At the time when they were being subjected to inhuman tortures, the blessed and pious Artemius, who had been appointed duke of Alexandria, was assigned to Syria as well on account of his just and blameless conduct.[5]

[3] The pious man, devoted as he was to Julian's government, approached him and said, "You should realize, your majesty, who it is that gave you the empire, if in fact it was God from whom you received it; as for me, I am convinced that, just as God gave Job to the devil when he asked for him, so also Satan has asked for you, to use you against us, so that the devil who inhabits you may make workers for himself out of those who are like you, those who have carelessly allowed themselves to trust you."

[4] When he heard this, Julian was filled with a rage and fury so uncontrollable that he ordered him to be stripped of his rank and beaten with rawhide whips until he had exhausted four teams [of torturers]. At the conclusion, he said to him, "You have forced me to do you this injury and to bring dishonor upon your people because of your rashness. Listen to me, then, and sacrifice to Apollo, and I will make you a praetorian prefect. If you do not listen to me, I will cut off your head. And we shall see what good the crucified one does you, the one you claim is a god."

[5] Artemius laughed, or rather laughed at him, and said, "You foul and inhuman brute, think who it was that protected you in Heliopolis during your insurrection! Was it not Christ, the God and Savior of those who hope in him and who has had patience with your wickedness?[6] Blind fool, wake up

---

3. On Julian's journey from Constantinople to Antioch, see 7.4c (*AP* 24). The "havoc" he wrought in Tarsus refers to his order to the bishop there to restore the temple columns (Zonaras 13.12.30–34). On his "arrogance" toward Christians, see 95 n. 27 and 94 n. 24 in reference to *AP* 23 in 7.4c.

4. The Greek passion of Eugenius and Macarius (*BHG* 2126) has been edited by François Halkin, "La passion grecque des saints Eugène et Macaire," *AnBoll* 78 (1960): 41–52. The Latin passion (*BHL* 5103) is an abridged translation of the Greek.

5. On Artemius's career, see 165 n. 1. As de Gaiffier ("Les martyrs Eugène et Macaire," 39–40) remarks, the primary sources for the trial and execution of Artemius do not say that they took place in Antioch and do not connect them with Eugenius and Macarius. If the connection was made later, it may have been in order to give a religious pretext for Artemius's death.

6. Heliopolis seems to be an oblique reference to the incident in which the pagans there, who had had much to endure since Constantine's time, set upon the Christians with savage glee when Julian came to power; the story is told in Gregory of Nazianzus, *Or.* 4.86–87; Sozomen 5.10.5–7; Theodoret, *Hist. eccl.* 3.7.2–4. Gregory, after recounting how the pagans had fed the Christians to the swine, remarks that

and realize how large the sky is, because it was not fashioned in any sequence of time but was spread out like a curtain in a single instant. Tartarus shudders at Christ's glance, the fearsome sea trembles when lashed from on high by the storm and moved in its depths, and, acknowledging the boundaries and decree of scripture, it does not trespass upon the land. And you, with the foolish wisdom you claim to have, do you dishonor God, the Maker of all things, and punish the saints? Blind fool! Reflect upon and recognize the God who created everything and worship and adore him alone, according to what is written."

[6] Julian listened to this but refused to accede to the saint's words; he ordered his back flogged with iron caltrops, his eyebrows pierced with hooks, and his sides skewered with red-hot spits. When the people of the city saw this, they cried, "Your majesty, you have not subdued the barbarian hordes or done anything good for the city, and will you cruelly and criminally punish a noble and holy man who has never done anything wrong?" When the foul and inhuman brute heard this, he ordered his tortures to stop; summoning the saint, he said to him again, "Behold, the city takes pity on you, and I feel sorry for you too. Sacrifice to Zeus and to Asclepius." But the holy Artemius said, "May anyone who listens to you and abandons the God who made heaven and earth go with you into hellfire, you sacrilege! Be persuaded, in the depths of your impiety, that I will not yield to your violence, nor will I sacrifice to your deaf and dumb idols. I worship the God in heaven, and him alone do I serve."

[7] The tyrant, when he heard this, ordered him to be locked up for fifteen days in a dark place and to be given neither bread nor water, while he decided what sort of death to inflict on him. And having conferred with his fellow triflers, he ordered him beheaded. But while he was in prison, Christ sent him food and told him, "Be brave and strong against the devil, for you have acknowledged me on earth before emperors and tyrants, and I will crown you before my angels. Take courage, therefore; today you will be with me in paradise."

[8] Now the tyrant banished Saints Eugenius and Macarius to Augasis, where forty days later they died in Christ on 20 December.[7] At that time a

---

Julian himself should have been fed to the demons he worshiped and then exclaims over Christ's long-suffering, which put up with such behavior. This is perhaps the background to the reference in section 5 of Christ's protection of Julian.

7. For "banished ... to Augasis," reading ἐν Αὐγάσει. Dufourcq ("Gestes d'Artemius," 5:187) regards "Augasis" as an obvious corruption of "Oasis," but de Gaiffier ("Les martyrs Eugène et Macaire," 35) points out that the converse is true, "Augasis" being the *lectio difficilior*. Likewise when *AP* 39 says that the martyrs were

great wonder occurred: there had been no water in the place at all, but many springs gushed forth that have continued to the present day.

[9] When the fifteen days were up, the tyrant took his seat in the judgment hall and ordered Saint Artemius to be brought out. And when he had been produced, the tyrant urged him, "How long will you continue in this madness, when you are so wise and abound in such wealth; will you not sacrifice to the gods?" Saint Artemius replied, "Have you gone mad, you scoundrel? You let the nations wage war and spend your time on me, God's servant? Pronounce against me whatever sentence you like. For I worship the God who is in heaven and his Christ, the Savior of all." Upon hearing this, Julian called in stone-cutters and stone-masons and told them, "Split a rock in two and put him in between." They did as they had been told and put him between the halves of the rock, which hid him so that he could not be seen, and so everyone said that he was dead.

[10] But he was giving voice to the psalm, "You have raised me up upon a rock, and now behold you have raised up my head against my enemies." And further, "You have placed my feet upon a rock, and you have guided my steps and placed a new song into my mouth. Receive my spirit, Only Begotten One." For his eyes had popped out from the pressure of the rocks.

[11] The tyrant, supposing that he had already died between the stones, ordered the stone-masons to apply their craft to opening the rocks. And the saint came out, giving voice to the psalm, "The Lord is my helper, and I shall not fear. What can man do to me?" It was only his eyes that had come out because of the pressure, and Julian said to him, "Now look at you, you wretch! Behold, you are deprived even of your eyes and are good for nothing. At least listen to me now and sacrifice, that you may become a friend of the gods and escape their punishment." But the blessed Artemius replied, "You shameless

---

banished to "Oasis," its author is correcting from "Augasis" because of his memory of Oasis as a place of exile of clergy during the fourth century (de Gaiffier, "Les martyrs Eugène et Macaire," 35–36). In the Greek passion of Eugenius and Macarius (Halkin, "La passion grecque," 41–52), Julian banishes the two to Mauretania, and they arrive at a place called probably "Gildona" or "Gildoba" (section 6; Halkin, "La passion grecque," 49 n. 1; de Gaiffier, "Les martyrs Eugène et Macaire," 35–37). They convert the pagans there and then go on to the mountain to which they had been exiled (section 7). A wheel of fire descends from heaven and splits the rock where they are, and a river of water gushes forth. A voice from heaven tells them to drink and they will no longer hunger or thirst (section 9). Thus, there may be no need to choose between Augasis and Gildona/Gildoba as the place where they died, if the latter is just a place they passed through on their way to exile. It is, however, worth noting that, according to de Gaiffier, the original Latin martyrology read: "In Mauretania civitate Gildoba (Gildona) passio sanctorum Eugenii et Macarii" ("Les martyrs Eugène et Macaire," 37).

dog, think up any other tortures you want, so that I may be crowned and you may be taken off to eternal hellfire."

[12] And he ordered him to be beheaded. As he was led off, he prayed, "You who are God from God, sole from sole, king from king, who are in heaven at the right hand of God the Father who begot you, and who dwelt on earth for the salvation of us all, the crown of those who contend for you in piety, hear me in my lowliness and receive my soul with peace and give it rest with the saints who were well-pleasing to you in the presence of your glory." A voice was heard, "Your petition has been received, and the grace of healing has been granted you. Hurry along your course, enter in with the saints, and receive the prize prepared for the saints and for all who have loved the appearing of Christ."[8]

[13] The blessed man was slain by the sword on Friday, 20 October.

[14] His blessed and holy body was requested from the emperor Julian by a pious and God-fearing woman, the deacon Ariste. He ordered that it be given to her. She made haste to prepare a leaden coffin, which is preserved even to the present day, embalmed his holy and blessed body, made it fragrant with costly perfumes and various incenses, put it in the coffin, and sent it to the all-blessed city of Constantinople, to a distinguished place [there], since she wanted to build a house worthy of the relics of the most saintly martyr Artemius, in order to hold a service in honor of the holy martyr.

[15] These things took place in the time of Julian, in Antioch in a place called Daphne, during the reign of our Lord Jesus Christ, to whom be the glory and the power for endless ages. Amen.

[16] [Nicephorus, *Hist. eccl.* 10.11]. [Julian] took personal charge of punishing Artemius, the noble combatant in the contest of piety who was duke and *augustalis* ["prefect"] of Antioch. [Theodoret, *Hist. eccl.* 3.18.1 inserted here.] The real reason for this was that he had smashed and destroyed so many idols' shrines in his divine zeal when he was in Constantius's service and that he had brought back the bones of the divine apostles Andrew, Luke, and Timothy from Patrae, Achaia, and Ephesus to Constantinople. The pretext, however, was that he was the one who had brought about the murder of his brother Gallus. So he stripped the martyr of all that he owned, degraded him from his rank, and after countless intolerable tortures finally beheaded him. Near Chalcedon he punished as well Manuel, Sabel, and Ismael, who had come as ambassadors from Persia, because they were representing Christian

---

8. The Psalms quoted by Artemius are, respectively, 60:3; 39:3–4; and 117:6 (= Heb 13:6). At the end of section 12, "all who have loved the appearing" is from 2 Tim 4:8. On the grace of healing given to Artemius, see 165 n. 2 (end).

interests, and he did not respect their dignity as ambassadors. [There follows Theodoret, *Hist. eccl.* 3.19.]

[17] [Zonaras 13.12.44]. The great Artemius, too, was punished by [Julian] because he was a Christian (although the charge against him was the murder of Gallus),[9] and the presbyters Eugenius and Macarius were punished by him, being granted the martyrs' crowns, along with those sent to him on embassy from Persia, Manuel, Sabel, Ismael, and many others.

[18] [Cedrenus 306D]. Artemius, duke of Alexandria, since he had shown great zeal in Alexandria against the idolaters in the time of Constantius, had his property confiscated and was beheaded after many tortures for the faith of Christ. The same thing happened to two presbyters, Eugenius and Macarius.

[19] [*Comp. chron.* 56.31]. [Julian] created many martyrs from those who refused to agree to his impiety, including Artemius, who was great among Christ's martyrs.

---

9. On Artemius's connection with the death of Gallus, see *AP* 36. On his decapitation, see A7.36a.

APPENDIX 4
BEGINNING OF THE LIFE OF THEODORE
HEGUMENOS OF THE MONASTERY OF CHORA
LIFE AND MANNERS OF OUR
SAINTLY FATHER THEODORE, MONK AND
SUPERIOR OF THE MONASTERY OF CHORA

The most blessed and holy fathers before and during our times, who were outstanding for their pure and blameless lives in Christ, were cultured men of the highest learning and read many of the histories and lives of the fathers; having gained a deep knowledge of everything there, they set down in writing the deeds of the saints. But when they reached the end of their lives and departed in the orthodox faith to be with the Lord, without being able to bring their project to completion, they left the books they had composed, and the unfinished life of our saintly father Theodore, to us as their genuine children, born of the Holy Spirit and sacred baptism; they had made some brief remarks about Theodore scattered here and there in their works to memorialize him, thereby inciting later generations to fill in what was missing. But we declined to undertake this work as being beyond our abilities, aware as we were of our scanty learning and inadequate style. But those who shared the memory of the saint, men most spiritual in the Lord, urged us fervently not to refuse and to leave the work unfinished, lest it be consigned to the depths of oblivion and vanish from sight, and thus they compelled us to undertake it. Our obedience to them having, therefore, forced us to turn our hand to what was beyond us, we invested ourselves in an extraordinary labor, for we too searched out and pored over many books to the best of our ability, like a bee collecting from many flowers, and thus we have written the life of Saint Theodore. We included nothing that came from ourselves but gathered [the material] from the holy fathers and historians Theodoret and Philostorgius and from the writers Hesychius and Dorotheus, putting it where it belonged. And I think I may say that those who read the lives of the saints derive no little benefit thereby.[1]

---

1. This biography (*BHG* 1743) in fact contains nothing from Philostorgius; see Bidez, *Philostorgius*, li–lii. On the monastery of Chora, see Georg Lippold, "Theodoros (127)," PW 5A.2:1909.

Appendix 5

From the Unedited *Life of Constantine*
of the *Codex Angelicus* A[1]
Concerning the Defeat and Death of Licinius

[Opitz, *Vit. Const.* 11]. … That was not all that Licinius did;[2] conceiving a desire for Constantine's realm, and learning that he had abandoned and spurned all of his ancestral gods and had preferred one [god], Christ, showing him every sort of honor and worship and placing in him his hopes of salvation for himself and for the entire empire, he grew scornful, reckoning that, there being only one of him, and one who had appeared recently, and had been in fact acknowledged as crucified by the very people who revered him, he would never prove superior to those whom he himself revered, great as they were and celebrated from time immemorial for their mighty deeds.[3] And having pondered the matter privately with his blasphemous thoughts, he decided to take the field against him, without stopping to give any consideration to what had happened in Maxentius's case.[4] For the absurd desire for

---

1. The text (*BHG* 365) has been edited by Hans-Georg Opitz, "Die Vita Constantini des Codex Angelicus 22," *Byzantion* 9 (1934): 535–93. His section numbers have been inserted for the sake of convenience, but the translation is, as usual, from Bidez's text. On the state of the text at the beginning of this excerpt, see Bidez, *Philostorgius*, 178, 344–45, 362.

2. The excerpt "That was not all that Licinius did" at the beginning of section 11 may have been preceded by a notice of his persecution of Christians. See 5.2a; Eusebius, *Hist. eccl.* 10.8.8–10; 10.8.14–18; *Vit. Const.* 1.51–54, 56; Socrates 1.3; Sozomen 1.7.1.

3. Eusebius (*Vit. Const.* 2.5) has Licinius's speech about Constantine abandoning his ancestral gods to worship some strange new one and about his (Licinius's) pagan gods outnumbering Constantine's one deity.

4. The reference to "what had happened in Maxentius's case" is the tradition that the latter had tried to defeat Constantine by magic but had been defeated at the Milvian Bridge by his adversary, who led an army bearing the cross against him

what belongs to others, giving rise as it does to mad hopes and making people trust in their attempts to realize them, leads those under the sway of this passion to execute their plans while they are blind and quite heedless to what is about to happen. That is what happened to Licinius, and it impelled him to push forward into great and evident dangers.

[Opitz, *Vit. Const.* 12]. But first he thought it best to consult the oracles, to find out how his gods[5] were disposed toward the matter. So he sent various persons to various places to consult them. And when they came back from wherever they had been sent, bearing oracular replies that all agreed in ordering him to take the field and promising to give him an uncontested victory, then he reviewed the armed forces and made his other preparations. And when all was ready, he arose and went with the army with the intention of crossing the mountain passes and falling upon the other's realm.[6]

[Opitz, *Vit. Const.* 13]. Now Constantine was aware of the attack before it came, since it was impossible to conceal an affair being pushed forward throughout the whole empire and requiring no little time, so he hastened to Illyricum and drove on as far as Macedonia; he did not think it right to attack first, lest he appear to break the pledges given under oath, but he testified beforehand that he was defending himself against attack.[7]

(Eusebius, *Vit. Const.* 1.36–38). *Bios* 333.22–23 also notices how Licinius forgot how the tyrants before him had been deposed.

5. "His gods" translates the reading οἱ αὐτοῦ θεοί rather than οἱ αὐτοὶ θεοί ("the same gods"). As here, Eusebius says the oracles gave encouraging replies (*Vit. Const.* 2.4; contrast Sozomen 1.7.2–3).

6. For the wars between Constantine and Licinius, see Zosimus 2.18–26, 28; commentary in Paschoud, *Zosime*, 1:89–101, 208–18. For the relationship between the two before this, see S II 6 and 244 n. 17, last paragraph. After Constantine allied himself with Licinius in 313, the latter defeated Maximinus, his co-ruler in the east who had sided with Constantine's enemy, Maxentius. The latter's defeat by Constantine the year before left two emperors whose alliance of convenience soon deteriorated to the point of war in 316, when Licinius lost Illyricum to the other. The account given here, however, is of their later battle in 324. Like Eusebius, *Hist. eccl.* 10.8.7, it suggests that Licinius tried to make ready in secret, and, like 10.8.8–9, it speaks of his mental blindness in the face of the examples of those before him who had ignored the fate of the others who had gone to war against Constantine. Also like 10.8.7 (but in contradiction to *Vit. Const.* 2.3), it says that Licinius made the first move. The story of Constantine's drive through Illyricum to Macedonia seems to preserve the recollection of his campaign to repel an incursion of Goths in 323 that brought him into Licinius's territory, giving the latter a reason to go to war (cf. Zosimus 2.22.1).

7. Libanius, *Or.* 59.21, supports the suggestion that it was Licinius who broke the

[Opitz, *Vit. Const.* 14]. They therefore encamped opposite each other. Constantine remained at ease because he did not want to start the battle, while Licinius, who was on the point of attacking, slaughtered victims to his gods, propitiating them with the sacrifices proper to each, examined the entrails, observed the movements and voices of the birds, and gazed at the stars, considering thence what fate held in store. He engaged deeply in such efforts, since he was facing the great contest. And when the business in which he was engaged had turned out to his satisfaction, and just as he had been hoping, he proceeded to attack.

[Opitz, *Vit. Const.* 15]. As for Constantine, once he too had made haste to draw up his lines opposite, he placed in front of his whole army the image of the cross shining upon a tall shaft that was covered in gold.[8] He bade those assigned to carry it in turns to take courage, since nothing fearful would befall them; the Christ who was honored by that image would, he said, be able to save not only them but the whole army.

[Opitz, *Vit. Const.* 16]. The clash, when it came, was terrific, but now there was a great wonder to be seen. Where the weight of enemy forces predominated most, and some company of Constantine's soldiers was hard pressed, the opponents, when the image was taken there, were forced to turn back. Thus those bearing the standard passed it on to others at intervals of time, so that it went through the whole corps as its bearers succeeded and relieved each other, until Constantine's men decisively turned back Licinius's army, broke its ranks, turned it to flight, pursued it, and struck it down; his men had no more courage. Thus almost all of Licinius's forces fell in that battle, and this was the greatest slaughter ever in the Roman army.[9]

---

oaths between Constantine and himself; *Bios* 332.19–20 understands his side of the agreement as the pledge to govern the east well and not to harm the Christians.

8. Eusebius, *Vit. Const.* 2.6–9, tells of the cross as Constantine's battle-standard against Licinius and of the safety of those who bore it. A similar story is told in section 21 below. For the shaft of gold, see S IV 3.

9. The battle described is that which took place at Chrysopolis on 18 September 324. Estimates of casualities are given as 25,000 in *Anon. Val.* 27, 34,000 in Zosimus 2.22.7, and 100,000 in Zosimus 2.26.3. The following account of Licinius's maneuvers after the battle of Chrysopolis (always supposing that that is what our author meant to relate in section 16) resembles Eusebius, *Vit. Const.* 2.10–18, in many respects, although in its general outline it is even closer to Zonaras 13.1.21–26. In all three histories Licinius is spared after defeat and is even allowed to continue to rule (*Vit. Const.* 2.11, 15; Zonaras 13.1.21; in contrast to Themistius, *Or.* 6.83b, where he is immediately stripped of the purple). In all three he proves faithless, raises another army (of barbarians), and is again defeated by Constantine (*Vit. Const.* 2.16–17; Zonaras 13.1.22). In *Vit. Const.* 2.18, however, he is executed after this second defeat,

[Opitz, *Vit. Const.* 17]. Licinius fled with a few members of his staff, and then, coming to the Thracian Bosporus and fearing for his own safety, he departed in haste for Bithynia. Arriving in Nicomedia, he put off the imperial regalia in the great fear and terror he felt at the moment, turned in earnest supplication to the bishop of the city, Eusebius, entrusted his case to him, and sent him to Constantine with the prayer that he would grant him his life, to lead it as a private person outside of the affairs of government.[10]

[Opitz, *Vit. Const.* 18]. Constantine, out of pity for him because of his changed circumstances and respect for their relationship through his sister, sent him back the purple robe, bidding him wear it and govern his realm, since he thought that his recent experience would amply suffice to chasten him for the future. Licinius, however, used his mildness and easy temper as fuel for his own arrogance, and, once he had reverted to causing even more trouble than ever, he did not deem it necessary to keep his peace but made his plans a second time as though to recoup the previous defeat.

[Opitz, *Vit. Const.* 19]. As for the gods who he had thought would give him victory, since he had revered them so greatly, and who in fact had promised to do so, he despised their weakness as showing that they had already grown old and were powerless to save, and even more their deceitful and fraudulent character shown in their making promises they could not fulfill, and he abandoned them as worthless. He sought out other strange ones from other nations, gods celebrated for illustrious deeds.[11] For he supposed that Christ too had been discovered because of his strange and novel character <and> especially because[12] he showed the freshness of his power in his deeds. And since those who made it their business to gratify his desires were not about to fail him in his delirious ravings about this matter, he made statues of all [the gods] they enabled him to discover whose names were known among various nations, even the most foreign, worshiped them in the way customary to each, and begged them to become his allies.

---

whereas in our account and in Zonaras 13.1.23 his life is again spared. Only after he tries yet again to rebel is he executed (also in Zonaras 13.1.26).

10. As in our account, Zosimus 2.26.3 has Licinius fleeing to Nicomedia after his defeat. Ours is the only one to name Bishop Eusebius as his intercessor; the other sources say it was his wife, Constantine's half-sister (Zosimus 2.28.2; Aurelius Victor 41.7; *Anon. Val.* 28).

11. As in Eusebius, *Vit. Const.* 2.15, Licinius seeks other gods for support when once again he begins to lay plans for rebellion.

12. The translation "<and> especially because" reflects the reading <καὶ> διὰ τοῦτο in Bidez, *Philostorgius*, 181.4 (see the corrections and additions listed on p. 361 of Bidez's edition).

[Opitz, *Vit. Const.* 20]. Now since his army had been destroyed and another could not at the moment be assembled that would be ready to fight, he hired a large force of barbarians and took the field against Constantine again.[13] Constantine made ready for a second contest, drew out his army in battle order again, and let the image of the cross shine forth, since he kept fresh and utterly holy in his memory the letters surrounding the standard he displayed, with their message: "Conquer with this."[14]

[Opitz, *Vit. Const.* 21]. Now while the battle was being fought most bitterly and those on either side were going at each other with great ferocity, a wondrous sight manifested itself in the neighborhood of the image <of the> cross. The enemy, especially the barbarians, kept shooting their arrows at the man carrying the pole on which the standard of the cross was fixed, and all of them made him their one target, but the shafts kept missing him, and none of those shooting could aim well enough to hit him. And so many men were grasping the shaft on which the standard was that it was clearly proven that it was by the assistance of the Christ they were revering that the bearers of his standard were protected, and not by the faulty aim of the archers. This same marvel had also been clearly seen at the first battle.[15]

[Opitz, *Vit. Const.* 22]. Now Constantine extended his lines, surrounded the barbarians with the wings on each side, and struck them down; the majority of them were now being pushed to the middle and were slaying each other in the confusion. Thus he overpowered them, turned them back, and cut down most of their army; charging hard upon those able to escape momentarily, he captured most of them, slew them, took Licinius alive, and seized the rest of his forces. Thinking him still worthy of leniency, he sent him to Thessalonica in Macedonia to be guarded [there]. For he himself had already made his way to Moesian territory and Thrace. But a great and dire fear had seized the barbarians living in places surrounding the Roman Empire, since the mightiest among them had been slain in greater numbers than was usual in war. For the swiftness, manner, and extent of the victory seemed the result of divine power rather than human effort.

[Opitz, *Vit. Const.* 23]. As for Licinius, not even in his extreme misfortune did justice allow him any tranquility at all, but when he tried once again to stir things up and hatch plots and was caught at it, he brought upon himself

---

13. As here, Licinius collects an army of barbarians in Eusebius, *Vit. Const.* 2.15; *Anon. Val.* 27.

14. For the motto "conquer with this," see 1.6.

15. As in *Vit. Const.* 2.16, the cross-standard protects those holding it, just as in the earlier battle (see sections 15–16; *Vit. Const.* 2.9). See also *Bios* 331.8–24.

the necessity of doing away with him, and he was killed in Thessalonica.[16] So ended Licinius's mad schemes.

[Opitz, *Vit. Const.* 24]. Constantine, after Licinius's death, took his sister in and treated her with due respect.[17] And now that he had assumed control of the entire Roman Empire all by himself, he put on a most beautiful crown,[18] symbol of monarchy and of his victory over his foes, and sent letters everywhere making an end of paganism[19] and calling to the true faith those deceived by the demons and their lifeless images and granting complete liberty to the churches of Christ, so badly injured during the pagan dominion, and to the preaching of the gospel. And in displaying this great and marvelous enthusiasm for the growth of the churches, he treated the bishops with the deepest respect. This was true especially of the westerners, since it was among them that he had first been instructed and exhorted regarding what is good, and of Hosius the Spaniard, who governed the city of Cordova in Spain and whose great fame had spread far and wide due to his age and splendid virtue, and of the most distinguished of the others with him from there. He paid them the greatest possible reverence at court and wherever he was, commending to their prayers the success of his enterprises.[20]

Opitz, *Vit. Const.* 25]. And crossing the Thracian Bosporus and arriving in Bithynia, he settled in the neighborhood of Nicomedia, where he saw to the affairs of state as he thought best. For that was the largest and most impressive of the cities there.[21]

---

16. On Licinius's attempt to stir up trouble once again in Thessalonica, see Zonaras 13.1.26; Socrates 1.1.4; Alexander Monachus, *Invent. s. crucis* (PG 87:4057BC).

17. Rufinus (*Hist. eccl.* 10.12) and Theodoret (*Hist. eccl.* 2.3.2) mention Constantine's honorable reception of Constantina after Licinius's death.

18. On Constantine's assumption of a crown, see S II 4; Eusebius, *Vit. Const.* 4.66; Aurelius Victor 41.14; Malalas 13.8; Cedrenus 295B–C (he says he was the first emperor to wear a diadem).

19. On the complex subject of Constantine's treatment of paganism, see Jones, *Later Roman Empire,* 1:91–92 and n. 138.

20. Constantine spent public money to repair and enlarge churches and to build new ones (Eusebius, *Vit. Const.* 2.45–46). It was Hosius of Cordova who oversaw the payment of the state subsidy to the churches (Eusebius, *Hist. eccl.* 10.6.2).

21. Constantine is attested for Nicomedia after the battle of Chrysopolis (Otto Seeck, *Regesten der Kaiser und Päpste für die Jahre 311 bis 476 n. Chr. Vorarbeit zu einer Prosopographie der christlichen Kaiserzeit* [Stuttgart: Metzler, 1919], 174).

APPENDIX 6

LIFE AND MARTYRDOM OF LUCIAN OF ANTIOCH[1]

1 [Opitz, *Vit. Const.* 52; *Suda,* Λ 685 Lucian]. Lucian's forbears were reportedly from Samosata in Syria and of noble blood. When he grew up, he met a man named Macarius who lived in Edessa and expounded the sacred books. Within a short time, he had mastered all of the best things he had to say about them.

[Simeon] Life and Martyrdom of the Holy Martyr, Saint Lucian

1. Samosata, a city of Syria washed by the Euphrates, was Lucian's native place. He was reportedly of noble blood. His parents, who were Christian, took care to train Lucian in piety from his earliest age.[2] When they both died, they left him a youth of about twelve. Finding that God was his only solace in the loss of his parents, he distributed all his wealth to the poor and sought refuge in a sacred temple.

And while young, he met one Macarius, who lived in Edessa and interpreted the sacred books, all of the best things from which Lucian collected within a brief time.

2–4 [Opitz, *Vit. Const.* 52]. He adopted the celibate life and achieved perfection in every human virtue, very quickly becoming the best known of those of his time. He was advanced to sacred orders, becoming a presbyter of

---

1. The Life of Lucian in appendix 6 is drawn not from Philostorgius but from the same source used by him (Bidez, *Philostorgius,* cxlvii–cli). Bidez reconstructed the main text, the one translated here, from two Lives of Lucian: one by Simeon Metaphrastes (see PG 114:397–416); and the other found in *Suda,* Λ 685 (Ada Adler, ed., *Suidae lexicon* [Lexicographi Graeci 1.1–4; 4 vols.; Leipzig: Teubner, 1928–38], 3:283–84), and from the *Vita Constantini* edited by Opitz, whose section numbers have been inserted for the sake of convenience.

2. On Lucian's ancestry, see *Synax.* 137.30. Eusebius (*Hist. eccl.* 8.13.2; 9.6.3) and Jerome (*Vir. ill.* 77) testify that he was a presbyter of Antioch and a keen student of the Bible.

the church of Antioch, where he founded a very large school; the most promising students came to him there from every place.

[Opitz = Simeon] Noticing that the sacred books had suffered much corruption, what with the extensive damage to them caused by time and by their
being moved about so much, to say nothing of the efforts of some thoroughly
wicked men, champions of paganism, who had wanted to subvert their meaning and adulterate them extensively, he took all the books and restored them
from the Hebrew, which was also a language of which he had the deepest
knowledge. He bestowed an enormous amount of labor upon the restoration.
Not only that, but it may be seen that of all those of his time, he was the most
careful to preserve intact the integrity of the sacred teachings.[3]

2 [Simeon]. When he first betook himself to the bath of rebirth and was
regenerated by water and the Spirit, he adopted the solitary life. Then when he
decided to abstain completely from wine and fine food, he as it were sprang
from the starting-blocks to do battle with all the pleasures of the flesh, chastis-
ing himself with fasts and making it his fixed habit to take food once a day at
the ninth hour. There were also stretches of days when he went without food
for a whole week. Indeed, most of his life was devoted to prayers and tears, for
the distance he kept from humor and laughter was the extent he judged these
things to be what was really laughable. On the contrary, he was eager to imi-
tate the grief-stricken, thinking that they were to be congratulated. Since he
welcomed silence and devoted himself to continuous meditation, he seemed
always preoccupied and sunk in dejection to those who met him, even though
in himself he was forever rejoicing and happy in the Spirit. And if ever he did
decide to utter a word, it was the sacred scriptures that he spoke. So deeply,
indeed, had he been smitten by a holy love for them that he was hardly willing
even to interrupt his continuous meditation of them for sleep.[4] Even when at
some point his body wanted some moderate rest, he allowed himself no sleep
until after extended prayer and hot tears while on his knees. And these are the
things the saint did while still young, still a boy.

---

3. Jerome mentions Lucian's work in providing a new edition of the Bible in
Praefatio in librum Paralipomenon (PL 28:1325A), *Praefatio in quatuor Evangelia* (PL
29:527B), and *Ep.* 106.2. The *Synaxarium* says he bequeathed to the church in Nicomedia a translation of the entire Old Testament and New Testament in triple columns
per page. His, it says, was the seventh translation of the Old Testament; he produced
it by checking all previous translations against the Hebrew original and making corrections and improvements accordingly (*Synax.* 139.24–26; 140.27–141.1). It is worth
noting in this context that Epiphanius thought that Aquila, Symmachus, and The-
odotion had corrupted the Bible with their new translations from the Hebrew (*De
mensuris et ponderibus* 11; 15–17).

4. On Lucian's love of the Bible, see *Synax.* 138.31–33; Sozomen 3.5.9.

3. But when he passed beyond that age and began to be reckoned a young man, he offered to the spirit, through the power of the Holy Spirit, his unrebellious flesh. He maintained his body with certain insubstantial foods, so that he had only bread a good deal of the time, and not even bread most days, but something even less substantial for his food. He thought water the most delicious drink. And there were even times when he made no use of fire.[5]

4. And thus, having achieved perfection in every human virtue, he quickly became the best known of those of his time. He offered himself to the church of Antioch and, having advanced to sacred orders, founded a very large school; the most promising students came to him there from every place.

He also practiced stenography, his earnings from which provided food both for himself and for the poor. Indeed, he thought it wrong that he himself should partake of food before others had been provided for from the work of his hands.[6]

5 [Opitz, *Vit. Const.* 53 = Simeon]. Now the emperor Maximian[7] learned about Lucian, his fame having spread everywhere, at the time when his fury against the churches of Christ was raging out of control and he had decided that it would be easy to obliterate the name Christian from human society if he got rid of those everywhere who were their leaders, and so he was seized by a fierce desire to lay hold of him. He sent men to arrest him. But Lucian, when he learned of it, did not walk willingly into danger but acted cautiously and took care to do everything he could to avoid giving any impression of being foolhardy and inflicting on the churches deep sorrow on his account. So he was as careful as possible, this being the way the Lord himself had acted and taught, and the apostles too. In fact, he withdrew secretly from the city and went into hiding on a farm. But one Pancratius, also from Antioch, who held the rank of presbyter but had been suborned by the Sabellian doctrine and had long envied Lucian his fame, betrayed him to his hunters.[8]

6 [Opitz, *Vit. Const.* 54 = Simeon]. He was taken to Nicomedia to be put to death (for that was where Maximinus was). Great was the number of those who refused to deny Christ and who were put to death in every possible way.

---

5. On Lucian's asceticism, see Eusebius, *Hist. eccl.* 9.6.3; *Synax.* 140.27.

6. On Lucian's practice of calligraphy, see *Synax.* 139.26–27.

7. In section 5 the emperor in question is undoubtedly Maximinus, whatever confusion may have entered into the manuscript transmission (see Bidez, *Philostorgius*, 188; and section 6).

8. The statement that Pancratius was an adherent of Sabellianism suggests that he was a follower of Paul of Samosata and hints at deep divisions within the church in Antioch long before those associated with Arianism.

There was, for example, Anthimus, bishop of Nicomedia itself, whom Maximinus burned to death; there was Peter, bishop of Alexandria; and there were many other good and noble men.[9] His savagery reached such a pitch that he even killed quite young boys because he could not persuade them to taste of the things sacrificed to the demons. For he did not persuade them; they resisted, braced by some obviously invisible assistance: [Simeon alone] an even greater proof not only of the wickedness but also of the weakness of the demons and their ministers, if indeed their inability to make their will prevail resulted from their manifest powerlessness after they had been so eager to succeed, and especially after they had put everyone to the test. The children's perseverance and resistance to the end was indeed the greatest help to those engaged in the struggle with their wits and judgment, since they would have been ashamed to appear inferior to children in not standing up to the onslaught of the terrors as they had. Those, on the other hand, who bowed to the threats were condemned by the children's sufferings, since they were shown to have been defeated, not by the grievousness of the terrors, but by the weakness of their own wits. Thus it is that none of the things allowed by God and his providence ever have been, are, or will be without purpose or apart from that reason that is sovereign. [Opitz, *Vit. Const.* 54 = Simeon] The children, then, underwent a variety of sufferings at that time, one of which is especially worth recording.

7 [Opitz, *Vit. Const.* 55 = Simeon]. Maximinus brought in two children who were brothers illustriously born and at first tried to entice them with the kind of promises he thought would be most attractive to children. And he ordered brought to them some of the sacrifices that had been offered by people while the boys were looking on, that they might taste them. But when they refused and wept and said as best they could, with their still-lisping voices, that this was not what they had learned from their parents, who, they said, had enjoined upon them something different, then he turned back to threats and in fact subjected them to various torments.

But when the children endured them also better than words can describe and yielded not an inch, the divine power giving them fortitude, then one of the sophists who was there, the one in particular at whose urging and direction these things were being done, himself undertook to make them eat of everything offered without delay. For it would be ridiculous if the Roman

---

9. On Anthimus, see A7.2; Eusebius, *Hist. eccl.* 8.6.6; 8.13.1; Simeon Metaphrastes, *Passio Anthimi* 3–5 (PG 115:173–84); all three sources say he was beheaded. On Peter, see Eusebius, *Hist. eccl.* 7.32.31; 8.13.7; 9.6.2; Athanasius, *C. Ar.* 5.9.1; Epiphanius, *Pan.* 68.1.2–3.5. *Bios* 338.6–8 speaks of 3,618 martyred in Nicomedia but ascribes them to Maximianus Herculius.

emperors were defeated by children not beyond the age of lisping. So he devised the following. Having fixed up a concoction of mustard that was extremely potent and quite unendurable, he shaved their heads. And having plastered the preparation on as thickly as possible, that the full concentrated power of the material that had been applied[10] might penetrate throughout to the fullest extent, he put them into a blazing hot furnace. There the children, as though their heads had been struck by lightning, immediately doubled up to the floor. Shortly afterwards the elder of the two fell down and died first, unable to stand the intensity of the fire kindled in his skull. The other, when he saw his brother fall, cheered with all his might, exulting in his brother's victory; he hugged him, kissed him, cried out that he was victorious, and shouted over and over, "You have won, brother!" until he too expired while speaking thus to him and embracing and kissing him, and he lay there then with his arms around him. And this was the greatest act of suffering of that time, and the one that struck most pity into the onlookers, the very age [of the children] moving most of them to compassion. Their relatives took them away and buried them with the other children, since they had died for the same reason. And now their martyrs' shrine near Nicomedia is still called the infant martyrs' shrine. Many are the miracles worked there down through the years unceasingly.

8 [Simeon alone]. Now Lucian, when he was brought to Cappadocia and met there some soldiers who were Christians but had somehow been forced to the act of denial, appealed to their consciences, pointing out that it was the most shameful thing of all for men, to say nothing of soldiers, to appear ignoble and quite lacking in the courage to face death; there were women and even children who had bested them. "How is it," he asked, "that you are willing to run risks for the mortal sovereign, when you have thus readily betrayed the heavenly one? Where is the stronghold or refuge that would protect you, if he should at once summon you hence? Do you not realize that he controls and governs the universe and that he is the steward of life and lord of death? That being so, it is far better to set less store by the present life and to attain endless bliss with him than it is to cling to your life here and fail of it nonetheless, since even the enemy will probably deprive you of it, and to lose the other life as well and furthermore suffer eternal punishment."

When they heard this, they recognized their error and repented of their denial. Returning to their senses, they spoke out openly, and most of them, not fewer than forty, suffered death for Christ. There were also some who bore up under every kind of torture and survived, their honor intact after

---

10. For "that had been applied," reading τῆς ἐπικειμένης ὕλης (see Bidez, *Philostorgius*, 190).

their second trial; indeed, they made up for their previous denial by the constancy they now showed for the faith.[11]

9 [Opitz, *Vit. Const.* 56 = Simeon]. So Lucian, having accomplished these and a great many other deeds while on the way, was brought to Nicomedia. [Simeon alone] Now he had a large number of disciples, some of whom were with him there in Nicomedia when he took part in the contest and some not. Some of them, when force was applied to them to make them conform to paganism, yielded, unable at first to stand up to the tortures. Afterwards, however, when the divine Lucian (who was still alive) summoned them and used the full range of his eloquence to bring them to a better mind, showing them how dangerous their transgression was and how no one who utterly betrayed his confession of Christ would escape the unquenchable fire of Gehenna, he caused them to repent and brought them back into the church.

10. Among those who came to Lucian in Nicomedia was Antoninus, his favorite disciple, whose services he used after his arrival for the writing of letters, as Lucian himself says in one of them.[12] Among those who were not there was a great number of men; among the women who were absent were Eustolia, Dorothy, and Severa. They say that Pelagia too, who lived in Antioch in Syria by Mount Amanus, was a disciple of his. She is said to have thrown herself from a very high roof when people came to seize her, out of fear that she might be forced to suffer something unspeakable (for she was a virgin), and so she died. Those devoted to the martyrs still revere her as a martyr.[13]

11. Lucian, then, was brought to Nicomedia.[14] [Opitz, *Vit. Const.* 56 = Simeon] Maximinus had heard from many folk that if he so much as caught sight of him, he risked becoming a Christian (so great was the reverence that attended his appearance), and, fearing that something of the sort might happen to him, he put a curtain between them during their interview and

---

11. *Synax.* 139.9–13 mentions those who had given up the faith out of fear and who were strengthened for suffering by Lucian's exhortation.

12. Jerome, *Vir. ill.* 77, mentions Lucian's letters; an excerpt may be found in A7.2.

13. Philostorgius 2.14–15 speaks of Lucian's disciples. Epiphanius, *Pan.* 69.5.2, says that Eusebius of Nicomedia lived with Lucian in Nicomedia. On Eustolia, see Athanasius, *Apol. de fuga* 26; *H. Ar.* 28.1; on Dorothy, Eusebius, *Hist. eccl.* 8.14.15 (she resisted the tyrant's lust and was exiled; Rufinus's "translation" *ad loc.* identifies her); on Pelagia, Ambrose, *De virginibus* 3.33–34; *Ep.* VII (37) 38; John Chrysostom, *De sancta Pelagia virgine et martyre* (PG 50:579–85; he confirms that she threw herself from the roof of the house); *Synax.* 120.3; 742.6.

14. On Lucian being brought to Nicomedia, see Eusebius, *Hist. eccl.* 8.13.2; 9.6.3.

spoke to him from a distance, using an interlocutor.[15] He began by promising to lavish upon him bounty beyond telling: he would take him as a counselor in his affairs and as a father, as associate in imperial rank and in the supreme government, and a host of other like things besides. He requested, he said, only one single thing in return: that he offer sacrifice to the gods. But when Lucian, spurning this largesse as worthless, said that he would not reckon the whole world as of equal value to faith in God, he went over to threats, stating that he would subject him to every form of human torture found in the annals of history, together with whatever could be devised by modern ingenuity. Lucian met this with unshakeable courage, and the emperor in his fury decided it would not do to put him to death quickly (for he thought he would welcome a speedy release from his sufferings). So he ordered him to be thrust into prison and his body racked with a variety of instruments.

12 [Opitz, *Vit. Const.* 57 = Simeon]. Those therefore assigned to this task took him and subjected him to a variety of tortures of many different kinds, [Simeon alone] which were to cause him a great deal of pain but under which he would hold out for a long time. One thing they did was put both his feet in the stocks (an oblong piece of wood used for racking), pulling them four holes apart, the most painful degree for this torture, since his buttocks were forced apart out of joint; at another time they maliciously worked his whole back with fearfully pointed shards joined closely together. And so that that just man could not even turn or move while being pierced by the points, they stretched out his hands and tied them to a piece of wood over his head.[16]

[Opitz, *Vit. Const.* 57 = Simeon] In many other ways they mistreated him as well, going so far as to deprive him of all food, unless he liked to partake of their sacrilegious offerings, which indeed they extended to him willingly. But he preferred to die countless deaths, and it was more pleasant for him to remain completely without nourishment and to be consumed by starvation than to have so much as to look at such things. And he persevered in the hunger that was wasting him for fourteen whole days, neither resting nor relaxing from his usual ways, but constantly encouraging those locked up in the same prison for the same reason by his words to them and engaging in unceasing prayers.[17]

---

15. According to *Synax.* 139.16–20, Diocletian interviewed him from behind a curtain lest he be vanquished by his words.

16. Pseudo-Origen, *In Job* 2 (PG 17:470D–471A) confirms that Lucian was racked apart in four directions on a bed of shards; see also *Martyrologium Hieronymianum* VII id. ianuar. (*AASS* Novembris II 29–30).

17. On Lucian's starvation, see John Chrysostom, *In sanctum Lucianum martyrem* 2 (PG 50:523); *Synax.* 139.20–24.

13 [Simeon alone]. Now when several days had passed, during which he was being mistreated in the way explained, and the Feast of Theophany[18] was drawing near, his disciples began to be downcast (many had gathered to him there from Antioch and other places), thinking that their teacher would leave them forthwith and depart, being no longer able to bear his prolonged fast, and that it would never be granted them to celebrate the day of Theophany with him (the feast seemed to them far off, and their teacher's bodily strength would never last that long, since his lack of nourishment had already consumed most of it). But that reverend man spoke against such thoughts, ordering them emphatically to take courage. "I will be with you," he said, "and I will celebrate Theophany Day with you and will depart on the next day." And in fact his words came true, which showed clearly the divine power that was his.

14 [Opitz, *Vit. Const.* 58 = Simeon]. When the awaited day of the feast had arrived, his disciples were eager to enjoy this last sacred rite celebrated by him. But it seemed impossible either to bring a table into the prison or to escape the notice of the many godless people who were there or who would come in. But he said, "This my chest will be your table, and I do not think that it will be of less value in God's sight than that of lifeless matter. And you will be my holy temple as you surround me completely."

And this is indeed what happened. The guards, as though he were now at the end of his life, relaxed their vigilance, and God, I would say, wanted to honor the martyr and refused to let the inconsolable longing of his disciples go unsatisfied and so brought it about that what had been planned came to pass unhindered. The martyr, that is, placed them all around him in a circle, so that they closed him in tightly and with perfect security, each against the other, and ordered the liturgical elements to be brought in and placed on his chest. When they had been put there, he looked up to heaven, barely able to lift his gaze there with his sight now failing, and offered the usual prayers. And having spoken at great length in an inspired way and consecrated all the offerings according to the supreme law, he partook of the sacrament, bade those of his disciples who were present to share it and partake of it, and sent it to those not there, as he himself explained in the final letter to them, for the writing of which he used Antoninus, the best of his disciples.[19]

And so he made it through that day with his friends, just as he had promised them.

---

18. The Feast of Theophany was Christmas or Epiphany; here it would be Christmas, given the traditional date of his death.

19. For Antoninus and his letters, see section 10.

15 [Opitz, *Vit. Const.* 59 = Simeon]. The next day some men came from the emperor to see if he was still alive (for they found it passing strange that his life had lasted so long); when he saw all those who had arrived standing by him, he cried out forcibly three times as loudly as he could, "I am a Christian!"[20] And the third time he gave up his spirit.

16 [Opitz, *Vit. Const.* 60 = Simeon]. Now there are those who say that he was thrown still alive into the sea. For Maximinus, astonished at his resistance to the end and his stubbornness, ordered those who take care of such matters to throw him into the sea after fastening a huge rock to his right arm, that he might perish by drowning and that his corpse might have no grave or any other burial rite. So he was in the depths for fourteen days in all, as many as he had been in prison engaged in the contest with his various bodily sufferings. But on the fifteenth day, a dolphin brought him to shore; it happened as follows. His disciples had been haunting the forelands and beaches, different ones in different places, to see if they could locate him when the sea, quite turbulent in winter, would cast him up. But as the time went on, they were ready to give up, and had now abandoned the search.

17 [Opitz, *Vit. Const.* 61 = Simeon]. It was just then, on the eve of the fifteenth day, that the martyr appeared in a dream to Glycerius, one of his loyal disciples, who was then staying on the mainland opposite Nicomedia. He told him, "As soon as morning arrives, get up, man, and go to this place" (telling him where on the shore he was to go). "I will meet you there when you have arrived." He awoke quickly because of the vividness and astonishing nature of what he had seen, and, dawn being already at hand, he got up, called together a large number of his comrades, and went to the designated place with them.

Just at that moment the dolphin emerged from the sea, a huge, strange-looking creature. Once upon the surface, it extended itself, blew mightily, and headed toward land. There was a great foam and rush about it as it came, the very waves sounding loudly as they were parted, one after the other.[21] It carried the corpse stretched out as though lying on a couch. It was quite a sight to see the corpse remain motionless on that round, slippery body without rolling off its transport under its own weight or from the force of the waves.

---

20. John Chrysostom says that to all the questions put to him under torture, Lucian answered only, "I am a Christian" (*In sanctum Lucianum martyrem* 3 [PG 50:524]).

21. 2.12 mentions the dolphin, which had a reputation reaching far back into pre-Christian times for bringing to shore the bodies of the dead so they could be buried (Erna Diez, "Delphin," *RAC* 3:669). The description of the great froth and rush it made seems conventional; see Plutarch, *Septem sapientium convivium* 18.160F–161A.

When the dolphin had reached land, the wave lifted it high and deposited it on the shore. And it stretched out and expired on the spot.

18 [Opitz, *Vit. Const.* 62 = Simeon]. The corpse, borne up upon the sand, lay there sound and complete, except that the right hand, to which the rock had been fastened, was not with the rest of the body at the time. And there are those who say that it was not sent up from the sea even later but remained in the depths where it was, as God saw fit. But others say that it too was returned not long afterwards, its fetters hanging around it, and when brought to land was picked up by those present, so that it could be restored to the rest of the body.

[Simeon alone] The incident with the hand took place, it seems to me, because God wanted to show it particular honor, pleased as he was with the work of emending the scriptures accomplished by its means. For among the sufferings undergone for Christ, that which is heavier is more honorable.

19. For let no one think that the corpse was brought out by the dolphin accidentally or that this happened by chance. That a dolphin really brought it out of the sea in the way described appears quite evident, since so many of those who lived at the time mentioned the event. And I myself have known from childhood the song about it that ends:

A dolphin took him on its back,
Expired while bearing him to land.

That this did not happen by accident is made clear not least of all by the very greatness of the miracle accomplished, as well as by the dream connected with it, to say nothing of what happened afterwards. For the corpse brought out of the sea was a huge surprise to those who saw it; it had remained quite unharmed except for what had happened to the hand, the sea having done it no damage in those many days and the fish not having touched it, and no unpleasant odor emanated from it, so that it was in every way obvious that God had done this deed and that it was not from negligence or inability to protect him that God had previously allowed the martyr to fall into such grave dangers, nor had he who had performed such a great miracle for him let his hand become separated from the rest of his body without a very good reason. It was rather that, in adorning his every virtue, he called him at that time to be a partner in the sufferings of his Son, thus providing him the best and fairest opportunity to be made a partner in his glory as well (this for me being the reason for all martyrs for the truth). Now, however, wishing to endorse the man's fervor for the sacred scriptures and to guarantee the great value of his labor, he granted the hand that had especially served him in this to be honored by special sufferings, just as, I think, spectators festoon the arms of athletes. If, however, anyone should believe that the hand remained in the sea, even he may take the occasion to reflect on these things and may also consider that often God combines natural phenomena with miracles, the latter serving to display the wonder-working power, the former to help nature retain our confidence.

But as for these things, and the reason why each of them happens, the One who governs them must know them clearly. Still, one may learn from each of his miracles and works that there is another reason that is ineffable and above us and a dispensation that is supremely good and incomprehensible and that nothing happens randomly or by chance.

20. Then, when the corpse brought in by the dolphin had been carried onto the sand, his disciples first ran up together, each from a different direction, and welcomed it fittingly, each of them kissing and embracing it fervently with all his strength. [Opitz, *Vit. Const.* 63 = Simeon] Then they carried it up, performed all the usual funeral rites, and laid it in the most celebrated place in that country. They set up a grave marker for it as best they could at the time; Helena later honored the place because of the martyr by establishing it as a city and calling it Helenopolis. She did so by gathering together those who lived in the surrounding area and as many as she could from elsewhere, put a stout wall around it, and built the great church for the martyr that is now clearly visible from land and sea to those traveling on either element.[22]

---

22. On the dedication of the martyr's burial place, see 2.12; A7.4, 7.4a–c; Jerome, *Vir. ill.* 77.

Appendix 7

Fragments of an Arian Historian[1]

1 [*Chron. pasch.* a. 253]. This tradition has also come down to us about Saint Babylas; it is one that was recounted to those before us by the blessed Leontius, bishop of Antioch:

"It was Decius who killed Saint Babylas, not only because he was a Christian but also because he dared to prevent the wife of the emperor Philip, and Philip himself, who were Christians, from entering the church.[2] The reason was that Philip had committed the following crime: this Philip the Younger, when prefect under the emperor Gordian who preceded him, had received from Gordian his son in trust. And when the emperor Gordian died, Philip slew the boy and took the throne."

2 [*Chron. pasch.* a. 303]. In the same year, many people everywhere, as we said, won through the contest and died, and this was just as true in Nicomedia,

---

1. Appendix 7 is a collection of material that may be seen to have been derived from an anonymous homoean history composed apparently in the later fourth century; see Bidez, *Philostorgius*, cxxxvi, cli–clxiii; Brennecke, *Studien zur Geschichte der Homöer*, 134–41; idem, "Christliche Quellen des Ammianus Marcellinus?" 226–50; and Barnes, *Athanasius and Constantius*, 209. Philostorgius was among those who drew from it. The excerpts are taken from seven chronicles, three of which will be familiar to students of the period: the *Chronicon paschale* and the Chronicles of Jerome and Theophanes. The Syriac chronicles may not be so well known, so it seems convenient to list them more fully: (1) *Chronicon miscellaneum ad annum Domini 724 pertinens* (Brooks and Chabot, *Chronica Minora*, 2:76–155) (abbreviated *Chron. misc.*; references to this work will be by page and line); (2) Jacob of Edessa, *Chronicle* (Brooks and Chabot, *Chronica Minora*, 3:261–330) (references to this work will be by page); (3) *Chronicon ad 1234* (= Chron. CE in Bidez, *Philostorgius*, 202) (Jean-Baptiste Chabot, ed., *Anonymi Auctoris Chronicon ad annum Christi 1234 pertinens* [CSCO 81; Scriptores Syri 3/14; Paris: Typographeo Reipublicae, 1920]); and (4) Michael, *Chronique de Michel le Syrien, Patriarche Jacobite d'Antioche (1166–1199)* (ed. Jean-Baptiste Chabot; 4 vols.; Paris: Leroux, 1899–1924) (references to this work will be by page and line).

2. On Babylas, see 7.8, 7.8a.

where the emperor was then staying, and where Dorotheus and Gorgonius, along with a great many others in the imperial service, died; a great choir of martyrs was formed together. And not long afterwards Anthimus too, the bishop of the church in Nicomedia, was put to death by decapitation. Others were burned to death, still more were thrown into the sea, and the executioners' strength failed before that enormous multitude.[3]

Concerning the immeasurable multitude of those martyred, the presbyter Lucian wrote to the people of Antioch:

"The whole choir of martyrs greets you together. I announce to you the good news that Pope Anthimus has reached the finish line in the martyrs' race."[4]

This is what took place in Nicomedia, and more besides.

3 [*Chron. pasch.* a. 325]. At that time [Constantine] took the field and won the victory by prayer over the enemies of the Christian faith. He therefore proceeded to erect churches in honor of the universal Savior Christ our God in various places for the conversion of the nations.[5]

3a [Theophanes 29B]. Hence he won the victory by prayer over all his enemies. He therefore proceeded to erect churches in honor of God in various places for the conversion of the nations.

The same year [a.m. 5815 = 322/3] Martinus too was killed after usurping power for three months.[6] And Licinianus, Licinius's son, was stripped of the title of Caesar by Constantine.

The same year, Narses, the son of the Persian king, overran Mesopotamia and took the city of Amida.[7] Constantius Caesar, Constantine's son, took the field against him and after a few setbacks finally won such a victory in battle that he even slew Narses himself.

---

3. On Dorotheus and Gorgonius, see Eusebius, *Hist. eccl.* 8.6.5 (they were in the imperial household and died by strangulation); on Anthimus, A6.6; on martyrdom by burning and drowning, Eusebius, *Hist. eccl.* 8.6.6.

4. On Lucian's letter, see A6.14.

5. On Constantine's construction of churches, see Eusebius, *Vit. Const.* 3.50.

6. "Martinus" is Martinianus, Licinius's Master of Offices whom he raised to Augustus of the west in July of 324 (the coinage shows he was proclaimed Augustus, not Caesar, contrary to the literary sources; see Paschoud, *Zosime*, 1:217). Licinius sent him with an army to Lampsacus to block Constantine's advance; he was executed in 325 when Licinius was. See *Anon. Val.* 25; 28; 29; Aurelius Victor 41.9; *Epit. Caes.* 41.6–7; Zosimus 2.25.2, 26.2, 28.2.

7. Narses was the brother, not the son, of Sapor II. In 335 he invaded Mesopotamia and captured Amida, but Festus (*Brev.* 27) confirms that he was killed while retreating from Constantius's counterstroke.

3b [*Chron. misc.* 129.14–19]. Constantine the merciful made ready against those who were fighting against the Christian religion, and he received the victory from God by his prayer, on account of which he also built churches everywhere to the glory of God, in order to further conversions to Christianity. And barbarian rulers and nations became subject to him.

[131.9–15] In the eighteenth year of his reign, he waged war against Licinius and conquered him and occupied his realm. The following year Martinus rebelled against him, reigned for three months, and was slain. And Constantine took over the entire Roman Empire, he and his sons Constantine, Constantius, and Constans, in the eleventh year of the peace of the churches.

4 [*Chron. pasch.* a. 327]. The emperor Constantine refounded Drepanum in Bithynia in honor of the holy martyr Lucian, naming it Helenopolis after his mother and granting immunity to it and to a considerable area facing it, in honor of the holy martyr Lucian, a privilege still enjoyed.[8]

4a [Theophanes 40B]. In this year [a.m. 5815 = 322/3],[9] Constantine, the most godly conqueror, took the field against the Germans, Sarmatians, and Goths and won a resounding victory through the power of the cross; he crushed them and reduced them to utter slavery.[10]

The same year he also refounded Drepanum in honor of the martyr Lucian there, naming it Helenopolis after his mother.

4b [*Chron. misc.* 129.20–22]. He renovated Drepanum in honor of the martyr Lucian, who had been placed there. And he called it Helenopolis, after his mother Helena.

4c [Jerome, *Chron.* 327]. Constantine founded Drepanum, a city in Bithynia, in honor of the martyr Lucian, who was buried there, and called it Helenopolis after his mother.

---

8. See also 2.12; A6.20; *Bios* 338.10–12. Drepanum was also where Constantine's father met his mother and begot him (*Bios* 308.11).

9. In Theophanes, where the *annus mundi* dates do not square with the indictional ones, the latter are almost always more reliable, Theophanes having found them in his source, whereas the *annus mundi* dates are of his own computation, continuing the system he inherited from George Syncellus; see Cyril A. Mango and Roger Scott, *The Chronicle of Theophanes Confessor: Byzantine and Near Eastern History, AD 284–813* (Oxford: Clarendon, 1997), lxiv–lxvii.

10. Constantine campaigned against the Goths and Sarmatians in 322 and 323 (*Anon. Val.* 21; Zosimus 2.21; Paschoud, *Zosime,* 1:93–94). He defeated the Goths in 332 and the Sarmatians in 334 (Rufinus, *Hist. eccl.* 10.8; Orosius 7.28.29). Eusebius (*Vit. Const.* 4.5) says he defeated the Scythians and Sarmatians through the power of the cross. Section 4a may be related to Constantine's undertaking in 5b–6b, 6, and 6a to secure the Danube frontier. See also Zonaras 13.2.42.

5 [Theophanes 41B]. In this year [a.m. 5819 = 326/7], work was begun on the octagonal church in Antioch.[11]

5a [*Chron. misc.* 129.22–23]. He built the great church in Antioch.

5b–6b [Michael 133, right column]. And he built in Antioch an octagonal church. And he built a bridge over the River Danube. And his army crossed over, subjected the Scythians, and made believers of them.

5c [Jerome, *Chron.* 327]. In Antioch, work was begun on the church that is called "the golden."

6 [*Chron. pasch.* a. 328]. The devout Constantine crossed the Danube many times and built a stone bridge across it.[12]

6a [Theophanes 41B]. In this year [a.m. 5820 = 327/8], the devout Constantine crossed the Danube, built a stone bridge across it, and subjected the Scythians.

7 [*Chron. pasch.* a. 330; P284D–285A]. In the 301st year from the Lord's ascension into heaven and the twenty-fifth of his own reign, Constantine the most devout, father of the Augustus Constantine the Younger and of the Caesars Constantius and Constans, founded a great, illustrious, and happy city, honored it with a senate, and gave it the name of Constantinople on 11 May, the second day of the week in the third indiction; it had formerly been called Byzantium, but he decreed that it should be called "Second Rome."

7a [Theophanes 42B]. In this year [a.m. 5821 = 328/9] the devout Constantine founded Constantinople, decreeing that it should be called "New Rome" and ordering it to have a senate. He also put up a porphyry column and upon it a statue of himself at the place where he had begun to build the city, toward the western part, by the gate leading out to Rome. He decorated the city, bringing into it from every province and city whatever work there was of art and statuary, bronze and marble.[13]

8 [Theophanes 42B]. In this year [a.m. 5822 = 329/30] the devout Constantine increased his efforts to destroy the idols and their temples, and he destroyed them in place after place. He gave their revenues to the churches of God.[14]

---

11. On the octagonal church, see A7.16, 16a; Eusebius, *Vit. Const.* 3.50; *Bios* 338.9–10.

12. On the bridge, see Aurelius Victor 41.18; *Epit. Caes.* 41.13; *Bios* 337.24–25; Wolfram, *History of the Goths,* 61: "On July 5, 328, Constantine opened a stone bridge across the Danube between Oescus-Gigen and Sucidava-Celeiu." Part of his project was to secure the border of the Diocese of Thrace, which was regarded by those of his time as of great military and political importance.

13. On the foundation of Constantinople and its porphyry column, see 2.9, 2.9a.

14. On Constantine's reputation for destroying pagan temples, see A1.5; A3.1.

7b and 8a [*Chron. misc.* 129.23–130.5]. Because of his love for God, he blotted out the memory of idols and destroyed their temples.

The fortieth bishop of Jerusalem was Maximus. Athanasius was the eighteenth bishop of Alexandria. The bishop of Antioch... The twenty-fifth after him...

Eusebius, son of Pamphilus and bishop of Caesarea in Palestine, became renowned as an author, and his many books may still be found.

Constantine built a famous and prosperous city, honored it with a senate, and gave it the name of Constantinople; it had formerly been called Byzantium.

7c and 8b [Jerome, *Chron.* 330]. The dedication of Constantinople was achieved by the stripping bare of nearly every other city.[15]

[331] The pagan temples were overthrown by Constantine's edict.

9 [Theophanes 42B]. In this year [a.m. 5823 = 330/1] the government hall in Nicomedia was destroyed by divine fire.[16]

10 [Theophanes 42B–43B]. In this year [a.m. 5824 = 331/2], on the eve of the seventh indiction, a severe famine gripped the east, so that villages gathered in large crowds in the region of Antioch and Cyrus, attacked and looted each other in nightly raids, and finally proceeded by day to enter the granaries and storehouses, plundered and looted everything, and withdrew. Thus a measure of grain cost 400 *argyria*. But Constantine the Great granted grain rations to the churches in each city in order to provide continual sustenance to widows, hospices, the poor, and the clergy.[17] The church in Antioch received 36,000 measures of grain. But the same year there was a mighty earthquake on Cyprus that brought down the city of Salamis, killing a large number.[18]

10a [Michael 133, right-left columns]. When the great famine struck the east, Constantine the victorious ordered that provisions be given at his own

---

On the wording of the reference about giving the revenues of the pagan temples to the churches, see *Bios* 324.16–19.

15. Eunapius's remark about the cities bereft of their people who had been moved to Constantinople (*Vit. soph.* 462) is perhaps closest to Jerome's words in 7c–8b. For other complaints about Constantinople costing other cities dearly, see Libanius, *Or.* 1.279; 30.37.

16. On the destruction of the government house in Nicomedia, see Eusebius, *Hist. eccl.* 8.6.6; *Oratio Constantini imperatoris ad sanctorum coetum* 25.

17. On Constantine's grain allowances to virgins, widows, and clergy, see Theodoret, *Hist. eccl.* 1.11.2–3; 4.4.

18. On the earthquake in Salamis, see A7.17.

expense to the poor and the clergy. And he gave the church in Antioch 36,000 measures of wheat.

10b [Jerome, *Chron.* 333]. A countless multitude in Syria and Cilicia died of pestilence and hunger.

11–12 [*Chron. pasch.* a. 335; P286AB]. The thirtieth-year festival of Constantine the devout was celebrated in Constantinople-Rome with great pomp.... He gave Dalmatius, the son of his brother, the censor Dalmatius, the rank of Caesar.[19]

11a [Theophanes 43B]. In this year [a.m. 5825 = 332/3] Dalmatius was proclaimed Caesar. Now Calocaerus usurped power on the island of Cyprus but was not equal to the Roman attack. He was defeated and put to death in Tarsus in Cilicia, along with the others involved, by being burned alive by Dalmatius Caesar.[20]

11b [Jerome, *Chron.* 334]. Calocaerus revolted in Cyprus and was put down.

12a [Theophanes 43B–44B]. In this year [a.m. 5826 = 333/4] the thirtieth-year festival of Constantine, the most pious and illustrious, was celebrated with great pomp. And in Antioch a star appeared in the sky by day in the east; it was smoking heavily as though from a furnace. It appeared from the third to the fifth hour.

13 [*Chron. pasch.* a. 337; P286C–287B]. The Persians declared war on the Romans. Constantine set out in the thirty-second year of his reign, heading east to counter the Persians, and when he reached Nicomedia, he departed from this life gloriously and piously in a suburb of that city on the eleventh of the month of Artemisios, having been granted the baptism of salvation by Eusebius, the bishop of Constantinople; he had reigned thirty-one years and ten months. He left behind as Caesars his three sons: Constantine was governing the regions of Gaul and in the twentieth year of his reign; Constantius, who was Caesar after him, was in the east and in the eleventh year of his reign; Constans, who was Caesar after him, was staying in the regions of Italy and in the third year of his reign. There was also Dalmatius Caesar, his brother's son, in Mesopotamia, who was also in his third year.

The thrice-blessed Constantine rested on 22 May, the very day of Pentecost. While the earthly dwelling of the devout Constantine was still lying unburied in the palace in Constantinople and being guarded until his sons could be informed, word was brought to Constantius in the east in Mesopo-

---

19. On Constantine's Tricennalia, see Eusebius, *Vit. Const.* 4.40; *Consul. const.* 335. On Dalmatius Caesar, see 2.16a; Jerome, *Chron.* 335. He was named Caesar on 18 September.

20. On Calocaerus's revolt, see Aurelius Victor 41.11–12; Orosius 7.28.30. He was executed by crucifixion.

tamia, where war with the Persians was still brewing, and he left at once for Constantinople. Upon his arrival, he brought out his father, the famed Constantine, with such pomp and glory attending the imperial procession that words cannot do it justice. The army was present bearing arms as though he were alive, and so was the whole city, since he had given it the name of Rome and bestowed on it all that was its glory, as well as its allowances of grain. Everyone was in such great grief that never did any emperor before him receive such glory in his life and after death. He was laid to rest in the Church of the Holy Apostles, in which lie the relics of the holy apostles Andrew and Luke the evangelist and Timothy, the disciple of the apostle Paul.[21]

The Persian king Sapor invaded Mesopotamia, intending to sack Nisibis, and after he had besieged it for sixty-three days and had not taken it, he withdrew.[22]

13a [Theophanes 49B–50B]. In this year [a.m. 5828 = 335/6] Eustathius, presbyter of Constantinople, who had adopted the apostolic life and risen to the summit of virtue, was recognized as outstanding, as was Zenobius, the chief of works, who had built the Martyrs' Shrine in Jerusalem at Constantine's bidding.

In the same year many of the Assyrians in Persia were sold in Mesopotamia by the Saracens.[23]

Now the Persians declared war on the Romans. The devout Constantine set out for Nicomedia and squared off against the Persians,[24] but falling

---

21. On Constantine's death, see 2.16a, b; 3.1a; *Consul. const.* 337. On Constantius's summons, see Rufinus, *Hist. eccl.* 10.12. Constantine called him to come to him when he was on the point of death (Julian, *Or.* 1.16C–D; 2.94B; Libanius, *Or.* 59.73–75). On the lamentation at his death, the word sent to his sons, the arrival of Constantius, the funeral procession and burial, see Eusebius, *Vit. Const.* 4.65–71; on his burial in the Church of the Holy Apostles, see 38 n. 4, second paragraph.

22. On the Persian attack on Nisibis, see Festus, *Brev.* 27: "Ter autem a Persis est obsessa Nisibis, sed maiore sui detrimento dum obsidet hostis adfectus est." Sapor laid siege to Nisibis ca. 16 June 337, less than a month after Constantine died. He had already planned an assault and was moving toward Nisibis when he was encouraged by news of the death. The siege lasted until 17 August, when Sapor was forced to retreat due to disease and short supplies. Bishop Jacob (James) had died on 15 July. See Richard W. Burgess, "The Dates of the First Siege of Nisibis and the Death of James of Nisibis," *Byzantion* 69 (1999): 7–17.

23. "Assyria" in 13a means the Persian province of that name; Saracen raids upon it were chronic at this time (Ammianus 25.6.8).

24. "Constantine set out for Nicomedia and squared off against the Persians," reading the aorist participle παραταξάμενος. Perhaps read the future participle παραταξόμενος: "to square off against."

ill, he rested in peace. Some of the Arian-minded say he was granted holy baptism at that time by Eusebius of Nicomedia, who had moved to Constantinople.... He [Constantine], at his death ... had reigned thirty-one years and ten months.

[51B] In this year [a.m. 5829 = 336/7], when Constantine the great and holy rested in peace, his three sons took over the government of the Roman world: Constantius in the east, Constans in Gaul, and Constantine in Italy.

13b [*Chron. misc.* 130.9–13]. Eustathius, presbyter of Constantinople, was living the apostolic way of life, and the archdeacon Zenobius was renowned.[25] He built a temple in Jerusalem, as Constantine had ordered.

In Mesopotamia, many of the Assyrians in Persia were sold by the Arabs.

13c [Jerome, *Chron.* 336]. Eustathius, a presbyter of Constantinople, was held in high repute; he it was who saw to the building of the Martyrs' Shrine in Jerusalem.

13d [*Chron. misc.* 130.6–9]. Afterwards he departed piously from this world, having reigned for thirty-two years. His sons Constantine, Constantius, and Constans followed him for thirteen years.

13e [Jerome, *Chron.* 337]. Constantine at the very end of his life was baptized by Eusebius, bishop of Nicomedia, and went off down into the Arian doctrine. From Eusebius stem the plundering of the churches and the dissension throughout the whole world, which continue still.

Constantine ... died ... in Ancyrona; his three children who survived him were called Augusti after having had the title of Caesars.[26]

13f [Theophanes 52B–53B]. In the same year, the Persian king Sapor invaded Mesopotamia, intending to sack Nisibis, and after he had encamped by it for sixty-three days and had not managed to take it, he withdrew.

Jacob, the bishop of Nisibis, easily achieved his desire by his prayers when he persevered in the path of piety.[27] He it was who caused the Persians to fail in their plans when they were hoping to destroy Nisibis. For they withdrew from the city at once, driven away by the spirit of prayer, and when they came to their own country, they found waiting for them the reward for the impiety they had committed: famine and pestilence.

13g [*Chron. misc.* 130.14–18]. Sapor, king of Persia, arrived in Mesopo-

---

25. Zenobius's title of "archdeacon" in 13b seems to be a corruption of ἀρχιτέκτων ("chief of works"); cf. 13a.

26. On Constantine's succession, see 3.1a. On the title of Augusti given them after having had that of Caesars, see Eusebius, *Vit. Const.* 4.68.

27. On Jacob, see Paul Peeters, "La légende de saint Jacques de Nisibe," *AnBoll* 38 (1920): 285–373; Gennadius, *Vir. ill.* 1; Theodoret, *Hist. eccl.* 2.30 (which, like Philostorgius 3.23, places him in the wrong siege).

tamia to capture Nisibis. He encamped by it for sixty-six days. And Jacob, bishop of Nisibis, drove away the army by his prayer. And when they returned home, they found famine and plague facing them in return for what they had done.

13h [Jacob of Edessa 289]. Sapor went up to do battle against Nisibis. But he returned from there, put to shame by the prayer of Bishop Jacob. And immediately he went forth in a rage and devastated and laid waste the entire region of Meso[potamia] in the year....

13i [Jerome, *Chron.* 338]. Sapor, king of Persia, having laid Mesopotamia waste for almost two months, besieged Nisibis.

13j [Same]. Jacob, bishop of Nisibis, was held in high repute; it was his prayers that had often freed the city from danger.

14 [Theophanes 53B]. In this year [a.m. 5831 = 338/9] Constantine, the son of Constantine the Great, invaded the territory of his own brother Constans and, joining war, was slain by the soldiers.[28] And Constans ruled the entire west by himself.

14a [*Chron. misc.* 130.19–20]. Gregory was the nineteenth bishop of Alexandria.

Constantine the Younger departed [from life] after reigning for twenty-five years.

15 [Theophanes 54B]. In this year [a.m. 5832 = 339/40], Constantius built Amida, providing it with an impressive wall. He also founded Constantia, which was previously called Antoninopolis, naming it after himself; it is 700 *stadia* south of Amida.[29]

15a [*Chron. misc.*131.4–8]. In Mesopotamia [Constantius] also built the city of Amida, giving it the name of Augusta Constantina. He also built a city in Osrhoene, which he called Constantina; it had formerly been called Antoninopolis.

15b [Michael 137, middle column]. In Mesopotamia he enlarged Amida and completed it, and called it Augusta. Tella, which had formerly been called Antoninopolis, he called Constantia.

16 [Theophanes 55B]. In the same year [a.m. 5833 = 340/1] Antioch was endangered by severe earthquakes for three days.

---

28. "Constantine ... was slain by the soldiers" translates ὑπὸ τῶν στρατιωτῶν. Perhaps read στρατηγῶν: "by the generals" (cf. Eutropius 10.9.2). On the episode, see 3.1, 3.1a.

29. On Amida, see A7.3a. On its fortification and the building of Antoninopolis, see Ammianus 18.9.1 (who tells us that the work was done while Constantius was still Caesar). On the distance between Constantia and Amida, see Mango and Scott, *Chronicle of Theophanes Confessor,* 59.

The round church that had taken six years to build was dedicated; the foundations had been laid by Constantine the Great, and it was completed and dedicated by Constantius.[30]

16a [*Chron. misc.* 130.21–26]. In Antioch in Syria, the church in the form of a rotunda was finished after fifteen years. Constantine dedicated it in the time of Bishop Flaccillus, on the day of the Epiphany of Our Savior.

The twenty-eighth bishop of Antioch was Stephen.

Antioch was subjected to repeated earthquakes for thirteen days.

16b [Jerome, *Chron.* 341]. Many Eastern cities were leveled by a terrible earthquake.

[342] In Antioch, the golden church was dedicated.

17 [Theophanes 55B]. In this year [a.m. 5834 = 341/2] Constantius conquered the Assyrians and celebrated a triumph.[31]

Sapor, the Persian king, added to his evils by persecuting the Christians subject to him.

Constans plundered the Franks in the west.[32]

[56B] A great earthquake occurred in Cyprus, and most of the city of Salamis collapsed.[33]

17a [*Chron. misc.* 130.27]. Sapor persecuted the Christians.

17b [Jerome, *Chron.* 344]. The Persian king Sapor persecuted the Christians.

18 [Theophanes 56B]. In this year [a.m. 5835 = 342/3] there was a great earthquake that brought down Neocaesarea in Pontus, except for the church and the bishop's house and the devout men found there.

The Romans went to war with the Persians and killed many of them.

18a [*Chron. misc.* 130.28–29]. Neocaesarea in Pontus collapsed, all except for the church, the bishop, and the devout men inside.

18b [Jerome, *Chron.* 344]. Neocaesarea in Pontus was destroyed, except for the church and the bishop and the others who happened to be there.

19 [Theophanes 56B]. In this year [a.m. 5836 = 343/4] there was a great earthquake that leveled the island of Rhodes.

20 [Theophanes 56B]. In this year [a.m. 5837 = 344/5] Dyrrhachium in

---

30. On the "round church," see A7.5.

31. The "Assyrians" of A.17 are the Persians; compare Zosimus 3.12.3. The victory in question was near Singara in 343. See Festus, *Brev.* 2; Mango and Scott, *Chronicle of Theophanes Confessor,* 61.

32. On Constans' success in quelling the Franks, see Libanius, *Or.* 59.127–135; *Consul. const.* 342.

33. On Salamis, see A7.10.

Dalmatia was destroyed by an earthquake. Rome was endangered for three days by the quaking. Twelve cities in Campania were destroyed.

20a [Jerome, *Chron.* 346]. Dyrrhachium was destroyed by an earthquake, and Rome quaked for three days and nights, and most of the cities of Campania were damaged.

21 [Theophanes 57B]. In this year [a.m. 5838 = 345/6] Constantius built the harbor in Seleucia in Syria by cutting through a great part of a mountain, and he rebuilt the city.

And he founded a city in Phoenicia that he called Constantia; it was formerly called Antaradus.

The Persian king Sapor invaded Mesopotamia and besieged Nisibis for seventy-eight days and then withdrew again in shame.

In the same year, there was an eclipse of the sun, so that the stars appeared in the sky at the third hour of the day, on the sixth of the month of Daisios.

21a [*Chron. misc.* 131.1–4]. Constantius built a harbor in Seleucia in Isauria by hewing off a great part of a mountain. And he built a city.

In Phoenicia he built a city that he called Constantia; it had formerly been called Antaradus.

21b [Jerome, *Chron.* 346]. A harbor was built in Seleucia in Syria at great public expense.

Sapor again besieged Nisibis for three months.

? [Eusebius of Emesa, standard-bearer of the Arian party, wrote many different things.]

There was an eclipse of the sun.

22 [Theophanes 58B]. In the same year [a.m. 5839 = 346/7] the sun again became darker at the second hour on a Sunday.

23 [Theophanes 58B]. In this year [a.m. 5840 = 347/8] there was a strong earthquake in Beirut in Phoenicia, and most of the city collapsed; as a result, a multitude of pagans came into the church with the promise that they would practice Christianity like us. Hence there were some who made innovations in the laws of the church, like plunderers, and left, and naming a place of prayer, they received the multitude there. They imitated everything relating to the church, becoming in regard to us like the Samaritan sect to the Jews and living like pagans.

24 [*Chron. pasch.* a. 350; P289B–292A]. [1] The blessed Leontius, bishop of Antioch in Syria, was a man who was completely faithful, religious, and zealous for the true faith; he had as well a concern for the hospices established to care for strangers, so he appointed religious men to take charge of them.[34]

---

34. Leontius of Antioch is praised for the purity of his doctrine in 2.3 and 2.15 and for his pastoral oversight in 3.18.

Among them were three who were extremely zealous for the faith. They had some occasion to travel to a place seventeen miles from Antioch that was called Thrakon Kome.[35] A Jew chanced to be traveling with them. The leader of the three brothers was a most reverend man named Eugenius.[36] As they were traveling together, Eugenius struck up a conversation with the Jew about belief in the only begotten Son of God. The Jew was ridiculing this, when they came across a dead snake lying in the road. The Jew immediately said to them, "If you eat this dead snake and do not die, I will become a Christian." Eugenius took the snake at once and divided it into three parts for himself and the two others with him, and they ate it in front of the Jew and went on living. Thus there was fulfilled with them the salvific Gospel saying: "And they will pick up snakes with their hands, and if they eat anything deadly, it will not harm them."[37] And the Jew went into the hospice with them, stayed there, and became a Christian of good repute.

[2] The Augustus Constantius, while staying in the east because of the Persian war, heard the news about Magnentius and left Antioch to head for Italy.

[3] The Persian king Sapor invaded Mesopotamia and besieged Nisibis for one hundred days. He attacked it in various ways, using many devices, even bringing up a herd of elephants trained for battle, mercenary kings, and all sorts of engines of war with which he threatened to level the city to its very foundations unless they were prepared to abandon it. But the people of Nisibis refused to surrender it, so Sapor then decided to flood it with the river flowing nearby. But the people of Nisibis conquered the enemy with prayer, since God was propitious to them. For when the waters had all but washed away the foundation of the walls so as to make them fall, a part of the wall did collapse, as God permitted, for the benefit of the city, as will be explained next. For the result was that the city was shielded and the enemy repelled by the water, so that many of them perished.[38]

---

35. On Θρακόων κώμη, see Ernst Honigmann, "Θράκων κώμη," PW 6A.1:552.

36. Is the Eugenius mentioned in A7.24.1 the same as the presbyter of that name martyred under Julian? See A3.2, 17–18; Bidez, *Philostorgius*, 274.

37. The Gospel quotation about snakes is in Mark 16:18 and Luke 10:19.

38. The siege is mentioned in 3.23, where, however, it is confused with that of the year 337, the one in which Jacob is said to have helped defend the city. For fuller accounts, in addition to the passages here, see Julian, *Or.* 1.26D–28D; 2.62B–67A; Theodoret, *Hist. eccl.* 2.30 (the latter also moves Jacob to the siege of 350); Zosimus 3.8.2; Zonaras 13.7.4. The different accounts agree that the Persians tried to undermine the city wall by damming the Mygdonius and then loosing it suddenly but that the attempt failed even though part of the wall was damaged. As A7.24.4 says, the elephants got bogged down in the mud left behind by the flood and became easy tar-

[4] But even after this had happened to them, they threatened to come in through the part of the wall that had fallen, bringing up the armed elephants and whipping up the horde to battle more fiercely, using every sort of engine of war. But the soldiers guarding the city won the victory through God's providence. For they filled the whole place with armed men of every sort and slew most of the elephants with catapults. Others fell into the mud at the bottom of the ditches, while yet others, when hit, turned and went back, killing more than ten thousand of their armed men. A lightning bolt from the sky fell on the rest of them, and everyone was so frightened of the dark clouds, the heavy rain, and the sound of thunder that most of them died of fear. Sapor, the new pharaoh, was hemmed in on all sides and defeated, drenched miserably beneath the waves of fear. And then, when he was on the point of destroying the city, with the wall having suffered a huge breach and the city finally about to surrender, a vision appeared by day to him at the time when he was giving battle: a man running around on the walls of Nisibis.[39] The one who appeared looked like the Augustus Constantius, so that Sapor became even angrier at the inhabitants of Nisibis. He said, "Your emperor is of no avail. Let him come out and give battle; otherwise, surrender the city." They replied, "It is not right for us to surrender the city in the absence of our emperor, the Augustus Constantius," which made Sapor angrier yet, since, from what had appeared to him, they were not telling the truth. He said, "Why are you lying? I see with my own eyes your emperor Constantius running around on the walls of your city."

[5] And in these circumstances Sapor, with whom God did battle in such various ways, withdrew frustrated, threatening to put his magi to death. They, when they discovered the reason for what had happened, decided what the purport was of the angel who had appeared with Constantius and explained it to him. When Sapor realized the reason for the danger, he was afraid and ordered the engines to be burned and all the equipment he had made ready for the war to be destroyed. He himself fled back to his homeland with his staff, most of his army having already been destroyed by pestilence.

A detailed account of this may be found in a letter of Vologeses, bishop of Nisibis.[40]

[6] The Augustus Constantius set out to wage war against Magnentius, but before he arrived Constantia, the sister of Constantius, invested Vetra-

---

gets for the defenders' artillery (Julian, *Or.* 2.64D agrees). Ammianus 25.1.15 supports the statement that the animals turned on their own troops.

39. The vision of Constantius is also found in Theodoret, *Hist. eccl.* 2.30.9–10.

40. Vologeses was consecrated bishop of Nisibis between 346 and 350.

nio[41] on 1 March with the purple and with imperial rank in Naissus in Italy, and raised up that revered man to challenge Magnentius in battle.[42] Afterwards, when Constantius arrived in the regions where the war was being waged in Italy, he received Vetranio with great honor; then he set up a dais high in the plain, and in the presence of the army and with Vetranio also at his side he gave a speech in which he said that it was fitting for the realm that power should be held by the same man who had received it from the emperors who were his forebears and that it also benefited the state to have public affairs administered properly by one authority and so on in this vein.[43]

[7] In all of these things God was with Constantius, prospering his reign. For he also showed great concern for Christ's churches. As for Vetranio, who had reigned for ten months, Constantius divested him of the purple robe, in accordance with the speech just described, and at the same time entertained him at his own table; loaded with honors and with a large escort and many gifts, he sent him to live in the city of Prusa in Bithynia, where he received provisions and allowances in generous measure. Now Vetranio was a Christian and attended church services, and so he gave alms to the poor, showing honor as well to the bishops of the church until the day of his death.

24a [Theophanes 66B–67B]. When Magnentius seized power in Gaul and slew the devout Constans, the Augustus Constantius was staying in Antioch when he learned of it.... Constantius set out for Italy against Magnentius.

24b [*Chron. misc.* 130.29–30]. The twenty-ninth bishop of Antioch was Leontius, a man of modesty.

24c [*Chron. misc.* 132.11–12]. Constantine and Constans died.

24d [Theophanes 59B–60B]. [1] In this year [a.m. 5841 = 348/9] the Persian king Sapor again besieged Nisibis and gave it a great deal of trouble, even bringing up a herd of elephants trained for battle, mercenary kings, and all sorts of engines of war with which he threatened to raze the city to its very foundations unless they were prepared to abandon it. But the people of

---

41. On Vetranio, see 3.22 and 57 n. 69.

42. On the dislocation of Naissus from Moesia to Italy in A7.24.6, see Michael Whitby and Mary Whitby, trans., *Chronicon Paschale, 284–628 AD* (Liverpool: Liverpool University Press, 1989), 29.

43. A comparison of A7.24.6 and A7.24f shows that their common source (see 205 n. 1) placed the divestiture of Vetranio after Magnentius's defeat. It also offered a summary of Constantius's address to the soldiers that suggests that he appealed to, among other things, their dynastic instincts, not unlike the references in Athanasius (in *H. Ar.* 50.1, Constantius claimed the right to inherit his brother's realm) and Zosimus (in 2.44.3, Constantius reminded the soldiers of his father's generosity to them and the oaths they had taken to foster his children).

Nisibis refused to surrender it, so then he decided to flood it with the river flowing nearby. But the men conquered the enemy with prayer, since God was propitious to them. For when the waters had all but washed away the foundations of the walls so as to make them fall, a part of the wall did collapse, and that happened as God permitted, as will be explained next. For the immediate result was that the city was shielded and the enemy overwhelmed by the waters, and many perished in the water.

[2] But even after this had happened to them, they threatened to come in through the wall that had fallen, bringing up the armed elephants and urging the horde to battle more fiercely with every sort of engine of war. But the soldiers guarding the city thereupon won the victory through God's providence and filled the place with armed men of every sort and slew most of the elephants with catapults. Others fell into the mud at the bottom of the ditches, while yet others, when hit, turned and went back, and more than ten thousand of their armed men died. A lightning bolt from the sky fell on the rest of them, and everyone was so frightened of the dark clouds, the heavy rains, and the sound of thunder that most of them died of fear. Sapor, the new pharaoh, was hemmed in on all sides and defeated by the waves of fear. While he was staring at the fallen part of the wall, he saw an angel standing on top wearing a shining robe and holding the emperor Constantius by the hand.

[3] He was immediately shaken and threatened to put his magi to death. They, when they discovered the reason for what had happened, decided to explain to the emperor the purport of the one who had appeared, saying that he was greater than they. Realizing, therefore, the reason for the danger, he was afraid and ordered the engines to be burned and all the equipment he had made ready for the war to be destroyed. He himself, with his staff, took flight for his homeland, his forces having already been destroyed by pestilence.

24e [Jerome, *Chron.* 348]. Of the nine hardest battles against the Persians, no war was ever <more serious> for Constantius [than this one]. For Nisibis was besieged, not to mention other matters.[44]

24f [Theophanes 67B]. The senate in Rome invested Nepotianus and loosed him against Magnentius.[45] He met Magnentius in Rome and was

---

44. Compare Jerome's statement with Festus, *Brev.* 27: "acriori Marte noviens decertatum est, per duces suos septiens, ipse [Constantius] praesens bis adfuit."

45. Julius Nepotianus was a nephew of Constantine who took advantage of the lingering resentment in Rome toward Magnentius's accession, to collect a makeshift army outside the city, overwhelm the provisional resistance put up by the usurper's praetorian prefect, and assume the purple on 3 June 350. He enforced his author-

killed by him after reigning for three months. But before the emperor set out for Rome, Constantia, also called Helena,[46] the sister of Constantius, proclaimed that revered man Vetranio emperor and raised him up to challenge Magnentius in battle. Constantius, though, having arrived in Rome and received Vetranio with great honor... [68B] While he was in Rome, he went out to the Campus Tribunalis, and, standing up above with the army and Vetranio with him, he gave a speech in which he persuaded the people that it was fitting that the power of the realm should be held by the man who had received it from the emperors who were his forbears and that it also benefited the state to have public affairs administered by one authority and so on in this vein.

Then he divested Vetranio, who had reigned for ten months, and at the very same hour entertained him at his own table; then, loaded with honors and with a large escort and many gifts, he sent him to Prusa in Bithynia. Being a Christian, he gave his time to the church and bestowed many alms on the poor. He also honored the priests until the day of his death.

24g [Jerome, *Chron.* 350]. As a result, the realm was thrown into confusion, and Vetranio and Nepotianus were made emperors, the former at Mursa and the latter at Rome.

24h [351]. Constantius removed the imperial tokens from Vetranio at Naissus.

25 [*Chron. pasch.* a. 351; P292A–C]. The Augustus Constantius, [now] the sole ruler, appointed his cousin Gallus to share his rule, with the title of Caesar, changing his name to Constantius on the Ides of March.[47] He sent him to Antioch in the east, where the Persians were threatening. The sign of the cross of Christ appeared in Jerusalem at that time, at about the third hour, on the day of Pentecost; it was radiant as it extended across the sky on 7 May from the Mount of Olives to Golgotha, where the Lord was crucified toward the east, the place where the Lord was taken up. The precious cross that appeared was encircled by a crown that looked like a rainbow. And at the same hour, it appeared in Pannonia to the Augustus Constantius and the army with him in the war against Magnentius. And when Constantius

---

ity with some exemplary executions, which quickly put the senate in the mood to give him any commission he requested. He reigned for twenty-seven days, eventually being put down by Magnentius's forces. See Aurelius Victor 42.6–8; *Epit. Caes.* 42.3; *Pan. Lat.* III (XI) 13.3; Zosimus 2.43.2–4; Socrates 2.25.10–11.

46. The confusion of Constantia (Constantina) and Helena (two different sisters of Constantius II) is found as well in A7.28a and c; the chronicle of Michael may have picked it up from Theophanes. See *PLRE* 1:222, 409–10.

47. The appointment of Gallus is mentioned in 3.25.

began to have the upper hand when Magnentius engaged him near the city of Mursa, Magnentius fled in defeat to Gaul with a few of his people.[48]

25a [Theophanes 60B–61B]. In this year [a.m. 5842 = 349/50] the Augustus Constantius, [now] sole ruler, appointed his own cousin Gallus to share his rule with the title of Caesar, changing his name to Constantius. He sent him to the east, to Antioch, where the Persians were still threatening. [62B–63B] In this year [a.m. 5847 = 354/5] Acacius of Caesarea and Patrophilus of Scythopolis, who were Arians, removed Maximus of Jerusalem and replaced him with Cyril, supposing him to be of one mind with them.[49] At this time, when Cyril was bishop of Jerusalem, the sign of the life-giving cross appeared in the sky on the day of Pentecost; it was radiant as it extended from Golgotha, where Christ was crucified, to the Mount of Olives, where he was taken up. The sign that appeared was encircled by a crown that looked like a rainbow. And on the same day, it appeared to Constantius as well. Cyril's letter about this to the emperor Constantius is preserved; in it he addresses him as "most devout."[50] Hence some people accuse Cyril of being Arian in his views, saying that he makes no mention of the word "consubstantial" in the catecheses that he published to assist the uneducated folk who sought the sacred fount of baptism on account of the marvel of the life-giving cross. But they are wrong, and they sin. [67B] The two of them [Constantius and Vetranio] fought Magnentius near Mursa. Magnentius was defeated and fled to Italy.

25b [*Chron. misc.* 132.12–14]. And Constantius, their brother, took over their entire realm, and he appointed Gallus Caesar, that he might govern the empire with him.

26 [*Chron. pasch.* a. 351; P292C]. Constantius, also called Gallus, the Caesar mentioned earlier, dwelt in the east and in Antioch.

26a [Theophanes 61B]. In this year [a.m. 5843 = 350/1] the Jews in Palestine revolted and killed many of those not of their nation, both Gentiles and

---

48. "Magnentius fled ... with a few" translates the reading μετ' ὀλίγων instead of μετ' ὀλίγον ("shortly thereafter").

49. On Patrophilus, see 1.8a; 4.10; A7.33, 33e. On Acacius's replacement of Maximus of Jerusalem by Cyril, see 4.12; Rufinus, *Hist. eccl.* 10.24. Maximus had offended Acacius by receiving Athanasius after condemning him at the Council of Tyre, but he may have died before he could be deposed; it was reported, however, that Acacius had driven him from Jerusalem and ordained Cyril in his place (Socrates 2.38.2). The report in Jerome (*Chron.* 348) that he died in office is probably false; see Gustave Bardy, "Cyrille de Jérusalem," *DHGE* 13.1181–6.

50. Cyril's letter to Constantius is in Bihain, "L'épître de Cyrille de Jérusalem," 264–96. The suspicion about his Arian leanings is reflected in Alexander Monachus, *Invent. s. crucis* (PG 87:4069B).

Samaritans. And they themselves were slain with their whole nation by the Roman army, and their city of Diocaesarea was destroyed.[51]

26b [Jerome, *Chron.* 352]. Gallus defeated the Jews who had seized the weapons of soldiers they had killed during the night in order to use them in their uprising. He slew many thousands of people, including even those too young to fight, and he burned their cities of Diocaesarea, Tiberias, and Diospolis, and many towns.

27 [*Chron. pasch.* a. 354; P292D]. In this year Magnentius again engaged in battle on Mount Seleucus, was defeated, and fled alone to the city of Lyons in Gaul. After he had killed his own brother, he then killed himself on 10 August.

27a [Theophanes 67B]. [Magnentius], who had often fought against Constantius's generals, engaged them in battle on Mount Seleucus, was defeated, and fled to Lyons.[52]

28 [*Chron. pasch.* a. 355; P292D–293A]. In this year Gallus, surnamed Constantius, who was Caesar, was summoned from Antioch by the Augus-

---

51. On the Jewish uprising, see Aurelius Victor 42.11; Socrates 2.33; Sozomen 4.7.5; Saul Lieberman, "Palestine in the Third and Fourth Centuries," *JQR* 36 (1945–46): 340–41; Menahem Stern, *Greek and Latin Authors on Jews and Judaism* (3 vols.; Jerusalem: Israeli Academy of Sciences and Humanities, 1974–84), 2:500–501; Joseph Geiger, "The Last Jewish Revolt against Rome: A Reconsideration," *Scripta Classica Israelica* 5 (1979–80): 250–57. The classic treatment is that of Michael Avi-Yonah, *Geschichte der Juden im Zeitalter des Talmud in den Tagen von Rom und Byzanz* (Berlin: de Gruyter, 1962), 181–87, which places the revolt in June of 351 and conjectures that resentment at Constantius's legislation forbidding Jews to own non-Jewish slaves (*Cod. theod.* 16.9.2 of 13 August 339), which put the Jewish textile industries at a great disadvantage in competing with others, found a promising opportunity to express itself during the political instability of Magnentius's revolt and the Persian siege of Nisibis in 350. Avi-Yonah's reconstruction has been criticized as overly conjectural by Peter Schäfer, "Der Aufstand gegen Gallus Caesar," in *Tradition and Reinterpretation in Jewish and Early Christian Literature: Essays in Honour of Jürgen C.H. Lebram* (ed. J. W. van Henten, H. J. de Jonge, P. T. van Rooden, and J. W. Wesselius; StPB 36; Leiden: Brill, 1986), 184–201. Schäfer also notes that there is no archeological evidence to support Jerome's claim that the three cities he mentions were destroyed by the Romans. They were, however, damaged or ruined by earthquake in 363, but Diocaesarea, at least, was quickly resettled, which probably would not have happened if the Romans had destroyed it and evacuated its inhabitants. Schäfer therefore wonders if Jerome simply assumed that the damage from the earthquake had been caused by the Romans in the earlier uprising. He fails, however, to notice that Jerome is here drawing from the homoean history (205 n. 1).

52. Magnentius's defeat is in 3.26; Mount Seleucus in Socrates 2.32.6; Sozomen 4.7.3.

tus Constantius and put to death on the island of Ister because he had been accused of killing a praetorian prefect and *quaestor* against the wish of the Augustus Constantius.[53]

The Augustus Constantius invested Julian, the brother of the Gallus who was surnamed Constantius, with the purple and appointed him Caesar on 8 October, giving him as wife his own sister Helena, and he sent them to Gaul.[54]

28a [Theophanes 68B–69B]. Constantius returned to Byzantium, and at the urging of his own wife Eusebia[55] he brought Gallus's brother Julian out of custody, appointed him Caesar, and sent him to Gaul, having joined to him in marriage his own sister Helena, surnamed Constantia.[56]

28b [*Chron. misc.* 132.14–15]. Shortly thereafter he killed him, and he appointed his brother Julian to take his place.

---

53. Gallus's downfall is in 3.28, 28a; 4.1, 1a; "island of Ister" is a confused reference to "island in Histria" (see 64 n. 3).

54. Julian's appointment is in 4.2, 2a. The date of Julian's elevation to Caesar is actually 6 November 355 (Ammianus 15.8.17; *Consul. const.* 355).

55. Julian himself says that Eusebia favored him (*Or.* 3.120C–121B; *Ep. ad Ath.* 274A–275C), and other sources agree that it was Eusebia who urged her husband to appoint Julian Caesar and post him to Gaul (Ammianus 15.8.3; 21.6.4; Zosimus 3.1.2–3; 3.2.3). The "custody" out of which he was brought in 28a means the close surveillance under which Constantius kept him in the years before his appointment (Julian, *Ep. ad Ath.* 271B–D; 272D). Eusebia's motives have been variously assessed. Among those who doubt she was acting disinterestedly, see J. F. Drinkwater, "The Pagan 'Underground,' Constantius II's 'Secret Service,' and the Survival, and the Usurpation of Julian the Apostate," in vol. 3 of *Studies in Latin Literature and Roman History* (ed. Carl Deroux; Collection Latomus 180; Brussels: Latomus Revue d'études latines, 1983): 348–87, esp. 368; and Noël Aujoulat, "Eusebie, Hélène, et Julien," *Byzantion* 58 (1983): 78–103 ("I: Le témoignage de Julien"), 421–52 ("II: Le témoignage des historiens"). Shaun Tougher ("The Advocacy of an Empress: Julian and Eusebia," *CQ* NS 48 [1998]: 595–99) assesses the evidence differently; he argues that Constantius in fact used Eusebia to persuade Julian to trust him and accept his appointment. He could not approach him directly because of the bad blood between them stemming from Gallus's execution and the suspicion that Constantius had also been responsible for the murder of Julian's other relatives in 337. See also Shaun Tougher, "In Praise of an Empress: Julian's *Speech of Thanks* to Eusebia," in *The Propaganda of Power: The Role of Panegyric in Late Antquity* (ed. Mary Whitby; Mnemosyne, bibliotheca classica Batava Supplementum 183; Leiden: Brill, 1998), 105–23.

56. On the confusion between Constanti(n)a and Helena in 28a and c, see 220 n. 46.

28c [Michael 138, bottom right-top middle]. When he had returned to Constantinople, he appointed Julian Caesar, and he gave him his sister Helena as wife; she was called Constantia.

28d [Jerome, *Chron.* 352]. Many of the nobility of Antioch were killed by Gallus.

[354] Gallus Caesar was sought out by his cousin Constantius, whose suspicions he had aroused by his outstanding qualities, and was put to death in Histria.

[355] Julian, Gallus's brother, was proclaimed Caesar in Milan.

29 [*Chron. pasch.* a. 357; P293C]. The Augustus Constantius, on his twentieth anniversary, entered Rome with a great show and retinue.[57] His wife, the empress Eusebia, entered with him, and they spent fourteen days in Rome.

29a [Theophanes 67B–68B]. At that time [a.m. 5849 = 356/7] Silvanus too usurped power in Gaul and was slain by Constantius's generals.[58] Constantius came to Rome and entered with a great show and retinue, acclaimed above the emperors before him. His wife Eusebia came with him, and he spent fourteen days in Rome.

30 [*Chron. pasch.* a. 359; P293C–D]. During their consulate [of Eusebius and Hypatius], in the month of Hyperberetaios, a great and violent earthquake occurred in Nicomedia around the third hour of the night, and the city collapsed and perished.[59] Among those who died was the bishop of the city, Cecropius.

30a [Theophanes 69B]. In this year [a.m. 5850 = 357/8] a great earthquake that occurred in Nicomedia around the third hour of the night destroyed the city and killed a great many. Among those who died was the bishop of the city, Cecropius.

31 [*Chron. pasch.* a. 360; P293D–294D]. [1] In this year the great church in Constantinople was dedicated on the fifteenth of Peritios.[60]

---

57. Constantius entered Rome on 28 April 357 (*Consul. const.* 357). See also Jerome, *Chron.* 357; Sozomen 4.8.1; 4.11.3.

58. Silvanus was an officer of Magnentius who went over to Constantius before the battle of Mursa; Constantius made him infantry commander in Gaul, but his enemies at court forged letters in his name that suggested he intended usurpation and thus forced him to that very deed in order to protect himself. He took the purple at Cologne on 11 August 355 and was slain on 29 August. See Julian, *Or.* 1.48B–49A; 2.97C; 2.98C–100B; Libanius, *Or.* 18.31; Aurelius Victor 42.14–15; Ammianus 15.5–6; Eutropius 10.13; Jerome, *Chron.* 354; Socrates 2.32.11; Sozomen 4.7.4.

59. The earthquake in Nicomedia is in 4.10.

60. The dedication of the great church in Constantinople is in 3.2. The "great church" in Constantinople is Hagia Sophia; see 3.2 and 38 n. 4. It may be noticed that the date of its consecration is given differently at the beginning of A7.31.1 and later

Macedonius, bishop of Constantinople, was deposed because of the long list of accusations brought against his own person,[61] and in his stead Eudoxius was ordained bishop of that church. He was installed on the twenty-seventh of Audynaios in the presence of seventy-two bishops: Maris, Acesius, George, Serras, Uranius, Theodosius, Eusebius, Pegasius, Leontius, Cyrion, Arabian, Asinus, Philotheus, Agerochius, Eugenius, Elpidius, Stephen, Heliodorus, Demophilus, Timothy, Exeuresius, Megasius, Mizonius, Paul, Evagrius, Apollonius, Phoebus, Theophilus, Protasius, Theodore, Heliodorus, Eumathius, Synesius, Ptolemaeus, Eutyches, Quintus, Alphius, Trophimus, Eutychius, Basiliscus, Theomnestus, Vetranio, Philip, Anastasius, Maxentius, Polyeuctus, Gratian, Leontius, Metrodorus, Eustathius, Jovian, Trophimus, Oecumenius, Menophilus, Evethius, and the rest.[62]

[2] At that same council of bishops, not many days after the installation of Eudoxius as bishop of Constantinople, the dedication of the great church of the city was celebrated thirty-four years, more or less, after the foundations had been laid by Constantine, the August Victor. The dedication was held during the aforementioned consulship of 14 February, or the fourteenth of Peritios.[63] The emperor Constantius Augustus offered many gifts for the dedication: large vessels of gold and silver and many cloths set with stones and interwoven with gold for the holy altar, as well as various golden curtains for the church doors and variegated curtains interwoven with gold for the outer porches. He also at that time gave many gifts with a generous hand to all the clergy, to the order of virgins and widows, and to the hospices. And for their maintenance and that of beggars, orphans, and prisoners, he added a grain allowance above that which his father Constantine had granted.[64]

32 [*Chron. pasch.* a. 361; P294D–295A]. At the beginning of the fourth indiction, he came to Mopsucrenae, at the first stage after Tarsus in Cilicia, because of the news brought to him of the revolt of Julian Caesar. He first received holy baptism from Euzoius, bishop of Antioch, whom Constantius himself had summoned to the way station, and then the Augustus Constan-

---

in 31.2; the fact that 360 was a leap year caused the problem. See Whitby and Whitby, *Chronicon Paschale,* 34 and 35 (nn. 107 and 111).

61. The deposition of Macedonius is in 5.1.

62. Among the bishops listed in A7.31.1, the editor queries "Acesius" and of course the remarkable "Asinus" (Ἀσίνου in the text, the names being given in the genitive; see Bidez, *Philostorgius,* 225, 261, and 266). For the former, perhaps "Acacius" is the correct reading.

63. In A7.31.2, the "aforementioned consulship" is that of Constantius (twelfth) and Julian (third).

64. On Constantius wishing to outdo his father in grain allowances, see 3.2a.

tius departed from life on the third of Dios, in the 410th year of Antioch, the fifth of the indiction, and the fiftieth year of the churches' peace, in the consulship of the aforementioned Taurus and Florentius.[65]

32a [Theophanes 70B]. In this year [a.m. 5852 = 359/60] the Persians took the stronghold called Bizabde.[66] But Constantius heard that Julian, renowned for his military talents in Gaul, had been proclaimed emperor by the army, so he left Antioch, where he had been staying because of the Persian war, and set out against the usurper Julian. And when he arrived in Mopsucrenae, at the first station after Tarsus in Cilicia, he died on the third of Dios.

32b [*Chron. misc.* 132.15–22, 29–133.5]. Julian waged war on the Goths and conquered them. And he rebelled against Constantius, and he ruled in Spain and Gaul. And Constantius made ready to go to war with him. And when he had come up from the east to wage war with him, he lay down upon the bed of his rest, and died, in the 673rd year,[67] and in the month of Tishri posterior. Constantius had reigned for twenty-four years.

<Constantius died> in the 673rd year and in the month of Tishri posterior; Constantius had reigned for twenty-four years. He died well before the Lord. He walked in the ways of his father Constantine, which is to say that he was an Arian. Julian took over his realm after him, when peace...[68]

33 [*Chron. pasch.* a. 362; P295A–296C]. [1] After the death of the Augustus Constantius, the peace of the churches was destroyed with the entry of Julian into Constantinople on the eleventh of Apellaios. The events transpired as follows. When Julian learned of the death of Constantius, he openly showed his apostasy and ungodliness, and, sending decrees against the Christians throughout the whole world, he ordered the restoration of all the idols. The pagans in the east, elated at this, lost no time in Alexandria in Egypt in seizing George, the bishop of the city, killing him, and impiously mistreating his corpse.[69] For they put it on a camel, carried it about through the whole city, then gathered the corpses of various animals along with the bones, mixed them with his remains, burned them up, and scattered them.

[2] And in Palestine they dug up the remains of Saint John the Baptist in the city of Sebaste and scattered them.[70]

---

65. Julian's revolt and Constantius's death are in 6.5 and 6.5a.

66. On the Persian incursions, see Jerome, *Chron.* 348 ("Bizabde et Amida captae sunt").

67. The 673rd year is of the Seleucid calendar.

68. Julian's accession after Constantius's death is in 7.1, 7.1a–c.

69. The death of George is in 7.2.

70. The mistreatment of the relics of John the Baptist is in 7.4.

They also dug up from his grave the remains of Saint Patrophilus, who had been bishop of the church in Scythopolis, and scattered all but the skull, which they mocked by hanging it up and fixing it in place as though it were a lamp.

In Gaza and Ascalon they killed presbyters and virgins and then cut them open, filled their bodies with barley, and threw them to the pigs.[71]

[3] In Phoenicia they killed Cyril, a deacon of Heliopolis, and ate of his liver, because he had destroyed their idols in the time of the blessed Constantine.[72] But it is worth recording how the one who had cut open the deacon and tasted of his liver destroyed his own life. He lost his tongue when it rotted away, spat out his decayed teeth, lost his eyesight after protracted and severe pain, and died in the midst of fearful agonies that racked his whole body.

They invaded the great church in Emesa and set up the idol of Dionysus.[73]

Likewise in Epiphania, a city in Syria, the pagans invaded the church and brought in an idol with flutes and drums. The blessed Eustathius, who was bishop of that church, a man pious and devout, heard the flutes and asked where this was happening. When he learned that it was in the church, his faith and piety were so ardent that as soon as he heard it, he fell asleep, having prayed that he would not see such things with his own eyes.

[4] In addition, when Julian entered Constantinople, Eudoxius being its bishop, he hatched a great variety of plots against the church and threw its affairs into confusion; his plan was to unleash upon the churches all of those deposed before his time for various absurd heresies and to garner allegations against the churches of God from the resulting disturbances.[74]

[5] Thus, for instance, Meletius, who had been deposed for heresy and other crimes, returned to Antioch and seized the old church, those clerics rallying to him who had previously been deposed lawfully by the holy council. Prominent among them was the former presbyter Diogenes, who outdid the others in taking his part, and the layman Vitalis, always an imposter, who had made great progress practicing his art and who sometime later had a falling

71. On the misdeeds in Gaza and Ascalon, see Gregory of Nazianzus, *Or.* 4.87; 5.29; Theodoret, *Hist. eccl.* 3.7.1; Sozomen 5.10.6; Barcellona, "Martiri e confessori dell'età di Giuliano l'Apostata," 67–69.

72. On the deacon Cyril, see Theodoret, *Hist. eccl.* 3.7.2–4.

73. On the incident in the church in Emesa, see Theodoret, *Hist. eccl.* 3.7.5.

74. Julian's plan to upset the churches by reprieving exiled bishops is in 7.4; see also Sozomen 5.5.7.

out with Meletius, separated from him, and himself founded a sect that was ridiculous. From him come those who are still called Vitalians.[75]

Apollinaris of Laodicea in Syria, the son of a grammarian, was also head of this sect.

33a [Theophanes 72B]. Then the pagans in the east, elated, lost no time in Alexandria in dragging off George, the bishop, killing him, and godlessly mistreating his corpse; putting it on a camel, they paraded through the city, and, mixing his remains with the bones of dead animals, they burned them up and scattered them.

33b [Theophylact 13]. Who could possibly recount what the usurper's ministers did to the servants of Christ in each place? For instance, they even dragged George, the bishop of Alexandria, through the street and killed him and then set him on a camel and exulted over his mangled limbs, and finally, having burned him to ashes along with the camel, they scattered the remains of the pyre.

33c [*Chron. misc.* 133.6–12]. In the fifty-second year of the peace of the churches, Julian reigned over the entire Roman Empire. He renewed the persecution of the Christians. And he ordered that the temples of the idols be opened, their altars built, their idols set up, and their services restored. And he removed the treasures of the churches and ordered the establishment of congregations of false doctrine. And he exiled bishops from their sees.

33d [Jerome, *Chron.* 362]. When Julian went over to idolatry, there was a seductive persecution that enticed people rather than forced them to sacrifice, and many of ours lapsed of their own free will.

When George, who had been ordained by the Arians in place of Athanasius, was burned to death in a popular uprising, Athanasius returned to Alexandria.

33e [Theophanes 72B–73B]. They dug up the remains of Saint Patrophilus, the bishop in Scythopolis, and scattered all but the skull, which they insolently mocked by hanging it up.

In Gaza and Ascalon, they killed presbyters and perpetual virgins and then cut open their innards, filled them with barley, and threw them to the pigs.

In Phoenicia, the people of Heliopolis killed Cyril, a deacon, and ate of his liver, because he had destroyed their idols in the time of the blessed Constantine. But the one who had cut open the deacon and tasted of his liver suffered the following: his rotted tongue dropped off, he spat out his teeth and lost his eyesight, and thus he died in agony.

---

75. On Vitalis's ordination by Meletius, separation from him, communion with Apollinaris, and foundation of a sect, see Sozomen 6.25.1–2.

33f [Theophylact 13]. They cut open the innards of someone else, stuffed him with barley, set loose the swine, and feasted them at that table.

33g [Theophanes 73B]. In Arethusa, [Julian] did fearful things against the Christians. Among them was the most holy monk Mark, who had saved and concealed Julian when the army was killing Constantius's family, and whose innards, while he was still alive...[76]

In Emesa, they set up the idol of Dionysus in the great church and destroyed the old church.

33h [Theophylact 13]. Not only that, but if any persons had destroyed an idolatrous temple during Constantius's reign or had broken up an idolatrous pillar, [Julian ordered] them to rebuild what they had destroyed and replace what they had broken, or else to submit to bitter tortures and capital penalties and punishments.[77] Among them was Mark of Arethusa, one of those who had saved <the> villain when his whole family was being slaughtered; he had destroyed an idolatrous temple. Pressed to restore it, he refused and so was subjected to many different tortures, finally being lifted up and passed from one group of boys to another, who used their styluses on his aged and revered body, he who was in truth higher than the earth and those upon it.

34 [Theophanes 74B–75B]. As for Dorotheus, the long-suffering bishop of Tyre who had written much about church history and excelled in eloquence, who had become a confessor under Diocletian and again under Licinius, and who had reached a great old age: the Apostate's officers, in the second year of his reign, found him in retirement in Odyssopolis, subjected him to many tortures because of his faith in Christ, and put him to death when he was 107.[78]

---

76. On the massacre of Julian's relatives after Constantine's death, see 34 n. 48, last two paragraphs. On Mark of Arethusa, see Gregory of Nazianzus, *Or.* 4.88–91; Sozomen 5.10.8–14; Theodoret, *Hist. eccl.* 3.7.6–10. Gregory in section 91 says that Mark was one of those who saved Julian and removed him secretly during the episode; see also Theophylact 10 (PG 126:165). For his martyrdom, see François Halkin, "La Passion de S. Marc d'Aréthuse," *AnBoll* 103 (1985): 217–29 (*BHG* 2248 and 2250; *Novum Auctuarium* 2250b–c).

77. On Julian's requirement that Christians restore pagan religious property they damaged or destroyed, see Libanius, *Or.* 18.126; Zonaras 13.12.31–32.

78. On Dorotheus, see Nicephorus, *Hist. eccl.* 10.9; Theophanes 35B–36B; *Synax.* 124.10. His literary output is attested by *Synax.* 731–733.1; Theodor Schermann, ed., *Prophetarum vitae fabulosae: Indices apostolorum discipulorumque Domini, Dorotheo, Epiphanio, Hippolyto aliisque vindicata* (Leipzig: Teubner, 1907), 132. The usual tradition of his martyrdom places it in Odyssopolis in Thrace (A7.34; *Synax.* 124, no. 10; 731.14; 732.12; Theophanes 36B) rather than in Edessa, as in 34a. The accuracy of

34a [Theophylact 13]. In Tyre, the bishop of that place was Dorotheus, who had quite a way with words, was the most notable historian among those of olden times, and was subjected to extensive tortures for the sake of Christ in the reigns of both Diocletian and Licinius when he was more than sixty years old; the enemies of the faith put him to death in the city of Edessa when he had reached a ripe old age, as the divine David says (for the saint was 107 years old).

34b [Michael 146 right]. The pagans put to death, at the age of 107, Dorotheus of Tyre, who had written a book about church history and who had undergone severe trials in the times of Diocletian and Licinius.

35 [Theophanes 76B–78B]. Julian, when he was staying in Antioch, kept going up to Daphne and worshiping the idol of Apollo, but he got no answer, he thought, from the idol.[79] Thinking that it was because of the relics of the holy martyr Babylas buried in Daphne that the idol was silent, he issued a decree that all the relics of the dead buried there should be transferred along with those of the martyr. And when this had been done, that very night the temple was burned down by fire from heaven, and the idol was so completely incinerated that not a trace of it could be seen (it was said to have been set up years before); as for the temple, it was so completely destroyed that people later saw its ashes and were astonished at how unexpected was the surprising thing God had done. Julian was stupefied by it and, suspecting that it was the result of a Christian plot, proceeded to interrogate the priests who had survived and to subject them to all kinds of tortures, so that some of them died; but the only thing they told him was that neither the Christians nor any human plot was behind what had happened but that it was fire come down from heaven that had kindled the temple and the statues. Thus the fire that had come down had been seen that night even by some people in the countryside. The emperor was incensed, and, as though fighting God, he locked up the great church and confiscated all the holy things. The two counts who were sent to see to this, the apostates Felix and Julian, said, "We thought there was some guardian power supposed to hinder us." And Felix said, "Look at the kind of vessels used to serve Mary's son!" Shortly afterwards, Felix suddenly brought up blood through his mouth and ended his life in agony, while Count Julian fell desperately ill the same day; his innards perished and he brought up excrement through his mouth and so died in agony.[80]

---

the tradition is doubted by Honigmann, *Patristic Studies*, 13, since it lengthens his life excessively and most of the stories about Licinius's persecution of Christians are in any case suspect.

79. Julian and the idol at Daphne are in 7.8 and 7.8a.

80. Felix and Count Julian are in 7.10.

35a [Jerome, *Chron.* 363]. The church of Antioch was closed.

36 [*Chron. pasch.* a. 363; P296C–297C]. In this year some even of those in the service, when put under interrogation, were led astray into apostasy, some of them yielding to promises of gifts and promotions and others to pressure added by their own officers.[81]

There was also Theotecnus, a presbyter of the church of Antioch, who was led astray by a promise and went over to idolatry of his own accord. God punished him at once in the following way: he was consumed by worms and plucked out his eyes, and, eating his tongue, he thus died.[82]

Then there was a bishop of Thebes named Heron who of his own accord apostatized while in Antioch; God's power, which works marvels, inflicted the following punishment on him to serve as an example and to instill fear in the many: it rendered him devoid of all support, struck him with a mortifying illness, and caused him to be brought into the streets to expire there in public in the sight of all.

During this time Valentinian, who was then tribune of the *Cornuti* legion, as the unit was called, distinguished himself by his confession of Christ. For he not only disdained his rank; he even accepted nobly and eagerly the exile imposed on him. How he was later honored by God when made emperor of Rome will be told afterwards.[83]

As for Artemius, governor of the diocese of Egypt, he had shown great zeal for the churches in Alexandria during his term of office in the time of the blessed Augustus Constantius, and so his property was confiscated and his head cut off, since Julian harbored resentment against him.[84]

Someone else who was martyred in Durostorum in Thracian Scythia was Aemilianus, a soldier who was burned to death by Capitolinus, the vicar. And many others in various places, cities, and regions distinguished themselves by their confession of Christ. It would be hard to number and name them.[85]

In this year one Thalassius, surnamed Magnus, who was noted for his licentiousness and profligacy and who went so far as to act as a pimp for his own daughter, died when his house collapsed on top of him.

---

81. On the pressure applied to those in the service to apostasize, see Jerome, *Chron.* 362; Rufinus, *Hist. eccl.* 10.33; Gregory of Nazianzus, *Or.* 4.81–83; Theodoret, *Hist. eccl.* 3.16.7; Sozomen 5.17.8–12.

82. Theotecnus is in 7.13, as is Heron in the following paragraph.

83. Valentinian is in 7.7.

84. For Artemius, see appendices 1 and 3.

85. Aemilianus was executed for destroying pagan idols (Theodoret, *Hist. eccl.* 2.17.5; *AASS* Novembris II 382–83; *Synax.* 827, no. 1; *AASS* Iulii IV 373–76).

36a [Theophanes 78B–80B]. In this year [a.m. 5855 = 362/3] some of those in the service were led astray into apostasy when put under interrogation, some of them by promises of gifts and promotions and others by pressure added by their own officers.

There was also the presbyter Theotecnus, who had charge of a church in a suburb of Antioch and who was led astray by a promise and went over to idolatry of his own accord. God punished him at once: he was consumed by worms and plucked out his eyes, and, eating his tongue, he died.

And Heron, a bishop of the Thebaid, apostatized of his own accord in Antioch; God immediately punished him in the following way to serve as an example and to instill fear in the many: his limbs were destroyed by a mortifying illness, and he was pitched out into the street to expire in the sight of all.

Also during this time Valentinian distinguished himself by his confession of Christ. He was then tribune of a legion, a unit of the so-called *Cornuti,* and he not only disdained his rank; he even accepted the exile imposed on him. Later God made him emperor. In the same way, Jovian undid his belt, crying, "I am a Christian!" He was a military commander whom the people loved so that they begged the emperor to do him no harm. He was made emperor after Julian.[86]

And as for Artemius, commander of the diocese of Egypt, in Constantius's time he had shown great zeal against the idols in Alexandria, so his property was confiscated and his head cut off.

Someone else who was martyred in Durostorum in Thrace was Aemilianus, a soldier who was burned to death by Capitolinus. And many others in various places and ways distinguished themselves by their confession of Christ.

There was also one Thalassius, noted for his licentiousness and profligacy, who went so far as to act as a pimp for his own daughter and who was honored by the emperor for his skill in the inspection of entrails; he lived in Antioch by the imperial residence. When his house collapsed on top of him, therefore, he alone perished along with one eunuch, in whose embrace he was found. All of those found with him were saved, the members of his household

---

86. There are several other stories about Jovian's confession. It is said that he was one of those who resigned from the service when Julian ordered the palace staff and governors to worship idols, but the emperor was forced to decline his resignation because of the impending war (Socrates 3.13.4; 3.22.1–3; 4.1.8–10). Theodoret (*Hist. eccl.* 4.1.2–3) alludes to his speaking up against Julian's paganism. Rufinus (*Hist. eccl.* 11.1) says he refused at first to succeed Julian because he was Christian and the army had been profaned by the Apostate's sacrilegious acts.

being Christians, and his wife and those with her. There was a child of about seven who was found there safe, and when asked how it had been saved, it replied that it had been carried by an angel.

Now the hateful Julian, in an attempt to disprove the divine oracle, ordered the Jewish temple to be built and put one Alypius, a pagan hostile to Christ, in charge of the work.[87] While he in turn was digging out the buried foundations, a strong wind blew through the excavation with such a blast that it destroyed the 200,000 measures of quicklime that had been made ready. And when the Jews persisted in their attempt to undertake the work, a fire came out that burned them to death, and thus they desisted from this arrogance.

36b [Michael 146 right]. The presbyter Theotecnus was led astray and sacrificed. And immediately he swarmed with worms, and they ate his tongue, and he died.

36c [Theophylact 13]. He ordered the churches of God to be seized all together and Christians to be accorded neither an education in the pagan disciplines nor senatorial rank.[88] There were many, therefore, who gladly removed their belts, considering all things rubbish that they might gain Christ alone;[89] such were Jovian and Valentinian, to both of whom God gave even the empire in his own good time. And there were many who renounced our true God and Christ out of the desire for empty glory.

36d [Jerome, *Chron.* 363]. Aemilianus was burned to death at Durostorum by the vicar for having destroyed altars.

36e [Michael 146 right]. When the Jews received the order to build the temple in Jerusalem and to sacrifice, they brought about 3,000 measures of quicklime, and a strong wind scattered it into the air, and the earth shook.

37 [Theophanes 80B–81B]. At this time, the divine cross appeared in the sky, luminous and surrounded by a crown of light; it stretched from Golgotha to the holy Mount of Olives and was brighter than in Constantius's time.[90] And the sign of the cross appeared of its own accord on the altar cloths and books and other church vestments and on the clothing not only of Christians but of Jews as well, and this not only in Jerusalem but in Antioch and other cities. The clothing of those Jews and pagans who made bold to disbelieve was found to be full of crosses. In some cases they were even black.

---

87. Julian's plan to restore the Jerusalem temple is in 7.9, 7.9a.

88. Julian's decree about Christians and education is in 7.4b (see also 93 n. 23).

89. The reference to "considering all things rubbish" in order to gain Christ is in Phil 3:8.

90. On the cross in the sky, see A7.25; Gregory of Nazianzus, *Or.* 5.4; 5.7; Rufinus, *Hist. eccl.* 10.40; Sozomen 5.22.12–13.

Julian sent many people in different places to soothsayers and oracles, that it might appear that it was at the bidding of the demons that he was engaging in war against the Persians.[91] And of the many oracles that had been delivered to him from different sources...

37a [Michael 146 right]. On account of the temple construction, an image of the cross appeared on all the garments of the Jews, as well as on those of the pagans and the Christians, and that not just in Jerusalem but in Antioch and in the areas surrounding them.

And there appeared the cross, which had a crown of light, from Golgotha as far as the Mount of Olives. It was fairer and brighter than the one that had appeared in the days of Constantine the Great.

38 [Theophanes 82B]. [Julian] was slain by divine justice in a foreign land. In this year [a.m. 5855 = 362/3], when he had reigned for two years and nine months, he was killed by divine decree in Persia [on 26 January] in the sixth indiction, [when he was thirty-one years old].[92]

38a [*Chron. misc.* 133.13–24]. And in the 674th year Julian the impure went down to the land of the Chaldeans, to Beth Aramaye. And there it was that the Romans brought it about that he perished. At that time, the Lord was angry with the cities of the pagans, the Jews, the Samaritans, and the teachers of falsehood in the south who had associated themselves with the madness of Julian the pagan. And wrath went forth from the Lord and began to bring down the impure and pagan cities upon their inhabitants, because they had defiled them with the blood unjustly poured out in them. It began to destroy cities to the number of twenty-one: some of them were overthrown, some collapsed, and some survived. It was in the month of Iyyar of the 674th year. [And on the twenty-seventh day of this month <Julian was killed>].

39 [Theophanes 83B]. In this year [a.m. 5856 = 363/4], Jovian was proclaimed ... emperor of Rome ... in the same place on Persian soil where the Apostate had been killed.[93] And after one engagement in battle, peace was declared by the Romans and Persians for a thirty-year period with a unanimity that seemed divinely inspired.

39a [*Chron. misc.* 133.24–134.9]. In the month of Khaziran of the year 674, on a Friday, beside the great River Tigris, on the north side of Coche and Ctesiphon, in the place called Beth Aramaye, Jovian put on the great crown

---

91. Julian's gathering of the oracles is in 7.15.

92. Julian's death is in 7.15; 7.15a. It occurred on 26 June in the third year of his reign (Socrates 3.21.17–18).

93. Jovian's accession is in 8.1; 8.1a.

of the Roman Empire.[94] And he made peace and concord and settled the hostility between the two mighty realms of the Romans and the Persians. And that there might be peace between them and he might rescue the Romans from the straits hemming them in, he gave the Persians the whole region east of Nisibis, some of the districts surrounding it, and all of Armenia, with the regions belonging to Armenia. And Nisibis was exiled, in the month of Ab of the year 674, to the region of Edessa. Nisibis was ceded to Persia when emptied of its inhabitants.

39b [Jerome, *Chron.* 364]. Jovian was forced by circumstances to hand over Nisibis and a large part of Mesopotamia to the Persian king Sapor.

40 [Theophanes 83B]. [Jovian] issued general laws for the churches for the entire Roman Empire, restoring to the Catholic Church the position and honor it had enjoyed under the blessed Constantine.[95]

40a [*Chron. misc.* 134.9–18]. Jovian believed in the Lord with all his heart, and he had begun to do what was good and right before the Lord and to walk in the ways of David and in the faith of Hezekiah and in the deeds of Josiah. And the Lord gave him rest as he deserved and rewarded him for his good deeds. He too had begun to put into effect his desire to make an everlasting name for himself and to pay honor to the whole Christian people of God. He ordered the church treasures to be returned, which Julian, in his madness, had removed. And he freed all Christians from taxes.

41 [Theophanes 84B]. The emperor Jovian went to Antioch in the month of Hyperberetaios.[96] And outside the city gate, in the place called Tripylon, there was born to a country gardener a baby girl in the womb for seven months having two separate heads, each completely formed, with each head divided from the neck up. It was born dead in the month of Dios, which is November.[97] Jovian set out from Antioch for Constantinople, and, having reached Ancyra in Galatia, he went on as consul with his son Varronian, whom he proclaimed *epiphanēs* without investing him with the purple. In that same year [a.m. 5856 = 363/4] the most Christian emperor Jovian died after reaching Dadastana, a place in Bithynia, having reigned nine months

---

94. On the location of Beth Aramaye and Coche, see Richard J. Talbert and Roger S. Bagnall, *Barrington Atlas of the Greek and Roman World* (Princeton: Princeton University Press, 2000), 91.

95. Jovian's church policy is in 8.5.

96. The month of Hyperberetaios is October. Jovian is attested in Antioch on 22 October (Seeck, *Regesten der Kaiser und Päpste*, 213).

97. On the portents, see Ammianus 25.10.1–2.

and fifteen days. And by proclamation of the army, the Augustus Valentinian became emperor for eleven years.[98]

41a [Michael 147, bottom right–bottom left]. He reached Antioch and from there went on to Ancyra in Galatia, where he made his son Varronian consul. He proclaimed him with great pomp, except that he did not clothe him with the purple.

42 [Theophanes 85B]. In this year [a.m. 5857 = 364/5] the Augustus Valentinian proclaimed his son Gratian Augustus and at the same time partner in his rule and consul.

42a [Michael 148 middle bottom–149 middle top]. He proclaimed his son Gratian Augustus and made him consul.

43 [Theophanes 87B–88B]. In the same year [a.m. 5859 = 366/7] the emperor Valens was staying in Marcianopolis in Moesia.[99] There was a great earthquake throughout the earth in the eighth indiction, during the night, so that in Alexandria boats moored to the shore were lifted high up and sailed over tall buildings and walls and came down inside into courtyards and dwellings. When the sea withdrew, they remained on dry land. The people who had fled from the city because of the earthquake saw the boats high and dry and had set about looting their cargo when the water returned and covered them all.[100] Other seamen related that they had been overtaken while sailing in the middle of the Adriatic at the time; their boat, while on the high seas, had suddenly settled to the seabed, and after a little while the water had returned, and they had sailed on.

43a [Michael 149 middle]. Valens made his way to Egypt, and while he was in Marcianopolis there was an earthquake such as had not been since the beginning of the world. The sea was stirred up and threw ships over the city walls; they fell into the middle of courtyards. The sea left its place, dry land appeared, the ships remained loose, and the people ran to loot them. But the sea came back over them and covered them. Some sailors related that this happened in the Adriatic Sea as well: the sea was stirred up and came up onto the land for many miles, swallowing up villages and their inhabitants, while

---

98. Jovian's death and Valentinian's accession are in 8.8; 8.8a.

99. Valens in Marcianopolis is in 9.7.

100. On the earthquake and flood, see Ammianus 26.10.15–19 (ships at Alexandria were driven two miles inland, with others landing on the tops of buildings); *Vita Athanasii* 29 (seafarers were left on the seabed [PG 25:ccx]); Socrates 4.3.4; Sozomen 6.2.14; *Consul. const.* 365; Jerome, *Vita S. Hilarionis eremitae* 40; John of Nikiu, *Chronicle* 82.21–23; François Nau, "Mélanges," *Revue de l'Orient chrétien* 13 (1908): 436–43. It occurred on 21 July 365. Ammianus's notice is studied by Gavin Kelly, "Ammianus and the Great Tsunami," *JRS* 94 (2004): 141–65.

all of its bed appeared to view. Ships dropped down onto the land, while those in them were frightened. But suddenly the sea returned to its place gently, and the ships were lifted up onto the sea and floated, and those in them were not harmed at all.

43b [Jerome, *Chron.* 366]. There was an earthquake throughout the whole earth, so that [the sea came upon the land] and countless people were killed in cities in Sicily and in many islands.

44 [Theophanes 89B]. Valens wintered in Marcianopolis during his campaign against the Goths [a.m. 5860 = 367/8].

45 [Theophanes 93B]. In this year [a.m. 5865 = 372/3], while Valens was staying in Antioch, some people were discovered hatching a plot against him, and a gang of impious folk was put to death, for they had been implementing their intrigue through soothsaying and sacrifice.[101]

46 [Theophanes 97B]. [Valentinian] died on the seventeenth of the month of Dios, in the third indiction.[102] Since Gratian, his son, was not there and Valens was staying in Antioch, the army that was there in the place where Valentinian the Great had died proclaimed his son Valentinian Augustus; he was about four years old, and his mother Justina was also there in Pannonia. When Gratian found out, he took his brother as co-emperor with himself, but he punished in various ways those who had made the proclamation, since it had been done without consulting him.

46a [Michael 151 middle]. When Valentinian died, and Gratian, his older son, was not there, but Justina was there, the army assembled and made Valentinian the Younger emperor when he was four years old.

46b [*Chronicon ad 1234* 168.7–11]. When he died, his son Gratian was not present. And his brother Valens was staying in Antioch. Now the army proclaimed his younger son Valentinian emperor,[103] a lad four years old, because his mother Justina was there.

47 [Theophanes 101B–102B]. In this year [a.m. 5870 = 377/8] the Goths … came out into Roman territory and laid waste many provinces, Scythia, Moesia, Thrace, Macedonia, and Achaia, and all of Greece, in all about twenty provinces. In this year there also appeared in the air clouds in the shape of armed men. There was as well a child born in Antioch who was fully formed

---

101. The plot against Valens is in 9.15.

102. The death of Valentinian I and subsequent events are in 9.16.

103. The Latin translation in Bidez, *Philostorgius,* 240, overlooks "younger" (*z'ūra*) in "younger son Valentinian."

except for having one eye in the middle of its forehead and four hands and four feet and a beard.[104]

Valens, who was staying in Antioch, heard about the Goths and went to Constantinople.

47a [Michael 152 middle]. At that same time, human beings were seen in the air, in the midst of a cloud; they had the appearance of armed men. And in Antioch a baby was born with one eye in the middle of its forehead, four hands, four feet, and a beard. And at that time the Goths went forth into Roman territory and plundered many provinces and Scythia, Moesia, Thrace, Macedonia, Achaia, and all of Greece.

48 [Theophanes 102B]. The barbarians caught up with [Valens], set fire to the house, and burned to death everyone in it without realizing it.[105]

48a [Michael 153 middle top]. And he fled to some farm. And when the barbarians surrounded it, he hid in a farmyard and concealed himself in a barn. And when they did not find him, they set fire to the whole farm, and that wicked man was also burned and departed into the fire of Gehenna.[106]

48b [*Chronicon ad 1234* 168.20–24]. And he fled and entered a field. And when the barbarians pursued him and surrounded the farm, he got into a mound of straw and hid himself in the straw. When the barbarians did not find him, they set fire to the whole field, and thus he suffocated in the smoke. And so he came to an evil end.

---

104. For more prodigies corresponding to those in section 47, see 10.11. In this section, "there ... appeared in the air clouds in the shape of armed men" translates ἐθεάθησαν ... ἐν τῷ ἀέρι [ἐν] ταῖς νεφέλαις ἐσχηματισμένοι ἄνδρες ἔνοπλοι. Removal of the brackets around the second ἐν would yield: "there also appeared in the air men arrayed in battle dress in the clouds."

105. Valens's death is in 9.17.

106. In section 48a, "concealed himself in a barn" translates what the editor seems to have read: *tmar nafsheh bbeit tebna* (in contrast to the printed text). The translation (by the editor) runs "se dissimula dans une grange" (Chabot, *Chronique de Michel le Syrien*, 295), and n. 1 adds: "Litt.: 'la maison de la paille.'" The text appears to need some revision.

Supplement
New Fragments of Philostorgius
on the Life of Constantine[1]

I

[*Suda*, K 2285 Constantine]: The great emperor, about whom Eunapius writes such nonsense; I have omitted it out of respect for the man.

---

1. Among the works that draw from Philostorgius is an anonymous and incompletely preserved Life of Constantine (*BHG* 365), the relationship of which to our author is lucidly expounded by Pio Franchi de' Cavalieri, "Di un frammento di una Vita di Costantino nel codice greco 22 della Biblioteca Angelica," *Studi e documenti di storia e diritto* 18 (1897): 89–131. Bidez included extracts from this Life in his edition of Philostorgius, after which Opitz published all the parts of it found in the manuscript in "Die Vita Constantini," 535–93.

The following year, however, Peter Heseler announced the discovery of a fuller (if still incomplete) copy of the same Life in Codex Sabaiticus 366 ("Neues zur Vita Constantini des Codex Angelicus 22," *Byzantion* 10 [1935]: 399–402), and in the same volume of that journal Bidez published extracts from the newly revealed additional parts of the Life that he identified as also dependent on Philostorgius ("Fragments nouveaux de Philostorge" 403–42). The latter article was reprinted in the subsequent editions of his *Philostorgius* (364–93 in the 1972 edition; 363–92 in the 1981 edition).

The remaining parts of the Life that are extant, and that were not edited by Bidez or Opitz, have been published by François Halkin, "L'empereur Constantin converti par Euphratas," *AnBoll* 78 (1960): 5–17 (the first appendix to which supplies the heading for pp. 10–17: "Les autres passages inédits de la Vie acéphale de Constantin").

The translation that follows is of the additional parts of the Life of Constantine published originally by Bidez in the article in *Byzantion* 10 referred to above and reprinted in the 1981 edition of his *Philostorgius* (377–81). The Roman numerals reproduce those in Bidez, while the Arabic numerals have been added for the sake of convenience.

II²

[1] Constantius feared that the young woman might be murdered with the child out of jealousy, so after taking thought he sent the boy [Constantine] with a letter to the emperor Diocletian and his son-in-law Maximian; they were staying in Nicomedia in Bithynia. His purpose was both that as a hostage the boy might guarantee unanimity among them and that his encounter with a number of different situations might bring him to be someone able to benefit the realm.³ For experience in several arts usually <trains?> the minds of those assigned to various tasks, rendering them more confident and reliable.⁴ In Diocletian's company, then, Constantine held the rank and honor of those whom the Romans call *domestici,* and he showed that he was by far the best among those of that station; where deliberation was required, he proved steady and reliable in discerning what to do, and where action was called for, he demonstrated great strength.⁵

[2] Indeed, as time went on and Constantine's outstanding qualities and ability were proven by his great undertakings—for he was by now a man—Diocletian, filled with envy and suspicious of his energetic character, plotted how he might do away with him as secretly as possible, keeping hidden his own guile.⁶ Now he was accustomed at certain festivals to have the soldiers of the division in which Constantine was enrolled contend with beasts that

---

2. For what precedes II 1, see Halkin, "L'empereur Constantin converti par Euphratas," 11–12: Constantius's envoys to Persia pass through Drepanum in Bithynia and lodge at the inn where Helena lives. There they meet the young Constantine and her and discover that he is Constantius's son from her earlier encounter with him. When they return to Constantius after completing their embassy, they tell him about Helena and her son, and he sends and has them brought to him. But the remarkable story spreads rapidly and soon reaches the ears of Constantius's lawful wife (Theodora).

3. Constantine's position as hostage (in the ancient sense of the word) at Diocletian's court is also related in *Anon. Val.* 2; Aurelius Victor 40.2; Zonaras 12.33.645A; *Bios* 312.9–16. Zonaras says Constantine was sent there to learn the military art. *Bios* likewise mentions Constantius's fear that his son might be murdered out of jealousy.

4. The phrase "usually <trains?> the mind" translates according to the editor's suggested reading: <ἀσκεῖν> εἰωθυῖα τὴν διάνοιαν.

5. *Bios* 312.15 also assigns Constantine a rank among the *domestici*; Lactantius, *Mort.* 18, says he was a *tribunus primi ordinis*. On the evidence of his qualities, see Eutropius 10.5; 10.6.3–7.1.

6. Diocletian's suspicion and envy are related or implied in 1.5; Eusebius, *Vit. Const.* 1.20; Theophanes 10B; *Bios* 314.5–6. *Bios* 312.20–313.5 also says that the court pagans were jealous of Constantine because they could forecast the future and tell that he would be the emperor who would abolish their religion.

were usually fearsome but that had had their teeth removed so that the contest would be free of danger and result in amusement and pleasure rather than wounds. So he himself first sent some others to take part in the contest and then ordered Constantine to do so, but he secretly ordered the keepers of the beasts to set upon him the animals that were in full possession of their natural powers.[7] Constantine, then, entered the contest with no inkling of the plot, and a lion was first loosed at him, a large and frightful beast. It then became evident that he had been granted that superior divine assistance that foresees the future, for he grabbed the lion and killed it. They then set upon him a most ferocious bear and then a leopard, but Constantine proved mightier than these as well, by the power of God's right hand rather than his own strength, and bore away from the dangers he had faced the prize of his own salvation.[8]

[3] Diocletian, then, failed of his purpose and thereupon pretended to be angry at those who had set the beasts upon him. Constantine, however, quite clearly perceived the plot against him, but for the present he too pretended to have no suspicion that it was in fact the emperor who was behind the threat to him. But as soon as he could get away, he took flight, and, having arranged everything, he withdrew, unbeknownst to Diocletian, and fled to the west and to his father, crippling the so-called public courier service on his way, so as not to be pursued.[9] For he chose the best of the horses that he needed, cutting the tendons of all the other horses and mules that he found and leaving them

---

7. Other sources say that it was Galerius who plotted to kill Constantine (Lactantius, *Mort.* 24; Praxagoras, *Fragmentum* (*FHG* 4:2a); Theophanes 12B; Zonaras 12.33.645A; *Bios* 314.1–4). He is said in one place to have withdrawn from a mock contest with beasts and soldiers and sent in Constantine in his place, having secretly arranged meanwhile for his adversaries to be in full possession of their usual weapons (François Halkin, "Une nouvelle Vie de Constantin dans un légendier de Patmos," *AnBoll* 77 [1959]: 77). For other notices of his contests with beasts, see Lactantius, *Mort.* 24; Praxagoras in *FHG* 4:2a; Zonaras 12.33.645B. This sort of stuff may go back to the tradition that Galerius put Constantine at risk by sending him out on campaign against ferocious barbarians (*Anon. Val.* 2–3).

8. On "the power of God's right hand," compare Lactantius, *Mort.* 24: "Dei manus hominem protegebat."

9. Both Lactantius, *Mort.* 24, and *Anon. Val.* 4 say that Galerius gave Constantine permission to leave but that his departure was a flight during which he took the public courier horses out of service; *Anon. Val.* speaks of mutilating them ("summa festinatione veredis post se truncatis Alpes transgressus"), while Lactantius speaks more generally and perhaps euphemistically ("post coenam properavit exire, sublatisque per mansiones multas omnibus equis publicis, evolavit"). Zosimus 2.8.3 also says that he crippled the relays in turn as he came to the several way stations. Aurelius Victor 40.2 and *Epit. Caes.* 41.2 say he killed them outright. The reason, according to *Anon. Val.*

unserviceable. And when he changed from the ones he had used to others, he crippled them in the same way.

[4] Thus his cleverness and daring made pursuit quite impossible to those who wanted to gallop after him, while he himself shortly after

arrived safely in his father's realm. Having there no more to fear,[10] and learning that his father was ill in that Britain which is called Albion,[11] he sailed across to him as quickly as possible and arrived in the nick of time, God's invisible providence obviously measuring out the length of his father's life by the time of his arrival.[12]

[Philostorgius 1.5]. Constantius died in Britain, which is called Albion. The youth Constantine reached him there while he was ill, having unexpectedly escaped Diocletian's plot, saw to his burial, and succeeded to his realm.

Thus he arrived just on time; when his father, who was ill and all but ready to depart from this life at the moment, saw his son appear unexpectedly, he rallied a bit, gathered his strength from his excitement, and placed the purple robe upon him.[13] For this is what the Roman emperors wore as a token of sovereignty. [Constantine is said to have been the first to put on a crown, but others relate that Diocletian was the first to put on both a crown and robes shot with gold, and his footwear was decorated with pearls.][14]

---

4 and Lactantius, *Mort.* 24, was his fear of pursuit and arrest by Severus, the Caesar in Italy. Zonaras 12.33.645B and *Bios* 313.12–15 mention that he fled with friends.

10. The editor notes that there is a verb missing in the sentence "Having there no more to fear...." The translation offers a probable sense.

11. Our author specifies that he is speaking of "Albion" in order to distinguish the island from Ireland.

12. The touching scene of Constantine's arrival at his father's death bed, derived from Eusebius, *Vit. Const.* 1.21–22, and endlessly repeated (e.g., Zosimus 2.9.1; *Bios* 313.15–17), may be relegated to the realm of historical fiction, as a comparison of *Anon. Val.* 4 and *Pan. Lat.* VI (VII) 7.5 shows that Constantine actually arrived in Boulogne just as his father was hoisting sail for Britain. After the crossing they went on to battle the Picts, Constantius then dying at York on 25 July 306.

13. On Constantius rallying at the sight of his son, compare Eusebius, *Vit. Const.* 1.22; *Bios* 314.11: ὥσπερ ἐπιλαθόμενος καὶ τὴν νόσον. See also Peter Heseler, "Hagiographica II," *Byzantinisch-Neugriechische Jahrbücher* 9 (1932): 320–37. *Bios* 314.16–315.14 also has Constantius transferring the tokens of sovereignty to his son: the purple, the crown, and the scepter. In Eusebius, *Vit. Const.* 1.22.1, by contrast, Constantine invests himself after his father's death.

14. The sentence in brackets is not considered by the editor to depend upon

[5] Constantius, then, departed from this life as soon as he had left his son Constantine as successor to his realm. Constantine, once he had received his father's scepter, showed honor to his brothers, allowing them to rule under him and giving Dalmatius the title of "Caesar," as the Romans call it, while to the other he gave the title some say of *rex nobilissimus* and others of *patricius*. In his affairs he combined gentleness and kindness with a great deal of energy.[15]

[6] Now after the death of Severus and Maximinus, the latter's son Maxentius held power in Italy,[16] as did Licinius in the east, so he formed a league and made a treaty with them for the sake of security, allying himself by marriage with both by giving his own sister to Licinius and taking Maxentius's to wife;[17]

Philostorgius, for whom Constantine put on a crown only after defeating Licinius (A5.24); see Bidez, *Philostorgius*, 383 n. 22. That Constantine did wear a crown, whenever he first put it on, is well enough attested (Eusebius, *Vit. Const.* 4.66; *Epit Caes.* 41.14; Malalas 13.8). Malalas 13.8 and Cedrenus 295B–C say he was the first emperor to do so, while *Anecdota Graeca* (John A. Cramer, ed., *Anecdota graeca e codd. manuscriptis Bibliothecae regiae parisiensis* [4 vols.; Oxford: Clarendon, 1839–41], 2:292) agrees with our passage at least as far as saying that Diocletian was the first to wear robes and sandals decorated with precious stones and gold.

15. The text implies that Constantine had only two brothers left. Socrates 3.1.6 in fact mentions only two (Dalmatius and Constantius), and Julian (*Ep. ad Ath.* 270C–D) suggests the same thing. He had three (half-)brothers originally, including Hannibalianus: the sons whom Theodora gave his father. The situation is stated correctly in 2.16a (see also 33–34 n. 48, first two paragraphs). There it also says that Constantine gave the titles *Caesar* and *nobilissimus* to all three. The title *rex*, however, went rather to his nephew Hannibalianus, proclaimed *rex regum et Ponticarum gentium* in 335 (see *Anon. Val.* 35; Ammianus 14.1.2; *Epit. Caes.* 41.20; *Chron. pasch.* P286B). The title *nobilissimus* was given only to Caesars in the third century, but in the following to the other members of the imperial families as well.

16. With regard to "after the death of Severus and Maximinus, the latter's son Maxentius held power," the editor notes that each of the occurrences of "Maximinus" is a confusion with "Maximian."

17. Diocletian's administrative reforms included an attempt to stabilize the transition of power by the appointment of a colleague, Maximian, in 286, and in 293 by the further appointment of two "Caesars" under the two Augusti: Constantius, Constantine's father, for Gaul and Britain; and Galerius Maximinianus for Syria, Palestine, and Egypt. In 305 Maximian and he retired from office (the former reluctantly), and Constantius and Galerius became Augusti, Diocletian having named Severus and Maximinus as Caesars in their place. Not long afterwards Constantine left Galerius's court to rejoin his father; when Constantius died, Constantine announced to Galerius that he had taken the title of Augustus in succession to him, but Galerius in response accorded him only that of "Caesar," a reduction that Constantine accepted.

from her he had a son named Crispus, who excelled in his father's virtues.[18] As for Maxentius, that most insolent and violent man, he practiced a savage tyranny toward his subjects, taking away those of their wives whom he learned excelled in beauty and violating them, including some whose husbands held the highest power after him, and stripping of their property those whom he discovered were the wealthiest; he even put some of them to death.[19]

III[20]

Thus did Maxentius behave. But as his arrogance in their regard increased, he planned to remove Constantine from the government as well, and he set himself to wage open war on him.[21] The agreement between them

---

On 28 October 306, however, Maxentius, the son of the retired Augustus Maximian, who was jealous of Constantine's irregular accession, revolted in Rome, assumed the purple, and called his restive father out of retirement to assist him. Maximian secured an alliance with Constantine by giving him his daughter Fausta in marriage in 307; Severus meanwhile died in his attempt to suppress Maxentius, and Galerius's invasion of Italy was likewise rebuffed.

In April of 308, Maximian himself tried to strip his son of power; upon failing he fled to Constantine. In the same year Galerius declared Maxentius a public enemy and appointed Licinius Augustus in place of Severus. And in 310 the ever-restless Maximian tried to supplant Constantine himself but was captured and hanged himself, perhaps with some encouragement. In 311 Galerius died, Licinius and Maximinus dividing his territory between them after nearly going to war over it. Constantine betrothed his own (half-)sister Constantia to Licinius in order to ally himself with him, and Maximinus in response recognized Maxentius in Rome as a legitimate emperor.

18. Crispus was not the son of Fausta but of Minervina, who had perhaps died before 307.

19. Eusebius also tells of Maxentius taking the wives of some even of the highest rank in the senate (*Hist. eccl.* 8.14.2; 8.14.16–17) and of killing senators in order to seize their property (*Hist. eccl.* 8.14.4; *Vit. Const.* 1.34). *Pan. Lat.* XII (IX) 4.4 mentions his rapes and his murders of senators.

20. After Bidez's extract II, the author of the Life sets Philostorgius aside to copy almost verbatim from Eusebius, *Hist. eccl.* 8.14.14, 16–17, the story of the Christian woman who committed suicide rather than let herself be led off to Maxentius to be dishonored. This part of the Life, the bridge between Bidez's extracts II and III, may be found in Halkin, "L'empereur Constantin converti par Euphratas." 13.

21. Maxentius initiated hostilities against Constantine, feigning (it is said) grief at his father's death (Lactantius, *Mort.* 43.4; Zosimus 2.14.1). The war began in the summer of 311; it is not known what moves Maxentius made or how Constantine countered them; see Timothy D. Barnes, *Constantine and Eusebius* (Cambridge: Harvard University Press, 1981), 40.

was abrogated, and their armies faced off against each other, drawn up for battle. It was then that Constantine, wanting to spy out and know precisely how large the enemy force was and what preparations it had made (for he took a great deal of thought about such things), made his way as secretly as he could out of his own camp late at night, got a wagon ready, filled a great ox-skin with wine, and put it on the wagon.[22] Then he dressed up like one of the locals, as though he were one of the peasants there, drove at daybreak to the enemy camp after circling around to arrive from the other direction, came up to them as though for the purpose of bringing them the wine, and sold it to them, cap on head, staying as long as he could and observing secretly everything he could about the enemy. Then when night fell and he had returned safely to his own camp, he was full of fear and dread, so impressed was he by the size of the enemy force and its preparations and dispositions....[23]

IV

[1] Such were the words he spoke, growling because he saw the great danger at hand that was nearly upon him, and then he fell silent and turned to other business. But as soon as night fell, he looked over to the enemy camp, where there were many fires burning everywhere and from which a great and confused noise came, both from the crowd in general and whenever the watches roundabout took up their battle songs. Thus with his fear increasing,[24]

---

22. The story of Constantine visiting an enemy camp in disguise was too good to be confined to one episode in his life and is also told in *Pan. Lat.* IV (X) 18.2, the enemy this time being barbarian: "Adis barbaros, et dissimulato principis habitu quam proxime poteras, cum duobus accedis." In the Life here it is to be placed in the following year, 312, when Constantine invaded Italy with forces far inferior to the total number that Maxentius could command throughout that country; see Zosimus 2.15.1–2; *Pan. Lat.* XII (IX) 3.3 ("Vix ... quarta parte exercitus contra centum milia armatorum hostium Alpes transgressus es...") (*Pan. Lat.* XII [IX] 4.2; 5.2).

23. Following extract III, the author of the Life again turns aside from Philostorgius to tell how the eunuch Euphratas encouraged Constantine to worship the one true God and to take Christ his Son as his ally, passing in review the history of the growth of Christianity and the downfall of its persecutors. Constantine replies that he believes and then begs Christ to grant him victory, or at least an escape from the looming darkness. This part of the Life, between Bidez's extracts III and IV, may be found in Halkin, "L'empereur Constantin converti par Euphratas." 6–10. Philostorgius himself, of course, attributes Constantine's conversion to the Western bishops (A5.24; Bidez, *Philostorgius*, 385 n. 34).

24. Constantine's fear of the approaching battle is mentioned elsewhere, although different reasons are given for it; sometimes it is Maxentius's sorcery that he

he once again turned to prayer, emitting repeated groans from the heart that was kindled within him: "If you have any power to save, O Christ, and if you are really a god, do not let me fall into the power of Maxentius, that most hostile of men, nor give me cause to regret that I have made you my champion in this danger."

[2] As he was thus speaking in prayer, a great and extraordinary portent appeared to him that signified victory beyond any doubt,[25] a victory over which Christ would preside, since he had listened to him favorably:

the figure of the cross appeared in the east, extending to a great distance and produced by a most brilliant radiance. It was encircled by stars like a rainbow, the stars not being arranged just anyhow but discriminately, as letters, and the letters formed the Latin words: "By this conquer!"	[Philostorgius 1.6]. ... in which [the victory over Maxentius] the sign of the cross appeared in the east, extending to a great distance and formed of a brilliant radiance. It was encircled by stars like a rainbow that were arranged as letters forming the Latin words: "By this conquer!"

All the air roundabout was bright and shining, with rays darting everywhere to a great distance. Seeing this, he was greatly relieved and, worshiping Christ and accepting this clearest proof of his divinity, he revived, having mastered and subdued the fear gripping him.

[3] Having now a firm expectation of victory, he at once made an image of the cross that had appeared.[26] What he did was to show a model of the sign of triumph to a goldsmith and thus raise up in the camp a trophy of

---

fears (Halkin, "Une nouvelle Vie de Constantin," 79; *Bios* 322.1–2). For the panegyrist telling of his visit to the barbarian camp, by contrast, his greatest fear is that the enemy will be too frightened of him to come out and fight: "Nil magis timuisti quam ne timereris" (*Pan. Lat.* IV [X] 18.2).

25. That the heavenly cross appeared to Constantine while he was at anxious prayer is also told in *Bios* 322.7–13; Rufinus/Eusebius, *Hist. eccl.* 9.1.1 ("cum igitur anxius et multa secum de imminentis belli necessitate pervolvens iter ageret atque ad caelum saepius oculos elevaret et inde sibi divinum precaretur auxilium, videt per soporem ad orientis partem in caelo signum crucis igneo fulgore rutilare"). See also Halkin, "Une nouvelle Vie de Constantin."

26. Constantine's battle standard against Licinius was to be a cross upon a golden shaft (A5.15). For its fashioning, see Halkin, "Une nouvelle Vie de Constantin," 80; Zonaras 13.1.11. *Bios* 322.25–27 also mentions the precious stones with the gold. For the fifty cross-bearers, see Eusebius, *Vit. Const.* 2.8. In Rufinus/Eusebius, *Hist. eccl.* 9.1.1, it is Constantine himself who bears the golden cross into battle.

purest gold and of stones most precious, since victory was quite certain. Fifty of the strongest men in the army were charged with taking it in turn to carry it in the line of battle, and it was the greatest display of faith amid such an overwhelming prevalence

of the polytheism and worship of demons of most people: some of the units bore the very names of the demons, such as those called the *Ioviani* and *Herculiani*,[27] which in Greek would be *Diasioi* and *Herakleioi* (among the Italians Zeus is "Jove" and Heracles is "Hercules"), while all of them carried idols on their standards, which the Romans

[*Suda*, I 403]. [*Ioviani* and *Herculiani*, names of units]: some of the [military] units bore a demon's name.

For among the Italians Zeus is "Jove" and Heracles is "Hercules."

call *signa*, different ones with different idols.[28] And amid all of this, Constantine placed his hopes for victory on the sign of the cross and the symbol of suffering.[29]

[4] He, notwithstanding,[30] derived confidence from the army under his command, with [its] change of belief resulting from the conspicuousness of

---

27. The *Ioviani* and *Herculiani* were two legions renamed by Diocletian and Maximian as a special honor after their accession (Diocletian being surnamed Iovius and Maximian Herculius); see Vegetius, *Epitoma rei militaris* 1.17; Zosimus 2.42.2; 3.30.2; Ammianus 22.3.2; 25.5.8; 25.6.2; 27.10.10; *Suda*, I 403. The comment about the Greek equivalents *Diasioi* and *Herakleioi* is a gloss from the author of the Life and is not from Philostorgius; see David Woods, "Julian, Arbogastes, and the *Signa* of the *Ioviani* and *Herculiani*," *Journal of Roman Military Equipment Studies* 6 (1995): 65–66.

28. The comment about the pagan *signa* implies that, as Eusebius, *Vit. Const.* 4.21, says, Constantine put the cross on his soldiers' shields and standards. See Michael DiMaio, Jörn Zeuge, and Natalia Zotov, "*Ambiguitas Constantiniana:* The *Caeleste Signum Dei* of Constantine the Great," *Byzantion* 58 (1988): 333–60; Hans Reinhard Seeliger, "Die Verwendung des Christogramms durch Konstantin im Jahre 312," *ZKG* 100 (1989): 149–68; David Woods, "Eusebius, *Vit. Const.* 4.21, and the *Notitia Dignitatum*," in *Historica, Theologica et Philosophica, Critica et Philologica* (ed. Elizabeth A. Livingstone; StPatr 29; Leuven: Peeters, 1997) 195–202.

29. For the "symbol of suffering," see Eusebius, *Hist. eccl.* 9.9.10: after his victory, Constantine erected in Rome τοῦ σωτηρίου τρόπαιον πάθους.

30. Regarding "He, notwithstanding...," the editor explains this as expressing the contrast between the suffering represented by the cross and Constantine's confidence in victory (Bidez, *Philostorgius*, 387 n. 40).

the marvel shown [to it] that had been clearly visible to all, and he had the firmest expectation of victory over his enemies, and so he was unshaken, exulting in his faith in Christ the Savior with a boldness firm and clear. Nor would he be disappointed, for Maxentius's entire army went over to him without bloodshed, everyone bowing down to him willingly and raising neither hand nor spear [against him].[31] For Maxentius, having aroused a great hatred for himself among all his subjects,[32] now offered the clearest demonstration of how bad it is for a ruler to want to control his subjects, not by gentleness and benefaction, but by arrogance and coercion; he did not understand how much better and firmer a foundation for governing is provided by kindness than by fear.[33] He met a sudden death, at any rate, in the Tiber River, carried off in the way I shall relate.

[5] For Constantine, even though he was thus buoyed up by such intense high hopes, did not think it right to attack first, since he respected his marriage connection and the treaties, but he drew up his forces for battle and waited. Maxentius, for his part, after rescinding the treaty and sending forth the army so that it might pitch its camp in a suitable place and ready itself for battle, made his other preparations while remaining behind in the city of Rome, since he reckoned that there would be all sorts of changes of fortune

---

31. "Maxentius's entire army went over to him without bloodshed"; not so, and this passage appears in fact to be contradicted by 1.6a, which speaks of "the bitterly contested battle against Maxentius" (see 9 n. 10). Other sources as well speak of a slaughter when the armies met before Rome, and most of Maxentius's guard was killed: *Pan. Lat.* IV (X) 29–30; XII (IX) 17.1; Zosimus 2.16.2–4; Zonaras 13.1.11. Bidez (*Philostorgius*, 387 n. 43) suggests that our passage here was influenced by Eusebius, *Hist. eccl.* 9.9.5, which speaks of Maxentius's flight from Constantine with no mention of a battle, and by *Vit. Const.* 1.38. *Hist. eccl.* 9.9.3, however, tells of three battles between the opposing armies before Constantine reached the city of Rome, although Rufinus's translation removes any hint of a clash of arms and lays stress upon Constantine's anxiety not to shed Roman blood; perhaps that is the earliest appearance of the tradition represented here. The apparent contradiction with 1.6a may be resolved, however, if one notices that the present passage is not talking about the final battle with Maxentius (who has still to try his trick bridge).

32. "Maxentius ... aroused a great hatred for himself among all his subjects" translates the corrected reading μέγα καὶ κοινὸν ἀρχομένοις in Bidez, *Philostorgius*, 381.36 (see also 392).

33. On Maxentius's tyrannical ways, see S II 6; Aurelius Victor 40.24; Eusebius, *Vit. Const.* 1.35. On Constantius's benevolent rule, see Opitz, *Vit. Const.* 9; Eutropius 10.7.2; Eusebius, *Vit. Const.* 1.45.

in the course of the war. Now Maxentius built the bridge on the Tiber River without connecting the whole thing....[34]

---

34. After Bidez's extract IV, the Life continues with a quotation from Zosimus 2.15.3 telling of how Maxentius ordered a bridge built over the Tiber River that was so constructed that it could be separated suddenly in the middle when Constantine's army was crossing it. Maxentius fell into his own trap and drowned in the river. The continuation is in Halkin, "L'empereur Constantin converti par Euphratas." 13–14; and Bidez, *Philostorgius*, 387–88 n. 48.

Bibliography

Adler, Ada, ed. *Suidae Lexicon.* 5 vols. Leipzig: Teubner, 1928–38.

Arbesmann, Rudolph Eugen. "Fasttage." *RAC* 7:506–24.

Amandry, Pierre. "La ruine du temple d'Apollon à Delphes." *Académie royale de Belgique: Bulletin de la classe des lettres et des sciences morales et politiques* 75 (1989): 26–47.

Amidon, Philip R. *The Church History of Rufinus of Aquileia: Books 10 and 11.* New York: Oxford University Press, 1997.

———. "Paulinus' Subscription to the *Tomus ad Antiochenos.*" *JTS* NS 53 (2002): 53–74.

Arendzen, John P. "A New Syriac Text of the Apocalyptic Part of the 'Testament of the Lord.'" *JTS* 2 (1901): 401–16.

Arnold, Duane W.-H. *The Early Episcopal Career of Athanasius of Alexandria.* Notre Dame, Ind.: University of Notre Dame Press, 1991.

Aujoulat, Noël. "Eusebie, Hélène, et Julien." *Byzantion* 58 (1983): 78–103 ("I: Le témoignage de Julien"), 421–52 ("II: Le témoignage des historiens").

Avi-Yonah, Michael. *Geschichte der Juden im Zeitalter des Talmud in den Tagen von Rom und Byzanz.* Berlin: de Gruyter, 1962.

Baldwin, Barry. "Olympiodorus of Thebes." *L'antiquité classique* 49 (1980): 212–31.

Banchich, Thomas M. "Julian's School Laws. Cod. Theod. 13.5.5 and Ep. 42." *The Ancient World* 24 (1993): 5–14.

Barcellona, Francesco S. "Martiri e confessori dell'età di Giuliano l'Apostata: Dalla storia alla legenda." Pages 53–83 in *Pagani e cristiani da Giuliano l'Apostata al sacco di Roma.* Edited by Franca Ela Consolino. Soveria Mannelli: Rubbettino, 1995.

Bardy, Gustave. "Cyrille de Jérusalem." *DHGE* 13:1181–86

———. *Recherches sur Lucien d'Antioche et son école.* Paris: Beauchesne, 1936.

Barnes, Jonathan. "Pyrrhonism, Belief, and Causation. Observations on the Scepticism of Sextus Empiricus." *ANRW* 36.4:2611–17.

Barnes, Timothy D. *Athanasius and Constantius: Theology and Politics in the Constantinian Empire.* Cambridge: Harvard University Press, 1993.

———. "The Collapse of the Homoeans in the East." Pages 3–16 in *Historica,*

Theologica et Philosophica, Critica et Philologica. Edited by Elizabeth A. Livingstone. StPatr 29. Leuven: Peeters, 1997.

———. "The Consecration of Ulfila." *JTS* 41 (1990): 541–45.

———. *Constantine and Eusebius*. Cambridge: Harvard University Press, 1981.

———. *The New Empire of Diocletian and Constantine*. Cambridge: Harvard University Press, 1982.

———. "Patricii under Valentinian III." *Phoenix* 29 (1975): 155–70.

Bastien, Pierre. *Le monnayage de Magnence, 350–353*. Wetteren, Belgium: Éditions cultura, 1964.

Baudrillart, Alfred, et al., eds. *Dictionnaire d'histoire et de géographie ecclésiastiques*. Paris: Letouzey & Ané, 1912–.

Bell, H. Idris. *Jews and Christians in Egypt*. London: British Museum, 1924.

Bidez, Joseph, "Fragments nouveaux de Philostorge sur la vie de Constantin." *Byzantion* 10 (1935): 403–42.

———. *Philostorgius. Kirchengeschichte: mit dem Leben des Lucian von Antiochien und den Fragmenten eines arianischen Historiographen*. 3rd ed. Revised by Friedhelm Winkelmann. GCS. Berlin: Akademie-Verlag, 1981.

———. "Sur diverses citations, et notamment sur trois passages de Malalas retrouvés dans un texte hagiographique." *ByzZ* 11 (1902): 388–94.

Bihain, Ernest. "L'épître de Cyrille de Jérusalem à Constance sur la vision de la croix (*BHG* 413)." *Byzantion* 43 (1973): 264–96.

Bleckmann, Bruno. "Constantia, Vetranio, und Gallus Caesar." *Chiron* 24 (1994): 29–68.

Boissonade, Jean François, ed. *Tzetzae Allegoriae Iliadis*. Paris: Dumont, 1851.

Boor, Carl de, ed. *Theophanis Chronographia*. Hildesheim: Olms, 1885.

Bouché-Leclercq, Auguste. *Histoire de la divination dans l'antiquité*. 4 vols. Paris: Leroux, 1879–82.

Bowra, C. Maurice. "ΕΙΠΑΤΕ ΤΩΙ ΒΑΣΙΛΗΙ." *Hermes* 87 (1959): 426–35. Revised and repr. as pages 233–52 in idem, *On Greek Margins*. Oxford: Clarendon, 1970.

Brakmann, Heinzgerd. "Axomis." *RAC* Supplement 1:5/6 (1992): 718–810.

Brennecke, Hans Christof. "Christliche Quellen des Ammianus Marcellinus?" *Journal of Ancient Christianity* 1 (1997): 226–50.

———. *Hilarius von Poitiers und die Bischofsopposition gegen Konstantius II*. Berlin: de Gruyter, 1984.

———. "Lukian von Antiochien in der Geschichte des arianischen Streites." Pages 170–92 in *Logos. Festschrift für Luise Abramowski*. Edited by Hans

Christof Brennecke, Ernst Ludwig Grasmück, and Christoph Markschies. BZNW 67. Berlin: de Gruyter, 1993.

———. *Studien zur Geschichte der Homöer.* Tübingen: Mohr Siebeck, 1988.

Brooks, Ernest W., and Jean-Baptiste Chabot, eds. *Chronica minora.* CSCO 1–6. 6 vols. Paris: Typographeo Reipublicae, 1903–5.

Buck, David F. "Eunapius on Julian's Acclamation as Augustus." *Ancient History Bulletin* 7 (1993): 73–80.

Burckhardt, August, ed. *Hieroclis Synecdemus.* Leipzig: Teubner, 1893.

Buresch, Karl. *Klaros: Untersuchungen zum Orakelwesen des späteren Altertums.* Lepizig: Teubner, 1889.

Burgess, Richard W. "The Dates of the First Siege of Nisibis and the Death of James of Nisibis." *Byzantion* 69 (1999): 7–17.

Burkert, Walter. *Lore and Science in Ancient Pythagoreanism.* Translated by Edwin L. Minar Jr. Cambridge: Harvard University Press, 1972.

Cabouret, Bernadette. "Julien et Delphes." *Revue des études anciennes* 99 (1997): 141–58.

Caltabiano, Matilde. "L'assassinio di Giorgio di Cappadocia (Alessandria, 361 d.C.)." *Quaderni Catanesi* 7 (1985): 17–59.

Cameron, Averil, and Judith Herrin. *Constantinople in the Early Eighth Century: The Parastaseis Syntomoi Chronikai.* Leiden: Brill, 1984.

Cantalamessa, Raniero. "Cristo 'Immagine di Dio.'" *Rivista di storia e letteratura religiosa* 16 (1980): 345–48.

Cardini, Maria Timpanaro. *Pitagorici: testimonianze e frammenti.* 3 vols. Fiorenza: La Nuova Italia, 1958.

Cathey, J. "Vom Analphabetentum zum Schreiber." Pages 88–98 in *Verschriftung und Verschriftlichung: Aspekte des Medienwechsels in verschiedenen Kulturen und Epochen.* Edited by Christine Ehler and Ursula Schaefer. Tübingen: Narr, 1998.

Cavalcanti, Elena, *Studi Eunomiani.* Rome: Pont. Institutum Orientalium Studiorum, 1976.

Chabot, Jean-Baptiste, ed. *Anonymi Auctoris Chronicon ad annum Christi 1234 pertinens.* CSCO 81; Scriptores Syri 3/14. Paris: Typographeo Reipublicae, 1920.

———. *Chronique de Michel le Syrien, Patriarche Jacobite d'Antioche (1166–1199).* 4 vols. Paris: Leroux, 1899–1924.

Chadwick, Henry. "The Fall of Eustathius of Antioch." *JTS* 49 (1948): 27–35.

Copenhaver, Brian P. *Hermetica: The Greek Corpus Hermeticum and the Latin Asclepius in a New English Translation, with Notes and Introduction.* Cambridge: Cambridge University Press, 1992.

Cowper, Benjamin H. *Syriac Miscellanies.* London: Williams & Norgate, 1861.

Cramer, John A., ed. *Anecdota graeca e codd. manuscriptis Bibliothecae regiae parisiensis.* 4 vols. Oxford: Clarendon, 1839–41.

Crisafulli, Virgil S., and John W. Nesbitt. *The Miracles of St. Artemios: A Collection of Miracle Stories by an Anonymous Author of Seventh Century Byzantium.* Leiden: Brill, 1997.

Cuntz, Otto, and Joseph Schnetz, eds. *Itineraria romana.* 2 vols. Leipzig: Teubner, 1929–40.

Dagron, Gilbert. *Naissance d'une capitale: Constantinople et ses institutions de 330 à 451.* Paris: Presses universitaires de France, 1974.

Daniélou, Jean, "Eunome l'arien et l'exégèse néo-platonicienne du Cratyle," *Revue des études grecques* 69 (1956): 412–32.

Delehaye, Hippolyte, ed. *Synaxarium ecclesiae constantinopolitanae: Propylaeum ad Acta Sanctorum Novembris.* Brussels: Carnandet, 1902.

Di Gregorio, Lamberto, ed. *Scholia vetera in Hesiodi Theogoniam.* Milan: Vita e pensiero, 1975.

Diels, Hermann, ed. *Die Fragmente der Vorsokratiker: Griechisch und deutsch.* Revised by Walther Kranz. 6th ed. 3 vols. Berlin: Weidmann, 1951–52.

Diez, Erna. "Delphin." *RAC* 3:667–82.

Dihle, Albrecht. "L'ambassade de Théophile l'Indien ré-examinée." Pages 461–68 in *L'Arabie préislamique et son environnement historique et culturel: Actes du Colloque de Strasbourg, 24–27 juin 1987.* Edited by Toufic Fahd. Leiden: Brill, 1989.

DiMaio, Michael, and Duane W.-H. Arnold. "*Per Vim, Per Caedem, Per Bellum*: A Study of Murder and Ecclesiastical Politics in the Year 337 A.D." *Byzantion* 62 (1992): 158–211.

DiMaio, Michael, Jörn Zeuge, and Natalia Zotov. "*Ambiguitas Constantiniana*: The *Caeleste Signum Dei* of Constantine the Great." *Byzantion* 58 (1988): 333–60.

Dionysius of Byzantium. *De Bospori navigatione.* Edited by Carl Wescher. Paris: Typographeum publicum, 1874.

Dobschütz, Ernst von. *Christusbilder: Untersuchungen zur christlichen Legende.* TU 18. Leipzig: Hinrichs, 1899.

Downey, Glanville. *A History of Antioch in Syria: From Seleucus to the Arab Conquest.* Princeton: Princeton University Press, 1961.

Drijvers, Jan Willem. *Helena Augusta: The Mother of Constantine the Great and the Legend of Her Finding of the True Cross.* Brill Studies in Intellectual History 27. Leiden: Brill, 1992.

Drinkwater, J. F. "The Pagan 'Underground,' Constantius II's 'Secret Service,' and the Survival, and the Usurpation of Julian the Apostate." Pages 348–87 in vol. 3 of *Studies in Latin Literature and Roman History.* Edited by

Carl Deroux. Collection Latomus 180. Brussels: Latomus Revue d'études latines, 1983.

Dübner, Friedrich. "Miscellanea." *Revue de Philologie* 2 (1847): 240–42.

Dufourcq, Albert. "Gestes d'Artemius." Pages 183–90 in vol. 5 of idem, *Étude sur les gesta martyrum romains.* 5 vols. Paris: Fontemoing, 1900–1988.

Dummer, Jürgen. "Fl. Artemius dux Aegypti." *APF* 21 (1971): 121–44.

Dzielska, Maria. *Hypatia of Alexandria.* Translated by F. Lyra. Cambridge: Harvard University Press, 1995.

Ebbinghaus, Ernst A. "Ulfila(s) or Wulfila." *Historische Sprachforschung* 104 (1991): 236–38.

Eitrem, S. "Hermes." PW 8.1:789–92.

Elliott, J. K., ed. *The Apocryphal New Testament: A Collection of Apocryphal Christian Literature in an English Translation.* Oxford: Clarendon, 1993.

Elliott, Thomas G. "Constantine's Conversion: Do We Really Need It?" *Phoenix* 41 (1987): 420–38.

———. "Constantine's Early Religious Development." *JRH* 15 (1989): 283–91.

———. "Constantine's Explanation of His Career." *Byzantion* 62 (1992): 212–34.

Faro, Silvano. "Oribasio medico, quaestor di Giuliano l'Apostata." *Studi in onore di Cesare Sanfilippo* 7 (1987): 261–68.

Fatouros, Georgios. "ΕΙΠΑΤΕ ΤΩΙ ΒΑΣΙΛΗΙ." *Hermes* 124 (1996): 367–74.

Fernández Hernández, Gonzalo. "La elección episcopal de Atanasio de Alejandría según Filostorgio." *Gerión* 3 (1985): 211–29.

Festugière, André-Jean. *La révélation d'Hermès Trismégiste.* 4 vols. Paris: Belles Lettres, 1949–54.

Fiaccadori, Gianfranco. "Teofilo Indiano." *Studi classici e orientali* 33 (1983): 295–331; 34 (1984): 271–308.

Fontenrose, Joseph E. *The Delphic Oracle: Its Responses and Operations, with a Catalogue of Responses.* Berkeley and Los Angeles: University of California Press, 1978.

Fowden, Garth. "Constantine's Porphyry Column: The Earliest Literary Allusion." *JRS* 81 (1991): 119–31.

Franchi de' Cavalieri, Pio. "Di un frammento di una Vita di Costantino nel codice greco 22 della Biblioteca Angelica." *Studi e documenti di storia e diritto* 18 (1897): 89–131.

Franco, C. "L'immagine di Alessandro in Giuliano imperatore." *Studi classici e orientali* 46 (1997): 637–58.

Fritz, Kurt von. "Pythagoras." PW 24:200–203.

Gaiffier, Baudoin de. "Les martyrs Eugène et Macaire, morts en exil en Maurétanie." *AnBoll* 78 (1960): 24–40.

Garzya, Antonio, and Denis Roques, eds. *Synésios de Cyrène: Correspondance.* 3 vols. Collection des universités de France 397. Paris: Belles Lettres, 2000.

Geffcken, Johannes. *Die Oracula Sibyllina.* GCS 8. Leipzig: Hinrichs, 1902.

Geiger, Joseph. "The Last Jewish Revolt against Rome: A Reconsideration." *Scripta Classica Israelica* 5 (1979–80): 250–57.

Gelzer, Heinrich, Heinrich Hilgenfeld, and Otto Cuntz. *Patrum nicaenorum nomina Latine, Graece, Coptice, Syriace, Arabice, Armeniace.* Leipzig: Teubner, 1898.

Geyer, Paul, ed. *Itineraria et alia geographica.* CCSL 175. Turnhout: Brepols, 1965.

Giet, Stanislas. "Saint Basile et le concile de Constantinople de 360." *JTS* 6 (1955): 94–99.

Ginzberg, Louis. *Legends of the Jews.* 7 vols. Philadelphia: Jewish Publication Society, 1909–38.

Graffin, René, and François Nau, eds. *Patrologia orientalis.* Paris: Didot, 1904–.

Grattarola, Pio. "L'usurpazione di Procopio e la fine dei Costantinidi." *Aevum* 60 (1986): 82–105.

Gregg, Robert C., ed. *Arianism: Historical and Theological Reassessments: Papers from the Ninth International Conference on Patristic Studies.* Cambridge: Philadelphia Patristic Foundation, 1985.

Gregory, Timothy E. "Julian and the Last Oracle at Delphi." *GRBS* 24 (1983): 355–66.

Gryson, Roger, ed. *Scolies ariennes sur le Concile d'Aquilée.* SC 267. Paris: Cerf, 1980.

Guidi, Michelangelo. "Un 'bios' di Costantino." *Rendiconti della R. Accademia dei Lincei* 16 (1907): 304–40, 637–62.

Guthrie, Patrick. "The Execution of Crispus." *Phoenix* 20 (1966): 325–31.

Halkin, François. "L'empereur Constantin converti par Euphratas." *AnBoll* 78 (1960): 5–17.

———. "Une nouvelle Vie de Constantin dans un légendier de Patmos." *AnBoll* 77 (1959): 63–107, 370–72.

———. "La Passion de S. Marc d'Aréthuse." *AnBoll* 103 (1985): 217–29.

———. "La passion grecque des saints Eugène et Macaire." *AnBoll* 78 (1960): 41–52.

Hansen, William. *Phlegon of Tralles' Book of Marvels.* Exeter: University of Exeter Press, 1996.

Hanson, R. P. C. "The Fate of Eustathius of Antioch." *ZKG* 95 (1984): 171–79.

Hefele, Carl J., and Henri Leclercq. *Histoire des conciles d'après les documents originaux.* 8 vols. Paris: Letouzey, 1907–52.

Henry, René, ed. and trans. *Photius: Bibliothèque*. 9 vols. Paris: Belles Lettres, 1959–91.

Heseler, Peter. "Hagiographica II." *Byzantinisch-Neugriechische Jahrbücher* 9 (1932): 320–37.

———. "Neues zur Vita Constantini des Codex Angelicus 22." *Byzantion* 10 (1935): 399–402.

Hobein, Hermann, ed. *Maximi Tyrii Philosophumena*. BSGRT. Leipzig: Teubner, 1910.

Holum, Kenneth G. *Theodosian Empresses: Women and Imperial Dominion in Late Antiquity*. Berkeley and Los Angeles: University of California Press, 1982.

Honigmann, Ernst. "La liste originale des Pères de Nicée." *Byzantion* 14 (1939): 44–48.

———. *Patristic Studies*. Studi e Testi 173. Vatican City: Biblioteca apostolica vaticana, 1953.

———. "Θράκων κώμη." PW 6A.1:552.

Jacoby, Felix, ed. *Die Fragmente der griechischen Historiker*. 3 vols. Leiden: Brill, 1954–64.

Janin, Raymond. *Constantinople Byzantine: Développement urbain et répertoire topographique*. Paris: Institut français d'études byzantines, 1964.

Jones, A. H. M. *The Later Roman Empire, 284–602: A Social, Economic, and Administrative Survey*. 2 vols. Oxford: Blackwell, 1964.

Jones, A. H. M., J. R. Martindale, and J. Morris, eds. *Prosopography of the Later Roman Empire*. Cambridge: Cambridge University Press, 1970–92.

Jungmann, Joseph A. *The Mass of the Roman Rite: Its Origins and Development*. Translated by Francis A. Brunner. 2 vols. New York: Benziger, 1951.

Kelly, Gavin. "Ammianus and the Great Tsunami." *JRS* 94 (2004): 141–65.

Kelly, J. N. D., *Early Christian Creeds*. London: Longman, 1972.

Kiessling, Adolf. "Hypasis." PW 9.1:234.

Kinzig, Wolfram. "Asterius Sophista oder Asterius Ignotus." *VC* 45 (1991): 388–98.

———. *In Search of Asterius: Studies on the Authorship of the Homilies on the Psalms*. Göttingen: Vandenhoeck & Ruprecht, 1990

Kopecek, Thomas A. *A History of Neo-Arianism*. Cambridge: Philadelphia Patristic Foundation, 1979.

Koschorke, Klaus. "Patristische Materialen zur Spätgeschichte der Valentinianischen Gnosis." Pages 120–39 in *Gnosis and Gnosticism: Nag Hammadi Studies*, XVII. Edited by M. Krause; Leiden: Brill, 1981.

Kotter, Bonifatius, ed. *Opera homiletica et hagiographica*. Vol. 5 of *Die Schriften des Johannes von Damaskos*. PTS 29. Berlin: de Gruyter, 1988.

Laffranchi, Lodovico. "Commento numismatico alla storia dell'imperatore Magnenzio e del suo tempo." *Atti e memorie dell'Istituto italiano di numismatica* 6 (1930): 134–205.

Lambros, Spyridon P., ed. *Excerptorum Constantini De natura animalium libri duo: Aristophanis Historiae animalium epitome.* Supplementum Aristotelicum 1.1. 2 vols. Berlin: Reimer, 1885.

Leadbetter, Bill. "The Illegitimacy of Constantine and the Birth of the Tetrarchy." Pages 78–85 in *Constantine: History, Historiography, and Legend.* Edited by Samuel S. Lieu and Dominic Montserrat. London: Routledge, 1998.

Leedom, Joe W. "Constantius II: Three Revisions." *Byzantion* 48 (1978): 132–45.

Lenski, Noel. "Initium mali Romano imperio: Contemporary Reactions to the Battle of Adrianople." *TAPA* 127 (1997): 129–68.

Leroux, Jean-Marie. "Acace, évêque de Césarée de Palestine (341-365)." Pages 82–85 in *Patres Apostolici, Historica, Liturgica, Ascetica et Monastica.* Edited by Frank L. Cross. StPatr 8; TU 93. Berlin: Akademie-Verlag, 1966.

Levenson, David P. "The Ancient and Medieval Sources for the Emperor Julian's Attempt to Rebuild the Jerusalem Temple." *JSJ* 35 (2004): 409–60.

Lieu, Samuel S., and Dominic Montserrat, eds. *Constantine: History, Historiography, and Legend.* London: Routledge, 1998.

Lietzmann, Hans. *Apollinaris von Laodicea und seine Schule: Texte und Untersuchungen.* Tübingen: Mohr Siebeck, 1904.

Lippold, Adolf. "Theodosius I." PW 13Sup:837–961.

Lippold, Georg. "Theodoros (127)," PW 5A.2:1909.

Lloyd, Alan. *Herodotus, Book II: Commentary 1-98.* EPRO 43. Leiden: Brill, 1976.

Luibheid, Colm. "The Arianism of Eusebius of Nicomedia." *ITQ* 43 (1976): 3–23.

Mango, Cyril A., *Studies on Constantinople.* Aldershot: Variorum, 1993.

Mango, Cyril A., and Roger Scott. *The Chronicle of Theophanes Confessor: Byzantine and Near Eastern History, AD 284–813.* Oxford: Clarendon, 1997.

Mansi, Giovan Domenico, ed. *Sacrorum conciliorum nova et amplissima collectio.* 35 vols. Florence: Zatta, 1759–98.

Marasco, Gabriele. "L'imperatore Giuliano e l'esecuzione di Fl. Artemio, *dux Aegypti.*" *Prometheus* 23 (1997): 59–78.

Meulder, Marcel. "Julien l'Apostat contre les Parthes: un guerrier impie." *Byzantion* 61 (1991): 458–95.

Micalella, Dina Lucia. "Giuliano e la 'paideia.'" *Rudiae* 7 (1995): 245–52.

Montfaucon, Bernard de, ed. *Opera omnia quae exstant.* 13 vols. Paris: Gaume, 1835–39.

Moreau, Jacques, ed. *Lactantius: De la mort des persécuteurs.* SC 39. Paris: Cerf, 1954.

Mortley, Raoul. *From Word to Silence.* Theophaneia 30–31. 2 vols. Bonn: Hanstein, 1986.

Müller, Karl, ed. *Fragmenta historicorum graecorum.* 5 vols. Paris: Didot, 1841–70.

———. *Geographi graeci minores.* 3 vols. Paris: Didot, 1855–61.

Nau, François. "Mélanges." *Revue de l'Orient chrétien* 13 (1908): 436–43.

Neumann, Alfred. "Cornuti." PW 10Sup:133–34.

Nobbs, Alanna. "Philostorgius' View of the Past." Pages 251–64 in *Reading the Past in Late Antiquity.* Edited by Graeme Clarke et al. Rushcutters Bay, NSW, Australia: Australian National University Press, 1990.

Nock, Arthur Darby, and André-Jean Festugière. *Corpus Hermeticum.* 4 vols. Paris: Belles Lettres, 1972.

Oberhummer, E. "Succi." PW 4A.1:513–14.

Oost, Stewart I. *Galla Placidia Augusta: A Biographical Essay.* Chicago: University of Chicago Press, 1968.

Opitz, Hans-Georg. "Die Vita Constantini des Codex Angelicus 22." *Byzantion* 10 (1935): 535–93.

———, ed. *Urkunden zur Geschichte des arianischen Streites, 318–328.* Vol. 3.1 of *Athanasius Werke.* Berlin: de Gruyter, 1934–35.

Palanque, J.-R. "Collégialité et partages dans l'empire romain aux IVe et Ve siècles." *Revue des études anciennes* 46 (1944): 54–58.

Papadopoulos-Kerameus, Athanasios, ed. *Varia Graeca Sacra.* St. Petersburg: Kirshbauma, 1909.

Parke, Herbert W., and Donald E. W. Wormell. *The Delphic Oracle.* 2 vols. Oxford: Blackwell, 1956.

Paschoud, François. "Zosime 2, 29 et la version païenne de la converion of Constantin." Pages 24–62 in idem, *Cinq études sur Zosime.* Paris: Belles Lettres, 1975.

———, ed. and trans. *Zosime: Histoire Nouvelle.* 5 parts in 3 vols. Paris: Belles Lettres, 1971–89.

Peeters, Paul. "La légende de saint Jacques de Nisibe." *AnBoll* 38 (1920): 285–373.

Penella, Robert J. "Julian the Persecutor in Fifth Century Church Historians." *The Ancient World* 24 (1993): 31–43.

Perrelli, Rafaelle. "La vittoria 'cristiana' del Frigido." Pages 257–65 in *Pagani e cristiani da Giuliano l'Apostata al sacco di Roma.* Edited by Franca Ela Consolino. Soveria Mannelli: Rubbettino, 1995.

Pietersma, Albert. *The Apocryphon of Jannes and Jambres the Magicians.* Religions in the Graeco-Roman World 19. Leiden: Brill, 1994.

Pohlsander, Hans A. "Crispus: Brilliant Career and Tragic End." *Historia* 33 (1984): 79–106.

Preger, Theodorus, ed. *Scriptores Originum Constantinopolitanarum.* 2 vols. Leipzig: Teubner, 1901–7.

Richard, Marcel, ed. *Asterii Sophistae commentariorum in psalmos quae supersunt.* Oslo: Brøgger, 1956.

Rougé, J. "Fausta, femme de Constantin: criminelle ou victime." *Cahiers d'Histoire* 25 (1980): 3–17.

Routh, Martin J. *Reliquiae Sacrae.* 5 vols. Oxford: Clarendon, 1846.

Rubin, Zeev. "Pagan Propaganda during the Usurpation of Magnentius." *Scripta Classica Israelica* 17 (1998): 124–41.

Ruprechtsberger, Erwin M. *Die Garamanten: Geschichte und Kultur eines Libyschen Volkes in der Sahara.* Mainz: von Zabern, 1997.

Rusch, William G. "À la recherche de l'Athanase historique." Pages 161–77 in *Politique et théologie chez Athanase d'Alexandrie.* Edited by Charles Kannengiesser. Paris: Beauchesne, 1974.

Salaville, S. "Un ancien bourg de Cappadoce: Sadagolthina," *Echos d'Orient* 15 (1912): 61–63.

Sathas, Konstantinos N., ed. *Anonymi compendium chronicum.* Vol. 7 of *Bibliotheca graeca medii aevi = Mesaionike vivliotheke.* Venice: Typois tou Chronou, 1894. Repr., Hildesheim: Olms, 1972.

Schäfer, Peter. "Der Aufstand gegen Gallus Caesar." Pages 184–201 in *Tradition and Re-interpretation in Jewish and Early Christian Literature: Essays in Honour of Jürgen C.H. Lebram.* Edited by J. W. van Henten, H. J. de Jonge, P. T. van Rooden, and J. W. Wesselius. StPB 36. Leiden: Brill, 1986.

Schäferdiek, Knut. "Die Anfänge des Christentums bei den Goten und der sog. gotische Arianismus." *ZKG* 112 (2001): 295–310.

———. "Das gotische Christentum im vierten Jahrhundert." Pages 19–50 in *Triuwe: Studien zur Sprachgeschichte und Literaturwissenschaft.* Edited by Karl-Friedrich Kraft, Eva-Maria Lill, and Ute Schwab. Heidelberg: Heidelberger Verlagsanstalt, 1992.

Schatkin, Margaret. A., ed., *Discours sur Babylas.* SC 362. Paris: Cerf, 1990.

Schermann, Theodor, ed. *Prophetarum vitae fabulosae: Indices apostolorum discipulorumque Domini, Dorotheo, Epiphanio, Hippolyto aliisque vindicata.* Leipzig: Teubner, 1907.

Schürer, Emil. *The History of the Jewish People in the Age of Jesus Christ (175 B.C.–A.D. 135): A New English Version.* Revised and edited by Géza Vermès and Fergus Millar. 3 vols. Edinburgh: T&T Clark, 1973–87.

Schwartz, Eduard, and Theodor Mommsen, eds. *Die Kirchengeschichte.* Vol. 2.2 of *Eusebius Werke.* Berlin: Akademie-Verlag, 1908.

Scott, Walter. *Hermetica: The Ancient Greek and Latin Writings Which Contain Religious or Philosophic Teachings Ascribed to Hermes Trismegistus.* 4 vols. Oxford: Clarendon, 1936.

Seaford, Richard, trans. *Euripides: Bacchae.* Westminster: Aris & Phillips, 1996.

Seeck, Otto. *Regesten der Kaiser und Päpste für die Jahre 311 bis 476 n. Chr. Vorarbeit zu einer Prosopographie der christlichen Kaiserzeit.* Stuttgart: Metzler, 1919.

Seeliger, Hans Reinhard. "Die Verwendung des Christogramms durch Konstantin im Jahre 312." *ZKG* 100 (1989): 149–68.

Sesboüé, Bernard, Georges-Matthieu de Durand, and Louis Doutreleau, eds. *Contre Eunome: Basile de Césareé.* 2 vols. SC 299, 305. Paris: Cerf, 1982–83.

Shepard, Odell. *The Lore of the Unicorn.* London: Unwin, 1930.

Simonetti, Manlio, *La crisi ariana nel IV secolo.* Roma: Institum patristicum Augustinianum, 1975.

Siniscalco, Paolo. "Ermete Trismegisto, profeta pagano della rivelazione cristiana." *Atti della Accademia delle Scienze di Torino* 101 (1966–67): 83–113.

Sirinelli, Jean. "Problèmes de la 'paideia.'" *Cahiers des études anciennes* 31 (1996): 135–46.

Sivan, Hagith. "Ulfila's Own Conversion." *HTR* 89 (1996): 373–86.

Smith, James D. "Reflections on Euzoius in Alexandria and Antioch." Pages 514–19 in *Critica et Philologica, Nachleben: First Two Centuries, Tertullian to Arnobius, Egypt before Nicaea, Athanasius and His Opponents.* Edited by Maurice F. Wiles and Edward J. Yarnold. StPatr 36. Leuven: Peeters, 2001.

Smith, Rowland. *Julian's Gods: Religion and Philosophy in the Thought and Action of Julian the Apostate.* London: Routledge, 1995.

Stead, Christopher. "Arius in Modern Research." *JTS* 45 (1994): 24–36.

Stern, Menahem. *Greek and Latin Authors on Jews and Judaism.* 3 vols. Jerusalem: Israeli Academy of Sciences and Humanities, 1974–84.

Szidat, Joachim. "Imperator legitime declaratus." Pages 174–88 in *Historia Testis: Mélanges d'épigraphie, d'histoire ancienne et de philologie offerts à Tadeusz Zawadzki.* Edited by Marcel Piérart et Olivier Curty. Fribourg: Universitaires Fribourg, 1989.

Talbert, Richard J., and Roger S. Bagnall. *Barrington Atlas of the Greek and Roman World.* (Princeton: Princeton University Press, 2000.

Tanner, Norman P. *Decrees of the Ecumenical Councils.* 2 vols. London: Sheed & Ward, 1990.

Thompson, D'Arcy W. "The Greek for a Zebra." *The Classical Review* 57 (1943): 103–4.

Thompson, Henry O. "Jordan River." *ABD* 3:953–58.

Tougher, Shaun. "The Advocacy of an Empress: Julian and Eusebia." *CQ* NS 48 (1998): 595–99.

———. "In Praise of an Empress: Julian's *Speech of Thanks* to Eusebia." Pages 105–23 in *The Propaganda of Power: The Role of Panegyric in Late Antiquity.* Edited by Mary Whitby. Mnemosyne, bibliotheca classica Batava Supplementum 183. Leiden: Brill, 1998.

Turner, Cuthbert H., ed. *Ecclesiae Occidentalis Monumenta Iuris Antiquissima.* 2 vols. Oxford: Clarendon, 1899–1939.

Uthemann, Karl-Heinz. Review of Wolfram Kinzig, *In Search of Asterius: Studies on the Authorship of the Homilies on the Psalms, VC* 45 (1991): 194–203.

———. "Die Sprache der Theologie nach Eunomius von Cyzicus," *ZKG* 104 (1993): 156–70.

Vaggione, Richard P. *Eunomius, The Extant Works: Text and Translation.* Oxford: Clarendon 1987.

———. *Eunomius of Cyzicus and the Nicene Revolution.* Oxford: Clarendon, 2000.

Velkov, Velizar. "Wulfila und die *Gothi minores* in Moesien." *Klio* 71 (1989): 525–27.

Vermes, Mark, trans. *Artemii Passio.* Pages 224–62 in *From Constantine to Julian: Pagan and Byzantine Views: A Source History.* Edited by Samuel N. C. Lieu and Dominic Montserrat. London: Routledge, 1996.

Vinzent, Markus. *Asterius von Kappadokien: Die theologischen Fragmente.* Leiden: Brill, 1993.

———. "Die Gegner im Schreiben Markells von Ankyra an Julius von Rom." *ZKG* 105 (1994): 285–328.

———. "Gottes Wesen, Logos, Weisheit und Kraft bei Asterius von Kappadokien und Markell von Ankyra." *VC* 47 (1993): 170–91.

Walford, Edward. *The Ecclesiastical History of Sozomen: Also the Ecclesiastical History of Philostorgius* London: Bohn, 1855.

Weissbach, Franz Heinrich. "Mesene." PW 15.1:1082–95.

Whitby, Michael, and Mary Whitby, trans. *Chronicon Paschale, 284–628 AD.* Liverpool: Liverpool University Press, 1989.

Wickham, L. R. "The *Syntagmation* of Aetius the Anomean." *JTS* 19 (1968): 532–69.

Wiles, Maurice. "Asterius: A New Chapter in the History of Arianism." Pages 111–51 in *Arianism: Historical and Theological Reassessments.* Edited by Robert C. Gregg. Cambridge: Philadelphia Patristic Foundation, 1985.

———. "Eunomius: Hair-Splitting Dialectician or Defender of the Accessibility of Salvation?" Pages 157–72 in *The Making of Orthodoxy: Essays in*

Honour of Henry Chadwick. Edited by R. Williams. Cambridge: Cambridge University Press, 1989.

Williams, Rowan D. "The Quest of the Historical Thalia." Pages 1–35 in *Arianism: Historical and Theological Reassessments.* Edited by Robert C. Gregg. Cambridge: Philadelphia Patristic Foundation, 1985.

Wolff, Gustavus. *Porphyrii de philosophia ex oraculis haurienda.* Berlin: Springer, 1856.

Wolfram, Herwig. *History of the Goths.* Translated by Thomas J. Dunlap. Berkeley and Los Angeles: University of California Press, 1988.

Woods, David. "Eusebius, *Vit. Const.* 4.21, and the *Notitia Dignitatum.*" Pages 195–202 in *Historica, Theologica et Philosophica, Critica et Philologica.* Edited by Elizabeth A. Livingstone. StPatr 29. Leuven: Peeters, 1997.

———. "Julian, Arbogastes, and the *Signa* of the *Ioviani* and *Herculiani.*" *Journal of Roman Military Equipment Studies* 6 (1995): 61–68.

———. "Three Notes on Aspects of the Arian Controversy c. 354–367 CE." *JTS* 44 (1993): 604–19.

Wright, Wilmer Cave, ed. and trans. *The Works of the Emperor Julian.* 3 vols. LCL 13, 29, 157. Cambridge: Harvard University Press, 1913–23.

Zecchini, Giuseppe. *Aezio: L'ultima difesa dell'Occidente romano.* Rome: Bretschneider, 1983.

———. "Filostorgio." Pages 579–98 in *Metodologie della ricerca sulla tarda antichità.* Edited by Antonio Garzya. Naples: D'Auria, 1989.

Index of Names

The index is keyed to the book and chapter divisions in Bidez's edition, although subdivisions have occasionally been introduced where it seemed convenient. Pr1 stands for Prologue 1 (the introductory material in Bidez, *Philostorgius*, 1–3), and Pr2 for Prologue 2 (the introductory paragraph in Bidez, *Philostorgius*, 4). A stands for Appendix (*Anhang*), and S for Supplement (the additional text printed on Bidez, *Philostorgius*, 377–81).

Ataulf: wedded to Placidia; killed: 12.4

Athanasius of Alexandria: unlawfully consecrated; tried; condemned: 2.11, 11a; returns from exile after Constantius's death: 2.18; driven out again: 3.3; Constans sends him back: 3.12; Constans punished for this by death: 3.22; defends consubstantialist doctrine: 3.17; condemned by Hosius and Liberius: 4.3; behind death of George of Alexandria: 7.2; replaces George: 7.2; A7.33d; ingratiates himself with Jovian: 8.6; compared to Cappadocians: 8.11a; bishop of Alexandria: A7.7b–8a

Athanasius of Anazarbus: disciple of Lucian and teacher of Aetius: 1.8a; 3.15

Athanasius of Ancyra: replaces Basil: 5.1

Athens: 5.2a; sacked by Alaric: 12.2

Attalus (rise to power and fall): 12.3–5

Augasis in Arabia: A3.8

Augusta (title): 3.22, 28

Augusta Constantina (= Amida): A7.15a, b

Augustus (Caesar): A2.26

Aurelian (one of Eutropius's judges): 11.6

Austuriani: 11.8

Auxentius of Mopsuestia: 5.2, 2a

Auxidianus (bishop, opposes Aetius): 8.4

Auxonius (praetorian prefect): 9.8, 11

Babylas of Antioch: 7.8, 8a, 12; A7.1, 35

Barbatio (general, sent to banish Gallus): 4.1, 1a

Barce (in Upper Libya): 1.8a

Bartholomew (apostle of India): 2.6

Basil of Ancyra: hates Aetius: 3.16; denounces Aetius to Gallus: 3.27; resents Eudoxius: 4.6; influence with Constantius: 4.8–12; 5.1, 4; 8.17

Basil of Caesarea: Pr1; 4.12; 8.11–13, 11a–12a, 11b–12b; 10.6

Basileus of Amaseia (Arian sympathizer at Council of Nicaea): 1.8, 8a

Basiliscus (bishop at Eudoxius's installation in Constantinople): A7.31.1

Baucalis (nickname for Alexandrian presbyter Alexander): 1.4

Bauto: 11.6

Beirut (earthquake): A7.23

Benjamin (tribe of): 7.14

Berenice (in Upper Libya): 1.8a

Beroea (Demophilus's native place): 9.8, 19

Beth Aramaye: A7.39a

Bithynia: 1.7a, 8a, 9a; 2.16a; 3.22; 4.1, 1a; A5.17, 25; A7.4, 4c, 24.7, 24f, 41

Bizabde: captured by Persians: A7.32a

Boeotia: 3.11; A1.16

Borborian: 3.15

Boreum (in Upper Libya): 1.8a

Borissus (in Cappadocia Secunda; native place of Philostorgius's grandfather): 9.9

Bosporus: A5.17, 25

Britain: Constantius the Elder dies there: 1.5; Constantine sails

Printed in the United States
200161BV00004B/1-96/A